EARLY MODER

Early Modern Italy: A Social History is a fascinating survey of society in Italy from the fifteenth to the eighteenth century – from the Renaissance to the Enlightenment. The early modern period was an exciting phase in the history of Italy, with the emergence of great artists, sculptors and architects and the flowering of culture generally. However, during this period Italy was not one coherent political unit, but was divided into many different states. Such divisions affected the population economically, socially and linguistically, but this social history considers patterns across these divisions, and contrasts within states.

Early Modern Italy covers the whole of the Italian peninsula from the Venetian Republic, Milan and Florence to Rome, Naples and the rural Italy of Calabria and Campagna. It spans a multitude of themes, including:

- the effects of geography on population and social developments
- the relationship between urban and rural Italy
- land systems, agriculture and rural communities
- urban society from professionals and artisans to pedlars and prostitutes
- the family and the household
- the church and religious life

Early Modern Italy is crucial to the understanding of the diversity, conflicts and incompatibilities from the past that still affect the stability and fragility of united Italy today.

Christopher F. Black is Senior Lecturer in Modern History at the University of Glasgow. He is author of *Italian Confraternities in the Sixteenth Century* (Cambridge, 1989).

A SOCIAL HISTORY OF EUROPE
Series Editor: Richard Evans
Professor of Modern History, University of Cambridge

A SOCIAL HISTORY OF MODERN SPAIN (1990)
Adrian Schubert

EARLY MODERN SPAIN: A SOCIAL HISTORY (1999)
James Casey

EARLY MODERN ITALY

A social history

Christopher F. Black

London and New York

First published 2001
by Routledge
11 New Fetter Lane, London EC4P 4EE

Simultaneously published in the USA and Canada
by Routledge
29 West 35th Street, New York, NY 10001

Routledge is an imprint of the Taylor & Francis Group

© 2001 Christopher F. Black

Typeset in Baskerville by
BOOK NOW Ltd
Printed and bound in Great Britain by
St Edmundsbury Press, Bury St Edmunds, Suffolk

All rights reserved. No part of this book may be reprinted or reproduced or utilised in any form or by any electronic, mechanical, or other means, now known or hereafter invented, including photocopying and recording, or in any information storage or retrieval system, without permission in writing from the publishers.

British Library Cataloguing in Publication Data
A catalogue record for this book is available
from the British Library

Library of Congress Cataloging-in-Publication Data
Black, Christopher F.
Early modern italy : a social history / Christopher F. Black.
p. cm. – (Social history of Europe)
Includes bibliographical references and index.
1. Italy–Social conditions. 2. Italy–Economic conditions. 3.
Italy–History–1492-1870. I. Title. II. Social history of Europe (Routledge (Firm))
HN475.B553 2000
306′.0945–dc21 00-055333

ISBN 0-415-21434-3 (pbk)
ISBN 0-415-10935-3 (hbk)

FOR
ELIZABETH AND TRICIA
FOR PAST SALVATION
AND
GRAND-DAUGHTER SOPHIE
HOPE FOR THE FUTURE

CONTENTS

PREFACE

A social history – or the history of society – is concerned mainly with the inter-relationships of individuals with each other, and the factors that affected these inter-relationships. These factors include the physical environment, the political, legal and institutional frameworks, agreed roles of behaviour, conventions and accepted ways of behaving, languages and other means of communication. There are different kinds of grouping of individuals: family and household, hamlet and city, work-places, guilds, confraternities, religious houses and so on. Social inter-relationships may be seen in terms of conceptual belonging or exclusion: nobility, 'order', class, rich and poor, clerical and lay, national groups. A general history like this can suggest to readers an abundant choice of ways of looking at society, and can include both wide-angle and microscope lenses. Readers then can follow their own inclinations and interests.

Social history has to be selective, by topic and geographical area. Each issue cannot be generalised and illustrated for all of the Italian peninsula, but my discourse should suggest some similarities and contrasts geographically. Current historical knowledge, understanding and perceptions – and my own biases – mean that more will be exemplified from north-central Italy than from the south, though the latter should have its share of attention in discussion of the rural scenes or household and kinship relations. In choosing examples, and highlighting certain historians' work, I have tried to represent different approaches and biases of other historians – in favour of 'mentalities' (more aptly the French *mentalités*), feminism, social anthropology, physical determinism, microhistory and so forth. Readers may well detect that chapters speak with different dialects. The authorial voice has many tones, including discords and dissonance. When not trying to convey others' approaches, I have favoured socio-religious matters rather than supposedly quantifiable economic dimensions. Social history concerns all in society, not just the lower orders and class warfare. I have tried to give a due share to women's history, but integrated into the whole, and not segregated into a separate chapter. The works of Fernand Braudel, and of historians working around the French periodical *Annales: histoire, sciences sociales*, have had their impact – when dealing with physical environment, structures, *mentalités,* but not when over-emphasising statistics, or excessively discounting the importance of events and individual actors. Other aspects seem influenced by Natalie Zemon Davis's work and approaches (though on France rather than Italy), on social groupings, popular religion and the importance of festivals and rites of violence; though I do not share her past Marxist and class-struggle interests.[1] I use works of art as evidence alongside written documents conventionally utilised by historians, though word limitations have curtailed sections that might have used them more, and have prevented discussion of problems of 'reading' the different kinds of evidence.

I am writing primarily for the English-speaking world, not the Italian (though I am mindful of the possibilities of an Italian version), in anticipation of a student and beginner audience (including that mythical beast, the General Reader). I also want to help professional academic readers with expertise elsewhere who want some guidance on early modern Italy, whether their primary interests are post-unification Italy, other parts of early modern Europe or the wider world. But I also consider Italian specialists – whether historians of certain cities and regions, or experts in art history, literature, music, political theory – who want some guidance about other areas, whether geographical or topical (while they can either challenge or educate me from their expertise). Italianist friends and contacts (as particularly at some recent transatlantic conferences) have encouraged me to consider them as well.

This last readership factor has added to the complications of bibliography, reference notes, language and detailed exemplification. The literature on virtually all I have covered is potentially large. Constraints of space mean that I have only been able to use a fraction, and to cite even less. I have included some archival references for the benefit of specialist colleagues.

Detailed examples have been used to arouse interest or to illustrate how a social situation worked (or failed), not to prove a generalisation. Some choices are of the unusual rather than the supposedly typical; but such examples should stress the complexities of social history, and probe simple generalisations; since many long examples cannot be paraded, I have tried to use some that cross-reference with a number of issues in different chapters, so that in the end they may illustrate both normal and abnormal situations.

The Italian university systems and archival organisation (state or ecclesiastical) encourage a concentration of research and writing on a regional basis. Given that the Italian peninsula has contributed more to Western history and culture than any other area (consistently from the Villanovans and Etruscans, through the Romans, the establishment of Western Christendom to the present), and has more surviving evidence on which to research, it is understandable that history writing remains regional. Italians are reluctant to produce Italian-wide studies, general histories or syntheses involving different areas, and they have mixed feelings about foreigners venturing to do so. If *Italian* history is to be written then it should be by teams of local specialists; hence the huge volumes in the multi-volume series published by the Einaudi and UTET presses are splendid in many ways, but lack overall clarity and synthesis. Leading cities and provinces produce vast multi-volume, many-authored volumes. A large thriving periodical literature is long on detailed information, short on analysis and synthesis. A foreigner working from abroad to produce overviews has much to master, with little intermediary help.

Anyone compiling a bibliography on all or part of early modern England or Scotland has a number of single-author and single-volume works to both help them and pit their wits against. For Italy I have little to build on, or compete against. There is one single-volume coverage of Italy in my period, helpful but somewhat dated – in French, by J. Delumeau (1974). There is a valuable modern single-volume study in Italian, using many eminent authors who do attempt Italian-wide syntheses for their areas: G. Greco and M. Rosa (eds) (1996), with Paolo Malanima covering the economy, and his friend Franco Angiolini, *La società*. In English the Longman series covers the early modern period in four volumes, with six authors: D. Hay and J. Law (1989), E. Cochrane (1988b), D. Sella (1997), D. Carpanetto and G. Ricuperati (1987). Each has merits, but there is no meeting of minds or series coherence. Here I offer one mind and authorial voice, if discoursed in various dialects!

In covering from the fifteenth to eighteenth centuries, I emphasise the central period from the late fifteenth to later seventeenth centuries. A suitable conclusion point for an 'early modern' period is the 1760s, when a number of states under the impact of enlightenment ideas and dire famine undertook serious attempts at reform of the old society. Arguably out of the intellectual debates and writings of the 1760s, and subsequent practical campaigns to reform inter-state trade, taxation policies, feudalism, legal procedures and punishments, agricultural production and so on, came sufficient changes that the foundations of modern Italian society and ideas were laid. So the 1760s–90s belong as much to the nineteenth century as to the early modern period, but several examples will be drawn from these late decades.

A suitable starting point is less clear. While it is tempting to accept 1494 – with the invasion of Italy by a large French army under King Charles VIII – as an often-used conventional breakpoint in Italian history, it has drawbacks for the social-history commentator. Many ideas, attitudes and procedures were developed in the course of the fifteenth century which need to be discussed with those of the post-1494 period: attitudes towards education, civility, the role of women, the uses of wealth, domestic living and conspicuous consumption, the relationship of the individual and the group and so forth. There is a more practical historiographical reason, connected with a precise historical development, for fully incorporating the fifteenth century into the chronology. In 1427 the Florentine government created a new register of its citizens' and subjects' possessions, the *catasto*, in order to have a more efficient and extensive foundation for taxation! It was a tribute to Florence's bureaucratic efficiency, and in some ways to the city's republican civility. The *catasto* records survived (and caused imitations – of lesser quality – in Tuscany and elsewhere, some of which also survive), and they have been the foundations of many studies in our century, including an early computer-based analysis in 1978 by the late David Herlihy and Christiane Klapisch-Zuber. Studies which started with this *catasto* record have moved on to wider investigations through the fifteenth century, bringing in other documentation such as wills, personal or family diaries and memorials (*ricordanze*) and notarial contracts. Many aspects of Italian social history have received illumination from the Florentine archival base of the fifteenth century –

population structures, family composition, wealth distribution and the position of women, children and servants. Some exemplification will thus come from that period.

Note

1 See notably her collected essays (1975) and her articles of 1974, 1977, 1981; and interview with her in H. Abelove and others (eds) (1983). For most of its history before 1993 the *Annales* periodical was subtitled *Economies, Sociétés, Civilisations.*

ACKNOWLEDGEMENTS

For funding travel, research and visits to international conferences I am grateful for grants from the British Academy, the Carnegie Trust, and research and travel funds granted by Glasgow University Court and the Faculty of Arts. I have worked in a number of different Italian archives and libraries, with varying degrees of co-operation and efficiency. I would particularly like to thank those who have helped me in Bologna; in its Archivio di Stato, Archivio Arcivescovile, the Archiginnasio library, and in the Istituto per Le Scienze Religiose/Biblioteca Giuseppe Dossetti.

My physical awareness of Italy has largely been focused, except for the Perugian *contado* years ago, on cities. More recently I have experienced the Tuscan *contado* through walking tours (with talk, visual delights and gastronomy!), organised by Alternative Travel Group; I would like to acknowledge my debt to two charming tour leaders in particular, Clare Lillingston and Frances Wolverton, whose knowledge of and enthusiasm for the area and its cultures, in many senses contributed happily to my (Braudelian) understanding. Most recently I am greatly indebted to Maria Bortoluzzi and Jenny Greenleaves Manco not only for caring hospitality, but for their expert guidance around Friuli and Tuscany respectively; and in Jenny's case for contributions to Chapter 2.

A significant amount in the book has derived from teaching students at Glasgow University. Students have been victims in lectures and seminars, but have also provided feedback, and new ideas or material through essays and dissertations submitted to me. While many students have wittingly or unknowingly contributed, invidiously I single out a few for their academic input, but also for the encouragement and friendship they have provided in dark moments: Helena Bruce, Alastair Dunning, Kate Griffith, Suzy Mercer, Liz Strachan, Jonathan Walker and most especially Carolynn Bain, who as my most dedicated Italianist ever served as a 'student reader' of several chapters in their early stages; her telling and frank comments along with her cheerful friendliness over several years have been a considerable help. Jon Walker has gone on to complete a Cambridge Ph.D. on 'Honour and the Culture of Male Venetian Nobles, *c.* 1500–*c.*1650'; I have benefited considerably from his research and ideas, especially about noble or gentlemanly attitudes, the Venetian elites, aspects of urban violence, immorality and corruption. Similarly Alastair Dunning's work for a Thesis for the Courtauld Institute in London has influenced my knowledge about Rome.

Among senior academics who have provided me with bibliographical suggestions, books, offprints, archival material, ideas – and encouragement – I would like to thank: Giuliana Albini, Stephen Bowd, Sam Cohn, Alex Cowan, Nick Davidson, Andrea Del Col, Aldo Colonello, Natalie Zemon Davis, Simon Ditchfield, Simon Dixon, Konrad Eisenbichler, Mario Fanti, Giovanna Farrell-Vinay, Costas Gaganakis, Marina Gazzini, David Gentilcore, John Henderson, John Larner, Richard Mackenney, Thomas Munck, Irene Polverini Fosi, Hamish Scott, Nicholas Terpstra, Marcello Verga and Danilo Zardin. Sam Cohn and Richard Evans, as series editor, read the (longer) penultimate text, and I am very grateful for their advice on what to cut, what to add and on some reorganisation and presentation. I alone have to atone for the sins of omission and commission.

But my greatest debt is to my former colleague Tricia Allerston. Her opportune arrival in the department in 1995 rescued the book from oblivion and me from despair. Reading what I had already written, discussing my problems in resolving blockages, providing critical assessments and encouragement, she helped me restructure certain chapters, and renew writing. In Glasgow, but also subsequently at Edinburgh University, she has exchanged information and ideas, especially in connection with the world of work, diseases and all matters Venetian. She has generously provided references, copies of recondite articles and transcripts of archival records. Limitations on footnoting preclude specific acknowledgements of all her significant contributions. Her practical help, her critical assessments, her willingness to listen and respond as a true colleague, her friendly and morale-boosting encouragement have contributed enormously to whatever merits this book finally has. So I include her in the dedication, with profoundest thanks.

Christopher F. Black
Glasgow
1st April 2000

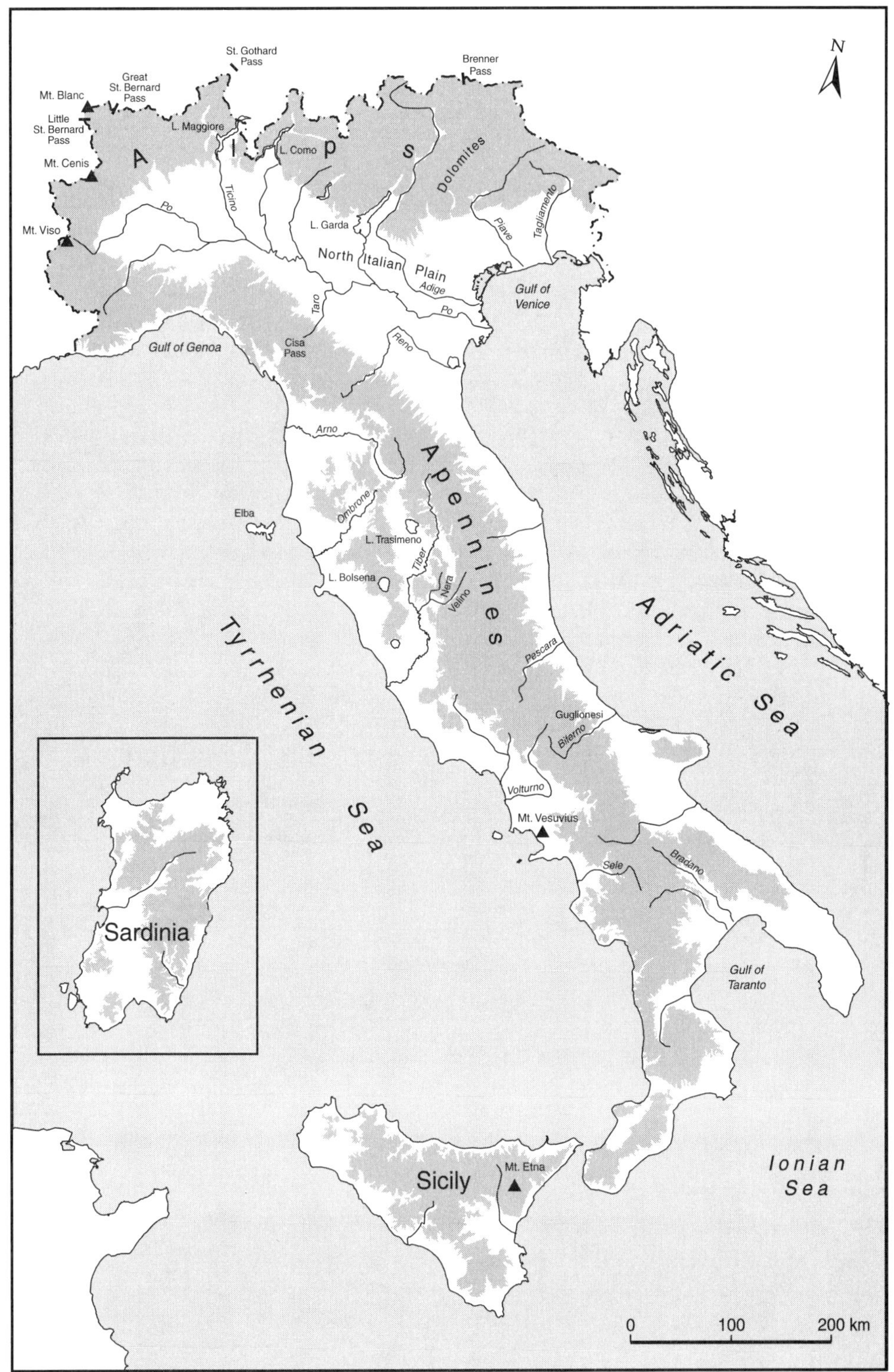

Map 1 Physical Italy.

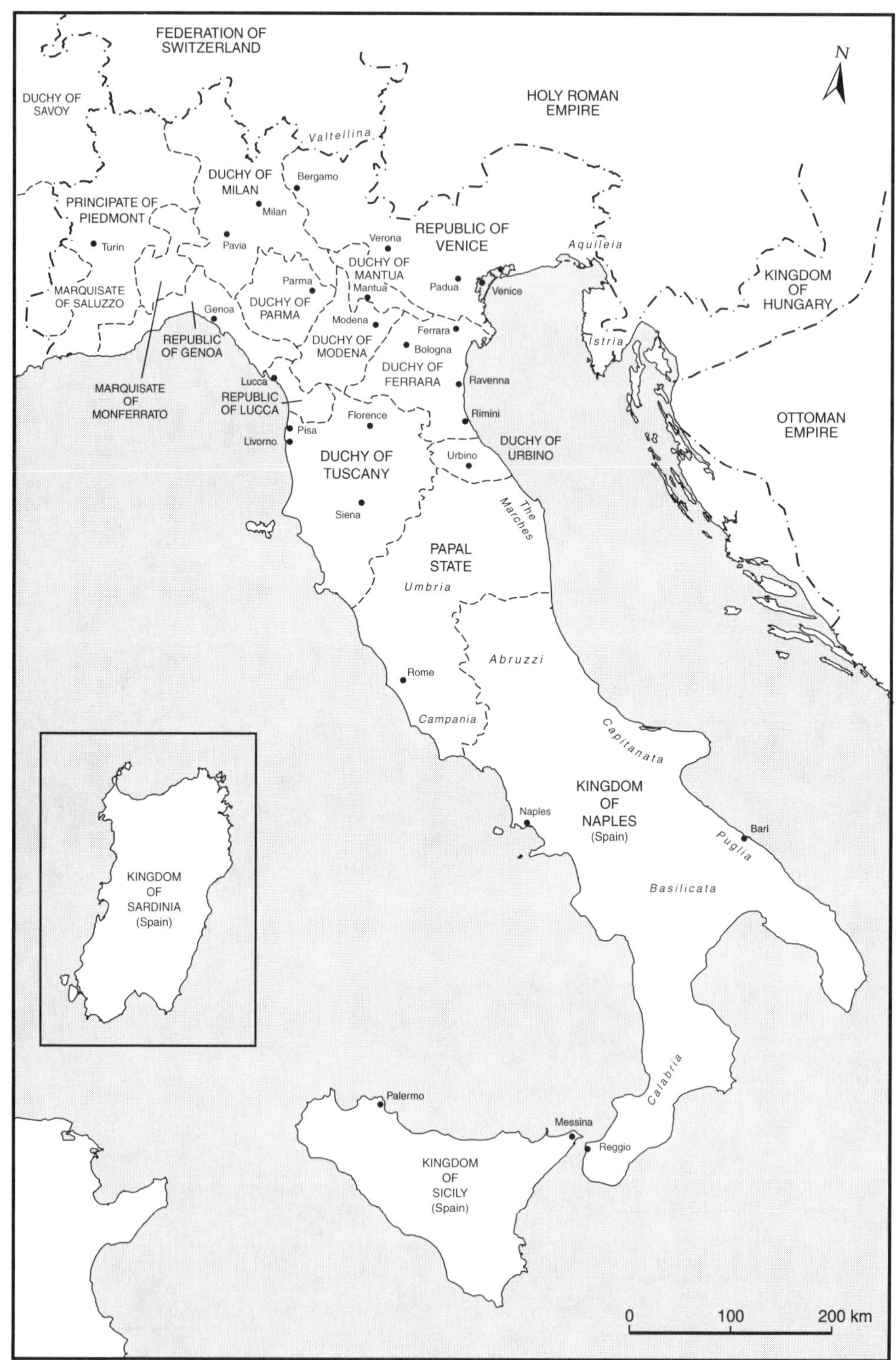

Map 2 The Italian States, 1559.

Map 3 Italian cities and towns.

Map 4 The Kingdom of Naples.

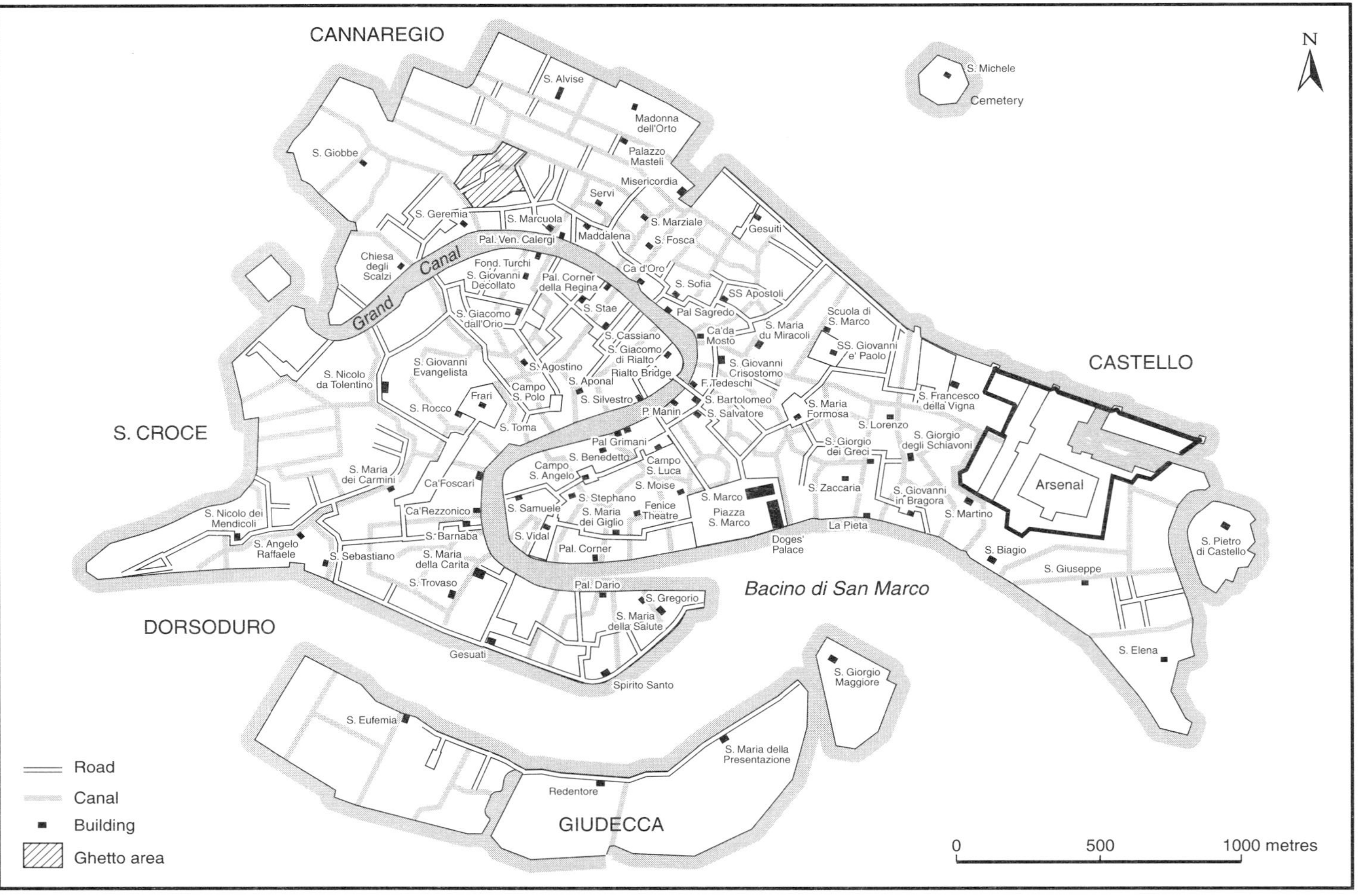

Map 5 The city of Venice.

1

DISUNITED ITALY

Unity and disunity

Italy in the early modern period, roughly from the fifteenth to eighteenth centuries, Renaissance to the Enlightenment, is not normally seen as a coherent unit. Politically it was subdivided into different kinds of States, as maps 2 and 4 indicate.[1] In the nineteenth century the dominant European statesman Prince Metternich notoriously stressed, when resisting nationalism, that Italy was merely a 'geographical expression'. It remained without political unity until 1870–71 when Rome itself was finally absorbed into United Italy, and became the capital. Even then the political state of Italy might arguably be seen as devoid of real Italian national feeling through the peninsula. It has been argued that there was a deep North–South divide within Italy, based on mutual ignorance, distrust or envy, that had made political unity of the whole geographical expression even more difficult for the few who desired it; and rendered such full unity unpalatable even to the majority of those who understood what was taking place in the 1850s to 1870s. Bitter civil war scarred the South in the 1860s.

Though the new Italy was supposedly based on linguistic nationalism and the sense of a common Roman classical past, very few spoke a common Italian language, and even fewer could have felt that they were heirs to a proud Roman past. Estimates of those who spoke 'Italian' at Unification vary from about 2.5 per cent to 12 per cent. The area is still possibly the most diverse linguistically in Europe. There are debates over definitions of 'language' and 'dialect', whether Italy has and had many languages (Florentine, Venetian, Sicilian, Calabrian, etc), or many dialects, derived from a common Latin origin. Some treat Ladino and Friulian as dialects, rather than separate languages. There are and were areas within Italy where other languages were spoken; southern areas where the common language was Greek or Albanian, and northern borders where French, German, Slavic languages and mixed dialects prevailed. All these languages had contaminated, infiltrated, or enriched (depending on your point of view) the speech and writing of wider regions.

These comments on linguistic disunity can be treated in various ways, and be misleading. Modern expectations of those living in monolingual societies, and wanting a common international language for instant communication, may exaggerate the difficulties of the past scene of linguistic diversity and mutual incomprehension. In our period the educated elites had the common language of Latin useable through the peninsula and further afield till the eighteenth century at least. Furthermore the sixteenth century saw, after some intense and interesting debate, the recognition of an educated Italian vernacular language, based on Florentine and Tuscan; though thanks to a leading Venetian writer, Cardinal Pietro Bembo, it was old-fashioned Tuscan literary grammar, syntax and spelling rather than contemporary sixteenth-century discourse. The spread of printing ensured a ubiquity of this more or less agreed Italian, whether the presses were in Florence, Milan, Rome, Naples or Venice; though the Venetian presses also printed literary texts in Venetian dialect. Public notices, legal, ecclesiastical, charitable, were printed in this Italian; one has to assume that in the market square or church porch there was the odd person able and ready to read out, translate into another dialect and explain them. Thereby, a knowledge of some standard Italian percolated through society, to be heard and spoken, but not read. As will be suggested at various points, the numbers of people from all levels of society who moved about Italy, between dialect areas, were considerable and many must have learned to cope with verbal communication quickly. A Calabrian arriving in Naples or Rome, a Roman, Florentine or Friulian reaching Venice, would initially find most speech around incomprehensible; by prior design or chance they might find a family or group from their own dialect and 'national' background. But they must have soon become comprehensibly involved with other languages.

Court records such as those of the Venetian Inquisition, the Roman Governor's criminal court, or the Bologna Torrone, suggest members of the lower orders from a variety of regions adequately communicated verbally – not just with knife and fist. Similar records throughout Italy put the evidence of the accused or witnesses in more or less standard Italian, though a few phrases and words might be in a local dialect. This was true even in the South. David Gentilcore, who has considerable experience dealing with investigative records, has found only one extensive record in a regional dialect (Calabrian). Some dialect comes through when a local scribe for the feudal court in the Calabrian village of Pentidattilo records a complex trial concerning murder and abortion in 1710; his record involved a complex translation procedure.[2] There are implications for those seeking to comprehend what 'voice' is coming through such records. But in this context I would stress peoples' abilities to overcome linguistic disunity, with the help of notaries and lesser scribes as communicators in society. Many travelled widely through their home region, towns and countryside, and were able to communicate, trade and intermarry.

Given the disunity even at the time of Unification, should we not confine ourselves – especially given the richness of local history – to reasonably coherent and cohesive sub-areas; based on old states, dynastic conglomerations or regional economies? One response is to say that because there is a modern united Italy – for good or ill, and under whatever threats over recent years – there should be pre-modern studies that illuminate the background of that same area, precisely explaining the diversity, conflicts and near incompatibilities from the past that still affect the stability and fragility of the present. Another response, especially from non-Italians, is that a perpetuated concentration on the famous sub-divisions – of Florence/Tuscany, the old Papal State, the Venetian Republic, or the Kingdom of Naples – distorts historical understanding by down-playing comparative analysis with near neighbours. The regional specialisation of many Italian historians, and fear of their professional rivals, means they would rather prove their breadth of learning, by alluding to French or English history than to a different Italian region.

More positively, a justification for an Italian-wide study of the very diverse peninsula rests on the realisation that at least among the elite of early-modern Italy there were concepts of the unity of 'Italy' and Italians. Florentines, Milanese and Venetians might regularly fight each other for control of northern Italy, but they were Italians with a common Roman past dominating an Empire – different from the barbarians, whether Christian French, German, Swiss north of the Alps, or heathen Muslims of the Ottoman Empire threatening across the Mediterranean waters or down from the Slavic north-eastern corner. This attitude of there being different kinds of foreigners, aliens and enemies lies behind the peroration of Niccolo Machiavelli's notorious *The Prince* (mainly written 1512–13); Machiavelli wanted the peninsula cleared of non-Italians, especially Swiss and German mercenary soldiers working with Imperial, Spanish or French princes. Despite the interpretations of nineteenth-century nationalists and more recent political scientists, it is difficult to accept that Machiavelli seriously envisaged a single Italian state as a permanent result, but he desired Italy to be free for Italians to contest among themselves. Like his fellow Florentine historian and friend Francesco Guicciardini, he was horrified at the ease of the French invasion of Italy in 1494 that left Italy dominated, if not fully occupied, by non-Italian rulers for the rest of our period. Machiavelli blamed lazy, luxury minded, Italian princes and patricians, and notably the Papacy which had not been strong enough to unite Italy, but strong enough to prevent another ruler from doing so. He wanted an end to Italian decadence, which might virtuously be achieved by a Medici prince from Florence uniting Italian forces against non-Italian barbarians. This reaction to the 1494 invasion generated an increased cultural and moral concept of *italianità*, but not a political movement for unity.[3]

Following the Reformation schism and the Catholic reform, church leaders (like Cardinal Roberto Bellarmino) saw Italy as a Catholic church unit; with the Alps and the Inquisition tribunals combining to create a *cordon sanitaire* to keep out heretics and heterodox ideas. But not till the eighteenth century (and hardly then) was a single Italian state perceived to be feasible or desirable.

The divisions and contrasts within the Italian peninsula were, and are, considerable; between the mainly mountainous areas and the smaller plains, between great cities on coasts and rivers, and numerous *città* perched on high hilltops; between great feudal monoculture estates growing grain or pasturing sheep, and tiny multipurpose terraced strips mixing vines, olive trees, goats and chickens; between large extended families and the widow-run room of children; between great palace complexes like the Vatican or the Gonzaga palace in Mantua, and the hovels or even caves of the rural poor.

For many historians the fundamental divide in Italy is between the North and the South (the *Mezzogiorno*). The *Mezzogiorno* might, for some, include Rome and the surrounding Campagna and the Abruzzi; but more consistently it refers to what was the Kingdom or Viceroyalty of Naples, with the islands of Sicily and Sardinia often included, (although I am largely excluding these islands from my 'Italy'). The concept of *Il Mezzogiorno*, or The South, is both geographical and attitudinal. The southern part of Italy has general geographical differences; more adverse climatic conditions, creating less diverse and less rich agricultural conditions; from these derive lower standards of living for most of the population, and more difficult communications. The south is often characterised as maintaining, or re-introducing a more intense 'feudal' structure socially and economically, nobles dominating large monoculture estates and having full feudal legal rights over towns and villages. Naples came to dominate the whole region, attracting the elite of feudal property owners, of educated professionals and adventurous international traders. The rest of the South was left with limited capital resources, less diverse occupations, less intellectual challenges; the south lacked the competitiveness of the rival city states and communes of the north. Thence derived the alleged torpor and unproductiveness of the *Mezzogiorno*. In the eyes of some Italian commentators – exemplified by the philosopher-historian who dominated Italy's intellectual world from the late nineteenth century, Benedetto Croce, and by a modern Marxist historian, Rosario Villari – the southern problem was exacerbated when Spanish control was consolidated from the early sixteenth century (and ratified in the peace settlement of 1559). Spanish influence supposedly consolidated feudal noble control, emphasising courtly manners, and chivalric codes of behaviour on the part of the elite, with accompanying disdain for hard work, manual labour, and capitalist entrepreneurship. With the addition of rigorous counter-reformation orthodoxy the South lost its renaissance humanism, its intellectual and commercial competitiveness, and lapsed into torpor except when it came to the preservation of 'honour' and the pursuit of vendettas.[4]

Various sections of this book will test these myths or realities. The South has been much less studied than the North, though there have been beneficial changes recently – as with the investigation of socio-religious history, or family and household structures. Hostile impressions have discouraged investigation of the southern past; fewer universities there have meant fewer local researchers. Images of the South, its poverty, its supposed violence and its distrust of outsiders, have discouraged the kind of foreign scholar who has so enriched the study of northern Italy. Within the south, Naples' past political, economic and cultural predominance seems to have led later historians to ignore Reggio Calabria, Nicastro, Potenza, Cosenza, Taranto, Bari or Lecce for example. These cities apparently rarely made the historical impact that, say, other cities in the Papal State besides Rome did, such as Perugia, Todi, Foligno, Orvieto, Spoleto, Ancona, all of which have attracted international scholarship for studies of our period.

The sources for studying the *Mezzogiorno* are also much more limited than for the North, because fewer documents and contemporary books were produced in the first place with a less literate, less urbanised, less politically fragmented society.

What was produced has suffered from greater attrition, through earthquakes, climatic adversities or German vindictiveness on evacuating Naples in 1944. When and where they do survive, poverty, indifference and ignorance have caused materials in feudal and ecclesiastical archives and libraries to be lost, eaten up, dampened or rendered inaccessible. So the southern problems dictate that attempts to test or change the image are made difficult.

For all the divisions within Italy, 'Italy' had an image in the eyes of non-Italians that was largely favourable and/or magnetic, even if the perception of Italy was normally of the nearer and more accessible northern, urban, Italy.[5] Through the period of our study, from the fifteenth to eighteenth centuries 'Italy' (like Europa pursued by Jove), was envied, admired, coveted, lusted, by rulers and the elite of much of Europe. If she did not satisfy or satiate, if gold proved mere gilt, if overtures were rejected, then admirers turned to despisers – as with Erasmus, Luther and Calvin, or Kings Charles VIII and Louis XIV of France. Italy and Italian based scholarship and the arts were central to the fifteenth-century classical Renaissance; for the rediscovery of lost manuscripts, the improvement in classical texts, in purifying the writing and speaking of Latin, and then Greek; for discoveries in anatomical sciences, in the portrayal of the human body, in perspective. From Italy came not only ideas and the means of their communication, but also commercial and industrial leadership, banking facilities utilising paperwork as well as gold coinage, florins from Florence and ducats from Venice. Italy also provided leadership in communication and commerce: transforming Germanic inventions in movable type from the world of secrecy into the realms of middle-class education and near-mass communication (with the printed illustrated newssheet).

Though Italy dominated culture and commerce less from the mid sixteenth to eighteenth centuries, plenty was left for non-Italians to envy. There were the courtly, gentlemanly and ladylike manners of *The Courtier* [*Il Cortegiano*, published 1528], the dangerous but exciting republican ideas of Machiavelli or the Venetian Republic; the canvases of great painters like Titian and Veronese who mastered the art of oil-painting (even if northerners had first developed the medium); the musical expertise of great composers like the Gabrieli, Monteverdi, Cavalli and Vivaldi (even if Netherlanders in the late fifteenth and sixteenth century had largely taught the Italians); there was Italian silk, damask, furniture, mirrors, drinking glasses, maiolica tableware, decorated pistols and daggers (preferably not to be used) for comfortable civilised living, and the imagery thereof. Those seeking classical erudition, scientific training, artistic treasures (classical or modern) headed for Italy, to be involved in universities – at least in the sixteenth and early seventeenth centuries – and academies, then salons, coffee-houses and theatres in the seventeenth and eighteenth. Those of a Catholic persuasion from the later sixteenth century might look to Italy (primarily Rome though not exclusively so) as offering religious leadership. There were books of all categories from Italian presses, especially Venetian.

Thus from an international perspective Italy, or key parts thereof, was central to European consciousness – to taste, education in the broadest sense, to manners and conduct, to commercial practice and procedures. Politicians – out to rape the peninsula – ensured that the Italian/non-Italian interchange was more complicated, involved and violent, as will become clearer below. The social and economic bases that produced the desirable Italy, and the way the pursuers also altered that society, will become evident as the book progresses.

The chronology and developments of early modern Italy

The social history developments have to be set within a framework of many different political units.[6]

The political geography of Italy in the early fifteenth century was extremely complex, and the political conflicts intense. Any map is inclined to mislead by implying the existence of coherent 'States' in a modern sense of reasonably structured political units; though by 1559 (Map 2) agglomerations of cities, towns and feudal estates had been consolidated into fewer, more integrated, political units. In the fifteenth century two major monarchical states covered the bulk of southern and central Italy, the Papal State and the Kingdom of Naples. The latter, (theoretically, until 1787, a feudal dependency of the Papacy), was ruled by members of the House of Aragon from Spain. Many overmighty feudal barons alternately had to be cajoled or beaten into accepting central direction from Naples (or Palermo or Barcelona). The coherence of the Papal State or States was even more problematic in the early century since rival popes claimed authority to rule both church and state. The situation was eased in 1417 when Pope Martin V was generally recognised as the single legitimate Pope. But it was long before he and his successors could seriously claim to have made themselves safe and secure in the Vatican within Rome, with moderate control over the territorial State with its subinfeudated families controlling some towns and countryside, oligarchic city communal governments and warlords or tyrants with more temporary control of other cities.

Italian areas north of the Papal State had a whole range of larger or lesser republican city states, dukedoms, marquisates or other princely regimes. The early fifteenth century involved a struggle between the Republics of Venice and Florence and the Dukedom of Milan to carve out and consolidate large territorial states based on their capital cities, with a competition to absorb lesser cities. Venice sought to dominate Padua, Verona or Vicenza; Milan to conquer Pavia, Como or Lodi; while Bergamo or Brescia might go either way. Florence struggled to conquer or entice Pisa and Arezzo, Prato and Siena. These northern struggles were not immune from intervention by Naples and the Papacy; and the northern republics or princes had their greedy eyes at times on parts of those southern territories. There were plenty of mercenary soldiers (*condottieri*) ready to get involved – for money, prestige, or even to create their own petty state. These *condottieri* had included foreigners, such as the English Sir John Hawkwood (known to Italians as Giovanni Acuto), whose unusually loyal services to Florence earned him a superb frescoed equestrian portrait in Florence Cathedral by Paolo Uccello (1430), as well as the splendid civic-sponsored funeral (1394), which had set new standards for the ritual treatment of death.[7]

A few exemplary events at the beginning of the fifteenth century can illustrate the political struggles of the period. In 1402 Duke Gian Galeazzo Visconti died unexpectedly, on the brink of capturing Florence. This unexpectedly ended one of the most serious threats to the Florentine republic. Out of this struggle, and fortunate salvation, Florentine humanist scholars and officials developed concepts of republicanism, freedom (for themselves if not Arezzo or Pistoia), civic humanism and the high virtue of the active life as opposed to contemplation and retreat from the sinful world. More politically, the setback for the Milanese–Visconti empire contributed indirectly to Venetian as well as to Florentine aggrandisement. Venice took Padua from the Carrara family in 1405, while in 1404 Vicenza had chosen Venetian republicanism rather than the Carrara dynasty. Verona also fairly willingly submitted. Later Venice encroached against the Milanese and Visconti, taking Brescia in 1426 and Bergamo in 1428.[8] From some of these events developed the greater territorial states, to be accompanied sometimes by the creation of wider economic conglomerates, and affecting the ebb and flow of Italian urban history and culture.

The Peace of Lodi of 1454, formally between Milan and Venice but also leading to a settlement between Florence and the Papacy, was a significant marker point. It brought a degree of peace to the Italian peninsula, although partly intended as a prelude to a new Crusade against the Muslim Ottoman Turks who had finally seized Constantinople (modern Istanbul) in 1453. The fall of the largest city of the period, the centre of the old Eastern Empire and of the Eastern Orthodox church, was a dramatic symbolic event – though the Ottomans had been eating away at Eastern Christendom in Asia Minor and the Balkans for a long time. From the Italian viewpoint there were benefits in the flight of Greek scholars and manuscripts to Italian courts and universities to buttress the classical revival: with significant effects not only on classical studies, but on broad scientific knowledge, theology, moral philosophy and social teaching, as on philanthropy. The sixteenth-century Florentine historian, Francesco Guicciardini, looked back on the period 1454–1494 as a golden age of peace, leading to major cultural achievements, and the benign leadership of the Florentine republic by the Medici family.

Guicciardini had wittingly exaggerated the degree of peace. There were continuing struggles within the Papal State and the Kingdom of Naples in the attempts to establish control. The Guicciardini and Machiavelli families within Florence had not only to confront the problems of war between Florence and the Papacy, but the considerable violence of the Pazzi conspiracy (1478). The Pazzi and others seeking to overthrow Medici domination killed Giuliano de' Medici in the Cathedral and wounded his elder brother Lorenzo *Il Magnifico*. Lorenzo and his supporters took bloody revenge on those conspirators they caught. This event is a reminder of the violent political struggles, the vendettas, the exiling, the painting of the hanged plotters as mural advertisements of their treachery that are part of the urban scene, even in periods of golden peace.

However the myth of peace was constructed at the height of much worse violence and depredation inaugurated by the 1494–5 invasion of Italy by the French under the personal command of King Charles VIII. This event is crucial for all aspects of

Italian history.[9] Charles claimed the throne of Naples. Invading Italy in September 1494, he and his considerable army reached Naples in February 1495. On the way they took control of Milan and drove the Medici out of Florence (with the aid of Florentines hostile to the Medici). Charles was soon back in France; but this brought no respite to Italy. The King had launched the peninsula into what has become known as the Italian Wars, lasting until 1559. Italy was the centre, or one of the centres, of international conflict. The French reappeared under Louis XII in 1499, and often dominated the north from Milan. The Spaniards, based in the south, contended for control of the whole peninsula, especially when King Charles of Castile, Aragon, Naples, etc. became Holy Roman Emperor in 1519 and brought in German resources as well. The Turks harried the Italian shoreline, and Sultan Suleiman I seems seriously to have considered taking Rome for his empire. Germans and Swiss fought also as mercenaries on all sides. Italian states manoeuvred between the outside powers, for and against each other, as alliances and leagues were formed, broken and reformed. Peace came in 1559 with the treaty of Cateau-Cambrésis, when the French and Imperial-Spanish sides were exhausted. Italy was left dominated by the Spanish, now under Philip II, sovereign over Naples, Sicily, Lombardy and coastal ports like Port'Ercole in Tuscany.

The effects of the Italian Wars were considerable and multifarious, both negative and positive. The 1494 French army was one of the largest so far known in European warfare; and it came with heavier guns for bombarding cities. Thereafter warfare was more intense and destructive than Italy had experienced before. The practices and threats of war caused new developments in the design and construction of city defences, castles and war machinery. This provided work for famous – or soon to be famous – artists: Leonardo da Vinci in Milan and elsewhere, Fra Giocondo in Naples and Padua; Antonio San Gallo the Younger and other relatives in Florence, Nettuno, Civitavecchia, Civita Castellana and Perugia; Michelangelo in Florence. From military architecture and machinery such designers developed ideas that soon influenced civil and ecclesiastical architecture, urban design and planning. The cities of Rome, Florence, Naples, Perugia and later Turin were to be among the beneficiaries. With larger armies and greater defence systems, the costs of war were considerably inflated. This required more taxation and levies, necessitating more efficient government officials, and/or more ruthless tax farmers and bankers. So political leaders were pushed towards greater centralisation, a better structured State with a semblance of a modern bureaucracy, and towards theories of the absolute state under which representative institutions, selfish privileged aristocracies and communal oligarchies, would not have the right and power to frustrate the will of the sovereign ruler supposedly acting for the good of all. These political theories and practices might be some time in the fulfilment, but the Italian Wars had pushed developments in those directions.

More immediately the war period 1494–1559 had had some devastating effects on people and places. The number of great set-piece battles was surprisingly small, but the wider effects of war conditions were often intense. The battle of Ravenna on Easter Sunday 1512, when the French defeated the Spanish, led to considerable casualties and the sacking of Ravenna. Other major examples of sacked cities were Rapallo by the Swiss in 1494, Brescia (by the French) and Prato (by the Spanish on behalf of the Medici) in 1512, and Rome in 1527. Cities might be besieged for lengthy periods: Pisa by the Florentines through the 1490s, Verona (occupied by Spanish and German imperial forces) by Venetian and French allies, Naples by the French 1527–8, Republican Florence by the Medici Pope Clement VII and his Imperial supporters 1529–30, Siena by the Medici and Spanish 1552–5. Some of these sieges were resolved without major destruction, but they still seriously affected normal life.

More insidiously the war periods saw the spread of diseases, starvation, as food supplies were plundered or peasants rendered unable to sow new crops, and economic recession. The 1520s in particular were grim years of plague, typhus (especially in 1528), bad weather and famine. From 1495 syphilis became a deadly and disfiguring affliction. The disease was allegedly brought back from the New World by Columbus' expeditions, though some medical historians have suggested that a strain was part of the European scene before, or that syphilis was a variation of yaws (still afflicting Africa) that became sexually transmitted.[10] However, without doubt it was the French march to Naples and back in 1494–5 that turned syphilis into a major scourge, transmitted by the soldiers and their camp followers. Italians tend to refer to it as the *mal francese*, the French pox, though the French and others blamed the Neapolitans. Initially syphilis had a high mortality rate, and created considerable fear and shock affecting the mood of the period, much like the modern AIDS epidemic.

The second major psychological shock to the mentality of the period, after syphilis, came from the Sack of Rome in 1527, when unpaid imperial troops (mainly German) went on the rampage, raping, sacking, looting and creating mayhem. The extent of the human suffering is obscure, especially as plague, malaria and food shortages added to the mortality and to the flight of survivors. The looting and destruction were considerable, especially of more decorative and portable works of art such as relics in lavish containers, jewellery, tapestries (such as the papal series for the Sistine Chapel woven to paper designs or 'cartoons' by Raphael, some of which are now in the Victoria and Albert Museum), stained glass, smaller antique statues and the like. Some works of art survived, to be preserved elsewhere, including some of the Raphael tapestries, but much ornate medieval gold and silver was lost. André Chastel (1983) and other commentators argue that the psychological impact was considerable, shaking Romans, Italians and other Europeans out of a complacent or over-confident mood, out of excesses of paganism and classical idealism, into a more reflective and serious Christianity. Artists, musicians and writers moved away from classical harmonies, into more emotional, tense, dissonant forms of expression. Moods of despair, anxiety or cynicism are detected in writers like Francesco Guicciardini or Piero Valeriano, and artists like Michelangelo, Rosso Fiorentino or Sebastiano del Piombo. While northern reformers might welcome the destruction of reliquaries, Catholic faithful were shocked by stories about the preserved heads of Saints Peter, Paul and John being laughingly kicked about the streets of Rome by drunken Germans. The sack was seen as the wrath of God; it almost certainly drove Italian religious leaders to take the threat of Lutheranism more seriously, and to seek reform of the church from within. Rome recovered, and some of the destruction acted as a stimulus for a new Rome, which gradually moved towards a more suitable environment for leading a reformed Catholic church.

The Sack of Rome had positive effects. It dispersed some influential people, or discouraged others from returning: artists, religious leaders, patrons. Rome's loss was Venice's gain. The sculptor and architect Jacopo Sansovino moved to Venice, contributed much to urban development and classicised Venetian architecture. Serlio, who had survived through the Sack, published in Venice inventories of Roman buildings, and promoted the images of classical architecture. Doge Andrea Gritti, Serlio's sponsor, was intent that Venice should be the new cultural leader of Italy in place of Rome. Pietro Aretino had left Rome for Venice before the Sack – forecasting its occurrence – and declined to return. Out of Venice he expanded his reputation as poet, dramatist, high-class pornographer, letter-writer, journalist and publicist for himself and artistic friends. In the somewhat freer atmosphere of mid-century Venice he was to have some impact on attitudes to vernacular literature, to artistic style and to women's roles and gender differences.[11]

By contrast, from the diaspora from Rome came serious, moralistic religious reformers, particularly Gaetano da Thiene and Gian Pietro Carafa (later Pope Paul IV); having started a society of clerics in 1524 to promote religious and social reform they and supporters dispersed from Rome in 1527. They took their reform ideas to Venice and Naples in particular. From their initiatives arose the new Order of Theatines that was to play a major role in Catholic reform, especially in the Kingdom of Naples.

The horrors of war that seriously disrupted society had a major impact on religious reform and philanthropic activity. Those who witnessed bodies lying unburied, the sick lying in the streets, raped women and orphaned and abandoned children wandering through city and countryside, were sometimes shocked and moved into starting lay confraternities or clerical societies to organise assistance; to found hospices, hospitals, conservatories and other refuges. The sack of Brescia in 1512, and particularly the raping of citizens by the soldiery, led Countess Laura Gambara to provide a refuge (eventually called the Conservatorio delle Convertite Della Carità) to protect vulnerable girls; this was to inspire many similar conservatories for girls and women. Later Girolamo Miani, a Venetian nobleman, similarly reacting to the effects of war in northern Italy, founded a company, the Servants of the Poor (Dei Servi dei Poveri) in 1534, to organise orphanages. Major ones were opened in Brescia, Pavia and Como. Friends and associates undertook similar work through lay confraternities, while Miani's immediate circle went on to create the Regular Clerks of Somasca, (the Somaschi). By the end of the century this Order had become notable for also offering educational facilities for poor slum-dwellers, as in Rome and Naples. So out of the disasters of war emerged major efforts to provide Catholic philanthropy.

The Peace of Cateau-Cambrésis of 1559 is another obvious marker in the history of the Italian peninsula (see Maps 2 and 4). It enabled the Italian states to restructure and consolidate themselves in relative peace. Philip II's Spanish rule, led by resident Viceroys in Naples and Palermo, or Governors in Milan, involved the native elites of the areas; and the southern areas were probably better controlled and governed (to the benefit of the average inhabitant) than they had been for ages. The extent of Spanish influence – often seen in the past as detrimental to liberty of thought, humanist culture and renaissance values – has probably been exaggerated, though it is now clear that Philip II had a Hispanicising policy even in Rome.[12] Spanish feudal attitudes, courtly manners and chivalric concepts may have accentuated existing tendencies towards economic and cultural 'refeudalisation'. A supposedly hostile Spanish attitude towards ignoble involvement in commerce and manual labour, which might have threatened the creation of wealth, can be balanced by other considerations. The South's involvement in the wider Spanish imperial enterprises – notably in trying to preserve the Netherlands – meant that the Spanish Italian areas provided men, materiel and materials for the imperial struggle. Capitalist northern Italians had opportunities for investment and commercial exploitation.

Outside the Spanish areas, the 1559 peace left the Venetian and Genoese Republics, the Duchy of Tuscany (under the Medici family again) and the Papal State as more integrated and centralised states. In effect north and central Italy had fewer centres of political power; the second rank cities and their dominant elites were more controlled; there was less factional fighting, less rebellion, and the general urban populace probably enjoyed a more placid existence than their predecessors in the centuries of communal 'liberty'. Siena, Bologna, Perugia, Orvieto, Verona, Vicenza or Brescia might for the rest of our period be less exciting places politically, have less local leadership, but they also had less civil war. There might have been cultural losses as patronage concentrated more on Florence, Rome or Venice. While some of these cities suffered economic decline, it is hard to argue that this was largely because they had lost *de facto* political control of their own destiny. The elites of the secondary cities redeployed their energies, their investments and talents, and many were incorporated further (as individuals, families or within corporations and local institutions) into the faster developing, pluralistic regional states.[13]

The peace of 1559 was followed by the conclusion of the Council of Trent in December 1563. This Council of the Church had met intermittently since 1545, (1545–7, 1551–2, 1562–3) either to produce some reconciliation with Protestants (for most involved a forgotten target or forlorn hope by the time the Council got down to business), or to define true Catholic doctrine, remedy acknowledged defects and immoral behaviour, and programme procedures for improving the church and its members. The ratification of the decrees, their printing and distribution to bishops and some other clergy by the summer of 1564 launched reform programmes of considerable consequences for society generally. Policies and implementation varied vastly through the peninsula, and worked at different rates of progress. Aspects of the impact of Trent and reformers inspired by it will be discussed further in various chapters; but it can said here that what generally emerged was a more coherent and regular religious–social life based on the parish church, through which society was more controlled and documented. There were major implications for the position of women, and male attitudes towards them, for marriage, education and philanthropy.

From the 1590s Italy faced growing pressures and tensions, economic, social and political, which suggest a general 'decline' in Italian fortunes and European influence. The modern cultural historian may counterattack with positive arguments that from then Tridentine puritanism and paranoic repression diminished, that painting, sculpture and music became more adventurous (especially in Rome and – at least for music – Venice), that conspicuous consumption on comfortable living generated activity in luxury crafts and trade. But the crises of the 1590s, and the sequels, had wider impact.[14] That decade saw as elsewhere in Europe, years of poor harvests under adverse weather conditions, famines, recessions in textile industries. The hunt for new food supplies brought in Dutch and English shippers, transporting grains from the Baltic. Their entry into the Mediterranean markets opened up opportunities and enticements that were not forgotten; so they remained to challenge the economic trading activities of the Venetians in particular, and to add to the problems of piracy on the high seas.

In 1618 the crises in the Holy Roman Empire, the Habsburg lands, and Bohemia in particular launched Europe into a war period that came to be known as the Thirty Years' War. The effects on Italy were complex. To begin with the Italian states were not directly involved, but they were affected economically. The Venetian Republic suffered through disruption to its northern markets – for textiles, luxury goods such as glass, or possibly foods. But Lombardy and Naples had benefits from helping to man and supply the Spanish armies. Also northern merchants were flexible enough to compensate for the loss of German trade by pursuing markets, especially for luxury textiles, in places further afield, such as Poland (at least until it faced crisis in 1655).

Conditions worsened for Italians when in 1627 Duke Vincenzo II Gonzaga of Mantua died without direct heirs. This produced a succession crisis, leading to war and the sack of the city by the Imperial army in 1630. It was not just that Mantua itself was a strategically important state; its Gonzaga rulers also had the marquisate of Monferrato with its crucial fortress of Casale, controlling north-western routes in and out of Italy. The succession with its properties were thus of considerable interest to the Spanish Habsburgs under Philip IV, the Habsburg Holy Roman Emperor Ferdinand II, (who was technically the feudal superior of Mantua), the French, and the House of Savoy ruling Savoy and Piedmont. The struggle for Mantua and Monferrato was intense, time-consuming and costly for all sides, devastating for the main cities and disruptive of the economy of northern Italy. This struggle coincided with a major plague epidemic (and typhus or typhoid in some places like Tuscany) 1629–32, and the armies exacerbated the spread and impact of diseases and death. The French Duke of Nevers was eventually recognised as the successor to Mantua, which gave the French a major excuse for intervening in north Italian affairs for the following decades.

As the Thirty Years' War ground on further north, the Spanish Empire became more hard-pressed, suffering more defeats and set-backs. One effect was to increase the financial pressures on its Italian states, Naples in particular, so that through the 1630s and 1640s the economic position of the Viceroyalty became worse, and the social tensions greater. The combination of long-term depression and short-term food and tax crises produced the major revolts in Palermo and Naples in 1647 (the Masaniello Revolt), and through much of the Kingdom of Naples. The Spanish authorities managed to resist both native rebels and French interlopers and to restore a semblance of order and authority. However the second half of the seventeenth century following the end of the Thirty Years' War in 1648, is seen largely as a period of economic and cultural stagnation, even if there was relative peace politically. Recent scholarship has been more inclined to highlight some intellectual and artistic vitality, in Naples, Venice and Turin, for example.

Italy was thrown into major political turmoil with the Spanish Succession crisis of 1700. Charles II of Spain died, as expected, without a direct legitimate heir. Fear that the whole world Empire would all pass to either an Austrian Habsburg or a French claimant had led to partition treaties ahead of the King's death, and then to war. The political fate of Naples, Sicily, Lombardy and Sardinia was at stake, and strongly contested. The Peace of Utrecht in 1713 left the Austrian Habsburgs in control of Naples and Lombardy, and the House of Savoy in possession of Sicily. But the logistical inconveniences of the latter occasioned an exchange with Austria in 1720, so that Savoy ruled Sardinia, and Austria ruled Sicily. The scene again changed when in 1735, as a by-product of the War of the Polish Succession, Austria ceded Naples and Sicily to a Spanish Bourbon, Charles III son of Philip V of Spain. Succession crises were fashionable in this period, to the further detriment of Italy. The end of the Farnese line as Dukes of Parma and Piacenza in 1731 led to Spain taking over these useful Po valley states within a few months; in 1748 it was recognised internationally that they should be ruled independently by Don Carlos. With the death of Grand Duke Gian Gastone in 1737 the Medici family finally petered out as rulers of Florence/Tuscany.This lazy alcoholic – though sometimes a well-intentioned and humane man – had become increasingly an embarrassment and scandal, as reputedly his court had become more and more dominated by riotous feasts with homosexual orgies.[15] Tuscany was handed over by the international powers to Duke Francis Stephen of Lorraine; but since he had married in 1736 Maria Theresa, heir to the Austrian Habsburg lands (who succeeded in 1740), Tuscany was soon part of the Austrian Empire.

It was not until 1763 that the Italian peninsula entered a period of peace, with agreed territorial settlements. Severe famine conditions particularly affected the Kingdom of Naples, Tuscany and Rome. This helped stimulate an interesting stage when serious attempts were made to implement enlightenment policies. Whatever the depth or shallowness of the economic and cultural decline of Italy from the mid-seventeenth to the early eighteenth century, a sense of *risorgimento* (revival) reigned from the 1760s, building on previous intellectual developments and reform moves, particularly in Naples. The weaknesses of Italian culture, in thrall to the French or to distant glories of the past, the economically unproductive results of outmoded feudal attitudes and institutions, the deficiencies of old legal procedures and practices all came under scrutiny from men as diverse as the long-lived Jesuit Saverio Bettinelli (1718–1808) (whose literary and historical critique *Il Risorgimento*, 1775, was to have such resonance), the Naples Professor of Political Economy Antonio Genovesi, the Modena cleric and historian Ludovico Muratori and the Lombard criminologist and state counsellor Cesare Beccaria. Rational analysis in much of Italy was accompanied by attempted remedies. The states of Tuscany, Lombardy, Naples, Modena and even the Papal States were to have ministers, counsellors and administrators who were themselves writers on reform, and/or were friends, collaborators and students of such writers and university teachers. Our early modern society was changed.[16]

The 1789–91 French revolutionary events had mixed effects on thinking Italians. If much had been achieved by reformers – particularly in agricultural improvements, legal reforms and the diminishing of conservative clerical teaching and influence – there were many frustrations. Most reformers, many of them lesser nobles and urban patricians, had secured action through absolutist princes, without many calls for a widening of political power – partly on the grounds that such a prince, if enlightened by suitable advisers, would secure action more quickly than a more democratic process involving benighted aristocrats and middle classes. However, by 1789 many reformers, like Beccaria and his erstwhile friend and associate Pietro Verri, were feeling frustrated by the limited changes that had been achieved, and what they heard out of France seemed inspiring. But as France degenerated into violence, and then liberated or invaded north Italy, attitudes towards France and new ideas became more mixed. Italy was again thrown into considerable chaos – intellectually, socially and economically – during the French occupation period. It was out of the combination of enlightened reform and of French-induced chaos and Napoleonic restructuring that modern Italian society emerged.

Though disunited politically through the period there was a sense of Italian identity, at least in high political and cultural circles, based on cultural identities, and a sense of geographical integrity. Resentment at trans-Alpine interference (as mention of another round of anti-French feelings in the eighteenth century has just suggested), could provide stimulus to action, and at least cultural vitality. The struggle to bring back the Pope, as a single agreed leader, to Rome, is one marker for the beginning of the period (1417), to be followed by a belated response to French invasion in 1494. Resentment at French cultural influences is one trigger for the *risorgimento* that helps end the era.

The fairly static and the changing political situations affect the social scenes in various ways. From the fifteenth to the eighteenth century the political geography was simplified, by external pressures and internal ambitions. The concentration of some political leadership in fewer cities affected urban demography and locations of economic activity, to the detriment of some intermediary cities, and impinging on all levels of society. More narrowly the simplified political scene changed the nature and roles of some of the elites, both within cities and in the rural world, though as we shall note, there were not the neat urban/rural, commerce/land divisions alleged for other states like Spain, France or Prussia. The political and military struggles of 1494–1559, besides eventually producing more centralised states, affected demographic patterns and economic activities (especially those connected with warfare). The evil effects of war and accompanying health problems dislocated society, added to banditry problems, but also generated welfare schemes and affected attitudes to morality and religious duties. The comparatively peaceful period, politically, from 1559 to 1700, to some extent under Spanish attitudes and threats, allowed new elites to entrench themselves, religious reformers to consolidate some Tridentine policies, and both to join political leaders in imposing more social control. As often before, climate threats and health crises were ready to disturb the stability, and endanger economic development, when serious wars did not. The last section of our period, from 1700, sees war and disease combine to produce more misery and dislocations; but unlike in the early sixteenth century, when reformers produced socio-religious palliatives, the new reformers were tempted to challenge the old society more fundamentally. Landholding and feudal systems, the dominance of aristocratic elites, the once revered contributions of religious education and welfare came under serious criticism, if not very effective execution. This was heading for a new era.

The political divisions overall, and local areas of cohesion, the impediments to political unity, the crises of demography, the distribution of economic prosperity and poverty, what dictated social mobility or immobility, were all significantly affected by Italian geography, which deserves a chapter of its own.

2

GEOGRAPHY AND DEMOGRAPHY

Physical geography

The social and economic history of any area is conditioned by that area's basic physical geography.[1] The Italian peninsula is predominantly characterised by mountains and high rugged hills; and few plains or rolling fertile downs (Map 1). No easy terrain for farming, or internal communication, the mountainous areas produced few profitable mineral resources in the period. The peninsula's long coastline is not that beneficial, with comparatively few natural harbours; rivers connecting mountains and the coast have hindered rather than helped the profitable use of the coastal plains. Much intervention by man has been needed to derive economic benefit from the rivers and coasts.

The mountain ranges of the Alps in the north, and the Apennines curving down the spine of Italy are the dominant features, leaving the valley of the Po and its tributaries, the most fertile plain area, as the key to northern agricultural prosperity. Crossing the mountains remained difficult and hazardous, especially in winter, until the late nineteenth and early twentieth centuries. Travellers have left telling records of the difficulties and dangers, but also of the intrepidity of many who did travel, and the employment of many who assisted them.[2] There were many Alpine crossings – Braudel calculated twenty-three for the sixteenth century, seventeen of which had been used since Roman times. In the western Alps the main routes to and from Italy and the Lombard plain were the Mont Cenis and St Bernard passes. Genoa, with its beneficial deep-water harbour, was protected by the northern end of the Apennines, through which there were reasonable passes (Giovi and Bocchetta) into the Lombard plain. But Genoa as a commercial Republic was hampered by having to rely on reasonably tranquil conditions in Piedmont and Lombardy to allow goods to be carried on to the Mont Cenis and St Bernard passes. Such factors tended to encourage Genoa to concentrate on sea routes. Venice, as the rival international trading power, developed a more beneficial situation from the fifteenth century. In land trading north through the eastern Alps, its goal was the Brenner pass, best approached via the Adige, Val Sugana or Piave. Rivers in between – the Po, Piave and Brenta – though not ideal were preferable to roads. Control of the Adige routes essentially required control of Verona; from the early fifteenth century the Venetian

Republic secured dominance over that city in its mainland, Terraferma, expansion. The Venetian Republic could thereby develop a more diverse economy than Genoa.

Further south the Apennines impeded north–south and east–west communications, and encouraged political fragmentation. South of Piacenza and Parma, men and goods could cross the Apennines via the Taro river and Cisa Pass to Sarzanello and La Spezia, and so down the coastal route through Tuscany. The French invading army under Charles VIII in 1494 took this route.[3] Those seeking access from the Bologna region to Tuscany and Umbria had difficult routes – whether via the rivers Setta and Stura to Prato, or through Firenzuola and Scarperia to Florence. Further south, the crucial links were from Faenza to Florence by the Val di Lamone; Forli to Florence via Castrocaro; Rimini to Arezzo through Borgo San Sepolcro. Umbria has been able to maintain adequate communication across the centuries, thanks to the Bocca Serriola and Bocca Trabaria passes from the Tiber valley across the Apennines. These routes explain the strategic, commercial (and ultimately cultural) importance of some smaller cities of north-central Italy. Further south communication routes would take advantage of the Tiber valley, then coastal routes on the Tyrrhenian sea or the Adriatic coast. Much of the south is rugged, arid, inhospitable – discouraging communication and perhaps civilised development – though river gorges such as those of the Bradano allow penetration inland.

Braudel and others have emphasised the importance of mountains, and the relationships with the foothills and plains for developments within Italy. Some caution is required here. The assumption that there was an almost automatic drawing down of hillbillies to the lower areas, except when hilltop cities had to be created, because mountain areas were poorer, is misleading. At least in late fourteenth and fifteenth century Tuscany and the neighbouring Bolognese areas, mountain inhabitants could be better off than those lower down and closer to the cities; and mountain people more often migrated from one mountain area to another, before moving down into plains or cities.[4]

The rugged Friuli region has achieved notoriety for its magical practices and beliefs investigated by the Inquisition, and effectively written up by Carlo Ginzburg in his studies of a heretical miller, Menocchio Scandela, and of *benandanti,* or night-riders who battled with evil forces.[5] The survival of pagan rituals and popular heretical beliefs is often attributed to remote mountainous territory. Yet Menocchio's home town of Montereale is in the foothills, with high Dolomite mountains behind, and the lower level of the great Tagliamento river bed south towards the Venetian lagoon. That river bed has been dried up through historic times; not very fertile but crossable without great impediment. Looking up above Montereale one can see paths and small tunnels, which date from the early modern period and further back. In fact this was an area that from Roman times saw much transit of goods and people, to and from the Germanic areas down to ports on the Venetian lagoon, to Aquileia, to the east and into the Istrian area and the Balkans. People and places in the Friuli and the Veneto could be remote, and snowbound in winter, but also they had significant contact with the wider world. Material goods and ideas moved and had their influence.

The river systems of Italy are crucial, but they present many problems, and are hardly as beneficial as a quick look at a physical map might suggest (Map 1). In summer many rivers dry up almost completely; in winter they are variable with erratic rainfall; many are prone to flooding, and sweep away beneficial soils. The Arno flowing through Florence is an obvious example of such problems. Italy has few lakes, and many catchment basins are meagre. Steep slopes, and the nonporous nature of many rock structures, render many river regimes unhelpful. For geographers the most satisfactory river regimes centre on Pescara, fed by the Nera and Velino and limestone springs in the Abruzzi, and the Tiber, as fed by the same rivers, with the Aniene as well. The Volturno and Sele render the Campagna region fairly fertile. The Po river with its tributaries has been the key to much of northern Italy's economic prosperity, but the irregularity of Alpine rainfall, seasonal fluctuations and flooding have produced major disasters. Human intervention – especially from the fifteenth century with canals, river re-routing and irrigation schemes – has tamed some of nature's excesses and improved the economic and social benefits.

The exit systems of the Po, however, highlight an additional problem: that many Italian rivers end in marshy, swampy coastland – eroding the coast and silting up lagoons (except where, as with Venice, the authorities over centuries have organised remedies). In the absence of adequate human intervention and control, areas further south like the Comacchio and Ravenna regions, or (on the Tyrrhenian coast) the deltas of the Tiber, Arno and Ombrone were insalubrious and under-productive, characterised through the early modern period by malarial conditions. Elsewhere along the coast, torrential river outlets have undermined the natural potential of bays to serve as ports.

Italy's physical geography helps explain the location and nature of the significant medieval and early modern urban centres: on key river locations, near passes and travel routes or high up on hill slopes or even tops – despite problems of water supply. Towns perched on hilly outcrops took populations away from erratic torrential rivers and streams, left lower slopes for productive agriculture and made the human communities more defensible against rival communities, feudal lords or robber gangs.

The mountainous and hilly nature of much of the peninsula should not indicate that all was barren and unproductive – leaving prosperity just for the Lombard plains, the Po valley, the Campania or the Puglian coast. Many mountain areas had arable land on hill-side terraces, or in the valleys: Braudel cited Spoleto as one of the best examples of a city in mountainous land, but with a fertile plain. Vines grow high up on Mount Etna, maize was brought to the Cosenza region in the sixteenth century, and grows at altitudes up to 1400 metres; wheat and barley are found at even higher levels in the Abruzzi. In central Italy when olive growing became marginal on higher slopes, hazelnuts and almonds contributed to the economy. Chestnuts were brought into the northern and central Apennines at high levels to be a staple of peasant diets, often to the detriment of older forest trees such as beech. Favourable climatic conditions in Umbria in association with intermontane basins (as in high points like Norcia or Gubbio) have enabled inhabitants to cultivate the terraced hills with wheat, beans and fodder, cutting back the old forests and bringing in almonds, olives, figs and then in our period, mulberries. This agricultural world sustained largish populations in cities high above, as in Todi, Perugia or Assisi.

Through the sixteenth to eighteenth centuries as foreign travellers to Italy more frequently recorded their impressions, they increasingly noted with admiration how hillsides in northern and central Italy were terraced, and intensely managed to utilise varieties of crops, trees and interspersed animals. Irrigation schemes, the way vines and fruit trees were cared for from Lombardy through the Papal States to Terra di Lavoro (north of Naples), were admired by careful observers like Arthur Young from England, the German Goethe or the French Charles de Brosses, who declared of the Vicenza–Padua landscape: '. . . there is no more beautiful or better decorated opera scenery than a country like this.'[6]

Contrasts came, then as now, when the South was surveyed. The South (the modern regions of Abruzzi, Campania, Molise, Puglia (or Apulia), Calabria and Basilicata, to which Sicily and Sardinia can be added) is predominantly mountainous and hilly, with only about 23 per cent plains. The mountainous lands are more arid than further north, their rock formations more unstable; speedy evaporation in summer, unreliable rainfall and the absence of permeable rock that might help trap water (except in the Campania), inhibit productive agriculture. The natural conditions, backed by policies of governments and feudal landowners from the late middle ages, encouraged the pasturing of sheep and goats over considerable areas – to the ultimate detriment of the soil. Deforestation and consequent erosion through the early modern period to the present has added to the poverty of the soil and the inhabitants. In the south the mountainous areas remained more isolated. The limited communication between human habitations further inhibited economic, social and cultural diversity in comparison with Umbria let alone the southern Alps and northern and central Apennine regions. Mountain snow and ice could be economically beneficial, and not just for those providing for ice-cream lovers at the Medici court in Florence. A Sicilian nobleman, Antonio Ruffo, was able to become a major art patron and collector in Messina (dealing with painters including Salvator Rosa, Poussin and Artemisia Gentileschi, and collecting Rembrandt works) – thanks in part to his monopoly control of ice supplies, derived from mountainous properties in Sicily and Calabria.[7]

The geographical scene changed through the early modern period from human intervention as well as climate. Deforestation, with its effects on climate, the soil and the structure of land, has been a constant detrimental factor, and not just in the south. In the northern Lazio until the sixteenth century an extensive forest of oak trees, the Selva di Manziana, stretched from the Tolfa hills to Bolsena; only a little survives.[8] However, mainly beneficial human interventions could affect the vegetation and water regimes of Italy. Mulberry trees were increasingly introduced from the later middle ages for silkworms; this particularly affected the Lucca, Florence and Bologna areas, then Piedmont, the Veneto (especially from Verona to Vicenza) and, by the eighteenth century, parts of the south. The ailanto was introduced from southern Asia in the eighteenth century for the same purpose. The mulberry tree became a major feature in peasant farming and the peasant economy – sometimes under direct government pressure, as when as early as 1440 the Florentine government on behalf of the silk guild compelled rural property owners or occupiers to plant at least 50 mulberry trees.

The cultivation of the saffron crocus increased in the period. Saffron was used for medicinal purposes, flavouring and colouring. While just another contribution to varieties of cultivation in Lombardy, Piedmont and Monferrato, it had more economic significance for other key areas, in Puglia and especially the Abruzzi. In the fifteenth century Abruzzi saffron became prized by German merchants operating out of Venice, and some (such as the Welsers and Baumgartners) established representatives in Aquila to organise the trade.

Controlling rivers, creating canals, draining marshes, had been part of medieval interventionism in the natural scene. In the thirteenth century various canals were built in the Milan area: the Chiaravalle, La Muzza and the Naviglio Grande. In 1400 Duke Gian Galeazzo Visconti of Milan ordered the building of the Milan–Pavia canal. Milanese authorities had various undertakings to control the waters of the Ticino and Adda, employing Leonardo da Vinci among others in such operations. The authorities in Arezzo in 1341 inaugurated schemes to drain the Val di Chiana, digging channels to the Arno. The Medici of Florence could consequentially develop a large estate there in our period. In the sixteenth century the Medici Dukes of Tuscany improved the health and agricultural conditions around Pisa by draining marshes, and in the early seventeenth century extended the work to marshes between Pisa and Livorno [Leghorn], which they developed thereby into one of the major Mediterranean ports by the eighteenth century. The course of the Arno was altered, the Navicelli canal constructed and Pisa thereby given easy water access to both Florence and Livorno. Similarly, Venetian authorities in the sixteenth century altered the courses of the Brenta and Piave rivers, (the latter judged in a 1552 government decree as 'the principal enemy of the lagoon'),[9] and then in 1605 the Po itself, to manage better the coastal area and save Chioggia from the adverse effects of water flows and silting. Through the sixteenth to eighteenth centuries the Venetians publicly and privately manipulated their parts of the Po valley with irrigation channels, canals, bank building, etc. as part of new land investment, agricultural experimentation and the development of villa and country-house living.

By the eighteenth century, travellers in Italy could contrast the beneficial effects of human intervention in the Po valley, in Tuscany (including the Val di Chiana) and in Umbria, with the neglect or failed interventions in the Roman Campagna, on which John Moore in his *A View of the Society and Manners in Italy* (1780) commented:

> After having traversed the fertile and cultivated valleys of Umbria, one is affected with double emotion at beholding the deplorable state of poor neglected Latium [Lazio]. For several posts before you arrive at Rome, few villages, little cultivation and scarcely any inhabitants are to be seen. In the Campagna of Rome . . . no trees, no inclosure, nothing but scattered ruins of temples and tombs, presenting the idea of a country depopulated by pestilence.[10]

The physical geography of the Italian peninsula dictated that there would be relatively few coastal ports to dominate international trade; that inland cities might thrive to control crucial river traffic – as with Florence, Verona and Mantua; that many other urban communities would be at high altitudes, and densely packed, for geographical reasons as much as for defence in the midst of social and political strife. Much ingenuity was required to control and improve water regimes for agricultural productivity, human health and personal or commercial communication. Geographical conditions helped dictate the continuing contrast between the more prosperous, progressive and mobile north and centre of Italy and the poorer more static south, with its latifundia estates, however much one might blame in addition political ineptitudes or cultural attitudes of the Aragonese and Spanish rulers of Naples and Sicily.

Demography

Through the early modern period, Italy was one of the most densely populated and urbanised parts of Europe – especially in the north – comparable with the Netherlands.[11] Population figures for the whole territory have to be tentative throughout; though for certain urban areas and their dependent more rural territories (the *contado*) fairly reliable figures survive from the later sixteenth century (see Appendix). Italy had a population of about 10 million in 1300 and rising; it plummeted by about a third in mid-century following the Black Death plague, rose more steadily to 11 million in 1500 and more dramatically to 12 million by 1600. It fell after devastating plagues again to 11 million by the mid-1650s and rose to 13 million by 1700.

Thus, through our early modern period the population rose, but dramatic mortality crises caused sudden dips. These crises were variable across Italy, and the patterns of recovery uneven. Normally mortality was less than the prevailing fertility, so there should have been a slow tendency towards population growth. 'Normal' mortality is seen as prevailing when there were no major famines, plagues and pestilences, or wars to create 'catastophic' mortality. The patterns of urban growth or decline were complicated. Cities were probably more adversely affected than rural areas by major epidemics; but complicated political and economic factors affect the figures for individual cities. As the Appendix indicates, a few cities grew dramatically from *c.* 1500 to *c.* 1700; some cities were surprisingly static, and some saw major slumps. Demographers argue that in the period mortality within a city outweighed fertility, so that a city or large town's population would need a balance of immigrants from countryside or small towns to sustain its overall level. Political, economic and cultural factors then explain why a Rome or Naples, for example, attracted far more immigrants through the sixteenth century than Florence, Siena or Lucca.

Italian demography in the period was characterised by high fertility and high mortality, with the mortality for babies and young children being very severe. A rate of 150–250 deaths of children in the first year per 1000 live births would seem to be normal; but a figure of 450–500 was not that uncommon, as shown by Fiesole in the seventeenth century. Death rates of children after the first year remained high as malnutrition, childhood diseases and hygiene problems took their toll. There were plenty of children around; Carlo Cipolla calculates that about a third of the population was under fifteen years old, who constituted about 90 per cent of the dependent population; i.e. there were very few old or totally infirm adults for the breadwinners to support. Children provided the pressure points, with families facing the problem of balance between not enough children and too many. The latter could lead to abandonment, and the growing foundling problem in Italy from the late fifteenth century; abandonment at least in the early months, meant death for most babies.

Italian adults mostly married surprisingly late; and late marriage was the key to population control or limited growth. Females might not marry until their early or mid 20s, males till their late 20s, or even early 30s. Figures on age of marriage for Italy are patchy, and show both status and regional variations. In the seventeenth century among nobles in Florence, Genoa and Milan the females tended to marry aged 19–20, but the males 33–36. In Empoli between 1650 and 1700 males married on average at just 29, females at 24. In Venice 1740–44 the average age for males was 31.4 and for females 29.3. But in Puglia females seemed to marry earlier: at 16.6 in Ceglie in 1603, 19.9 at Lucera in 1621. Late marriage tended to limit the period of child-bearing. Some of the abandoned children were illegitimate children whose birth reflected the pressures of these late marriages, since from the later fifteenth century there was increasing reluctance to accept illegitimate children as part of family and household. But premarital conception may equally have led to the marriage or to publicly agreed and permanent cohabitation. The late age of male marriage was seen as causing problems, particularly in fifteenth and sixteenth century Florence where, authorities argued, it fostered the male homosexuality for which the city was notorious. Italy through the period maintained a population section of unmarrieds – as secular clergy, monks, friars and nuns. This would in particular affect the population profile, and fertility, in towns and suburbs. Recent evidence suggests also that in cities a fair number of other adults, including women, never married.

The major factors in the fluctuations in the population were the mortality crises, which tie in with many areas of social history. The mortality crises were caused by plagues and other diseases, famine and war; sometimes by all of them coming together. The great plague crisis of 1347–50, the Black Death, was the most devastating, reducing the population by about a third. In demographic terms the later fourteenth and fifteenth centuries witnessed a long slow recovery. Arguably Italy had been overpopulated, and the slower recovery was beneficial. For the surviving families it had meant more opportunities for land ownership or control, for job opportunities and prosperity.

Many plagues occurred subsequently through our period, but the term plague (*peste* or *pestis*) was, and is to be, used vaguely. It is unwise to assume that many, if any, of a variety of disease epidemics were of bubonic plague involving the bacillus

Yersinia pestis, as identified and studied from the later nineteenth century. The medical conditions, patterns of mortality and the spread of epidemics as reported by competent and observant medics and health officials at the time seldom tally with modern data and analysis; more careful, unprejudiced, analysis is needed to identify different serious epidemics.[12] Contemporaries were aware of a number of epidemics, human and animal, that were fatal, and they used various terms. Some doctors or government officials recording many deaths seemingly affected by fevers, buboes, skin lesions or blotches, etc. were loath to declare it *pestis*, because this brought into play strict quarantine regulations that could have major economic repercussions, as will be discussed later.

Plague remained an intermittent crisis factor – and certainly a fear – through the fifteenth century in local areas (as for example in and around Perugia in the 1480s), though possibly not of major demographic significance. But plague produced some catastrophes on a broader scale in the next 150 years. Pestilences were devastating in the 1522–8 period for nearly all Italy – though linked with other epidemics and diseases for humans and cattle, and the impact of war. Then mortality rates were 7 or 8 times the normal in some of the worst affected areas like Tuscany. In 1575–7 Venetia, Lombardy and Sicily were badly affected by plague; in 1629–31 most of northern Italy except Friuli and Romagna; in 1656 Genoa, Rome and Naples. According to Venetian records 46,721 people died in Venice during the main plague period from July 1575 to February 1577. At the height of the next great visitation, from July 1630 to October 1631, 46,490 died in the city or special plague hospital zones (*lazzaretti*). During a great panic on the 14–15 August 1630, allegedly 24,000 persons fled the city. It is estimated that half the population of Mantua, Milan and Padua died from plague in 1629–31, 56 per cent in Verona, and a third of Bologna and Venice. M. Barbagli suggests that 1,100,000 people throughout Italy died from this epidemic. The Naples epidemic of 1656 (heavily concentrated in the period from the end of April to late September) generated some of the most horrendous estimates of its mortality, though many fail to distinguish between those who died and those who fled. More rational calculations suggest that the city's population in 1657–8 was two-fifths what is had been in 1654–5, with 240–270,000 persons out of 400–450,000 in Naples and its vicinity dying of plague or allied causes. Similarly, Genoa and its dependent littoral territory dropped by about 90,000 in its population from 440,000 to 350,000; the city of Rome fell from 120,000 to 100,000.[13]

The impact was devastating beyond the immediate deaths. Government actions to prevent the spread of plague (whose vehicles of contagion were not understood) could virtually close down the economy, as victims and their families were isolated, houses shut, clothes and other goods burned to prevent contamination, cities closed off from neighbours and travel curtailed. Food supplies became a serious problem, further affecting health and life. The next season's sowing, pruning and harvesting were endangered. Though fewer mouths needed feeding, fewer farmers were available to act quickly, and it was harder to get food into beleaguered cities. It is unclear which sectors of society suffered most, or recovered best. Some detailed Venetian studies do not substantiate the old argument that the upper classes, especially nobles could survive better, because they could more readily escape the city into supposedly safer villages. The younger generation apparently suffered less than the older in Venetian epidemics, especially in the 1630–31 crisis. The Jews may have been proportionately the worst affected sub-group in Venice in 1575–7, because of the density of occupation in the Ghetto, though the calculations are affected by the problem of establishing who fled, never to return to Venice.

The rapidity of demographic recovery after plague was dependent on other variables. Plague probably hit whole families, or left others largely unscathed, except maybe for the elderly. Those who survived plague and immediate food/health conditions were comparatively healthy – fit to procreate again and take advantage of new economic opportunities. If the general economic climate was favourable soon the population might rise, and immigration into key cities be hastened. Venice recovered well in most ways after 1575–77; but recovery after 1631 was slower because the wider economic climate in northern Italy – affected by the Thirty Years' War north and south of the Alps – was less favourable. Venetian families were smaller on average than before.

After plague, *tifo*, which might have been typhus or typhoid involving rashes and fever, was probably the next most serious epidemic for the sixteenth and seventeenth centuries. Typhus, a microbe (*rickettsia*), was spread by lice and fleas, while bacterial typhoid involved *salmonella typhi*, largely spread through faeces.[14] The major epidemics identified by Massimo Livi Bacci (1976) were in 1505, 1528, 1590–1, 1620–1, 1628–9 (immediately preceding plague in some areas to complicate interpretations, as for Florence or Turin), and 1648–9 (especially in Florence), then in 1817–18. In 1590–1 the death rate in certain districts of Florence was four times the normal; 1620–1 was less dramatic because sanitary officials were more vigilant. Typhus and typhoid killed less than plague; of those affected only 20–40 per cent died, while 70–80 per cent of those identified as having plague died from it. But typhoid left survivors seriously debilitated – so presumably more susceptible to secondary illnesses, less fertile and less economically productive. Survivors could retain *rickettsia*, in some cases enough to damage others again. *Tifo* induced less fear and hysteria than plague (which led to the scapegoating of 'anointers' (*untori*) and other supposed spreaders) – or for that matter syphilis in the early years of first epidemic when communicated by soldiers and their camp followers during the Italian wars of 1494 and after. Quarantine regulations against *tifo* were less severe, and so the economic disruption was less.

While *tifo* seems to have declined as an Italian scourge in the later seventeenth century, it was to be followed by smallpox, which has not been identified as a problem, if existent, in the fifteenth and sixteenth centuries. The major crises of smallpox so far noted by Livi Bacci were in Milan in 1707 and 1719, Verona in 1716 and Bologna in 1729. It was lethal for children under the age of ten or so; for adults it was aesthetically disfiguring but seldom fatal. There were some areas in the eighteenth century which have been identified as having endemic smallpox; notably the ports of Livorno and Portoferraro. In Livorno between 1767 and 1804 a steady 10 per cent death rate was attributable to smallpox; while in Portoferraro there were five occasions in the eighteenth century when smallpox was given as the cause of 40–50 per cent of deaths. Such death-dealing, particularly to children, would have had a longer term effect on the overall population than many other epidemics.

The direct impact on mortality, fertility, and general health of other illnesses and diseases – of fevers, syphilis, tuberculosis, malaria, cholera, dysentery, etc. from contaminated water supplies, fetid housing and bedding – have received little study, though Cipolla has shown that public health officials and doctors were as aware as many poor of their existence and debilitating effects. Malaria, linked as we saw above with Italy's physical geography, explains the underpopulation and economic backwardness of areas like the Tuscan Maremma, the Roman Campagna, or Calabria.

Food crises led many to die of starvation, but Livi Bacci (1990) has challenged some older views about their long-term demographic effects. Chronicles, diarists and government edicts indicate that throughout the fifteenth to eighteenth centuries cities and rural areas suffered from major harvest failures – caused by bad weather, insect infestations, or warfare and pillage – and that local people starved or came close to starvation. Basic grain stocks might run out, or the prices of grains and bread rocket beyond the means of all but the richest, or those with access to some charitable handouts. Such food crises might be fairly localised, or affect large parts of Italy in the same year or years. General food crises can be declared for the 1520s, 1549, 1555, 1590s (as for much of Europe), 1602, 1637, 1648 (a general European crisis year), 1678, 1694, 1709–10, 1764–7 and 1816–17 which is seen by Livi Bacci as the last of the great food crises for Europe.

Perugia in the Papal State provides a good example for studying crisis years between 1480 and 1540. Chroniclers and officials recorded the following years as crisis ones for grain supplies: 1484, 1489, 1491, 1496, 1505, 1509, 1511, 1519, 1523–34 without relief of a good harvest, 1536, 1538–9. Locusts created major damage in 1491 and 1495. It can be added that 'plague' (including some animal epidemics), contributed to mortality and ill-health in 1482, 1486–7, 1487–9, 1493, 1496, 1504–5, 1522–9 – though the nature of the plagues cannot be convincingly determined from the vague terminology.[15]

Chroniclers, diarists, ambassadors, local historians and polemicists all described people dying in the streets of starvation in particular cities. The Venetian sources report Romans starving in the winter of 1504–5, despite serious attempts by Pope Julius II to secure grain supplies from far afield. The famous Venetian diarist and historian Marin Sanuto lamented how poor men and women were dying in the streets even of Venice itself in 1527, as well as in less well-organised and charitable areas like Rome and other cities of the papal State. Reports through the 1590s comment on those starving to death in cities like Ferrara, Modena and Bologna; or barely surviving as they tried to live off 'bread' made from flour adulterated with tares and darnel.

The population fortunes of individual cities, and the balance between city and its dependent territory (*contado*), were also affected by political and economic factors (see Appendix). Political developments from the fifteenth to sixteenth centuries caused a shift of emphasis from many middle-sized urban communities to a few much larger ones. Through the fifteenth century, north and central Italy was politically fragmented, with many independent or quasi-independent cities run by communal oligarchies, dominant families or petty military *signori*. Amidst conflict and tension territorial states were consolidated, based on Milan, Venice, Florence and Rome. The Peace of Lodi recognised one stage in the consolidation of the territorial state, but it was only after the 1559 peace that the more modern concept of a centrally organised, 'absolutist' state was more fully realised. Then Rome, Milan, Florence and Naples emerged more obviously as capital cities; they attracted the most politically active, those who wished to serve in a fuller bureaucracy, those seeking a court environment. Servants and the service industries followed, especially in a changing cultural environment more disposed towards conspicuous consumption. The political centralisation and the decline of communal oligarchies or petty tyrants with their own courts, diminished the importance and population attractiveness of cities like Siena (absorbed into the Tuscan state of the Medici Dukes), Pisa, Arezzo, Perugia, Viterbo, Rimini, Orvieto, Brescia, Bergamo, Salerno and so on. Ferrara's demographic position changed after 1598 when, with the ending of the legitimate line of the ruling D'Este family, the city reverted to direct papal control as an integrated part of the Papal State, losing its political and cultural importance.

There were complications and anomalies. Florence should have increased its population like Rome and Naples as the capital of a larger, absolute state. But here a rise of a bureaucratic and court-centred population was offset by a failure to return to the great textile producing activity of the middle ages. Genoa's continuing prosperity in the sixteenth century – based on banking and trading – did not lead to a major urban population increase, in part because its location on the littoral with mountains behind restricted growth physically. It only slowly recovered from the 1656 plague disaster. Its chief economic rival, Venice, although limited by its lagoons, could expand to its islands with engineering ingenuity. Venice, Rome, Milan, Naples could recover from disasters of plague and disease. Rome revived after the major sack by plundering troops in 1527; Brescia, sacked in 1512 (and hit badly by plague in 1630–31), was less resilient.

Rome grew as it became the centre of a more consolidated Papal State, and benefited from the revival of the Papacy and the desire of successive popes to show Rome as a fit city to lead the Catholic world. It attracted more pilgrims (who needed to be welcomed, cared for and persuaded to buy goods if they did not remain), artists and craftsmen working on palaces for cardinals and their relatives or major new churches for the new religious Orders, but also peasants driven from surrounding farms as landowners shifted from arable to pastoral farming. Naples similarly with its Viceregal court dominated the politics and culture of a wide territory, and was the Mecca for the noble elite of the whole Viceroyalty and those who wished to serve them, and for the peasants escaping feudal depredations, shifts to arable farming and the extreme misery of remote areas.

The effects of economic fortunes on particular cities and their populations will become clearer in later chapters, in discussion of industrial and agricultural changes and developments in rural proto-industrialisation from the later seventeenth century.

Though debates abound about the causes and effects of diseases and food crises for Italy as a whole, and some areas in particular, there is no doubt that disease and dearth generated many fears, from which some cities and state governments were spurred to attempt preventive and remedial actions, and philanthropic organisations were developed. Better provided and organised cities tended to attract people from less well-off cities and villages seeking help, and notably basic food supplies. Italy had a great variety of food sources, though securing access and a fair distribution was inevitably problematic.

The supply of food

Italy's geographical features and demographic factors indicate potential problems over basic food supplies.[16] Human ingenuity was needed to maximise the use of difficult terrain and erratic water supplies, but when so employed considerable food diversity could result. As elsewhere in Europe, adequate increases in food production did not keep up with the population in the sixteenth century, and it was difficult in many areas to maintain the standard of living in food consumption. In Italy's case from the late sixteenth century grain supplies were increasingly sought from outside the peninsula and Sicily (notably from the Baltic). Meat consumption may have declined. Greater diversity of agricultural production in the eighteenth century resolved some basic supply problems – giving cheaper, but less nutritional foods (such as maize and rice) for the poor.

The staple foods for Italians were grains and wines. Wheat was produced in the grain-growing areas of northern Italy, Romagna, Umbria, Puglia or Sicily and Sardinia; but almost never alone as a grain crop. Wheat (*Triticum vulgare*) was for the best flour and bread, and for the richer sectors of society, predominantly in the major cities. Cheaper grains were spelt (particularly in the earlier half of our period) and millet which was more widespread. Millet produced a coarse flour, but it was more long-lasting; the Venetian Republic in the sixteenth-century led the way in choosing this for storing in warehouses to cope with years of dearth. Barley, which features for example in Umbrian records of the fifteenth and sixteenth centuries alongside wheat and millet, was more for horses than humans, but it was also made into a mush, or barley water for feeding the sick. Rye, grown in northern Italy by the fourteenth and fifteenth centuries, became a more important food ingredient when Venetian and Roman governments started importing it from the Baltic in the crisis of the 1590s. By and large within Italy wheat did better in the drier southern and central regions, while the lesser grains could succeed in the more humid air and soils of the north.

Mainland Italy had since Roman times imported basic grain supplies; from Egypt, north Africa, Sardinia and Sicily. By the sixteenth century the encroachments of desert and the Ottoman Turk limited the first two areas as sources, while soil exhaustion and erosion reduced the exports from Sicily. The Ottoman areas still supplied Italians; the Genoese in the eighteenth century used locally grown wheat for the richer classes, importing cheaper grains from the Levant for the poorer. Venice imported its bean supplies from Alexandria. The Baltic trade came into major use in the 1590s and 1600s. The Dutch and English, rather than Venetians or Genoese, were the major carriers, and their involvement in this crisis trade gave them openings into Mediterranean seafaring and trading that they maintained – to the long-term detriment of the Venetian economy in particular. This long-distance hunt for grain supplies was dramatic in its organisation and broad impact, though its contribution to Mediterranean food supplies may have been exaggerated, along with the decline of Sicilian contributions.[17]

Rice had been introduced into Italy in the fifteenth century, and was soon a cheaply sold food in the Ferrara market; by the seventeenth it was a significant crop in Lombardy, Piedmont, Venetia, Romagna, Tuscany, Naples and Sicily. Rice flour was mixed with other flours to make poor people's bread; it was rarely eaten by the rich. The introduction of rice crops became part of capitalist development, and was seen by Braudel as creating peasant proletariats. Maize or indian corn (*Zea mays*) was another new food, for the poor and animals. Maize, originating in southern America, arrived in Venetia about 1539. Confusingly it came to be called *gran turco*, which had been one of the names for buckwheat (*grano saraceno*, *Fagopyrum esculentum*) which had been brought from the east in the fifteenth century and grown in northern Italy as well as more prevalently in France. Maize was soon commercially developed in the Polesine area near Venice, and by the end of the century was found across most of the Venetian mainland territories growing among other crops. Maize was primarily made into corn-meal cakes and polenta for the poor, and rarely provided food for the rich. By the eighteenth century Venetian peasants were selling their good quality wheat for export and living off less appetising maize. Other crops that could provide basic food and nutrition were pulses, lentils, beans, chick peas (known in Venetia as *menudi* or *minuti*, minor foods). In hilly areas, and elsewhere in dearth conditions, the main flour became that made from chestnuts, the *albero del pane*, 'bread tree'. Nuts were also used to produce edible oils – as much as olive-oil. How much the population derived from these foods, as from vegetables, herbs, wild fruits, fungi, remains unstudied. Most of these food sources were local, and on a small scale; therefore not well documented, unlike the main grains of large-scale production, trade and transport.

Wine and olive oil of varying qualities was available locally throughout most of Italy. Olive oil in its different qualities from successive pressings and treatments was a food, a cooking medium, a fuel for lighting, a lubricant and the basis of soap. Olive-soap was seen as crucial for washing wools, and promoted as such in Tuscany and Piedmont from the later middle ages. Olives for multi-purpose uses did well in subalpine regions, as around Lake Garda, Como and Monferrato. In the eighteenth century improvements in olive production became the target of enlightenment reformers in the Kingdom of Naples.[18] Wine was a necessity of life, as food with a significant calorific contribution to the average diet, and as a safer liquid that water for much of the time. As a generally critical English traveller, Samuel Sharp, noted in 1767:

> The people in Italy . . . spend more than you would believe on wine, but neither their abilities nor the example of their betters, lead them into

> drunkenness: They have a great notion that [wine] is wholesome, so they give it to their children at the breast.

It was also seen as a key to social harmony and well-being, the key to good secular and religious festivals and good labour relations.[19] Italian wine production was plentiful not only in northern and central Italy as now, but the Kingdom of Naples also produced considerable quantities. There were wine connoisseurs in the fifteenth and sixteenth centuries, ready to praise local vintages – of Montepulciano or Orvieto for example – but the pursuit of vintage productions as in Tuscany dates from the eighteenth century. By then travellers in Italy also praised the skill and attractiveness of the terracing and planting of vines and olive trees on hillsides.

The extent of meat-eating in Italy is hard to gauge. Seemingly Italians were major meat-eaters until the end of the fifteenth century, and there was then a steady decline to a low point in the nineteenth. Within Italy beef cattle were not that prevalent, and the large herds in northern Italy in the eighteenth century were more for diary produce – cheeses – than meat. However northern Italy secured meat supplies from far afield – the Balkans, Poland and especially Hungary, from which huge herds were driven or brought by ship, to be slaughtered on the Lido of Venice for example. Elsewhere there were sheep flocks, for meat as well as wool. It was the basis for Rome's high meat consumption in the seventeenth and eighteenth centuries. Puglia supplied mutton to places like Perugia and Florence in the fifteenth century. There were pigs, for which the cuisine of parts of Umbria was and is famous; or wild boar, which was cheap and plentiful in Sicily until at least the sixteenth century. In the later part of our period a decline in the consumption of fresh meat may have been balanced by an increase in salted or smoked meats and sausages: Parma hams, zamponi, or salami (the centre of much competitive selling and monopoly battles among the guildsmen of eighteenth-century Rome). A Perugian writing in 1607, Cesare Crispolti,[20] considered that the Perugian *contado* was well supplied with meat: cattle, pigeons and poultry. The prevalence of these last two (and smaller birds that modern Italians are so keen to shoot to extinction) in the diet is hard to gauge, but was almost certainly significant.

Fresh fish, from tuna and squid to anchovies and sardines, presumably provided a basic food for some coastal areas, though the Mediterranean was not that prolific. River fish were also in limited supply. The major inland lake of Lake Trasimeno, serving Umbria and Tuscany, provided pike, carp, eel, tench and chub. Again according to Crispolti, who itemised this stock, the supply of fish was plentiful in the neighbouring river systems of the Tiber, Chiascio, Chiani and Nestore. Smoked and salted fish from afar added to the diet elsewhere, as in Venice which consumed herrings from northern seas so treated. Much had come through France, but in the seventeenth century the English merchants took over the main supply of preserved fish, smoked herring, salted pilchards, cod and sometimes salmon; they were primarily brought during the winter to Livorno and distributed from there by sea or land for the high demand during Lent.[21]

Fasting was likely to affect the males and females in monastic houses most, and one might be tempted to feel sorry for those so deprived of meat for up to 120 days a year, and restricted in food intake in many other ways. Many picture a few well-fed abbots and priors offering hospitality to distinguished visiting laymen and women, while most nuns and friars were near starvation or malnourished. But a recent study of food in monastic institutions in southern Italy at the end of period reveals a more complex situation. Though in a supposedly poorer part of the world, the male and female inmates appear to have had an abundant, healthy and varied diet through the year, even with days of only bread and water. Many had access to fresh fish of considerable variety; the Clarisse nuns of Francavilla listed 21 different fish at one point. The terms *verdure* (greens) and *legumi* (vegetables) imply a restricted diet, but in fact can cover a range of vegetables, pulses and salads that would put many modern greengrocers and supermarkets to shame. They were well supplied with eggs and dairy products. Nunneries in southern Italy as in Venice could produce a considerable range of cakes and sweets; needed to reward the visiting priests, confessors and sometimes workmen, they were unlikely to have passed by the mouths of nuns and their *converse* helpers. Attempts by the Patriarchate of Venice to curb such supplies, or the keeping of chickens within convents (treated as pets as well as egg suppliers), were clearly in vain. While monks, friars and nuns might have been thus better fed than their peasant and artisan lay neighbours, the evidence from their sources reminds us of the variety of food supplies that could be available in country and town.[22]

Briefly looking at food and drink supplies that might be brought into the larger cities at least for the wealthier, one might highlight – besides the salami, sausages and smoked fish already mentioned – Campagna cheeses like *cacio cavallo* that were sent to Rome, Livorno and Naples; the Cretan and Dalmatian cheeses imported into Venice; or maraschino liqueur from Zara over which Venetians established monopoly control in the eighteenth century. By the eighteenth century brandy, coffee and chocolate were part of the consumption of the not so rich as well as the elite of leading cities, especially Venice and Rome.

The rich could enjoy a considerable variety of foods derived from various parts of Italy or abroad, and the less well off might similarly indulge during major festivities. The Venetian writer Orlando Lando in the 1550s cited the food that might satisfy the gourmet in Italian cities: sausages from Bologna and Monza (its fine sausage, *luganica sottile*), zampone (bacon hock) from Modena, cheeses from Florence and Piacenza, pheasant and chestnuts from Chiavenna, special pies from Ferrara, *gnocchi* from Piacenza, mince (*tomarelle*) from Monza, quince jam from Reggio, marzipan from Siena, fish and oysters from Venice. In 1600 the Perugian confraternity Della Morte organised a pilgrimage to Rome for the Jubilee celebrations, a long account of which survives written by one of its leading organisers, canon Marc'Antonio Masci. The confraternity received hospitality from confraternities of other cities as it marched in orderly fashion down to Rome; and the canon was particularly impressed by the food, wine and music offered. At Deruta they were given a meal in the main square which included roast kid, sausages, ham, cheeses, omelettes, expensive vegetables (unfortunately not specified); near Rome they were welcomed by cartloads of food for a meal sent by marchese Ascanio della Corgna, which included capons, sausages, hams, loaves of bread, cheeses, a great quantity of artichokes and barrels of both red and white wine.[23]

The contrast with this good living and celebration is what was eaten when the poor were desperate with hunger and poverty. With a shortage of grain, even the coarsest bread was adulterated in many ways, but particularly with darnel seeds, with *ghittone* – a herb with black grains normally used as chicken feed – and unripened vetch grains. Piero Camporesi has recently suggested that these ingredients could readily lead to hallucinations and drugged conditions. A late sixteenth-century Bolognese poet, Giulio Cesare Croce – from the poor, writing of the poor and to some extent for the poor – called darnel bread 'dazed' bread. In addition, bread even in more normal times might have additions of sesame, fennel, cumin and poppy seeds. While much of this was for seasoning, poppy seeds in particular could lead to hallucinations. Poppy seeds were readily available as the sixteenth-century writer Pietro Andrea Mattioli stressed – in Tuscany, Lombardy and the Trentino mountains where poppies grew with broad beans. Concoctions from poppy seed were also used to calm fretting, teething babies – and their nurses. Children were fed with a pap made from hemp or linseed with apples and pears.[24] From the literature and chronicles of the sixteenth and seventeenth centuries, Camporesi has suggested that many of the poor would have existed in drugged states, by deliberate commission in normal or abnormal times or the unconscious results of famine conditions. Hunger and pain might be dulled, but imaginations might readily be stimulated to wild fantasies and sensual dreams. Adult peasants in particular would be rendered less fit for work; they and their children were ready to imagine the unreal, to absorb and elaborate on improbable tales. This mental and physical environment may explain how people could confess, without torture, to the most unnatural and improbable actions raised in witchcraft trials. I suggest also that the religious ecstasies of ascetic holy women and men could be affected by stale mouldy bread and putrid water, equally likely to distort and challenge the imagination. The drugged state of the urban poor might also be a partial explanation for violent collective action – particularly the bizarre crowd behaviour in the Masaniello revolt in Naples in 1647.

This knowledge of food supplies, of their origins and of their deficiencies, should provide understanding of the causes of social prosperity, of the wheels of commerce, of the richness and poverty of human imagination and mentalities. Italy's geography provided many contrasts between barren, dangerous areas, and those able to provide considerable diversities of food, especially when aided by human ingenuity to control water supplies. Many Italians could be well fed, but most could be rendered vulnerable and endangered by cruel changes in weather and by disease epidemics. Those able to control the natural resources, and access to them, could generate much prosperity, and support large urban areas, but geographical conditions in much of Italy also enabled many more rural areas to prosper from a diverse economy. Such fundamental structures help explain why, despite vagaries in international economic developments, adverse political interventions from outside and natural disasters, the overall economic scene through the early modern period was generally prosperous, and could recover from crises better than sometimes alleged.

3

THE CHANGING RURAL AND URBAN ECONOMIES

General economic trends: decline and shift

The state of the Italian economy, or economies, through our period has been much debated, notably whether there was a decline or shift in the seventeenth century, as part of a wider debate about the shift of economic leadership from the Mediterranean to the north-west Atlantic.[1] There is the interlinked argument from Braudel and Immanuel Wallerstein that world economies shifted their '*superville*' epicentres from Venice and Antwerp in the early and mid-sixteenth century to Amsterdam at the close, and then London from the later seventeenth century. I favour the view that, while Italy (notably Venice, Genoa, Milan and Florence), in the course of the seventeenth century did lose leadership in many economic matters, such as international trade in pepper and spices, in shipbuilding and capital investment and insurance, there were some compensatory shifts and gains, and no absolute decline, economically or culturally. Standards of living, physical and of *mentalité*, should be more important than economic league tables; as Braudel stressed; 'from the point of view of quality of life . . . I would certainly rather have lived in Tuscany, than in Spain under Philip II or even in France under Louis XIV'.[2] Here I will outline the main trends as they affect urban and rural society, highlighting those affecting rural society's vitality or stagnation.

The mortality crises associated with plague and other epidemics of the Black Death period produced a major drop in population across most of Italy with depopulation of many rural areas, and a disinvestment in land on the part of urban investors. Surviving rural populations could, however, use the shortage of labour to improve their incomes and standard of living, and the conditions under which they worked the land. As the fifteenth century unfolded urban and rural populations rose, surplus urban wealth was reinvested in the land and urban dwellers consolidated rural properties, dispossessing smallholders, or renegotiating share-cropping and leasing contracts to the detriment of the *contadini*.

In the fifteenth and sixteenth centuries economic vitality and wealth was heavily urban, as Franco Angiolini (1996) stresses. Michel de Montaigne touring Italy in 1580–81, noted the wealth of many very populous Italian cities and their inhabitants (in contrast to native France); and was aware of serious brigandry in rural areas, testimony to poverty and chaos outside the cities (though of course there were many banished townspeople as well as disgruntled peasants in the bandit gangs). By the eighteenth century, Grand Tour travellers were less complimentary about urban vitality (outside a few pleasurable places like Venice and Rome); by then Italy was hardly an urban manufacturing economy, the Italian economies had their strengths (relatively weakened in comparison with western and north-western Europe) based on agricultural development, and some associated rural industries. The shifts had taken place as a result of crises through the seventeenth century.[3]

The fifteenth and early-sixteenth century saw attempts to create and consolidate territorial states, especially centred on Florence, Venice, Milan and the Papacy in Rome, while petty princes, military *condottieri* and lesser communes strove to avoid central domination. Such struggles could disrupt economies through the effects of military conflicts, civil unrest and sieges. Where power was more effectively concentrated in key cities economic leadership might pass to a narrow elite in one city prominent in conspicuous consumption, to the detriment of lesser cities or towns. Within Tuscany, where Florence sought to consolidate a territorial state (Republican or Medicean), Volterra and San Gimignano for example suffered by the sixteenth century, though Prato, Pescia and Borgo San Sepolcro seemed to have gained relatively in population and prosperity since the fourteenth century.[4] Milan failed to assert its economic pre-eminence within Lombardy; Vigevano, Cremona and Lodi gained in size and economic strength by the sixteenth century. Parma and Piacenza similarly improved, though they were to be lost to the Lombard state by the mid sixteenth century, as were Bergamo and Crema, which became part of the Venetian Republic. The continuation of a multifarious urban scene in Lombardy, backed by the princely policy of the Visconti and Sforza to favour seignieurial aristocrats (and ex-soldiers), possibly helped spread wealth across the region, and encouraged a widespread urban investment in rural properties.

This trend continued through the sixteenth century in most of Italy. The Italian wars, threats from the Turks in the Mediterranean, the expansion of European contacts around the world, the discovery of new sources of supply of silver, gold, spices, luxury silks, etc., all had adverse effects on Italian manufacturing in key areas and Italian overseas trade through the sixteenth century. However, there may have compensating trading developments within Italy once war effects diminished or ceased. While wool manufacturing declined in Florence and then Venice (from the 1610s), silks, glassware, pottery, furniture, musical instruments and book production developed their output.

Through the sixteenth century Italy probably produced most of its own manufactured goods, and expanded the range; a diversity of imported raw materials (cotton, silks, materials for dyes, soda for glass) fed the Italian manufacturing industries. As Richard Goldthwaite (1993) argues, the increased enthusiasm for conspicuous consumption by the rich fed the expansion of luxury goods. Venetian elaboration on dyeing, with government-fostered reorganisation of the industry from the late fifteenth century, boosted demand for ever more varied clothing, bedding and hangings. Jewellery, glass and furniture became more elaborate, fashion conscious and expensive – and repeated sumptuary legislation to curb the expenses had limited effects. Venetian practice, and printed publicity in the mid-sixteenth century, boosted the cosmetics and luxury soap industries.[5] Capital earned by leading banking families, particularly among the Genoese, who invested in the wider Spanish Empire, fuelled both urban manufacturing and new land investment. Goldthwaite's argument that the rich got richer applied to cities like Venice, Rome, Genoa, Cremona, Bari and Lecce as well as to individuals. There were losers among cities that used to thrive on manufactures (Brescia in metals, Perugia in cloth and leather goods), among patricians, small wool producers and artisans, and among many peasants.

In assessing variable economic fortunes, one of the key variables was the extent to which capital was reinvested in land and then put to use with some entrepreneurial initiative and efficiency – as in parts of the Veneto, but not in much of Umbria or Campania. There was a continuing investment in land by private urban families, ecclesiastical organisations, hospitals. But there were complicated variables as to how this affected those in the small towns and rural areas, which tended to see a population expansion. Entrepreneurial investment in land, with irrigation schemes, planting of mulberries and fruit trees and expansion of dairy farming, could prove beneficial for the rural population in providing variety in the sources of income and employment (including paid work for women in silk-producing areas for example), and bring some compensation for the growing population pressures on the land, the inflation of basic food prices and the lowering of real wages for the landless labourers. In other areas the re-investment in land by the elites meant changes from labour-intensive arable to pasturage, driving peasants off the land and into cities like Rome and Naples where (without major expansion in urban industries) they swelled the ranks of the poor. Changes in fiscal policy through the sixteenth century may often have allowed the urban elites to lessen their own burdens (and so spend on luxuries, art patronage or land investment) and pass the burden to rural tax payers, whether through taxes directly imposed on individual families, or mediated through levies on rural communities. Resulting indebtedness further diminished the numbers of small proprietors, and the stock of common land, and expanded the numbers of share-croppers (as in Tuscany or Umbria), and of *coloni* working on large farms and *latifundia* estates (as in Lombardy or much of the Kingdom of Naples). Expropriation and exploitation of peasants was the main characteristic of the period through much of Italy. The result could also be an increase in rural violence, brigandage and banditry.

In counterbalancing some arguments about economic decline in the South, some commentators have pointed to the growth of fairs and large markets, and the expansion in size and wealth of southern towns continuing through the sixteenth century and later (as with the Puglian cities of Bari, Lecce, Taranto, Matera and Barletta), assisted by capital investments from Venetians, Genoese and Tuscans.[6] The existence of multiple fairs should have benefited rural areas, giving rural inhabitants a greater variety of goods, incentives to experience urban society, if briefly during the periods of fairs, and knock-on effects (legal or illegal) of having merchants and their supporters travelling through lesser villages.

From the 1590s the Italian economy is judged to have lost pre-eminence in long-distance trade (especially in spices and oriental luxuries), in associated banking and insurance expertise and profits. The Dutch and English entered the Mediterranean carrying grain supplies from the Baltic to cope with the 1590s' food crises, and failed to leave. The English in particular took over as transporters of goods in and out of Italy, especially using the port of Livorno. They joined the Turks, Berbers, Uskoks and others in depredating Italian, especially Venetian, shipping. Italy declined as an exporter of manufactured goods, especially woollen textiles and metallurgy. Maintaining high standards of production, and protecting reasonably high wages as in Venice, Italian cloths lost out to cheaper if less durable Dutch and English materials. But equally problematic was how Venetians could prevent competitors, notably the English, cheating by passing off cheap and shoddy cloths as Venetian by using false stamp marks in the Levant market which still appreciated high quality, if expensive, cloths, or stop them counterfeiting soap in a similar way. The French tried deceiving the world with imitation Venetian glass, when they could not bribe or cajole Venetian glass-blowers to emigrate.[7] Banking crises on the eve of and through the start of war in Germany from 1618, the subsequent disruption of overland trade to and through the German states, the increased taxation imposed on its Italian possessions by the Spanish government to finance its war operations, all contributed to difficulties for Italian trade and manufacturing. Typhus and plague through the 1620s and early 1630s in northern Italy, and major war activities associated especially with the struggle for the Duchy of Mantua, brought catastrophic drops in population, especially in the large cities like Venice and Milan, followed by major problems in economic production whether of manufactured goods or rural produce.

Recent work suggests that after the mid-seventeenth century the overall picture in northern Italy is less gloomy than once alleged.[8] Lesser towns and rural areas picked up what was lost in great cities like Milan and Venice. Out of war could come benefits for armaments makers in Brescia and northern valleys, where manufacturing was added to basic mining activities. While Italians, especially Venetians lost out in major sea transport, land routes for silk exports, for example, remained active, and transport costs were not that significantly different. Cities like Bologna and Milan gained by the willingness of Venetians and others to use land routes. A post-plague shortage of labour briefly saw better conditions in wages for rural survivors; many city or feudal-elite families in Lombardy went into crisis, and were forced to sell properties. After a shake-out, surviving old landowning families and accumulating new ones took over; they invested in agricultural development with a keener sense of profit; they more ruthlessly re-negotiated contracts with peasants and communes, who became more suppressed. But in economic terms this released profits that from the eighteenth century funded new industrial development, especially in silks. If Venice again lost out in silk production, into the eighteenth century Bergamo or Vicenza gained, learning from the Dutch among others. Later Turin and other parts of Piedmont moved towards a more capital intensive and factory-like production.

The economic shifts in the seventeenth century away from the major manufacturing cities led to more rural-based processing and manufacturing, providing wider sources of income for families, especially with additional female labour. So the countryside became the mainstay of Italian economies, through the production of food and raw materials, and the processing of them. C. M. Belfanti (1993) has stressed that the process of 'rural decentralisation of manufacture', or proto-industrialisation, was under way from the mid sixteenth century in some northern areas, such as the Duchy of Mantua, the Republic of Genoa, or the Bresciano under the Venetian Republic. Proto-industrialisation regionally could be the product of merchant entrepreneurial vitality, or occasioned by desperation in city and countryside. Mantuan and Genoese merchants, facing strict city guild restrictions and high labour costs, shifted various processing and manufacturing activities to produce knitwear in the Mantuan *contado*, or velvets through the Genoese Riviera di Levante (centred on Zoagli near Rapallo). The plague epidemic of 1579–80 caused many Genoese silk craftsmen to flee Genoa; they remained in the inland villages to create a rural silk processing and weaving industry that survived many vicissitudes till the eighteenth century. Small landholders also became weavers.

Poor agricultural land tempted urban investors to develop rural industries using cheap labour free from city guild controls, especially if there was a good water supply, and accessible raw materials. The Bergamo area with its valleys saw the development of middle quality woollen cloths and iron. In 1620 the region had 84 mines, 11 blast furnaces and 100 forges.[9] The valleys of the Bresciano similarly had rural iron production; the Camonica valley kept up 90–100 forges throughout the period from the 1560s to the 1780s, producing pots, horseshoes and cuirasses. The Trompia valley manufactured firearms, agricultural implements, wires and nails, while the Sabbia valley produced steel.

The western shore of Lake Garda, poorly situated for food production, developed flax spinning. Salò merchants organised raw supplies from across Lombardy, distributing them for semi-manufacturing by peasants through the winter to be finished back in Salò. The rural inhabitants could also earn from paper making, and minor iron workings, with 70–80 forges, producing nails and hardware for Venice and other cities.

In various parts of the Veneto, northern Papal State, and Lombardy enclaves, combining poor food agriculture, with feudal privileges, freedom from guild controls or with government tax concessions could develop profitable rural industries: cotton manufacturing in Lombard areas around Gallarete and Busto Arizio; cordage and hemp sailcloth in the Cento region between Bologna and Ferrara; hat making from willow shavings in the Pio family's little seigneury of Carpi; hemp production in the Bolognese *contado* areas around Budrio and Castel S. Pietro. Thus rural industry could be of considerable importance for the overall Italian economy, and for the configurations of work and income in the land of the 'peasant'. Major city organisers put a significant amount of work and income into poverty-stricken rural areas, and continued to profit themselves when the major city manufacturing faltered. The numbers involved are hardly established yet; but it was reported that there were 10,000 iron workers in the Camonica valley in 1609–10; over 7000 people were producing 60,000 cloths in Busto Arizio in 1767. At the end of the century a Friulian entrepreneur, Del Fabbro, employed 11,000 weavers on looms producing flax and hemp cloth, and 18,000 women were involved in the domestic silk industry in the Como area. Rural families thus had variable sources of income from different skills, were interlocked with an urban economy and international trade and were in contact with urban dwellers and urban material culture.

For the debate about shifts in the Italian economies from the last third of the seventeenth century, Gigliola Pagano De Divitiis' vision of the scene through the activities of English merchants and the views of English merchants, is valuable.[10] Within Italy the north–south divide or contrast was accentuated, whereby the south provided agricultural produce, and the centre-north remained the manufacturing area, even if the locales changed (as above). English merchants were primarily interested in importing (from Naples and Puglian ports like Gallipoli and Bari) olive oil for cloth processing and to a lesser extent soap making. They obtained currants directly from Venetian dependencies like Zante and Cephalonia, from Puglia (which in part remained in the Venetian economic sector) or indirectly through Venice. The English also imported, whether by sea or by land, silk threads and silk manufactures, derived from Tuscany, Lombardy and Piedmont. They took full advantage of Livorno, which the Grand Dukes of Tuscany developed as a modern port, (effectively a 'free port', though not officially so until 1675). The English ships in the winter months largely brought fish to Livorno and Naples, for distribution across Italy thereafter – smoked herring, salted pilchards, cod, salmon, predominantly for Lenten fasting. Here English 'fish-boats' were replacing fish supplies that had come overland from or through France. Some English woollen cloth entered Italy, but seemingly the Spanish industry suffered much more than the Italian from this competition.

In broader economic terms the Italians, especially the Venetians, lost out as carriers of the imports and exports, though by the late seventeenth century small coastal vessels from Venice regained some share of the carrying of olive oil. Livorno residents developed insurance expertise at the expense of Venetians. In port facility terms, Livorno's gain was often at the expense of Genoa as well as the already silting-up port of Pisa, though Genoa fought back in the 1660s. Except at the height of war activity a considerable amount of northern Italian exporting went overland, with Bologna, Verona and Milan being major interchange points. Venetians and others argued that it was safer, and hardly much different in costs, to send silks overland as far as the Netherlands ports. This lessened the impact of English control of shipping, and complicates assessments of northern Italian trading, especially in lesser towns.

While the English sought to compete with Italians in producing silk threads and manufactured silk cloths (which were very fashionable in England throughout much of the sixteenth century), they failed to learn certain secrets, such as spinning organzine silk – which continued to come from Bergamo, Bologna, parts of Piedmont and Sicily. Florentine (and wider Tuscan), silks or Genoese velvets held up quite well in the new competition. Venetian silks lost out against the English, but competed in the Levant market (even against English fraudulent activities in stamping their cheaper and poor quality goods with the Lion of St Mark). Some

Venetians (and English observers) were aware of the dilemma of either maintaining quality and standards for their best Levant markets, or cheapening their production to compete in the more fickle and insecure English (and presumably French) markets. The Venetian secretary in London in 1672, Girolamo Alberti, warned that Florentines had recently made the mistake of trying to compete with inferior silks; they had lost their market and their reputation, and the city's looms that had been adapted now lay idle. The Florentines were seeking to replace the southern Italian manufacturing industries, used to producing light silks, and may not have been quite as unsuccessful as Alberti implied, though his advice for Venetians may have still been valid. They wanted to maintain a variety of target markets, while the Florentines were almost entirely geared to England. When England had been hit by plague in 1665, with its disruption of commerce, Florence had been badly affected.[11] As long as Italy could produce raw silk, various kinds of silk threads, and manufactured silk cloths, garments and hangings, the city and dependent rural workers could prosper.

A recent emphasis by early modern European historians on consumerism and material culture has widened the horizons and targets of economic history, moving beyond capital, raw materials and major manufacturing which might be more readily quantified.[12] We are encouraged to look more carefully, through inventories and testaments especially, to what people possessed in their homes, what they wore, what they ate and drank beyond necessities. Alison Smith's recent study (1998) of Verona inventories revealingly reproduces that of the movable goods in Count Gasparo Verità's house in 1578, but warns that clothes enclosed in chests will probably be under-recorded. There is little doubt that consumer demand increased through our period. The consumer revolution from the later seventeenth century has been noted for England and France. Less study has been made of Italian inventories, but visual evidence might suggest that northern and central Italian cities shared in the rising consumer demand, and little momentum was lost from the consumerist pull that Goldthwaite saw as helping generate the 'Renaissance'. Shops and retail outlets both in large cities, and smaller ones like Prato, we know expanded in numbers and became more elaborate, presumably responding to desires, and encouraging demand. The desires for better, more fashionable clothing and footwear, for more comfortable seating and bedding, for hangings, pictures and prints on the wall, for food varieties, may all have started in the elite secular houses, but repercussions are found in the gloomy seventeenth century in rural areas, or the cells of monks and nuns supposedly disdaining worldly goods and elaborate foods, as well as in the inventoried houses of lesser Venetian artisans.[13] The second-hand market allowed goods and desires to be passed on. Those who start with the good second-hand are likely to aspire to the new, so the economy moves.

Rural and urban inter-relationships

Physical mobility was extensive in and out of cities and villages within a few kilometres, but also over great distances through the peninsula, or across the Alps, and over the seas. All levels of society could be involved from patrician ambassadors to shepherds leading their flocks over considerable distances. There were well-to-do women who moved through marriage strategies, and humbler ones who flocked to cities to be servants or prostitutes; hopefully trying to make money or contacts in preparation for marriage, or dolefully fleeing some disaster or disgrace, or seeking errant husbands. For some, regular movement was part of their livelihood: seasonal workers on harvests, the myriad of 'officials' sent out to administer justice, collect taxes or rents, transport goods, peddle wares, sell potions and quack remedies or round up criminals and bandits. Some had skills to sell and sought a better employment situation, or were enticed to move by governments or merchants seeking to develop silk making, glass blowing, or ironmongery, and patrons (individual or institutional) seeking a well-reputed artist or musician to enhance their prestige and delight their fancy. Many moved voluntarily and under legitimate economic imperatives. Others were driven out of city or village, as undesirable Jews, prostitutes or beggars who could not claim long-term residency and protection. Courts (or political opponents) condemned significant numbers to permanent banishment or short-term exile, while even more fled fearing a court because of a crime committed or alleged, considering it unwise to stay in an attempt to prove innocence – given the vagaries of justice. Some moved as part of a family, but most travelled as individuals.

The interchanges between *contado* and city were unbalanced, in numbers and mental outlook, and not necessarily welcomed. Urban dwellers could despise the caricatured dumb and dangerous peasant/*contadino*. The *contadino* might fear most people coming from the neighbouring town, whether as somebody demanding payments of taxes, rents and dues, or as a *bandito* seeking refuge from city magistrates and police. The Bologna tribunals of the Torrone and Della Plebe record city officials making visitations round the *contado* to check on bandits and criminals, or on whether locals were trading and crafting under genuine licences, using correct measures, preparing food supplies for themselves and the city in a proper way.[14] As parish priests from the later sixteenth century were arguably better educated (in towns), and more resident, they could bring back to the *contado* different ideas, tastes, religious and social practices that would have an impact whether favourable or distrusted.

The Bergamo province provided many migrants in our period, escaping the poverty of mountainous areas. In popular literature, such as the short stories of Bandello and Straparola in the 1550s, such Bergamaschi were coarse, money-grubbing and sponging on others. They provided manual labourers for Brescia and Verona. But more surprisingly people from the Valdimagna area of the province ran about three-quarters of the shops down in Ancona in 1596. In the eighteenth century skilled workers from the iron mines, now underfinanced, moved to mines on Elba, in Piedmont, Lombardy and Switzerland, and remitted profits to families back home. The image, and reality, of the Bergamaschi abroad becomes complex.[15]

Arguably through the period the inter-relationships became more beneficial as well as more complicated. The urban image of the rural scene (if not of all its inhabitants) may have become more positive, as a greater proportion of the urban population went backwards and forwards between areas and read about the rural scene in literature (based on a classical idyll) that romanticised the simple peasant and rustic life, as the concept of villa life spread.[16] A renewed interest from the sixteenth century in active investment in, and exploitation of, the resources of the countryside by well-to-do urban residents changed the complexion of that countryside, but also attitudes. By the eighteenth century, at least in parts of northern Italy, the urban involvement in changing the scenery, through terracing and irrigation, but also in trying to educate the 'peasantry', brought even more interchange and involvement. More urban dwellers came to see the rural air and diet as healthier, so sent more children to country wetnurses – however disastrously in practice. While historians tend to be aware of movement from country to town, they have been less aware of those who emigrated to the countryside to improve their position. In the early eighteenth century Anguillara in the Agro Romano absorbed a significant number of immigrants, mainly from Rome, though artisans also came from Lombardy, Venice and the Marches. Both elite and plebeian families were seeking land or salaried work; many were marginalised by the communal council or a confraternity, and marriage was an agency to gain both acceptance and land, through a dowry.[17]

Commerce and those involved with it provided much interconnection between city and *contado*. For example Donato Ferrario from Pantigliate moved from that part of Lombardy into Milan, possibly with some expertise in metal work since in 1403 the city gave him a post scrutinising money makers. He settled in the Porta Nuova area and (aided by his Milanese wife) became involved in a whole range of commercial activities and investments, including animal husbandry, water mills and textiles. He utilised many different people who moved back and forth between city, near and more distant countryside operating his enterprises, conducting merchandise and supervising his investments.[18] Mills provided a major contact point between *contadini* and townspeople, and the miller – when not threatened by reluctant tax payers or those worried about fraud – might be the communicator of urban ways, and novel ideas. 'Cheese and Worms' Menocchio was not the only miller challenging religious orthodoxy in the Veneto.[19]

In some cities the official organisations catered for guild members who might work both in the city and in the *contado*; and recognised the different remunerations that might be involved. In 1549 the Florentine guild of *Linaioli* (of linen workers, but also for second-hand clothes dealers [*rigattieri*], sellers of old-iron [*ferravecchij*], tailors and mattress makers) allowed those wishing to exercise the different aspects of the guild in the *contado* to pay half-fees to the guild. It also ruled that women who had previously been allowed to operate as tailors, cutting, sewing, and keeping open shops (*botteghe aperte*) as well as dealing privately, without paying guild fees, should now have to contribute. They paid less than the men did; and paid very little if they worked from home rather than from a shop.[20]

The inter-dependence of urban and rural life was enhanced by the development of proto-industrialisation, whereby various manufacturing processes leading to the production of cloth in particular were put out from the cities into the countryside, partly to avoid strict guild regulations and utilise cheaper, often female, labour. It brought more sophisticated production techniques into rural economies, instead of just taking raw produce away. Urban agents more frequently visited the countryside promising work. They may have exploited cheap labour in comparison with guild regulated labour in cities, but also brought a higher standard of living for the rural dwellers, with knock-on effects in consumer terms. A greater awareness of what might improve living conditions and comforts (initially to be bought new or second-hand from the city), might lead a small local community to create its own imitations.[21]

As part of the mobile scene within Italy and European-wide were the long-distance pedlars. For obvious reasons our knowledge of them and their activities is usually limited. Some were destitute individuals who picked up various cheap wares and travelled around seeking to sell them – haberdashery and trinkets, prints, pamphlets and books. Those peddling devotional images might also provide magical healing remedies; or also be *cantastorie*, people who went round telling or singing stories, spreading accounts of monstrous births and strange event as prognostications, and peddling images of them, or copies of the stories. Pedlars in fact or under accusation operated on the fringes of legality, connected with smuggling and thieving, as discovered through police records in Tuscany. They might link up with city guilds, as with Turin tailors, to handle banned and smuggled fabrics, for mutual advantage. For some pedlars this precarious mobile life was their whole existence, for others a seasonal activity, supplementing the family income, while for others it might be the path to permanent emigration. The more successful became small merchants operating a sort of network of mountain village shops. Other pedlars were part of a well-developed network, organised by (sometimes related to) families in various cities; and they might trade in more substantial and profitable goods – most notably, by the eighteenth century, books and pamphlets, legal or illegal. Family networks organised the peddling of goods between northern Italy, France, Switzerland and even remote Scotland. These families might operate over several generations, and use marriage strategies to extent their networks. Early seventeenth century documents record the Bittot family, originally from Montagny in Tarantaise, that operated routes between Venice and Lyons, Lyons and Haarlem, Haarlem and Gdansk, Gdansk and Venice again. Some years later the Brentano family emerged in the Lake Como area, with branches in Gnosso, Troccia, Cimaroli and Tremezzo. They started in the late sixteenth century selling spices and citrus fruit. They penetrated into Basel and Frankfurt where they were allowed to open a shop in 1678. By the eighteenth century another noted international family, the Gravier, with key figures in Genoa and Rome, organised the circulation of books and pamphlets of all kinds, but could also deal with gloves. A lesser branch based in Turin diversely peddled haberdashery through the winter, or dealt with the supply of mules. Earlier, in the later sixteenth and the seventeenth century the village of Pontremoli in the Tuscan Apennines was a centre for peddling books and pamphlets, in conjunction with printers from the Duchy of Parma. Such selling operations point to a mobility of people and ideas across Italy and Europe more widely.[22]

A specialist kind of pedlar was the charlatan and mountebank, (*ciarlatano* and *cerretano*). The English implications of these terms are con-men, tricksters, the travelling salesman or much patter and little honesty. While in Italian from the fifteenth century the words have similar implications, we can also here be dealing with licensed pedlars of powders, potions, unguents and elixirs. They were an element in the medical profession, with senior medical officials seeking to control their activities, and allow for the spreading through city and countryside of medical remedies; though a *vice-protomedico* in the Papal State in 1632 might still describe a *ciarlatano* as one of 'those people who appear in the square and sell various things by means of entertainments and buffoonery'.[23] While superior medics despised them, and city officials expelled them like vagabonds in plague crises, some were well-educated, and not much different from apothecaries and physicians with a more respected and permanent position in urban society. They were just as likely to produce curative remedies; and Venetian health officials were ready to sell their remedies for plague. In their selling techniques they drew on the theatre, such as the *commedia dell'arte*, and were part of the popular entertainment of the cities and villages. Sellers of a remedy called *orvietan*, supposedly invented in the late sixteenth century by a Lupi of Orvieto as an antidote (for whatever real or imaginary illness the seller might select), became renowned from southern Italy to Paris and London. Serious sellers sought government licences to sell and perform on stages. Girolamo Ferranti of Naples, and his son were among the most famous travelling charlatans. In 1616 Gregorio, who had a shop in Rome, was selling in Florence, with the assistance of entertainers, including an attractive woman, according to a printed news-sheet (*Avviso*):

> The amiable Vettoria, cleanly and neatly dressed as a young boy, has large numbers of people running to her, with the somersaults she does, her divine dancing and singing, such a sweet and beautiful sight, that the enchantment touches and lulls everyone, so that, sighing, they cry: alas, alas my heart, what is this? And most of all certain old men, who look at her with mouths agape, because they would like to flirt with her and partake of that tasty morsel.[24]

Subsequent chapters are divided for convenience between rural and urban society, but it should never be forgotten that there was much inter-connection at first or second hand. Urban and rural economies were linked to their mutual advantage, whether through major investors, or these minor pedlars or performers. International trade, and urban economies were the main motors for economic growth, the sources of Italian economic domination in the later medieval and early modern period up to the early seventeenth century, but when these sectors declined relative to parts of northern and western Europe, some investments and productive activity moved into the smaller cities and rural areas, so spreading material benefits there. The urban elites continued to exploit the *contado*, but some benefits accrued to the latter. Shifts and adaptations were made easier because the rural scene in much of Italy was already in itself diverse, and experienced significant mobility, even in the supposedly monocultural agriculture of the south, as we shall see.

4

THE LAND AND RURAL SOCIETY

Prelude: *contadini*, peasants and landowners

The complexity of Italian rural society was considerable.[1] The common word *contadino* which is often used as the equivalent of the English *peasant*, has some of the same derogatory connotations for modern users, as it did in the past. The English term assumes a rural dweller living in a small village or an isolated farm or huts. In Italy the *contado* meant the whole area dependent on a main city or town; and it could mean quite considerable communities of many hundreds or even thousands of inhabitants in a kind of urban community such as Prato. Perugia (population 19,234 in 1582) had in its official *contado* (population 57,234 in 1582) towns or villages such as Deruta, Marsciano, Castiglionfosco, Corciano, Paciano, Passignano, Piegaro, Antria, Fratta (modern Umbertide) and Sigillo with well over 500 persons, and Panicale with over 1000, through the sixteenth century.[2] Many inhabitants would not have been primarily dependent on agricultural work (*peasants*) – the *maiolica* pottery makers of Deruta for example – but still be called *contadini*, with or without adverse connotations.

The *contado* had land owned by people and institutions based in the large cities, or in lesser urban centres, and land owned by villagers. There were elite landowners who alternately lived in the *contado* and a city. In the actual operation of the land numerous systems of tenancies, share-cropping and direct labour schemes existed. There was much inter-connection between *contado* and city, though this varied through different kinds of terrain. Cities could incorporate fields and vineyards, and there was industrial production in the *contado*. This chapter is designed to demonstrate the variety of land-holding systems in the *contado*, the considerable variation in types of rural communities, and different social categories between simple peasants and great landowners inhabiting there.

Types of land systems and agriculture

Given the diversity of Italian geography, the variations of social compositions and the disparities in the prevalence of urbanisation, it was not surprising that there were considerable differences in the types of land-holding systems, and of agricultural organisation. One type, primarily in the South, was that of the large *latifundia* estate, where a feudal baron owned vast hectares of land, and employed landless labourers who lived in large villages or small towns and went out into the fields as required. A share-cropping system characterised central Italy. Everywhere there could be small-holdings with peasant owners, and properties leased out for varying periods from a few years to generations, by urban institutions or individuals, the church and monasteries.

A common system in much of central-northern Italy was the *mezzadria* (share-cropping, *métayage*). This involved a contract between the landowner (individual or institutional) who provided the land (*podere* in Tuscan), the housing, usually (in Tuscany and Umbria) oxen for ploughing, a plough and other equipment; one or more *mezzadri* would undertake to work the land, and the main produce (wheat, barley, beans, grapes or wine, olives, etc.) would be shared on the completion of harvest. In the classic Tuscan system the contract usually was annually renewable, but for efficiency might remain in the same family for years or generations. The peasants were required to live in the farm-house on the property to protect it. The size of property was related to the labour required to work it, and the size of the family-household contracting for it. The contract might be with a father and son(s), or a group of brothers; if the basic family was not large enough to work the property, then the contractors would be required to take on an assistant (*garzone*), who might be vetted by the proprietor. The family was expected to be self-sufficient on the allocated property. A change in the size of the household could lead to the non-renewal of the contract; this might involve an exchange with a better matched *podere* owned by the same proprietor, or severance and the family's hunt for a new proprietor and *podere*, near or far.

Mezzadria contracts might stipulate that the family seek permission for any marriage in the household, that it should provide the proprietor with a certain amount of pork or poultry in the year, that certain improvements should be undertaken (new ditches, draining channels, planting more olive or mulberry trees, etc.),and how this would affect the share of the produce to be handed over to the proprietor. There were regional variations. Around Bologna the landlord retained the produce of pasturage and woods, but allowed the *contadino* some foraging for a limited number of animals. In parts of Lombardy and Piedmont the *contadino* had to rent from the proprietor pasturage for his beasts, and even his house and garden. But in the Valpolicella the proprietor might have to guarantee grazing land on his directly farmed property for his share-cropper (*lavorente*) to use. Some *mezzadria* contracts could be longer than a year at a time, as frequently in Umbria; in 1527 Bonifatio Corgna provided a piece of land in Castel Pila, (or Castel del Piano, Perugian *contado*), with vines, a house, an oven and a well; the labourer was to work for four years for half the produce.[3] This four-year period seems common in Umbrian contracts. The Valpolicella version (*lavorencia)* ran for three to five years.

There has been much debate about the growth of the *mezzadria* system through the middle ages, and its subsequent development through to the present.[4] It has been variously seen as a system of gross exploitation of the peasants, or as a relatively beneficial sharing system replacing exploitative forced labour. In Umbria and Tuscany in the fourteenth and fifteenth centuries urban communities and the well-to-do used this to take over control of rural areas, liberating peasants from servitude under older systems, but also depriving them of free land. Many contracts favoured the proprietors and exploited peasant labour, creating kinds of forced labour on domain properties. But in the Valpolicella and others areas of the Veronese the share-cropping system until the late eighteenth century appears a balanced system, where the peasants were far from down-trodden. The 'memoir' of a fifteenth-century Tuscan peasant, Benedetto del Massarizia, indicates he preferred share-cropping to leasing because it gave him some insurance in bad times; half the produce was kept, whereas a fixed rent might take away all the return.[5]

From the later fifteenth century in Umbria *mezzadria* contracts show more involvement, and more contribution from the proprietors; and go into considerable detail about how the *mezzadri* or *coloni* should work the properties. Alongside the standard *mezzadria* contracts were a whole variety of agreements – *di lavoreccio* (primarily concerning tilling), *di cottimo* (for mixed farming) – varying the length of time of contracts, the amount and methods of investment by proprietor and *contadini* and the methods of payment in kind, money and labour. Some contacts were open-ended – but with a heavy penalty payment if the *colono* wished a quick exit. Some contracts were for life or three generations. In 1525 Ser Pacifico di Andrea leased to Valentino di Francesco and his family some land in Panicale (near Lake Trasimeno), tilled, wooded and with olives, to be worked for three generations. Within two years Valentino had to plant 40 new olive trees, and build a house about 5 × 4 metres; he was to pay annually a third of the produce to Ser Pacifico and his successors. This seems a beneficial contract for Valentino, in a fairly prosperous area, with Panicale having an annual three-day fair where surplus produce might be sold.[6] When reading the intricate Latin notarial contracts one wonders how well the illiterate peasants remembered the stipulations and orders of farming procedure. But Benedetto del Massarizia, unable to write (though possibly competent to read), had notaries and others compile a family business memoir; and he was clearly adept at dealing with notaries, complex contracts and disputes with abbeys over land.

Through the Veneto, Lombardy and the Republic of Lucca simple renting contract systems operated rather than the *mezzadria*, or existed alongside, with different time lengths. Renters might be obliged to work on the proprietor's domain land, to use his mill, to bottle wine in his house. Some cultivators in return for a fixed rent had considerable freedom over how they farmed; others were hemmed in with restrictions. With freedom went some risks; the cultivator might be bound to pay the full amount however bad the harvest. Other contracts built in a sharing system based on the harvest, some helpful to the peasant, some not; in Paduan cases this meant if the harvest fell below a certain level the landowner would just take half (so reducing from the normal rent). Valpolicella tenants paying fixed rents (*affitanze*) might still secure from the landlord payment for abnormal damage from storms and floods.

Some contracts mixed *mezzadria* with rent systems for the same family, as in Como or the Veneto: a fixed rent on cereals, and a sharing of the produce of fruits, grapes, mulberry leaves, wood. In Valpolicella mulberry leaves might be under a separate contract alongside the normal *lavorencia*; or an equivalent of the share-cropping system for raising silkworms or pigs (*soceda*) alongside a cash-rent (*affitanza*) for cereal production (rye or wheat). In Friuli the sharing element became more common through the period, as landowners tried to gain more control over smallholdings. In parts of Lombardy there was a shift from *mezzadria* elements to a mixed system, with an easily collectable fixed rent on one main harvest. And here rent was increasingly paid in money rather than kind – as in Tuscany and Emilia from the sixteenth century. In the Valpolicella in the late seventeenth century there was some movement from share-cropping to direct renting, and then from the 1730s back to share-cropping, because it was more flexible and responsive to fluctuations in a volatile agricultural and general economic climate. The Tuscan Benedetto del Massarizia and his relatives around Siena worked some land as share-croppers, rented some, laboured for others – and he owned from 1476, among other properties, a vine-yard with orchard, olive-trees, woods, arable land, and a house with a vat.[7]

Many owners in north-central Italy from the sixteenth century had difficulty securing suitable families to work the land, so the share-croppers and tenants could secure reasonably favourable conditions; hence the longer periods for share-cropping contracts, the agreements for proprietors to cover abnormal damage, the foregoing or postponing of rents when harvests were poor. The adverse reputation of the share-cropping system derived particularly from eighteenth-century Enlightenment campaigns for agricultural reform to be led by actively involved, economically well-educated landowners; and from the late eighteenth and nineteenth-century conditions of rising population, land hunger, social and political disruption that worsened conditions for the rural populations generally.[8] In reality over the period the *mezzadria* systems had operated very differently, affected rural families variously, and was probably most beneficial for the workers (and even the landholders), when mixed with other forms of land management.

Direct farming by large landowners in north and central Italy was limited. Much land was owned by the urban elites and by ecclesiastical institutions, who rented their land. Some large landowners did have home farms around the rural castles, villas and hamlets where they resided some of the time. Here they would use labourers (*braccianti*, *braccenti* etc.); some would be permanently employed, and provided with estate houses, others were hired as day labourers from the villages and small towns as needed, and were the most vulnerable. But given the mixed farming and mixed economy in many parts of north-central Italy they are not all to be classed as proletarian landless labourers. Many of those working on a day-rate as *braccianti* for the local landowner also had their own smallholdings, or were the unmarried children of a tenant household. In a mixed rural economy when agricultural tasks could be staggered through much of the year, a *bracciante* could be employed by various landowners, large and small, on a variety of tasks: sowing, reaping, pruning, gathering wood, building or repairing terracing, drainage channels, moving flocks.

The direct farming, and the control of the share-cropping and renting schemes, could be in the hands of powerful officials working for the landowners, as *fattori* or *gastaldi*, etc. They organised the drawing up of contracts by notaries, acted as rent collectors, checked on the fulfilment of contracts, listened to complaints, and dealt with claims for compensation for damage. A factor might serve one large landowner and be part of his estate (with free housing and food), and be somebody to be feared by tenants; or work for a group of lesser landowners. In the latter case, living in a village, he might be closer to the tenants. In the Veronese there were dynasties of estate managers; some became powerful landowners and/or commercial dealers. In Tuscany the factor was sometimes required to be celibate, so as to concentrate on his onerous duties, taking him afar through scattered properties. But a professional factor of the seventeenth century (Giacomo Agostinetti) thought a factor should be married, with a wife to take care of him, to avoid scandals. When a leading Bolognese prelate Monsignor Innocenzo Malvasia drew up instructions in 1609 for his factor, Paolo Rangone, he assumed that this already experienced factor might be succeeded by his son. Malvasia had a substantial, largely compact, estate at Panzano di Castelfranco Emilia (now in the province of Modena). His manual shows he was actively concerned with his properties (despite a busy ecclesiastical career), had read other manuals, and knew the peculiarities of Bologna farming practices. Aware of the power of the factor, and opportunities for deceit and corruption, as well as the merits if honest and faithful, he was detailed in his warnings and instructions. The complications of running a mixed farming estate (with hemp and animal farming seen as the main areas for profit and expansion) – involving *mezzadria* and other contracts, and day labourers – emerge from this manual, and show the social and economic importance of the professional factor in the *contado*.[9]

The powerful role of a factor is evident in a study of Altopascio, which also reveals much about the complexity of rural society. Altopascio was a village and estate complex in Tuscany (north of the Arno river, south east of Lucca) which in our period passed in effective control from the small Order of San Jacobo to the Capponi family, and then (1584) to the Medici Grand Dukes of Tuscany.[10] The 'village' or Estate covered about 3000 acres, centred on a *castello* as a small urbanised community of 40-odd houses and 600–700 persons through the 1615–1784 period. The Medici estate-manager (*fattore*) dominated from this castle village, with an administrative elite group separate from the rest of the village society. By the eighteenth century the factor's household included two assistant managers, a scribe and a female housekeeper; but also the priest and his servant, the bell-ringer and his assistant, the estate guard and a dispenser. The 1767 register designated four heads of household as 'gentleman' leasing out land (and one such family had a surgeon). The head of the Vettori family was said to be a merchant dealing in silk, cattle and other things; and resident within his household were the baker, the manager of the grocery shop and a carter. Among heads of household there were five shoemakers, two blacksmiths, a general shopkeeper and two delicatessen sellers (*pizzicagnoli*), a carpenter, two weavers and a plate seller. Shopkeepers and artisans had housing above their work. Some also leased land, and there were labourers living within the *castello* who worked land rented outside the walls. Wives and daughters were also weavers. A hospice or hospital (the original basis of the early medieval community) remained to cope with the poor.

The fields started from the castle walls of Altopascio; to the south-east was an area of poor hard yellow earth leading to low hills and a forest area (the Cerbaia). North and east was the plain area with the river Ralla and the Sibolla canal, a low fertile alluvial area, which, however, required careful draining. Part of this land operated with long-term leases, the leaseholders building their own housing on the spot and living in isolated farms. Other parts of the plain were worked directly by the grand-ducal factor; but these were divided into plots (*poderi*), of which there were 38 in 1784, with isolated farms. Here the housing was often just a large primitive hut, though by the eighteenth century there were well-planned solid houses being erected to a common plan; multi-occupancy, multi-purpose, with accommodation for animals in stables, hen-houses and pigsties incorporated in the complex building.[11] The forest areas provided wood for various purposes, and grazing for animals. Two sizeable water areas (lakes Bientina and Fucecchio), and a swamp were useful for fishing and processing flax. An estate oven produced bricks. There was an estate mill – which peasants often tried to avoid to circumvent taxes and monopoly prices.

Altopascio was an area of multi-crop farming, including wheat, rye, oats, beans, barley, flax and sorghum; maize successfully appeared in 1710. Grapevines bordered the fields, and there were mulberry trees to feed silkworms. The different levels of agricultural workers included: *garzoni*, or apprentice farm labourers (who were often bastards from the foundling home); day-labourers (*pigionali*) who were hired as needed and lived in rented housing; the *mezzadri*, share-croppers, on the grand-ducal land who paid in kind or money; and those who rented or share-cropped land from other leaseholders living outside the Altopascio estate. Families outside the *castello*, according to the detailed 1767 *status animarum* record, were supplemented by women spinning flax or weaving linen (for the linen industry based in nearby Fucecchio). One woman made shoes, and another was registered as a householder who sold fruit and vegetables, and several were servants. Wetnursing was also a source of income, whether the women were taking children into their home in the estate, were entering private houses, or going off to foundling homes in Pisa and Lucca.

Altopascio was important for the Medici income, providing about 13 per cent of total private estate income in 1650; but it was recognised to be a 'poor' village – especially as nobody resident there owned his property. Though poor and rural-agrarian it was not an isolated community. It lay on an ancient route from southern France to Siena and Rome: the Via Francigena or Via Romana. A hospice or hospital for pilgrims and travellers had given rise to the medieval community and its associated religious Order of San Jacobo. Other useful roads linked with towns and cities. Rivers and canals gave cheap and easy access by water to the Lucchese, the Arno and the port of Pisa. It was on the frontier zone between the Grand-Duchy of Tuscany and the Republic of Lucca, vulnerable in moments of state conflict, but having benefits as well as dangers from contraband trade. So the inhabitants had contact with a wide world, for economic, social and cultural benefit. The intercommunication is shown by the high and increasing level of marriages where a partner was chosen from outside the Altopascio parish.

The neighbouring Republic of Lucca illustrates a different mix of *contadini*, and some tense social relations. This Republic essentially consisted of a merchant city, a small port – Viareggio – of varying fortunes through the period, and a mixed rural area. Part of the rural area, that surrounding the city, the Sei Miglia, consisted of fertile plains and low hills; other parts in the Vicariates were more rugged, mountainous, but with some value in producing chestnuts, pasturage, and (in the Camaiore) olives and vines. The Sei Miglia was dominated by city landowners (private or religious), with some of the patricians from the sixteenth century having villas at the centre of active farms. In times of food crises the *contadini* here could hope for 'some help . . . from the landowners (*patroni*), who had an interest in maintaining their peasants (*salani*)', as the city's General Council noted in the seventeenth century. The *contadini* in the mountains fared much worse in bad harvests; they were made to help the grain-short city and Sei Miglia with chestnut-flour, and themselves live off 'vegetable roots and wild garlic' ('radiche d'erbi et agletti salvatici'). While they had more common land than in the plains, this was often pledged to citizens to cover communal debts. These distant *contadini* had to sent representatives to the city to seek food relief; having little credit to raise money to buy what was available, and not having self-interested or charitable landowners to help them, they returned to mountain villages empty-handed. Faced with such situations the mountain people were intent on hiding their meagre supplies from city officials from the Annona commandeering food; they thus fulfilled the urban view of them as fraudulent and criminal. Their fastnesses gave protection to 'bandits', adding to the hostility between *contadini* and urban officialdom, and to the atmosphere of violence. While rural inhabitants in the plains and lower hills close to Lucca, especially women, could supplement incomes from processing, spinning and weaving silk, the remoter mountain *contadini* had few such opportunities.[12]

The rural and agrarian scene in the South is conventionally seen as having been very different. Yet generalisations about the mainland South (the Agro Romano or Roman Campagna, and the Kingdom of Naples) and Sicily, as being dominated by great *latifundia* estates (called *tenute* in the Roman Campagna) in the hands of feudal barons, who were largely resident in Rome, Naples, Palermo and Messina – and so neglectfully absentee – have to be qualified[13] (see Maps 1 and 4).

A *latifundia* system is generally understood to mean an extensive property owned by a major landowner, relying on semi-servile, low paid labourers. It was often single crop, under-used and under-capitalised, and provided limited profits. Neapolitan nobles had such extensive estates in parts of the Kingdom such as the Tyrrhenean plain – north of Naples (Terra di Lavoro), south to Salerno, across towards Nola and Avellino; in the Calabrian plain; in the Adriatic or Puglian plains. The Tyrrhenian plain was reasonably well irrigated, productive and fairly easily worked. Calabria and parts of the Adriatic plains were much poorer for crops, but they provided great areas for pasturing migrating sheep, as did the Roman Campagna. Elsewhere, however, the feudal landowners had scattered, more subdivided properties, as in the poorer regions of Abruzzi and Basilicata. Other parts of Puglia (Terra d'Otranto), and the Caudina valley near Benevento (from the seventeenth century) saw *latifundia* estates broken up into large farms involving mixed farming, and mixed ownership and tenancies; with benefits in productivity and earning power even for the labourers.

The *latifundia* estate, and a mentality behind it, is frequently blamed for the backwardness of the south in both economic and social-civilising terms. But many problems stemmed from the geographic deficiencies of southern Italy outlined before: extreme summer heat, landscapes denuded of trees, poor rain supplies and inadequate river systems. The South therefore by and large lacked the variety of hillside agriculture, or forest-based arboreal and animal economies, that made central and northern Italy more diverse. The southern plains could grow grains, but mainly wheat with limited returns on yields. The lack of oats meant lack of food for cattle or horses; a paucity of oxen and horses (to pull heavy machinery) meant a heavy reliance on manual labour. The plains could provide pasturage for sheep, alternating with grain growing. This encouraged a major capitalist investment in huge herds, and noble control over extensive areas of land, with legal powers to direct the movement of the flocks between valleys and hills. It was in the interests of governments to facilitate the organisation of large herds. As G. Delille argues, the basic geographical facts of most of southern Italy precluded the development of an arable–pasturage–viticulture system based on smaller herds (which elsewhere was more efficient and progressive), with the use of oxen or horses to help work the land.[14] Retention of the *latifundia* system was thus logical and economically understandable for much of the south. The Neapolitan feudal baronage generally took little interest in land management, or in raising the profits of their agricultural possessions, at least until the enlightenment campaigns of the eighteenth century.[15] The *latifundia* system encouraged the concentration of people in large communities, rather than in small hamlets or villages as found in north-central Italy. But in parts of the Kingdom like Terra d'Otranto, where the land was more subdivided, there were episcopal cities like Alessano, Castro and Ugento which were really villages (with 161, 51 and 151 households in 1561).[16] Day-labourers would be based there, and hired to go out into the fields as required. Others moved out with the flocks for the major migrations. Many labourers were only employed for limited days in the year for seeding and harvesting. However considerable areas of common land remained for labourers as well as tenants to keep their animals, or have tiny plots for their own crops.

Most inhabitants of the Kingdom of Naples lived in substantial population centres, whether cities (*città*), large villages (called *terre*) or hamlets (*casali*). The last were usually dependencies of the other two; *città* and *terre* were in administrative terms *università*. The *università* were predominantly feudal, under baronial control. In 1531 out of 1563 such communities only 55 were royal cities under direct royal jurisdiction. The Spanish rulers increased the number of *università* to about 2000, but only 50–60 of the most important in size and strategic location were royal. By the 1780s there may have been 3000 *università*, of which 2300 were feudal (after some campaigning to shift some back into royal control). Then about one million out of the 4.8 million population lived in royal communities. The feudal communities were most predominant in Basilicata, Terra di Lavoro and Calabria, and least in Terra di Bari and Principato Citra.[17] The feudal *università* were local municipal authorities with their own officials and councils; sometimes with wide citizen voting population, sometimes with narrow oligarchies, with tax-raising powers, some control over common lands and some legal jurisdictions.

The feudal barons who had these *università* in their fiefs had more jurisdictional power than feudal nobles in other Italian states; and they had feudal levies and contributions that could be significant sources of revenue (and more profitable than farming). They often had considerable monopoly rights; vassals might have to use the lord's mills, ovens and inns, to process cloth in special places. The baron could impose taxes on goods and people passing through his territory, or on goods sold on his property, as in a market. Hunting and fishing rights were under baronial control. Forced labour had ceased by the sixteenth century, though in some fiefs the vassals were required to present 'gifts', as at Christmas, instead. The baron could require vassals to defend his castle (or pay in lieu), or fill certain offices, such as revenue collectors, though salaries were paid. Barons controlled various legal and administrative offices in the *università*, and received proceeds. Appeals could be made from feudal courts to royal appeal courts, but in practice the feudal system was a major buttress to the local power of barons over the vassals (*vassali*, as all the inhabitants in their territories were officially called).

The Neapolitan and Sicilian barons, as also the Roman nobles in the Campagna, generally only kept a small proportion of their land under direct farming. The Borghese, the dominant feudal family in the Campagna, by 1763 had 93 per cent of their lands in tenancies. The large estates had considerable areas of common land for the vassals to graze animals, and other unenclosed land where peasants could rent tiny plots. Then other areas were rented out under various kinds of contract, for payment in fixed amounts of rent in money or kind, or in shares of harvest. In Calabria many such contracts were for eight years, closer to Naples four, in Sicily three to five. In the Roman Campagna leases by the eighteenth century were for 9 to 12 years on baronial property (but less on ecclesiatical possessions). Middle-rank tenants might sub-let. In some areas simple *mezzadria*-type contracts existed but, as in Sicily, the division was much more favourable to the proprietor (two-thirds), than in north-central Italy. Much of the ecclesiastical land on the mainland, as in Puglia, was rented out at very favourable levels of payment from the peasants' point of view, sometimes in the eighteenth century to minimise anti-clerical attacks. The extent to which inhabitants of the large rural *terre* had access to tiny pieces of land on the hill-sides, under what conditions, for growing vines, olives, fruits or keeping animals, remains unclear.

A consideration of some southern fiefs can counter-balance simplistic views of the *Mezzogiorno* of *latifundia* estates and sheep migration. The Caracciolo Brienza branch of the greater Caracciolo clan ranked among the top 50 Neapolitan families, having 15,000 vassals by the end of the eighteenth century.[18] Their power was centred on four main fiefs: Atena and Brienza (Principato Citra), and Sasso and Pietrafesa

(Basilicata), in neighbouring *università*, but across two provincial boundaries and three dioceses. Within the provinces they were distant from the capitals, Salerno and Matera (Map 4). Atena was far from its episcopal centre, Capaccio; and the other dioceses were poor (Campagna-Satriano and Marsico Nuovo). So the Caracciolo Brienza had limited rivalry from lay or ecclesiastical powers. Like many Neapolitan barons – and unlike Tuscan, Roman or Lombard equivalents – the Caracciolo Brienza barons spent considerable periods in their fiefs, in the castles at Brienza, Pietrafesa and Sasso, and (from 1612) a palace built at Atena. The castles were prominent on hills dominating the village; besides being the domestic residence they contained offices, law courts, jails and storage space. The Caracciolo discouraged visits by equals, and there were no fiefs of equals close by. They returned to Naples, where they had palaces, for major social and business negotiations such as marriages.

The fiefs were not particularly large or wealthy. Brienza (at 713 metres) and Pietrafesa (630 metres) were on high hills between the Vallo di Diano plain and the Lucan Apennines. The properties produced grain, oil and wine; there was pasturage and many wooded areas. Atena (the smallest in size) was mainly in the plain of the Vallo di Diano; it produced grain and wine, but had little pasturing; it suffered from being marshy and swampy, from frequent flooding of the river Tanagro. Atena was close to the royal road to Calabria, and the baron's privileged inn was economically significant. It was the centre of the Caracciolo commercial activity. Sasso (higher in the mountains, at 940 metres) was the poorest *università*, with the smallest population, which eighteenth century officials judged to be savage and very poor. It relied mainly on pasturage, but produced some silk. Like Atena it also had buffalo for producing cheese. At Atena the Caraccciolo created some sub-fiefs, leading to the formation of a small elite society; but otherwise there were few above a low level of peasant farmers. Though resident in the fiefs, the Caracciolo Brienza showed little direct interest in the land, were unadventurous, and accepted declining returns from the land in the seventeenth century. Little of the land – of the barons or the commune – was enclosed or rented out as autonomous farms. Much land was open to grazing by all vassals, and other areas were open to whoever wished to grow crops in return for a proportion of the harvest (*terraggio*), which was usually only a tenth. The family also had allodial land and houses, rented out for money or kind, except where they directly farmed vines. Giovan Battista (d.1620) was the exceptional active land-owner, buying up land within the fief, trying to create more coherent properties, especially at Atena (where he built a palace). He increased wheat production for commercial sale to Naples. He also made some nine-year contracts with groups of residents in Pietrafesa and Brienza, supplying oxen and some initial seed for wheat and barley growing, designed to boost overall production. But his successors did not follow his enterprising approach. The Caracciolo were no more adventurous in livestock, unlike the Doria, Princes of Melfi, with fiefs in Basilicata and Puglia.

The herding of great flocks of sheep dominated some key southern areas. Animal husbandry (sheep, goats, oxen, cows, buffaloes, mules, horses, pigs, etc.) all over Italy served various purposes and played varyingly significant roles, providing food variety (meat and dairy), clothing (wool and leather), fertilisation for crops, work and transport animals. As part of mixed farming, animals were the salvation for many small tenants, share-croppers and labourers. Where sheep became a significant feature the size of the flocks caused different effects. Small flocks of sheep were primarily useful for fertilisation and local food supply; but not leading to great profits. However, large flocks of sheep and cattle could serve major industrial enterprises and create considerable wealth. By the sixteenth century in Calabria, the Salerno-Eboli plains of the Neapolitan Campagna, and Puglia, and the Papal Campagna, considerable capital was put into the building up and organisation of flocks of thousands of sheep, which had to be moved from plains and valleys to hills and back. The plains in summer were too hot and arid to support sheep and cattle, which were taken to the hills and mountains, which in turn were too cold in winter. In Calabria Citra flocks that spent the summer in the Morano mountains and Sila area, came down to the plains and coastal areas around Crotone. Sheep were moved from the heat of Roman Campagna in June up to the central Abruzzi and Umbrian hills till late September. The most capitalised and organised transhumance was that from the Abruzzi mountains to the plains of Puglia, organised by the Dogana of Foggia.[19]

The effects of the large-scale transhumance systems were considerable and various. In the Papal State the leading landowners from the fifteenth century, under government incentives (until there were some second thoughts in the 1580s), shifted considerable areas from arable to pasturage, to the detriment of the cereal food supply, and leading many dispossessed and underemployed peasants to migrate to Rome and other cities. In Calabria and Puglia arable and pasturage combined better, and the sheep used fallow land in the plains, without major depletions of the farmed land. The movement of the large flocks required many males to leave home for months, affecting family and household. The large-size ventures encouraged some entrepreneurial and capitalist ventures in areas not otherwise noted for this, and set up wide networks for the commercial distribution of wool.

The large-scale sheep movements were organised through various government-created institutions – the customs house (*Dogana*) – for its own tax-raising purposes. There were the *Dogana dei pascoli* for the Patrimony of San Pietro in Tuscia (in existence from at least 1289, and significantly developed from the fifteenth century), a *Dogana* in Salerno (for the western part of the Kingdom of Naples) and most prominently the *Dogana delle pecore* for the eastern side, which moved its headquarters from Lucera to Foggia in 1468.

The *Dogana* at Foggia was intended to regulate the transference of large flocks from the Abruzzi mountains to set pasture lands on the Adriatic plains for the winter months (with staging areas of pasturage in transit); to control the sheep owners, shepherds and farmers providing pasturage on fallow land; to prevent opposition from fief holders, communes and arable farmers who resented the dominance of sheep and other animals; and to collect taxes. Though the size and prosperity of the operation fluctuated considerably through our period (the growth periods being 1447–94, 1550–1612, 1686–1806), the enterprise was always extensive. There were 1,700,000 sheep involved in 1496, and as many as 4.25 million reported in 1580/81.

In 1783 there were 2315 families with *locati*, places allocated for pasturing their sheep. Some 6000 other families were involved in shepherding, or 4 per cent of the Provinces involved with the Foggia *Dogana* (Abruzzi Citra, Abruzzi Ultra, Capitanata and Molise).[20]

Flocks were brought down from the Abruzzi at the end of September, along different regulated sheepwalks starting at places like Aquila, Celano and Pescasseroli; negotiating six passes (Ascoli and Candela, Biccari and San Vito, Guglionesi, La Motta, Melfi and Spinazzola, Ponterotto) and rivers (especially the Biferno and Fortore) and resting at various holding pasture stations, the sheep (and some mules and horses) were dispersed from late November to one of twenty-three main pasture locations in the Tavoliere di Puglia (from Lesina and Castelnuovo in the north to Andria and Minervino in the south). The return journey started at the end of March and was completed in early May. The specialist livestock farms were complex to house the humans, the sheep, dogs and horses, to provide facilities for milking and cheese-making and to provide market gardens. The nearby cereal farms were simpler, though some also had pasturage. The animals provided manure for the cereals, and improved the arable production rate. One full-time shepherd per 500 sheep was seen as the best working arrangement. Smaller sheep-owning families might amalgamate to send off such a flock, or a small owner just accompany his own flock. Other individuals or companies created very large flocks, developed a hierarchy of full-time and part-time shepherds (sometimes specialising in lambs, pregnant ewes or rams); wood-gatherers, cooks, dog-watchers were also required. A full-time shepherd was assumed to work 360 days a year; any other worker would have a working-year of much less, given obligatory feast-days when they should not work on the land or in the workshop.

Shepherds might start before they were ten, and have a career on the sheepwalks until their 60s; many were literate (to cope with complex negotiations, taxation, record keeping imposed by the *Dogana* system), and they could end as substantial sheepowners themselves. Virgilio de Colangelo of Pacentro started in the *Dogana* in 1524, and 59 years later aged 75 was a rich possessor of 6000 sheep when he was awarded his *locato*. Substantial sheepowners may have started as a paid shepherd, or owner of a small flock, or were nobles and notaries organising major companies and enterprises, and acting as syndic officials on the governing body. The Doria family, Princes of Melfi, provided the leaders in the seventeenth century; from 1672–1763 they averaged 9844 sheep (with a maximum of 15,533), 904 goats with eighty-seven shepherds, of whom twenty-seven were full-time.[21]

The range of those involved in the Foggia *Dogana* operation, and superintended by the representative body, the *generalità*, that governed and negotiated for those owning sheep and rented pasturage, was wide; the *generalità* superintended the pastoralists and agriculturists, and also their families, servants, guards on horseback, shearers, surveyors, bakers, cheesemakers, shoemakers, accountants and more. For the Puglia-Abruzzi regions the *Dogana* produced a fairly harmonious balance between agriculturalists and pastoralists, and fended off the opposition of nobles and communes who were not part of this corporate system, and resented its power. By the eighteenth century (and especially after the famine of 1764), leading enlightened reformers such as Ferdinando Galiani and Melchiorre Delfico attacked the *Dogana* monopoly control, as detrimental to the agricultural reforms needed to ensure a steady food supply for a rising population.

Not all southern communities in the feudal system were predominantly agricultural, and some focused on small industrial complexes, or artisan specialities. For example Solofra, on the route between Salerno and Avellino (an Orsini *feudo* from 1558), benefited from the Salerno sheep system. Noted for producing parchment in the sixteenth century, it became both a tanning centre, and a producer of beaten gold. It conducted much trade through the fairs at Bitonto, Foggia and Salerno. In 1658 (after the cruel plague), it had about 500 households; 101 were headed by tanners, 58 by shoemakers, 19 by gold and silver beaters, 23 by tailors. There were four doctors and notaries, but now only one parchment maker. Its variegated employment profile would do credit to a Tuscan or Veneto *città*, but for having only one lawyer.[22]

The social and economic complexities of a southern feudal territory can be exemplified by neighbouring Eboli, which was judged a potentially prosperous and happy fief in a report about it in 1640, when the Doria d'Angri succeeded the Grimaldi.[23] It was well located geographically, extending from the gulf of Salerno in the south 40 miles to the Picentini mountains in the north, with the river Tusciano to the west, the river Sele to the east. There were easy communications with Salerno (17 miles) and Naples. At the mouth of the Sele, eight miles from Eboli, was a landing-stage, facilitating transport of produce to and from the annual Fair at Salerno, and the local San Bernardino fair. Eboli, with about 600 households in 1648 was on top of a hill, easy to reach; a baronial castle was across the Telegro valley, and well protected. Around the town were various sizes of cultivated property, with vines, olives and gardens. Below the hills and down to the sea was a large plain, partly wooded and partly swampy, for pasturage and common usage. Few true *ebolitani* worked the land, but lived civilly ('si vive civilmente, senza servizio manuale'); they brought in seasonal labourers (*braccianti*), from Campagna, Montecorvino, etc.

But all was not so happy in Eboli. The swampy plain, plus a warm climate meant serious malarial problems. This discouraged the feudal lord from living there; and when his Vicar General came to administer the fief he tended to reside in the neighbouring Doria *feudo* of Capaccio. In the later sixteenth century a bandit leader, Benedetto Mangone, from a lair near Eboli, was the scourge of the province until captured and executed in Naples in April 1587. There were many conflicts between landholders and pastoral farmers, between large sheepowners and local *contadini*, over disputed boundaries and common lands. The 1640 reporter also stressed that Eboli was full of social-political tension, with the vassals constantly litigating against the lord. The Eboli *feudo* had had a number of changes of lordship over the previous century and more, facilitating the development of a noble elite, which had secured some subinfeudated property from the Grimaldi, in conflict with lesser citizens The latter petitioned Nicolò Doria not to draw distinctions, and he declared 'all my sons are of a kind, and so I will know how to castigate Nobles like the commoners (*plebei*), if they should commit crimes'; but he soon established new rules for local elections that ratified the distinction between privileged families (*delle prerogative*) and the body of the community (*università*), which also accorded the former some tax exemptions. The tension between the local nobility and the populace grew during the 1640s, and exploded during the general revolution in Naples and the Kingdom in 1647–8. Eboli was badly affected by the 1656 plague (recovering to only 355 households in 1669). The Doria gradually took a greater interest in this *feudo*, supervising direct farming and improvements, but so inducing conflicts with the well-off proprietors who had tried to enclose large areas for their exclusive pasturing.

Eboli has been noted as an open society, not only in terms of importing seasonal workers, but with marriage systems also open to outsiders (geographically exogamous, unlike Solofra to the north). Women played significant roles in family strategies and economically in the control and transference of property, especially among less well-off families; this helped tie incomers to the land and property. Conjugal solidarity, assistance for widows to remarry and the use of godparent relationships, gave social protection. Different strategies were used so that sons could marry and set up small conjugal families with some substance, and that premature deaths should not leave partners or children unprotected. So in Eboli political conflict and violence characterised the public life, but the domestic scene had more social cohesion.

This section should have shown that landholding systems were complex throughout the peninsula, the types of agricultural production diverse and consequential employment opportunities varied, even in a supposedly unsophisticated southern society. Some implications for types of households and families will emerge later.

Landownership

From the owning family's and institution's perspective ownership was of great significance, as the source of prosperity (or debt), of prestige and status, the occasion for disputes with governments over taxation, and as the basis for social bargaining, especially through marriage alliances and dowries. From the governmental viewpoint the main concern was whether the land was owned by ecclesiastical institutions or the laity, since the former might be exempt from taxation. A significant shift from lay to ecclesiastical ownership, as happened in the Veneto in the sixteenth century, could alarm governments worried about their tax base. Governments also were interested whether the land was owned by a citizen or recognised urban resident, or by a country or *contado* dweller, since the former might be more lightly taxed than the latter. The distinction of recognised nobility as such mattered less in Italy than in some other countries (as in many parts of France), since it did not necessarily or usually mean any automatic exemption from land tax. In that sense Italian states suffered less from the social tensions between privileged, tax-exempt, nobility and tax-paying middling classes.

Most large-scale landowners, whether lay or ecclesiastical, were not directly and actively involved in land management; most land was contracted out in various ways to small tenants or share-croppers, or was controlled by factors. When and where landowners did take a personal interest – as with some patricians in Venice, Padua and Vicenza from the sixteenth century, the Doria family as Dukes of Melfi in the seventeenth, or the Tuscan nobility of Chianti in the eighteenth century developing terracing and quality wine-growing – it might lead to more adventurous farming, with benefits for many including those peasants who remained on the land. In the last case at least, and elsewhere under enlightenment agricultural reform, many *contadini* suffered by being driven off the land or into serious underemployment through agricultural efficiency requiring fewer workers. The lack of direct interest by many aristocratic landowners could on the one hand contribute to economic stagnation, on the other to less onerous exploitation of peasants in times of crisis.

The concentration of land in the hands of leading noble families and the church generally increased through to the eighteenth century. According to Stuart Woolf's summary the nobility owned about 20 per cent of the landed income of Naples, 70 per cent of the Bolognese plains; in Lombardy 42 per cent of the plateau, 46 per cent of the plains and 49 per cent of the hills; in Venetia the Venice patricians and the local nobilities owned (in 1740) 55 per cent of the plains, 38 per cent of the hills. In the Agro Romano 61 per cent of the land was held by 113 families, and 37 per cent by 64 ecclesiastical institutions (in 1783). In Lombardy 20–23 per cent of the land was in the hands of the church, hospitals and confraternities, and these groupings controlled 20–30 per cent of the lands of the Kingdom of Naples. But within the nobility through the seventeenth and eighteenth centuries more control was concentrated in fewer families; three-quarters of the Neapolitan feudal lands were held by only 15 families, from nearly 1500 titled noble families.[24] This imbalance became the target of enlightened reformers.

Eighteenth-century reformers attacked ecclesiastical landowners for neglecting the productivity of what they leased out, for exploitation of peasants in some cases, and for lax 'generosity' to lazy and threatening peasants. Concern for having prayers and masses said for departed souls, led individuals to leave property (or money that would be invested in property) to churches, monasteries, hospitals and (to a lesser extent) confraternities to help finance the priests, and to be registered as a 'good work' that might help secure remission from the stay in Purgatory. Land held by the church was likely to be held in mortmain, inalienable and unchangeable in its usage. So church land might pass on from generation to generation in the same family, or with similar kinds of tenants and *mezzadri*, without much concern for improvement, productive shifts in usage or changing farming methods. A polemical study of Puglia – where about a third of cereal production was under ecclesiastical ownership – suggests that ecclesiastical properties there suffered from all faults; the need to finance the counter-reformation revival led ecclesiastical managers to seek short-term increases in returns, impoverishing many *coloni*, and turning many from small lease-holders to day-labourers. But the ecclesiastical managers were often too inept and/or fraudulent to ensure long-term productivity or true profit for worthwhile ecclesiastical enterprises. The Jesuit Order from the mid seventeenth century may have been agriculturally the most efficient of the ecclesiastical institutions. Strident claims for ecclesiastical immunity over taxation led to debilitating clashes with both communal (*università*) governments and rival lay noble landowners.[25]

While general accusations about conservative church ownership might be valid, the picture can be misleading. Some institutions could be considerable landowners demonstrably active in improvements, productivity and enterprise. The great Roman hospital of San Spirito in Sassia, the wealthiest ecclesiastical institution in the sixteenth–seventeenth centuries after St Peter's, had large land possessions in the Papal State, especially north of Rome. An on-going study is revealing that from the late sixteenth century the hospital brothers had some very active administrators, who well supervised the properties and their returns, creating large farm-houses, granaries and mills; they employed significant architects like Ottaviano Mascarino and Gasparo Guerra to build churches, or fortresses (as at Risparmini), to protect the properties and peasants from pirates raiding the coastline. The fraternity was also concerned that their extra-Roman properties should enhance the image and reputation of the Hospital.[26]

The Neapolitan monastery of the Certosa di San Martino (with beautiful Baroque buildings and paintings implying rich incomes) was a landowner in Puglia, and a significant player in the shepherding system of the Foggia *Dogana* (as were Jesuits). The Cassinese Congregation of the Benedictines were notable for land reclamation schemes, irrigation and variable land usage. The Perugian monastery of this Congregation, San Pietro, was a major landowner in Umbria; its surviving archival records show major work in re-routing and controlling the flow of the Tiber river, the creation of new farm colonies, especially at Casalina, and the introduction of cattle farming. Leading monks who served as officials there (and in other Houses, especially that at Padua, since they had to move regularly), are revealed as active entrepreneurs in the sixteenth–seventeenth centuries. But the War of Castro (1641–4) sent them and many others in the Papal State into economic crisis, and they gave up direct control of their key properties. However in the later seventeenth century the monks were experimenting with cheese production and tobacco growing.[27]

Church landownership could be significant. From the sixteenth century most of the Perugian *contado* was owned by the nobles, but a quarter was owned by monasteries, churches, hospitals and confraternities.[28] The proportions of ownership between nobles, other city dwellers, ecclesiastical institutions and local *contado* dwellers varied considerably through the length of Italy, and even within narrow territorial bands. Much depended on the quality of the land, on the relative resources of leading urban families (or existing fief and castle-based nobles), on the adventurousness or otherwise of leading ecclesiastical institutions. From the early sixteenth century nobles and patricians tended to accumulate more land, especially where commercial-based elites shifted resources into land. From the mid sixteenth century the proportion of land in ecclesiastical hands increased significantly in some areas. The Venetian authorities from the 1560s were particularly worried by the way testamentary dispositions put more property – urban and rural – into church ownership (if not direct control), to the detriment of the tax base.

What tended to diminish was the proportion of land owned by rural smallholders, as secular urban investors, and ecclesiastical institutions took control. A local Pisan case study can illustrate the decline of ownership by *contadini*. The *podesteria* of Palaia (with 12 communities) was the most fertile of these areas and had already been targeted by leading Pisan and Florentine families in the later fifteenth century. The powerful Riccardi nobles of Florence account in part for the further shift – especially around the commune of Villa Saletta, where the Riccardi possessed 36 per cent of the property (by value) in 1563, and 90 per cent in 1620. (That of religious institutions fell from 28 per cent to 4 per cent, of other proprietors from 36 per cent to 6 per cent.) The Pisans in 1585 complained formerly at the inroads into their territory made by leading Florentine families. The Florentines owned (by value) 29 per cent of Peccioli, 10 per cent of Lari and 32 per cent of Palaia in 1560; by 1637 they had 41 per cent, 17 per cent and 45 per cent. The urban Pisans had to be content with buying up from local peasants in the less economically attractive hill area of the vicariate of Lari. The *contadini* ownership between 1560 and 1637 fell from 38 per cent to 27 per cent in Peccioli, from 61 per cent to 30 per cent in Lari, and from 34 per cent to 17 per cent in Palaia.[29] The loss of ownership was of course significant for the *contadini*, but the detriment to their welfare varied according to what kind of tenancy or contract followed with absentee owners or factors.

Ecclesiastical and noble landowners could be both adventurous and debilitating in their effects on economic production, and the social well-being of their tenants, share-croppers and labourers. No easy pattern can be discerned over time or geography, contrary to past polemical assumptions. What has to be noted is that even when a peasant was tied to a fief holder and his land, seemingly vulnerable to exploitation, he (and sometimes she) often had the opportunity to own a little land and to own animals that could be nurtured on feudal and common lands. This applied, as recently stressed, to the remote village of Pentidattilo, on a rugged hillside on the southern tip of Calabria. Thereby some feudal peasants under the Alberti in the early eighteenth century could enjoy some material benefits.[30]

Inhabitants of the *contado* and living conditions

The Italian *contado* was thus very diverse, and had a great variety of inhabitants. Some communities (like Altopascio) have the social-economic appearance of a small town. Villages, Neapolitan *terre*, hamlets (*casali*), Tuscan farm complexes show considerable ranges and types of peasants: very poor day-labourers unemployed much of the year, poor and rich smallholders and herdsmen; some of these and their families were involved in textile processing and manufacturing. There were the professionals involved in the farming, the factors, managers, grain dealers; there were smiths, cobblers, tailors full-time or part-time, depending on the size of a village community and its wealth; there were notaries, doctors, apothecaries and teachers in the larger villages or *terre*; all sorts of levels of clergy; there were nobles, their families, retinues and soldiers.

Whatever the ownership of the land, the extent to which owners had significant contact with the land and the world of the *contadini* was very variable. Many Italian elites – the patricians of Milan, Genoa, Turin, Palermo, Messina – were based in the cities, owning rural property but rarely visiting the countryside. A shift from commerce to land-holding and entitled fiefs as the basis of wealth and status for urban elite families seldom led to a *contado*-based existence. Some were urban-based, but had villas, castles or palaces away from the large cities – for brief visits to escape summer heat, to hunt, to indulge in fashionable bucolic entertainments – as from Florence, Rome, Naples or Venice; though some such patricians, especially from Venice or Vicenza were active gentlemen farmers fully involved in rural activity.

But some elite landowners lived more in the *contado* than in the large cities. These fall into various categories. Many were poorer nobles – with titles and fiefs, but limited rich land – who could not afford to maintain a civilised urban lifestyle; they lived in the more mountainous areas of Piedmont, Liguria, Friuli, Tuscany, Umbria, the Romagna and the Kingdom of Naples, or the coastal Roman Campagna. But as was noted with the Caracciolo Brienza, richer Neapolitan families were ready to spend long periods in their remoter fiefs; they did not treat their Naples palaces as the prize civilised residences in the way their Roman, Genoese or Florentine equals did. Poorer nobles resident in their castle fiefs could there organise money-making banditry, with a degree of immunity. Neapolitan, Umbrian, Romagnol and Venetian nobles were also noted for involvement either in outright banditry, or strong-arm extortionate practices using tough retainers (*bravi*) against local peasants, as Venetian officials supervising the Terraferma reported back about local nobles from Brescia, Bergamo, Padua, Treviso or the Friuli. The *contadini* could be caught up in the factional fights of elites, such as the Brescian Martinengo, Colleone and Avogadro families, or the Friulian Savorgnan clans.[31]

Where the nobles were resident in rural areas, and interested in the land, as with the Venetian Barbaro at their Villa Maser (designed by Palladio, frescoed by Paolo Veronese), there were beneficial effects on a wide-ranging economy, with adventurous agricultural development. Economic and social diversification inevitably followed if powerful, comparatively rich families, conditioned to conspicuous consumption and elaborate living, rebuilt castles, or created elaborate villas and palaces on the *contado* properties, and lived there at least part of the time. Building operations, staffing the properties, providing greater varieties of food, clothing and furnishings would all affect the local economy, even if much was also brought in from further afield.

The development of Medici villas in Tuscany from the fifteenth century (at Careggi, Poggio a Caiano, Poggio Imperiale, Pratolino or Caffaggiolo where *maiolica* decorated pottery was developed), had major consequences for the local economies, and for the whole image of rural living, market-gardening and formal garden development. Other patrician families like the Ginori were to follow a similar path from the early sixteenth to the eighteenth century whether as art patrons, market gardeners, active villa inhabitants, through to creating a porcelain factory near their favourite villa di Doccia in 1737. Cardinals and their families from Rome redeveloped villa life on Roman precedents at Frascati and Tivoli. In the Veneto villa life became the vogue for many patrician families from Venice and Vicenza especially;

but Palladio, Scamozzi and successors built most of them to be the centre of working farms and adventurous agriculture. On a lesser scale one has to consider the probable beneficial effects of the Caracciolo Brienza deciding to reside in Brienza or Atena; the Farnese establishing a palatial residence at Caprarola; of members of leading Perugian families like the Baglioni or Della Corgna retreating to (respectively) Spello and Castiglione del Lago; or the Vitelli building a palace at Città di Castello.[32]

The living conditions of the peasants and rural artisans clearly defy easy categorisations. Some peasants were packed into multi-occupancy buildings in compact large communities on the hillside; others lived in caves, in flimsy wooden huts; others in fairly substantial farmhouses scattered across the landscape of Tuscany or parts of Umbria. Up until the 1960s touring through central or southern Italy – hill-top towns or farmland – could still give some idea of what physical conditions might have been like for centuries. The background scenes of Tuscan and Umbrian paintings of the fifteenth and sixteenth century can give some idea of the hamlets and isolated farms of the period; fairly simple stone structures; living areas, animal housing and storage co-mingled; wells and ovens outside. Mills appear as more substantial structures, as befitting somebody of above average prestige and wealth, but in need of protecting produce, and himself and family from irate customers resenting his role as tax collector for commune and landowner. Sketches and detailed drawings survive from the period, as in the Siena archives, of what farms and buildings on the estates looked like. Some leading architects and theorists became interested in rural architecture for individual peasant families, or composite farm communities, such as Bernardo Buontalenti in the sixteenth century for the Arno valley, or F. Morozzi of Siena in the eighteenth, leading to probably better housing conditions, but maybe less autonomy. Benedetto del Massarizia and his clan had living spaces and 'luxury' possessions (beds, clothing, fancy shoes, silver buckles, mirrors, painted boxes), enough for Balestracci to see him as of a peasant middle class.[33]

From the later sixteenth century in the Lombard plain farm settlements were increasingly developed based on courtyard principles (rectangular complexes up to 120 × 150 metres or so), which enclosed the peasants and their animals at night, and imposed a degree of social control by the landowner and his agents. Areas around Rome had known similar complexes in the fifteenth–sixteenth centuries, and returned to them in the eighteenth where arable farming was reintroduced. Flatter areas of the South (the Capitanata, Sele) show similar complexes, to contrast with the hilltop fortress communities. These large farm communities testified to the efforts of landowners and institutions developing capitalist farming.

Many southern communities were 'dormitory towns for agricultural workers', with very simple basic housing.[34] Montefusco, on the old Appian way from Avellino to Naples, seems typical of one category in physical structure, though it had artisans (e.g. potters and shoemakers) and upper class residents. Perched around a castle up in the mountains, little streets radiated down from the central public buildings. An early eighteenth-century description indicates that most housing along these lanes were single storey stone, with storage basements, with some two or three storey structures up the hillside behind. Most would have been single-room for a nuclear family. In 1631 the community had 1125 people, in 275 households. Marriage meant moving out, finding a vacated, or building a new, primitive, abode. There were fourteen nobles and twenty-five *borghesi* or doctors, who would have had more substantial housing; but geography and poverty dictated simple housing and simple household structures for most here, whether artisans or farm workers.

In the worst conditions *contadini* lived in primitive wooden shacks, tumble-down stone hovels and caves. For shepherds and forestry workers these dwellings were for part of the year while away from a family base. We have no real idea of the numbers who lived their lives in remote and very primitive dwellings outside communities; just as we find it hard to tell the dire rootless poor in city basements and alleys.

Italian rural society was very complex throughout most of Italy. Land-holding systems, and the organisation of agricultural production varied considerably, creating a multi-layered peasant society. The terrain often encouraged, or necessitated the diversity. There was much flux between systems of agricultural organisation. As far as limited detailed knowledge indicates trends over the period, it seems that the proportions of land owned by urban-based elites and institutions increased from the sixteenth to the eighteenth century; the *mezzadria* systems marginally declined, tenancies and labour contracts become more monetary, and the level of material well-being increased, (partly through proto-industrialisation and more inter-connections with cities), if not at the rate enjoyed by the leading cities.

5

THE URBAN ENVIRONMENT

Throughout the early modern period, Italy had the largest number of major cities in Europe. If one takes 10,000 people as a rather crude dividing line, Italy had at least twenty-nine such cities in 1500, thirty-four in 1600 and forty-five in 1700. The comparable numbers at those dates for France were thirteen, twelve and eight; for the Netherlands twelve, fifteen and eleven, and for England four, five and three cities.[1] Over the period Paris, Amsterdam and London grew into very large cities, but so did Naples and Rome (see Appendix). Below the 10,000 figure all western European areas had many communities that can be called urban, on the basis of the diversity of a non-farming economy, and England had many market towns with under 1000 people that might be judged more 'urban' than, say, Cosenza at 12,000 in 1600. But within Italy one might claim a community like Altopascio or Poppi as urbanised as well at under 1000 people. As already noted, some large Italian cities declined in size through our period, and in terms of complexity of economic activity within sizeable communities, the Netherlands and England probably grew proportionately more urban. This chapter will concentrate on the top category of cities, and derive evidence from them, but much can apply to some *città* below that level (see Map 3).

Housing, living conditions and material culture

Urban living conditions varied considerably from spacious rooms in grandiose palaces to jam-packed basement hovels, shacks in waste areas of Rome, and on roofs perched over more substantial buildings. Most housing was probably high density, cold and damp in winter, stifling hot and fetid in summer, with primitive sanitary conditions – as became clear in reports during epidemics. Housing, mostly stone or brick not wooden, could be many storied and complex – as with the buildings piling up the hillsides in great cities like Genoa and Naples, or numerous Umbrian hill cities like Perugia or Todi. For the most part rich and poor lived in fairly close proximity. Great palace complexes could isolate the rich families: the Strozzi and Medici palaces of fifteenth-century Florence, the Genoese sixteenth-century *palazzi* off the Strada Nuova, enclaves in eighteenth-century Turin. Similarly isolated were the urban villas of Rome built or expanded throughout the period, or a retreat on the edge of the city like the Palazzo Te in Mantua. Such palace households could be of considerable size, with many servants of different statuses living in, with limited privacy for the leading family members.

Powerful extended families developed enclaves within a city, whether as groups in interconnected buildings along a street, or based on squares. By the fifteenth century Genoa had a number of fortified noble family compounds, as noted by Pero Tafur, visiting in the 1430s. Most were to be broken up or altered in later urban developments, but there are partial survivals of the Doria complex around piazza San Matteo. These enclaves consisted of the houses or palaces of the senior branches of the family (with maybe fifty close relatives living together), with more distant and poorer relatives living in narrow streets running off the square. Shops, ovens and storage facilities, possibly a market, a loggia, common bath facilities and a church or chapel could be part of the complex. This organisation provided a powerful, defensible, social grouping, based on an aristocratic clan, with many dependants, from lesser family members to skilled artisans, shopkeepers, retainers, servants and slaves. With some internal political stability after about 1528, with tendencies towards more conspicuous consumption and display, with desires for more privacy, the leading families made the housing more palatial (as along the Strada Nuova), and diluted the size and importance for wider society of these enclaves. The Genoese patricians, long after others, had a considerable control over 'public space', which they arrogantly dominated. Their Venetian counterparts were more subtle. Despite the dominant *palazzi* on the Grand Canal, Venetian patricians from the sixteenth century tended to build complexes away from the centre, combining a less ostentatious *palazzo* for the main family, with middle rank and more modest housing for dependants, and for general renting. This allowed for a more consensual control of space and local society. Leonardo Moro's development from 1544 of the 'Island [Isola] of Ca' Moro at S.Girolamo', has been seen as paradigmatic of this strategy.[2]

In the main urban space the social orders co-mingled in various cities; or at least the upper orders came close to the *popoli* since the street floor might have artisan workshops and their living accommodation, as in central parts of Venice. In sixteenth–seventeenth century Milan the patricians tended to avoid the area around the Duomo, where much commercial activity was concentrated, and a certain amount of manufacturing, as of metallurgy and textiles. In fifteenth-century Florence or Perugia the fairly close proximity between the leading families and the artisans encouraged hierarchical social relationships, and patronage systems, that diminished economic–class conflicts in contrast to neighbourhood and factional struggles.[3]

Commercial, artisan and domestic accommodation structures interrelated in diverse ways. Larger cities in particular had specialist locations for dominant craft-cum-commercial operation, combining work and living quarters, and producing streets of tailors, shoemakers, booksellers (as in Naples), jewellers or retailers (the Venetian *Merzeria*). Some of these more prestigious activities might be close to the city centre, where professionals like notaries or medics might also live and work – as in Bologna, Milan and Venice. Noisome and dangerous activities were banished to remoter parts of a city, where their specialist workers would also live – tanners, fullers, butchers (if involved in slaughtering and preserving). As humanist architect Leon Battista Alberti said 'Goldsmiths, silversmiths, and painters may have their shops in the public place, and so may sellers of drugs, habits, and other creditable trades; but all nasty, stinking occupations should be removed out of the way.'[4] The zoning of such activities might be dictated by the water supply from rivers, streams and canals – as in Bologna, Perugia or Milan. Dangerous activities such as glass-making could in the case of Venice be confined largely to one island – Murano.[5]

At least from the fifteenth century growing pride in spending money on housing and decoration was voiced. The Florentine merchant Giovanni Rucellai commented, having built a palazzo to the design of L. B. Alberti (who also defended the morality of costly building expenditure): 'I think I have done myself more honour by having spent money well than by having earned it. Spending gave me deeper satisfaction, especially in the money I spent on my house in Florence.'[6] Michelangelo later argued that: 'A noble house in the city brings considerable honour, being more visible than all one's possessions', and he was keen to have a spectacular house of his own in Florence to emphasise his (exaggerated!) noble ancestry.[7] Elite householders varied in the degree of ostentation on the outside of houses. The noble and merchant houses of Florence, Genoa or Perugia might be fairly austere outside, and hide splendours within. Milan buildings were noted as being generally spacious, deep rather than high, with narrow and unimpressive entrances, but more splendid within, and with interior courtyards and small gardens in wealthier constructions.[8] In contrast the Venetian facades along the canals were elaborately and idiosyncratically showy, as were the street facades of the seventeenth-century palaces of Lecce, with their sculpted festoons of nature. The exteriors of more humble citizens' dwellings were in some places more colourful and decorative than they now appear in cityscapes: colourfully painted, and decorated with arabesques, grotesques, mythological scenes and frescoes of marital and domestic virtues. Faded or damaged survivals have recently attracted my attention in diverse cities like Florence, Prato, Venice, Verona, Belluno, Bassano del Grappa, Cividale, Spilimbergo or Udine.

Changing attitudes to material culture and conspicuous consumption, evident from the mid fifteenth century, led to greater comfort and display within buildings. Interior decoration and furnishings were increasingly prized, with tapestries on walls as much as paintings, and spectacular beds and bedding. By the eighteenth century elaborate mirrors, chandeliers and upholstered furniture were also prized for display to visitors for those who could keep open house. Both inventories and illustrative detail from paintings and prints suggest a growing variety of goods through the period. Some examples of vulnerable goods like bedding, clothing and wall and floor coverings have survived, along with greater quantities of more durable goods, whether of metal from iron, copper, pewter to gold and silver, or ceramic and glass, which enhance the pictorial evidence of growing luxury and display. Peter Thornton's work, and the catalogues for a travelling exhibition of Venetian fashion, the Murano glass museum collection, and a Venetian exhibition of gold and silver provide good evidence of elaborate interiors and possessions available for wealthier consumers.[9]

Room structure was gradated, with rooms for the inner family providing more privacy, other chambers that might serve family and privy meetings with select outsiders and rooms for full public display and social presentation. In palaces, notably in Rome, elaborate etiquette affected interior design, and how people (inhabitants and visitors) met and moved between rooms.[10] Bedrooms could be open to visitors or double as a study. The development of the 'study' may be seen as ideal exemplar of status, display and privy sociability. A small, comfortable room, dominated by a desk (though it might also have a bed), it was a place for contemplation (present delights and consolations, and the uncertain future); and it would contain prized books and exotic or unusual objects, scientific and musical instruments. The study could be a secret retreat, and a cosy location for entertaining select erudite friends. Some studies were suitable for intimate concerts. As Dora Thornton stresses, much thought and delight was involved in planning this special living and thinking space. Though seen as primarily a male retreat – *his* study – Vittorio Carpaccio, a painter who clearly liked study-scenes, suggested also a female ideal study–bedroom in his *Vision of St Ursula* (Venice, Accademia, *c.* 1495). Castiglione's learned mother had her own study; so too did a Venetian courtesan, Julia Lombardo, wishing to provide a classical, refined environment for entertaining her clients and lovers.[11]

Though living conditions for many improved through the period, conditions for the poor and unfortunate could remain grim even in the wealthier and better regulated north-central cities like Bologna or Florence. These conditions were known by governments, and come down to us in the records through heath officials and those called on to help them (such as charitable confraternity members) when facing morbidity crises. They pointed to dank, dirty basement housing where the poor lived in putrid water and excrement. They described women who collected manure from the streets to sell, and kept it in their houses while it accumulated. They noted a butcher in Montopoli in 1607 who had 'a gully inside his house which is full of all kinds of filth, excrement, guts and other muck, which made the most cruel stench, together with a heap below the shop entrance on to which all the bloody waste falls, giving off an unbearable stench'. The Florentine fraternity of San Michele was called in by the government in 1630 during the plague to assess the poor in Florence, and see who needed new bedding and mattresses (especially to replace what might have been burned in anti-plague precautions). They reported on many 'houses' (cramped rooms) 'where because of misery there is not even the comfort of a bed, people sleeping on a little uncovered and filthy straw, and some others have foul and fetid straw mattresses'.[12] Such conditions were alarming to doctors and other officials worried about the health hazards to the population at large, and sometimes to charitable souls genuinely worried about the wretched conditions of some deserving poor.

These conditions for the poorest in the most densely packed buildings probably varied little across the centuries, while interior comforts improved for the majority. As we have noted, it depended on the city whether the fetid poor were in basements just beneath the richer, or in totally different buildings.

Organising the urban scene

Urban space was increasingly controlled in several cities.[13] Control was governed by combinations of ideals and practicalities, by plagues, politics and propaganda that might encourage a scenic display. Towns had been planned in the high middle ages – as with new towns in Tuscany – but Renaissance neo-platonism, mathematical theorising and new concepts of perspective led to ideal plans for new cities (which could seldom be realised). These had effects on urban redevelopment in existing cities and towns. While an ideal might be a circular or octagonal shaped city (in part realised from the 1590s in Palmanova in the Veneto), practicalities favoured grid plans with straight streets, and prominent squares in front of the major civic buildings or churches. When Pope Pius II in the 1460s started turning his small Tuscan birth-place of Corsignano into a gem-like small *città*, re-named Pienza after him, he set a precedent for a combination of ideal city theory, dynastic propaganda and practicality that bore in mind the housing and working needs of those outside the Piccolomini family. This was to affect much later urban activity. Theoretical concepts of social place, appropriate size of housing, and location within a city were taken up by architects such as Francesco di Giorgio Martini and Sebastiano Serlio, who designed houses suitable for nobles, merchants and artisans. In practice Italian planners and builders in cities like Rome and Venice did not segregate the social orders in different zones.[14] Motivations behind planning were complex, leading to different configurations where natural features allowed choice, ease of access to public buildings, churches and markets; and thoroughfares which were suitable for the policing of crowds and the domestic population; but did not allow too easy an access for any enemies from without the gates.

In theory, and considerably in practice, the period saw robust municipal controls over urban space and the location of urban populations in the major cities. Rome from the pontificate of Nicholas V (1447–55) developed a body of rules and a bureaucratic system under the Maestri di Strada that led the way in control systems; Venice (with additional problems of canal and water supply control) followed, and then Turin with its later seventeenth-century planned expansion (once firmly established as the single capital of the House of Savoy's state) followed. In these cities officials sought the orderly development of streets and frontages, and prevented the invasion of public space (whether at ground level or by balconies) by competitive building. Property owners unwilling to 'modernise' could be expropriated and entrepreneurial developers and decorators rewarded. There could be incentives for, and controls over, street cleaning and paving. In our period competitive display into street and square spaces replaced the sky-high invasion by competitive 'defence' towers in medieval cities like Florence, Siena, Bologna, Perugia and San Gimignano (which retains the most significant number today). Governments and powerful families battled over public display and spatial control, notably in Rome.

In Rome, Popes Julius II (1503–13), Paul III (1534–49), Sixtus V (1585–90) and later Alexander VII (1655–67), had major concerns over suitable pilgrimage routes. This was not merely for practical access and control, but was also meant to offer impressive uplifting inspiration for pilgrims, with suitable vistas opening to statues, obelisks or church facades, and imaginative decoration on the way. The control of street systems, with varying building plot sizes, allowed for the suitable development of palaces and substantial tenements for the richer orders, and moderately sized but more hygienically regulated housing and working places for the middling sort and poor. Sixtus V, aided by architect–engineer Domenico Fontana, laid down the basic structures of modern central Rome. He linked the major ecclesiastical and classical sites, and set street and zonal guidelines for housing the rapidly increasing population. Followed notably by Paul V (1605–21), Sixtus and Fontana ensured a suitable water supply for domestic and commercial purposes, restoring the ancient Roman aqueducts and creating new ones, and allowing impressive fountains to dominate public outlets, to the glory of the papacy, and also of some local families (like the Mattei and Barberini) who utilised them for zonal control. Paintings and prints from the eighteenth century remind us that many of the chief Roman areas remained unpaved, messy and muddy for all the planning and bureaucracy. But Rome's planning throughout was a prominent example of carrot-and-stick development that went beyond propaganda for Church and Papal State, and benefited the social and economic life of many thousands of Romans.[15]

Throughout the period Republican Venice similarly experienced governmental restructuring of the city, with a combination of commercial, communication, health and propaganda motivations. Like Bologna, its control systems were medieval, but they became more extensive from the fifteenth century, as standards and requirements of republican and private display became more ostentatious. Dangerously unregulated palace building on the Grand Canal, affecting the canal bed and flow of water, led (especially in the wake of the Ca'Foscari development), to government orders from 1462 that infringed on even the leading families.[16] Considerable expertise was needed and developed to control the waters of the lagoon, to maintain shipping lanes, to clear alluvial deposits from the rivers and canals feeding into it; to control and keep usable the inner canals (since refuse and sanitation went straight into them); to ensure wooden piles maintained the increasingly heavy brick and stone buildings (as Venice replaced wooden buildings from the fifteenth century); and to guarantee the elaborate systems whereby fresh cleaned water flowed up into the numerous well-heads in the courtyards and *campi* (of which there were 6782 in 1858). As with Roman fountains, the Venetian wells and *campi* were social foci, neighbourhood meeting points and centres for network control by leading patricians.

From 1486 the Venetian government tried to ensure the use of stone to shore up canal banks, wharfs and bridges; some walkways were paved, then increasingly the Campi; the 1500 great Jacopo de'Barberi printed map shows the large Campo San Polo paved. Development of the Zattere (1519–31) and Fondamenta Nova (1590s) took heavier and commercial shipping away from older residential and small-craft areas. The wooden Rialto Bridge across the Grand Canal, centre of the commercial zones, was finally replaced by the stone structure that still exists today, with its prestigious shops, in 1588–91. In the course of the sixteenth century the San Marco area around the Basilica and Doge's Palace was reconstructed to make it the show area for the city. Old ramshackle and dangerous buildings were destroyed and around the paved *piazze* impressive government offices (porticoed for access to shops and later coffee houses) were built. These included the Mint (with well-ordered cheese and salami shops on the ground floor), and the Library. Venice gained a spectacular central space, highlighting its republican religious virtues, providing an administrative centre linked to the Republic's capitalist roles in the Mint and the commercial shopping Merzeria zone and forming a cultural and social centre for the well-to-do.

Other cities witnessed noteworthy urban restructuring under diverse motivations. In the late fifteenth century Naples redeveloped the Castello area – for defence, commercial benefit, new housing, policing control and the easement of the fresh water supply. Street developments and the encouragement of concentrated palace building came in the Via Larga of Florence under Lorenzo de' Medici, the Strada Nuova of Genoa, parts of Pisa, Vicenza or Verona in the sixteenth century, Lecce and Turin in the seventeenth and eighteenth centuries. In the sixteenth century Bologna developed a central civic and religious centre around the Piazza Maggiore, rather like Venice's; with the old basilica of San Petronio, governmental palaces of the Podesta and Capitano del Popolo, the Archiginnasio for scholars, a Mint for the continuance of financial leadership, the Portico dei Bianchi clearing away messy old shops and offices, and Giambologna's vast Neptune statue for symbolic pride. It should be stressed that Bologna (like Milan), then had canals (now hardly detectable) and a nearby port, especially the Reno canal linking the Reno and Savena rivers, facilitating silk manufacturing and exporting, and transit by water to Ferrara and the Po river.

Bologna's development of its famous arcade or portico system – providing protection from the sun and heat in summer and the snow and rain in winter – which had housing or offices above the walkway took place under strict regulations from the thirteenth century, and continued throughout our period (running to about twenty miles by the end of it). Other cities of the period, from Padua and Modena to little Asolo, had arcaded streets to a greater or lesser extent, but Bologna's system was the most extensive and organised. The Bentivoglio family which ruled Bologna in the fifteenth century found the porticoes an impediment to police control and troop movements. But in the sixteenth century papal and municipal government legislation made clear that they were developed with twin motives of commercial-social utilitarianism and the beautification of a proud city, to the delight of visitors like Montaigne, who declared: 'this is a city all enriched with handsome wide porticoes and a very large number of beautiful palaces'. Montaigne was also impressed by the well-ordered brick-lain streets of cities like Ferrara and Venice, and their freedom from mud (unlike Piacenza, unpaved though it was a large city); whereas Florence's streets were paved with flat stone slabs 'without method or order'.[17]

Urban planning and restructuring, and the organisation of water supplies, were crucial aspects of urban social development in the period. They affected population location within cities, the zoning of commercial operations and the profitability or otherwise of certain industrial, craft and commercial enterprises. They could affect hygiene conditions, and lessen dangers of typhus, typhoid and dysentery. Fire hazards were reduced in cities like Venice. Rebuilding and the regulation of house sizes and materials improved housing conditions for many. Facilities became available for better retail shops, more conspicuous display, and (by the late seventeenth or eighteenth century) more open social gathering points, such as coffee and chocolate houses. The more elaborate developments of *piazze*, *campi* or broad streets affected public gathering and social inter-relationships, as well as facilitating the better control and integration of corporate bodies (such as confraternities and guilds) in religious and civic processions. The creation or expansion of governmental bodies – such as the Roman *maestri delle strade* and the Venetian *Savii delle Acque* – with the employment of experts in water controls, canal and lock building and other building operations, contributed significantly to the professionalisation of urban society from the sixteenth century, at least in cities like Bologna, Milan, Naples, Rome, Turin and Venice.

Some leading professionals were aware of the disparity between the well-regulated public places and fine palaces and the condition of back streets and poor hovels. The voices came loudest in the face of health epidemics and morbidity crises, with calls for the paving of streets, the clearance of cess-pools, the removal of animals (cattle, buffaloes, pigs and geese as Dr Perinto Collodi listed them in 1615)[18] and their dung from the urban streets back to the countryside, the clearance of cemeteries to without the city walls, and the promulgation of orders banning the throwing of excrement and refuse straight into public streets and canals. Following the Black Death (1348–50), first in Tuscany, then elsewhere, medical leaders and government officials developed various strategies for dealing with health scares, especially 'plague'. Florence and other Tuscan cities like Prato, Pistoia or Siena, might have led the way with health boards and control regulations. Milan followed, but by the sixteenth century Venice probably provided in its Sanità organisation the most active and effective permanent institution, operating fairly consistently through crisis and non-crisis periods. This was partly because of the additional complications of a canal-based city, its major international port (with close proximity to the Ottoman Empire from which plague often came, and which did not believe in warning systems or controls), and its high profile in bureaucratic organisation. The Venetian Sanità accumulated many powers and responsibilities as a major agent of social control in the city; it controlled or investigated prostitutes, syphilis, midwives and wetnursing, as well as problems of epidemics and the behaviour of doctors.[19]

As already indicated, many health scares and calamities occurred through our period. If a plague epidemic was feared in the neighbourhood or along major lines of communication, or actually diagnosed, then major cities (and the lesser cities, towns and villages in the better organised states like Tuscany and the Venetian Republic) brought into play drastic measures for health control.[20] Cities, towns and villages might be sealed off; incomers and potentially plague-carrying goods from any suspect area could be banned. Infected persons were carted off to *lazzaretti*, isolation hospitals and locations such as special islands in the Venetian lagoon. Still healthy members of the household were boarded up in their houses. In full crises artisan shops and other workplaces where people might contact each other were closed, and attempts were made to curb all but very essential movement through the cities. Police bodies, with criminal courts, normal or special, acted to control the populace. They tried to ensure confinement orders were obeyed, that people did not sneak off to their shops to make things to sell, move in or out of the city without control, that neighbours did not rob each other, body-carriers plunder the dead or dying, prostitutes seek clients, nor *untori* spread plague through their ointments. By the 1590s the Venetian authorities had military guards controlling the borders, shooting those transgressing border controls by crossing or sending goods from infected Ottoman territories. By the seventeenth century within Italy the major states and cities – notably Genoa, Milan, Florence, Lucca, Rome, Venice and Naples – contacted each other over plague. They had agreements on warning systems, on the control of movements of people and goods. However, given the dire economic consequences if the normal manufacturing and retailing systems were stopped, there could be tense relations, breakdowns in reporting processes and mismanagement, as in Genoa and Naples in the late 1640s and 1650s.

The effectiveness of health controls is debated among modern commentators. The medical experts were right to highlight the problems of basic sanitation, involving cess-pits, stagnant water or foul bedding as they affected general health, fevers, typhoid and typhus. In practice, and under political economy restraints, not enough was done about faeces hosting typhoid bacteria. Depending on the plague(s) involved, burning clothing, bedding and carpeting and so purging human and rat fleas (plus lice and mites) might also have helped, especially if the *rickettsia* organism was around. But quarantining may well have confined far too many close to the vectors of plague, and increased the casualty rate. This quarantining also had dire economic consequences. Carlo Cipolla argues that the blockading and quarantining in the 1630 Florentine epidemic increased unemployment by 150 per cent, and the number of needy from about 12,000 to 30,000 among the 80,000 inhabitants. Food somehow had to be provided for them, as well as bedding and clothes. It is of course impossible to assess what the controls on movements of people and goods between and within cities and towns did to stop or limit epidemics; we know the results when the precautions failed. The increased urban planning, water regulating and street paving probably improved the normal hygiene and health conditions of the cities.

The organisation and production of goods and services

The larger urban communities in Italy produced a great range of goods and services. These might be generated by an individual and his or her immediate family, by the interaction of various individuals and families (as particularly in textile production) who were co-ordinated by merchants and factors, or by a few major production units such as shipyards and factories. Factories in the modern sense of large buildings with machines and intense labour operations were rare before the later eighteenth century, when silk manufacturers in Piedmont started them. In our period the biggest production system was the shipyard, particularly the Venetian Arsenal – though the less studied Genoese and Livorno complexes were also notable. Most production was small-scale, based on units that combined workshop, retailing and domestic living. But behind such production there could be important and sizeable guild corporations, controlling the social as well as the economic lives of full members, apprentices and interlocking non-members. The guilds can be a key to much of the life of the urban dweller, and they affected the relationships with rural areas.

The general argument until recently has been that Italian guilds (*arti*, sometimes *università*) – as economic corporations controlling the production of goods and services and the economic lives of the producers – reached their peak by the fifteenth century. Thereafter they have been seen as declining in political power. They ceased to be the key to municipal government, giving way to dominant ruling families or a select oligarchy divorced from direct economic activity. The central political forces increasingly controlled the guilds, or made them irrelevant for overall economic policy of the city and state. However, they still has some control over who could or could not practice a particular craft or trade in a given city; they became increasingly conservative, hostile to innovative techniques and entrepreneurial capitalism. Thus enlightened writers and ministers in the eighteenth century sought to abolish the guilds.

Recent research is modifying the above picture of guild activity and importance. For some leading Italian cities, but notably not Florence, it is clear that the number of guilds increased through to the eighteenth century when they were abolished in some states. New creations matched the elaboration of craft production and the variety of service activities in an increasingly consumerist and materialist culture. Elite guilds of merchants, wool merchants and bankers did mainly become exclusive, protectionist and conservative, but more for social-political purposes than strictly economic ones. Entrepreneurial businessmen and manufacturers could evade guild controls, and move from Milan to smaller towns like Como or the *contado*. Most lesser guilds seemed more flexible over membership and working practices, and concentrated on such matters, along with philanthropy. They were less political in some local governments like Perugia's. Highly skilled and prized craftsmen, such as artists and gold–silver smiths, could escape when more mundane guild members proved restrictive, and work freelance or with powerful patrons. Lesser skilled men and women losing out in one occupation could move to a wide-embracing retailing sector, and as in Venice join the flexible mercers' guild. Guilds spent much time on demarcation disputes with each other, whether over strictly economic confrontations, or social precedence; but this could suggest flexibility and choice for individuals able to play between guilds. Guilds could be promoters of change, guarantors of skills, production standards and living-standards, or (at other times and in other places) impediments to change. The enlightenment and later liberal claims that guild systems stifled the economy and hampered the development of a progressive society are becoming harder to sustain.

Guilds were legally recognised entities subject to statutes, and they tended to become more controlled by the centralising states from the sixteenth century. Each guild should have had its own statutes; and the overall role of guilds within a given city would be governed by the general urban statutes, which by the sixteenth century might be conveniently summarised in a printed form as in Perugia.[22] Each guild controlled entitlement to membership, conditions of work, apprenticeships, the quality and often the quantity of production, and the physical and moral health of members. In economic terms the guilds could control the lives and activities of non-members involved in any way with the craft or trade of the particular guild. Apprentices, labourers and servants, though not members, were affected by guild rules and their legal courts. Those entering into a contract with a guild member could come before the guild's own court. Each Perugian guild had its own tribunal, where rules were enforced with summary justice. A sampling of some early sixteenth-century guild court records in Perugia (for taverners, notaries and hat-makers) showed that most cases concerned the settlement of debts and contracts. Women hat-makers (*berettari*) were involved on both sides in some cases.[23]

Such guild courts were run by the leading guild officials. The statutes indicate the perceived importance of hierarchies of officers within a guild, and often their election involved complicated processes. Office-holding could clearly satisfy the power instincts of some members, though also being time-consuming and distracting from business for others (hence fines could be imposed for not taking up a balloted post and fulfilling official duties). Some guilds were overloaded with officials, others managed with very few. The Roman *tessitori* (weavers) in 1574 had twenty-three officials (for ninety-three members), and the Roman *speziali* (spice-sellers and grocers) in 1607 had forty-four, though admittedly they had an important church and a hospital to run. But the important and powerful silk guild of Catanzaro only needed six officials in 1569, while in Turin the tailors only needed four syndics to run them in 1612. Given that guilds had many functions, that some were rich – like the wool guild in Florence – in property, and could exercise considerable power and influence in a city, office-holding could have major social attractions. The guilds were often important for the social and religious welfare of their members and relatives, helping widows, marriageable daughters with dowries and the sick and old. Guild officers thus played roles in charitable amelioration and social control.[24]

Guilds could cover almost any kind of activity, as Rome's growth demonstrates. The fourteen guilds founded in the fourteenth century incorporated people like merchants, hoteliers and innkeepers, notaries, painters and sculptors, but also wool-workers and various agricultural workers. The fourteen fifteenth-century creations included bankers, industrial workers like glassmakers, blacksmiths, furnacemen, but also German bakers. The twenty-three new guilds in the sixteenth century organised many more food producers, but also public writers and copyists, printers and booksellers. With an urban transport revolution, coach drivers were bonded together. Humbler folk like cleaners, refuse collectors and second-hand dealers now had their own guild organisation. In the next century the twenty-four foundations recognised the greater variety of food suppliers, as of fish, sausages or vermicelli and other pasta, but also hatters and sellers of delicate slippers. Finally the thirteen creations up to the 1760s recognised those indulging themselves thanks to sellers of wine, spirits, tobacco, or seeking adornment from wig-makers and hair-dressers.

Guild support was clearly necessary for those battling in the new competitive drinks market, as Roman society became more refined and, in some ways, public in coffee houses and brandy shops.[25]

Venice saw some similar patterns of guild growth until it had about 130 guilds in the seventeenth century. But this total included large guilds with various semi-autonomous subsections, whereas Rome had allowed such to break away completely. The Venetian Arte dei Fabbri by the seventeenth century combined twelve different kinds of metal workers, hitherto independent: workers in iron, copper, bronze, brass, tin, pewter, gunsmiths, scale makers, tinkers, used-iron dealers, hardware dealers and nailmakers. The Arte dei Depentori similarly now combined painters, miniaturists, leather-gilders (*coridoro*), gilders and frame-makers (*indoradori* and *soazeri*), cloth pattern designers (*desegnadori*).[26]

The appearance of new guilds, or recognised sub-sections, reflected new products, trades, and refinements of living. From the fifteenth century we have a surge of hat-makers; the appearance of guilds for printers, paper makers and sellers and book-sellers from the sixteenth century, as printing became very much more widespread; musicians from the sixteenth century as they moved away from church domination. Wig-making moved onto the scene in the seventeenth century, in Milan and then Rome especially. The growth of the silk industry led to diversification in guilds, as did the armaments industry in Brescia and Milan, and dependent areas; not only because guns and other weapons became more complicated, but because some purchasers wanted status-implying decorations and refinements, beyond functional purposes. Merchants might battle against old entrenched corporate bodies within a major city, putting out work for lesser towns and villages. In response to what was at times a cheap labour exploitative situation those involved might in turn become essential experts, and respond with their own guilds; this happened in 1758 with the gunlock makers of Lumezzane who were part of the armaments industry of Brescia and the Val Trompia.[27] The rising importance of Turin from the later sixteenth century, as the House of Savoy transferred its power base from France to Italy, from Chambery to Turin, is shown by the late foundation of important guilds such those for bankers (1589), tailors (1594) and saddlers (1658). The eighteenth century incorporation of watch-makers, makers of gold and silver buttons, or locksmiths suggests a degree of industrial diversification and specialisation.[28]

The guilds as they had developed by the fifteenth century varied considerably from city to city in whom they included as members. The main issues were whether major merchants, employers and masters were in their own exclusive corporations (as in the Florence wool-guild, Calimala), or were in the same guild as the associated journeymen and assistants (as in many Venetian guilds); whether subsidiary workers in the wool, linen and cotton industries were in one or two guilds, or had their own independent guild for each specialism; whether the least skilled workers were incorporated with legal rights, or formed a vulnerable proletariat. Many guilds had three main categories of members, masters, workers (*lavoranti*) and apprentices/assistants (*garzoni*). Statutes dictated the length of apprenticeship, the conditions needed to move to the *lavorante* status, and then full mastership. Mostly decisions were made by the guild masters themselves, but through the early modern period outside governments, notably in the Papacy and Savoy, controlled those allowed to operate a craft, trade or profession. Typically the *garzoni* was a teenager, a qualified *lavorante* in his 20s and 30s (and hoping to be a master), and a master in his late 30s or older.

Relations between the different levels of artisans probably followed no easy pattern. Some small enterprises, such as a printing works, may have been 'family' and co-operative; but we can balance (below) fraught situations around artist studios. Many craft occupations involved dangerous operations, with fires, dyes, presses and cutting machines suggesting a need for co-operation and trust. But there could be major tension between, say, master bakers and workers, though a Venetian example had the added complexity that Venetian masters were using German assistants – with religion, 'nationalism' and rival guild pretensions involved.[29] Where, as in textile operations, a heavy imbalance existed between a select group of powerful masters, and numerous workers and apprentices – often outside a guild structure and its protections – relations could have been tense, and exploitation harsh, directly or through managers. The 1378 Ciompi revolt in Florence may have warned the masters to be more accommodating. We know that a leading Florentine silk manufacturer, Andrea Banchi, in the fifteeenth century was solicitous about his workers, male and female; trying to keep good workers, reducing pressures when they had difficulties and fostering loyalty by securing cheaper wine and oil for them.[30]

A workshop or *bottega* had its hierarchies, whether all, some or none were controlled by a guild. Insights into a 'workshop' – though not one now under guild control – can be gained from knowledge of the painter Agostino Tassi (d.1644), now hardly known but in his day well patronised. Information is derived from his various trials – for rape (of the young painter Artemisia Gentileschi), and incest (with his sister-in-law Costanza Cannodili).[31] Tassi, despite his violent record, died as a rich man in Rome with a house on the Corso, servants, carriage and horses. But much of his life can illustrate the artisan's world – and its tensions – partly because, though a talented fresco painter, he seems primarily to have made his wealth through organising art workshops. Though he exaggeratedly claimed a thousand apprentices and assistants, he certainly had many. They worked on major fresco cycles for palaces (including the Quirinal, Lancelotti and Patrizi-Clementi), cartoon designs for tapestries and ephemeral decorations for religious and secular festivities. Unlike (allegedly), the more famous painter Cavaliere D'Arpino, Tassi himself worked and lived on site for distant fresco projects and painted ephemera, while co-ordinating many projects. While Tassi organised a number of site workshops (*cantieri*) at the same time for several Roman palace projects, much focused on a household and workshop that promiscuously mixed family life, training, production and immoral pleasures. When Tassi was on trial for incest in 1619 he was living in a rented apartment on via della Lungara, with his sister-in-law Costanza, her painter husband Filippo Franchini, their two daughters and a wet-nurse. Three assistants were part of the household, but others temporarily slept about the place when business was brisk. Agostino's well-lit bedroom was also the main studio, while bigger paintings were produced in the darker dining-room. Later he had larger premises, with slightly more privacy for the immediate family, but with other trained, assistant painters and apprentices living in the household. Boys might start aged about 11, be employed to grind colours, keep the studio tidy and be general 'servants', and be taught to draw, in return for food. Some, like G. B. Primi, for a while paid to be trained as draughtsmen and painters; but ended up receiving lodging, food and payment as assistants. The Tassi studio systems – involving different kinds of working and payment arrangements, depending on age, skills, needs and ambitions, in a linked household and workplace environment – were probably typical of more than the artists' artisan world, even if tailoring, smithing or selling drugs and groceries did not have such a fluctuating need for extra assistants for projects.

The social environment of sex and violence was less typical. Even if some charges were exaggerated, the Tassi circle was involved in much fighting and violent sexual activity; some assistants with mixed feelings had to accept the services of Agostino's mistresses instead of financial rewards and payments. Agostino's wife Maria (sister of Costanza) had fled in 1610 with another man, and Agostino was rumoured to have murdered her. He was accused in both 1611 and 1619 of incest with Costanza, but this did not break up the household-studio. Had Agostino and Filippo Franchini agreed to share Costanza? Agostino's condemnation in 1612 for raping Artemisia Gentileschi (while teaching her painting in the absence of her painter father) seemingly led to a sentence of exile; but the patronage of the papal Borghese family had the sentence revoked. Freed from prison he continued his studio work, which grew apace. His assistant Primi had fled to Genoa when Agostino threatened to amputate his arms (either for stealing drawings or for denouncing the incest), but years later (1641) after some successful work in Genoa he was back in Rome, living with Tassi and Franchini. While Claude Lorrain might be the only recognised top rank artist to have been trained by Tassi's workshop, it is clear from the experience of Primi and others that – despite the unseemly ambience – the workshops and dependent artistic networks provided comfortable careers for many middling artists, such that it was unwise to break out of the connection. Tassi largely got the named credit, and highest share of the payments, as the master painter.

The above example reflects on a workshop scene, though not one in this case subject to guild controls, since most painters were by the seventeenth century outside the strict guild system – for good or ill. The extent to which it was mandatory to be a guild member to exercise a trade or craft varied over time and place. In most cases involving specialisms, membership would be compulsory, and so stated: for example all goldsmiths, soap-makers, linen-workers, innkeepers in Rome; all tailors, shoemakers, masons in Bologna; all silk-workers in Catanzaro. But in Venice from 1517, fustian producers who worked at home without employees were exempted from membership, as in Verona were various dealers in paper from 1674. Governments could also readily exempt individuals they wished to favour. While Prato had some twenty-one guilds in the late fourteenth–fifteenth century, they hardly feature in the lives of a group of seventeen diverse minor local merchants and retailers whose account books have just been studied; they were innkeepers, cheese sellers, druggists, butchers, a waller, a grain seller and a second-hand dealer. If they were guild members, it seemingly mattered little.[32]

Membership figures, for the active or passive, are hard to establish. For Perugia in the later fifteenth century, I estimated about 1900 guild members for a city of 16–19,000 persons; or 4–5000 adult males. Perugia in the early fifteenth century could record 165 members of the Mercanzia (dealing mainly with wool, leather and cereals), 182 taverners, 25 potters. For Venice, R. T. Rapp calculated that about two-thirds of the work-force belonged to guilds that were required to provide men for galleys; in addition there were members of the Arsenal and other exempt guilds (lawyers, notaries, hatters, distillers and others).[33]

Guilds frequently conflicted. The diversification of guilds and the incorporation of specialisms, added to the potential areas of dispute, as to who could do and sell what, or utilise what materials and suppliers. Could guild-organised purveyors of food monopolise the selling of produce in the major squares of Bologna or Rome (as around the Piazza Navona), or could *contadini* come in and sell directly from their own stalls, barrows or mere baskets? In Bologna and Venice, makers of new shoes conflicted with those who repaired and adapted the old; while all these challenged specialist tanners and butchers as to who was allowed to tan the hides for shoe leather. Silk manufacturing, as in Genoa, Lucca, Naples or Milan, saw many conflicts between different guilds, or between guilds and independent merchants organising putting-out work; while arguments over tailoring in Turin or hat-making in Bologna, Modena and Carpi have recently been highlighted. Much of this might seem socially and economically detrimental; not conducive to efficient and cost-effective production, and so contributing to Italy's 'backward economy'. However, some disputes probably defended standards and efficiency, saved individuals from gross exploitation and provided corporate protection that contributed to a more stable society balanced between extremes of rich and poor. The fact that wrangles were lengthy suggests nobody was totally victorious, nobody totally defeated. However protectionist, conservative and male-dominated some guilds might have been, most urban economies seem to have had room for innovative entrepreneurs, for illegal or semi-legal interlopers (from within or outwith the state), for pedlars (whether legally incorporated or not) and for women to have their roles and some prosperity, especially in retailing.[34]

The Venetian Arsenal was the largest industrial complex in Europe for much of our period, to be overtaken by London only from the later seventeenth century (see Map 5). The government inevitably was more interventionist over guild activity than elsewhere. The surviving outer walls still give an idea of its immensity, while many surviving drawings, prints and paintings show its internal structures in our period.[35] Further it was a more complex, integrated and controlled industrial area than anything in London, Amsterdam or Livorno. It involved not only ship building and repairing, but also the making of sails, ropes, pitch, and the manufacturing of guns. In many ways it was socially a separate city, with a degree of loyalty and identity of its own. The complex was governed by officials responsible to the Senate, though three major powerful guilds of shipwrights, caulkers and oarmakers on the ship building and repair side controlled much of the labour force down the line. The workforce was fluid, difficult to control and calculate – as much from its privileged position as from the vagaries of employment. The numbers working on a daily basis fell far short of those officially enrolled in the guilds. Once accepted as masters or even apprentices the men might split their activity between the Arsenal and private shipyards elsewhere. When the latter were suffering, there were guaranteed jobs, or payments, back in the Arsenal. A recognised master might work most of his life in the private sector, but return to easy jobs in his old age. In 1559 the three guilds had 2183 enrolled masters, but only 960 seem to have been regularly active in the Arsenal. The government through the seventeenth century attempted to curtail this discrepancy, as shipbuilding in the Arsenal declined, and ensure a smaller but more consistently active work force. In 1696 the three major shipping guilds had 1282 enrolled masters and 486 apprentices, with 984 masters and 282 apprentices active.[36] They tried to insist enrolled members worked a minimum of 130 days, out of a normal working year of 265 days. Inducements such as special wine rations were used, doubtless explaining the difficulty of getting workers in on Mondays – 'Saint Monday' – after Sunday celebrations.[37] The full workforce in the Arsenal was possibly double the above number, when members from other smaller guilds – such as mastmakers, smiths, gun-carriage makers (*carreri*), cask makers – and non-guild labourers and porters are counted. Women appear as workers in the main industrial activities of the Venetian Arsenal, as well as being landladies, brothel-keepers and shopkeepers in the district. One unusual worker was Marrieta Battaglia Rubini, sentenced by the Inquisition in 1639 to a whipping and one year's imprisonment for practising magic. After three months she petitioned to be released to serve the rest of her sentence stitching sails in the Arsenal, at half pay – as apparently had been allowed for other prisoners. She duly served seven months.[38]

In the seventeenth century the building of new ships seriously declined, though repair work and gun-making might flourish. The Arsenal workforce was smaller but it had a more close-knit hereditary family structure, and state employment offered some security. Many smaller private shipyards (*squeri*) existed elsewhere, but their prosperity was more precarious. A moderately substantial wooden *squero* of the seventeenth century survives in San Trovaso. The living quarters were above the construction and storage areas.[39]

By the seventeenth century Livorno was the most advanced *port* in Italy, though not such a diverse industrial complex.[40] From 1544 it had been developed as the main Tuscan port to replace the silting-up port of Pisa. Jetties, a customs house and an arsenal were soon built; deep docks, a new fortress (1590), a well planned city and storage areas followed. A canal (started in 1560), gave ready access to the Arno river. Grand Dukes through the period fostered this port, with special tax concessions or tax exemptions, though it was not officially a 'free port' until 1675. In the interests of commerce and international trade Counter-Reformation scruples were overcome and Jews (and converts, *conversos* or *marranos*) were encouraged to settle, and trade from there. They had little difficulty shifting between Jewish and Christian identities as required in their travels. Armenians with similar international connections and access to the Ottoman Empire were likewise attracted; in the 1660s the Armenian Antonio Bogus may have been the biggest ship owner in the city. To populate the city, the Tuscan government allowed criminals and *banditi* (see Chapter 11) to be absolved of court verdicts, or to live safely as exiles from scenes of crime elsewhere, and settle. It became the centre for disposing by many nationals of plunder gained from raiding each other's ships. As the dragoman Giovan Battista Salvago told the Venetian Doge in 1630:

> Algiers and Tunis are full of merchants of all nationalities – Livornese, Corsican, Genoese, French, Flemish, English, Jewish, Venetian and others. These merchants buy the plundered goods and send them to the free port of Livorno where they are distributed throughout the whole of Italy . . . Trade in plunder is the real incitement to piracy; if it didn't exist, the plunder would go to waste in Barbary and the pirates, with their useless booty, would lose interest.[41]

If Venice was the main loser, the Tuscans gained. Livorno, as we have noted, became the centre of English operations. They benefited in particular from the modern storage facilities, especially for olive oil and fish. For much of the seventeenth and eighteenth centuries Livorno was a polyglot, international city, fostered by the Tuscan Medicean and, later, Habsburg governments.

Meeting places: buying and selling

Much social intercourse outside the home combined business, leisure and social manoeuvring, whether in streets and piazzas or indoors. Sociability in indoor public places became more varied from the later seventeenth century in larger cities, especially with drinking establishments for coffee, chocolate and brandies.

Tomaso Garzoni's *Piazza Universale* (1585) is emblematic of the social intercourse of urban Italy in the middle of our period. He envisaged all classes meeting, but located with due gradations in their stance and movement from the central position of the nobles and gentlemen, to the fringe positions of the latrine and refuse cleaners. The *piazza*, or main central thoroughfare, as meeting place for all saw changes through the period. City planning made them safer and healthier, with paving and cleaning, as well as more visually spectacular. Stalls, carts, shacks as points of sale were often removed (except intermittently for major markets), and more secure shops established on the perimeter. Use of the *piazza* for small or large gatherings was affected by religious reformers seeking to clear the churches of non-religious meetings, throwing out the money-changers and lawyers, if not lovers on trysts. Concentration of power in regional states, with their princely and elitist rule, removed some of the 'political' meetings, the *parlamenti*, that had existed to ratify government decisions, new councils, or the take-over by a new *signore*. The *piazze* and large thoroughfares remained the locations for major religious parades and for theatrical activities, where all levels of society could gather together; even if the nature of the religious gatherings changed, or gross frivolity in the fifteenth century gave way to more serious saintly festivals from the later sixteenth. The latter need not exclude street parties, and fountains of wine.[42]

Different levels of society met in business establishments, workshops and retail shops. *Bottega* was the word used then for such places, not just a modern 'shop'. The same location could be used as home, workshop and retail outlet. Counting *botteghe* has proved problematic, given the problems of definition, and the huge turnover in selling points. Florence in 1561 had 2172 officially recognised *botteghe*, for a population of 59,023, though some of these were clearly for manufacturing only and not selling. Among the most numerous involving retailing, there were 96 shops of shoemakers or cobblers, 31 hosiers, 131 bakers, 99 wood-sellers, 101 mercers (6 classified as large-scale), 69 tailors, and 66 second-hand clothes dealers (*rigattieri*). Rome in 1622 (population about 120,000) had over 5500 *botteghe*, with 1582 selling cloth and clothing, with or without other goods. The speed with which new shops could emerge is shown by some Venetian figures: 517 *new* retail outlets were registered in the years 1561–8, including 170 mercers, 95 druggists – and even 27 surgeons. Bologna in 1758 had 1232 *botteghe* and '*banchetti*' from about 89 guilds; these included 200 outlets for shoemakers and cobblers, 31 for tailors, 54 mercers, about 166 food retailers (including 25 selling bread) and 78 for second-hand dealing, but only four bookshops and one printing shop. The numbers of individuals involved is not clear.[43]

Documents from Pistoia for the late fifteenth and early sixteenth centuries show us very simple retail points tacked onto houses, displaying goods on the street, with no public entry into the building. A significant Florentine palace like the Palazzo Ginori had its own commercial outlet – for selling the 'house' wine produced by the family properties of the Sesto Fiorentino and elsewhere.[44] Surviving old shops in Venice show the more substantial combination of workplace and selling point that would have been a feature of several commercial cities. Good examples in Venice of two-storied shop and housing complexes can be found in the Castello area: along the Calle del Paradiso (based on fourteenth-century structures), Salizzada S.Lio, Salizzada dei Greci for example. The shop inventory (1653) of a second-hand clothes dealer, Girolamo Targa, records shelving all around, a bed, bench, cupboards, ladders and fire-irons. An awning protected shoppers and the display from the sun.[45]

Because of the interaction of creation and selling, working conditions by the end of our period in large cities at least could be elegant. In an anonymous eighteenth century painting in the Ca' Rezzonico, Venice, *The Lace and Embroidery Workshop*, a male customer is discussing with a woman details about a coat, *velada*, on the embroidery frame; elsewhere in the room women are spinning, winding and bobbin lacemaking. Another visitor plays with a dog, watched by an elaborately dressed lackey. Paintings hang on the walls, and padded furniture awaits customers.[46]

Buying and selling took place on streets, as well as in *botteghe*, at market stalls or by makers and sellers coming into houses. Itinerant sellers of many kinds were clearly part of the urban (and to a lesser extent village) scene. From the seventeenth and eighteenth centuries images of pedlars and specialist street-sellers, men and women, abound, as shown by the eighteenth-century engraver G. Grevembroch,[47] or Venetian painters, including the notable Pietro Longhi, and more obscure Gaetano Zompini, who produced prints and *terze rime* poems about their activities. Sellers came round to houses or stood on the streets with their baskets, selling breads, cakes and doughnuts, fruit, nuts and vegetables, eggs and cheese. Itinerant cobblers or carpenters made repairs at the door; there were pedlars dealing in second-hand cloths, clothing or utensils. In Venice and Turin by the eighteenth century the shop-based shoemakers and cobblers had bitter conflicts with the ambulatory shoe-repairers and sellers of second-hand shoes. Attempts to clean up urban spaces, to discourage the hassle of street-selling, encouraged the development of some permanent retail outlets, such as food shops in San Marco and the Merzeria in Venice.[48]

In Venice at least some pedlars (*revendigoli*), who traded in a whole range of goods, including foods, were officially recognised as part of the guild of second-hand dealers (*strazzaruoli*). This allowed them to sell old furnishings and clothes as well as other goods. Such pedlars admitted to this guild lacked the apprenticeship training (five years) of the *strazzuaroli*, which would have allowed them to alter, repair and refashion their goods. Their poverty meant they could not set up shop like proper second-hand dealers, they stated in 1621; they seemingly were unskilled male and female workers on the fringes of the commercial system, both scraping their own living, and probably benefiting the master *strazzaruoli* by helping the distribution of goods they had acquired.[49]

Public auctions were part of institutional business and ways for private individuals to raise money. These might cover properties, offices and tax contracts, but also personal goods. The Florentine Office of Wards held auctions to settle estates. Pawn-broking institutions (Monti di Pietà) auctioned off unredeemed pledges after a given period, to add to the cash supply for loans, or help (in Perugia's case) the local hospital. Courts through auctions raised money from confiscated properties of criminals. On a death, property and goods might be auctioned to raise money to fulfil the testaments. Sales and auctions were held in the streets and under porticoes, or in hostelries, involving a wide social mix of persons. The living, rich or poor, resorted to auctions similarly to utilise assets; and purchasers could obtain luxury goods as well as necessities. Auctions were a significant, and well-regulated, part of the second-hand economy, for Christians and Jews.[50] Obtaining second-hand goods from economic or social superiors could enhance one's own status and prestige; the acquisition of antiques, books, works of art could be a way of entering a new cultural milieu.[51]

Shops and workshops could be centres for recreation and long discourse. A Venetian apothecary at the Due Colombini (the two little pigeons) in the 1580s had his premise used for playing chess; behind this activity a dissident priest organised meetings of like-minded evangelicals.[52] Bookshops were useful meeting places for discussion, for playing games and for the circulation of new, maybe dangerous, ideas. A bookseller in Venice called Vincenzo had people playing chess and tarot in his shop; and the Inquisition in 1570 suspected they also held heretical discussions. The numerous tiny bookshops of Naples fulfilled such roles from the seventeenth century to at least the mid 1970s. The great Neapolitan philosopher of history, Giambattista Vico, was self-educated in a whole range of old and new ideas in the bookshops run by his father and friends. Some idea of such an environment is given in an anonymous painting exhibited at a 1996 London exhibition on the Grand Tour, showing Bouchard & Gravier's bookshop in Rome, about 1774, with louche intellectuals and earnest monks studying books and prints.[53]

The restrictions on public sociability for women, especially for the young, of course remained considerable until very recently. For them meetings in church might count as the most favourable respectable opportunities for encountering others, whether secret lovers or female friends. Visits to a confessor in the Counter-Reformation period provide the one real opportunity to escape the home; to him they might pour out their sexual, marital and domestic problems as to nobody else – and then find themselves taken advantage of by the equally frustrated and lonely confessor. Involvement in Christian Doctrine teaching in the confraternities of Christian Doctrine or just alongside the parish priest and curate might provide more opportunities for social contact. In a more secular context, the development of the horse-drawn carriage from the sixteenth century allowed richer females to take to open places in the key cities, under some male escort – most notoriously the older male friend or lover, the *cicisbeo*, in seventeenth and eighteenth century Rome or Naples, who might also be the escort in the opera boxes of these cities or in Venice. Attempts to converse from out of carriage windows contributed to the traffic-jams of Rome. Visual evidence suggests that by the eighteenth century well-to-do women in Venice (where earlier they had been fairly restricted) or Rome could go shopping in a fairly leisurely way, and visit coffee or chocolate shops, presumably under escort.

Inns and taverns were meeting spaces for all sorts and conditions of men, and a more limited choice of women; places full of excitement and danger, surprises and routine business. They could be scenes of murder and mayhem, especially in remoter areas, or of encounters between foreigners and natives in the cities, or places where local residents could borrow money, pawn goods, or purchase second-hand goods (legal or illicit). Both Garzoni in his *Piazza Universale* (Discorso 98) and Venetian authorities attacked taverns as places where all sorts of vicious practices were perpetrated, including the fencing of ill-gotten goods. In 1599 an official from an employers' organisation in the woollen industry confiscated cloth being offered in an auction of tavern pledges, alleging the cloth had previously been stolen. Through to the eighteenth century second-hand goods were profitably interchanged between the Ghetto Nuovo and neighbouring Christian taverns of some dubiety.[54]

The Venetian inns could also be gambling dens, with dire effects, The government in 1571 alleged that gamblers went to inns 'to satisfy their immoderate appetites [and] leave their wives and children to die of hunger in the house, because in these conventicles of drinkers they speak without respect of any quality of person, they blaspheme, gamble, luxuriate, and finally indulge in every sort of depravity'.[55]

Inns were good meeting places for the exchange of ideas, and could rightly attract the attention of worried authorities. John Martin has argued that: 'The Tavern was a haven of unhampered discussion in the early modern world'.[56] In the 1540s and 1550s Venetian authorities were concerned with discourse in taverns such as the Aquila Nera (Black Eagle) and Leon Bianco (White Lion) near the Rialto, where Germans might spread heretical ideas. Investigations of a tavern near the Rialto fishmarket in 1569 unearthed a network of contacts with Modena; the inquisitors there then heard from a witness about tavern discussions of Lutheran ideas back in 1565. When the Venetian inquisitors investigated evangelical craftsmen in the San Moisè parish they were told about such religious discussions not only in confraternities, but in the local taverns. Many of these were workmates who had learned to trust each other, and moved their social-religious discourse into a more public domain.

Inns were of course primarily for travellers rather than residents. Northern and central Italy had many, of varying quality as foreigners often commented. Rome had 236 recorded inns in 1526, and 360 in 1615; in 1561 there were forty inns in Florence (stable population about 60,000), and Como (population 8000) had sixteen in 1553.[57] One of Milan's eighty-eight inns could hold 1100 travellers. Southern Italy was seen as short on inns for travellers until well into the eighteenth century. What might be encountered there is illustrated by Louis Ducros in a sketch of an inn at Barletta, and his journal entry. He and his Dutch companions ate in a cavernous room serving as a large kitchen and storeroom:

> full of all kinds of filth, besides our muleteers; the wind and rain were coming through holes in the roof of the house made by the weather, and sometimes pieces of it were coming through the roof into our soup or stew. We were quite convinced that the beds we had been given were normally home to a good part of the town's bedbugs.[58]

Through the seventeenth and eighteenth centuries the variety of drinking establishments where people might meet expanded considerably in the major cities, to include coffee houses, chocolate shops or brandy dens, to add to more long-standing wine bars and inns. Venice had a major coffee house (All'Arabo) in the Piazza S.Marco from 1683, and this square alone soon had about thirty-five (some selling acquavita and ices as well). But it was the establishment in 1720 of Florian's that launched the famous refined society coffee-house fashion. Bologna had thirteen *Caffettieri* in 1758, all in the city centre. Roman archives document the intense competition in the eighteenth century to open such establishments, to manipulate the rules to diversify the supply of such beverages, as Roman authorities sought to limit the numbers per *piazza* or main street and to protect privileges accorded particular guilds. A drawing by David Allan reveals a more sedate coffee house in Rome, about 1775; it allowed space for reading, or convivial conversation over the billiard table. The exterior of the notable Caffe degli Inglesi appears in another of his drawings of the Piazza di Spagna. Pietro Longhi and other Venetian artists depict luxury and gentility in coffee houses, sometimes implying seduction and flirtation.[59] A periodical called *Il Caffè*, published in Milan 1762–4, made significant contributions to the Enlightenment.

Far more dubious were the *ridotti* and *casini* of Venice as social gathering places; these words covered a variety of occurrences and/or places primarily associated with gambling. They varied from reasonably respectable salons in palaces, to seedy dens; places for gambling, flirtation and sexual activity. Pietro Longhi's paintings provide us with the luxurious, louche, image of a *ridotto* or salon of the Ca' Giustinian; but Jonathan Walker's archival researches reveal more sordid evidence on major gambling, cheating, violence, prostitution and rape. While the government might licence *ridotti* and *casini* as semi-permanent organised places for controlled gambling and 'honest conversation', the Senate and other bodies frequently attacked the excesses of such gatherings, and 'prohibited places, where public and infamous *ridotti* are held, with gaming, drunkenness, and other dishonesties, from which *ridotti* those that hold them . . . obtain profit and income' (1598). Such places could lead to fraud and deceit, especially of foreigners, to violence, to the ruination of families through excessive gambling and to sexual depravity. Attempts, as in 1615, were made to prevent courtesans and prostitutes holding *ridotti* in their houses, or organising gambling. The repetition of legislation and orders for investigation highlight their significance in the social life of Venetian patricians, their *bravi* and lesser associates. However some *ridotti* were important meeting places for intellectual discussion, not just for sensual pleasure and the noble mania for gambling. A foreign visitor like John Evelyn could readily secure entry to the San Felice *ridotto*, as part of Carnival celebrations, before going to the opera. The San Trovaso casino was in the seventeenth century a useful place for political gossip. A Mocenigo father introduced his son to political contacts by financing modest losses. Social gambling was a way of learning etiquette in a republic without a recognised court; and a writer in the 1620–30s, Antonino Colluraffi, stated that patricians had (unfortunately) to go to the *ridotti* in order to secure suitable offices.[60]

The Venetian *casino* allowed women (of some respectability as well as courtesans) access, with a certain amount of equal competition and involvement by the later seventeenth century. The French ambassador Saint-Didier recorded the presence of noble women in the San Moise *casino* in the 1670s; but frowned on this as much else as part of the excessive liberty or libertinism of Venetian high society, and love of entertainment. This sort of 'immoral' behaviour produced heavier attacks against Italian decadent 'effeminate' society in the eighteenth century.

This chapter has indicated that the physical environment of leading Italian cities was well regulated in the early modern period, starting out of hygienic necessity, but increasingly affected and complicated by concerns for social and political control and for propagandist embellishment, public and private. The regulation of urban lives owed much to the guild systems. In many cities the growth of the guilds testified to the diversification of artisan activity as it met the expanded material culture. Through the seventeenth and eighteenth centuries there were many more places for men (and to some extent women) to meet for work, commerce and pleasure.

Sometimes political and religious leaders had cause for concern over such social contacts. This chapter has concentrated on physical structures within cities – living areas, places of work and of meeting – and the single most obvious organisation of urban work, the guild. The next chapter will consider other working groups through the social hierarchies, down to the economically most vulnerable workless.

6

URBAN SOCIETY

The variety of urban occupations

The variety of activities in urbanised areas in the period was considerable, as the discussion of guilds in Chapter 5 highlighted. These organisations were often at the heart of urban working society, but many occupations existed economically and socially above and below them. Contemporaries enthusiastically categorised occupations and status. This is best seen in Tomaso Garzoni's *La Piazza Universale di tutte le professioni del mondo*, which was first published in Venice in 1585, and had about 30 editions over the next century. He created an imaginary *piazza*, a sort of world theatre, in which all occupations are represented from the most noble and respectable at the centre, to the most ignoble, like latrine cleaners on the edges. He mentions about 400 different occupations under 155 separate *Discorsi*, which mix occupations sometimes in strange ways. Garzoni's occupations cover the most obvious ones like lawyers, smiths, barbers, dyers, butchers or printers that one expects from the world of guilds; but many less obvious ones like charlatans, charmers, buffoons, bandits, beggars; and even lovers, drunks, layabouts (*Otiosi di piazza* in Discorso CXVII), pimps and whores, or guards and spies, inquisitors and heretics. He has 18 different kinds of prophets, soothsayers, fortune tellers (in Discorso XL). Godmothers (*comari*) are brought in with midwives, wetnurses and other nurses as all dealing with pregnant women (Discorso CXXX). Garzoni provides a very complicated view of society, with multiple gradations based on moral worth (partly in a Counter-Reformation spirit) and concepts of nobility and ignobility, as much as economic importance. He stressed both the integration of activities, whether within the city or between city and countryside, and minute differentiations.[1]

Outside the fictional world, one should emphasise also that a particular family might cross several occupational demarcation lines, be classifiable at different status levels and occupy different spaces in and around the piazza. A businessman or merchant and his family might be involved in a whole range of occupations, as also a nobleman, notary or cleric; few were specialists. Andrea Arnaldi of a fifteenth-century family in Vicenza, was a notary, tax farmer and legal agent, also a wool merchant and silk retailer, and organised the raising of livestock and selling of agricultural produce. The Arnaldi family over the decades had a whole range of shops around the Piazza Maggiore, frequently changing location and what they bought, sold and exchanged. As they sought to rise in status in the city they moved out of some of the smaller trading activities, moving from diversified retail to specialised wholesale.[2]

This chapter will focus on a number of occupational groups or classifications, bearing in mind earlier discussion and exemplification through the guild structures, and forthcoming comments on some elites of city and countryside.

Women and male occupations

The previous discussion of guild organisation stressed a male world, though women were involved in some guilds. The historical records have tended to underestimate the extent and variety of women's work outside the immediate family. Given recent unveiling of evidence about where women worked with men, and debates about women's hidden work, some comments on women working and earning with men may be helpful in a focused section. Female servants, midwives and prostitutes will feature elsewhere below in appropriate places.

The close, but easily hidden, female involvement with male work was highlighted by Deborah Parker's study of women in the book trade in early modern Italy, stressing their important activity in many processes alongside fathers, brothers and husbands in what could be a family enterprise involving masculine physique, feminine delicacy and the learning and literary skills of all. Family living conditions and the workplace, the printing atelier, were often closely integrated.[3] The workshop production of books involved a complex co-ordination of skills and specialists; and involving a degree of secrecy. The full role of women as 'the printer' is disguised by their not being named as such, but recorded as heirs of the master male printer – husband or brother usually. A few like Girolama Cartolari (in Rome after working with her husband earlier in Perugia and Pesaro), and Elisabetta Rusconi (in Venice), did eventually publicise their own name as printer. The printing enterprise was often, maybe usually, an extension of the master printer's house – and household. Guild rules and family pressures encouraged keeping presses within the family and also encouraged intermarrying between printing families. This was facilitated by the tendency to cluster printing establishments in a particular neighbourhood of a city (in Florence around the Badia, around the Piazza Parione in Rome). Only males could officially be apprenticed; they might live in with the family and work, unless near neighbours – and end marrying a daughter of the house. Wives and daughters in printing families were taught to read and share in the production, even if not paid and formally trained. If they usually lacked the strength to operate large presses, they could be compositors and proofreaders. Having to be literate, and sharing in a complex co-operative venture within the supposed security of the household, meant these women could take over operations and maintain a family enterprise if the male master-printer died with a going concern. While family interests might stimulate an unusual female input from adolescence onwards into the workshop system, it should be noted that larger-scale enterprises such as Paolo Manuzio's in Rome in the 1560s brought in a significant number of women printers, when trying to cope with post-tridentine official publications, notably the Breviary.

Recently social historians have become more aware of female activity in the economy and broader ranges of society outside the family and cloister. Many mature women were neither married nor in convents. Many were widowed or abandoned without male support.[4] One has to explain how unprotected women, young and old, survived. There is much debate on the nature and extent of female employment, and whether work opportunities rose or declined from the sixteenth to the eighteenth century – especially with declines or shifts in textile production, and possibly changes in attitudes towards living-in female house servants. Historians of poverty often argue that the numbers of vulnerable women increased from the sixteenth century; though changes may be distorted because of a greater concern then for the problems of the vulnerable poor who 'deserved' assistance.

Documenting female employment and 'work' is difficult because of the nature of surviving records; and the female contributions are almost certainly heavily under-recorded. Many females were part of the domestic family workforce, unpaid as such and so unrecorded. Just as in the countryside women worked alongside men in the fields, so in the city they contributed in the artisan workshops. If widowed they could sometimes utilise technical or managerial skills so learned to continue the shop and craft as the leading income earner. Urban parish records show considerable numbers of female heads of households; while some record keepers might indicate the employment (or at least formal skill) of a male head of house, they much more rarely indicated a woman's skill or source of income, whether head of house or independently working wife or daughter. One cannot assume that such women were not earning money, nor know whether when a widow was given an 'occupation' she really worked as a sail-maker or blacksmith in the Venetian Arsenal, or merely presided over the establishment using male labour. Many urban women heading 'houses' probably supported themselves as landladies, as has been argued for the Venetian Arsenal area, and as is suggested by Roman parish records at the turn of the sixteenth–seventeenth century, when house lists give non-family members who must have been lodgers and/or apprentices.

Several issues concerning urban female occupations can be illustrated from the start of our period from the Tuscan *Catasto* record of 1427.[5] For Florentine Tuscany it registered 7114 female heads of households (against 52,661 male heads): 3755 in the cities (1536 in Florence itself), 3359 in the countryside; but only a few female heads were given an occupation. The largest numbers were servants (116 household-heads). The only two categories that might involve major new income are wool merchant (2) and innkeeper (3). Those recorded as uncloistered religious (59 *pinzochere*), or dependent on a religious house (41), had a reasonable high tax assessment, which presumably implies past resources, investments and grants. *Pinzochere*, as independent women living in small female communities but in the world, were later to come under attack from Counter-Reformation leaders, and pressurised to enter nunneries taking full vows. They might be suspect as prophesiers and healers – from which activities they might have derived an income.

Laundresses and hairwashers sometimes alternated as prostitutes in reality or in the accusations of civic leaders, as in Perugia.[6]

Some women were in top guilds, though the degree of their direct involvement cannot be ascertained. In the industrial and commercial sector women were most likely to be involved with textiles: processing wool, cotton and silk, weaving, cloth making and tailoring. In Venice women were active even at the full guild level, where they were noted among fustian weavers, comb-makers, cappers, tailors and doublet-makers.[7] In Florence after the Black Death there seemed to be a decline in the female labour force; but the work of Judith Brown and Jordan Goodman suggests that from the sixteenth century women had a larger proportionate involvement in both woollen and silk textiles again. By the mid seventeenth century women constituted between a third and half the labour force in Florence. In 1604 62 per cent Florentine weavers were women, and about 40 per cent of all textile workers; in 1662–3 39 per cent wool workers, and 84 per cent silk workers. And a large number of female silk weavers and throwsters were 'masters', i.e. fully qualified and legally recognised producers. One explanation of this rise is that males were moving into more skilled luxury crafts – ceramics, furniture, jewellery, coach-building – leaving women with lower-paid and nastier jobs. The lower skill, and lower pay, aspects of female employment are highlighted by the evidence that, among the Florentine weavers in the 1610–20 period it was women who mainly wove taffeta, producing 10 *braccia* a week for 70 *soldi*; while men mainly wove the more luxurious satin velvet, producing 4 *braccia* a week for 210 to 280 *soldi*.

That 'unsupported' women sought to finance themselves through skills in tailoring, stocking-making or as seamstresses is indicated by Turin records on the poor in the eighteenth-century, when single women or women with children attached applied for poor relief, having fallen ill and being no longer able to work fully at these activities. If such women and children were taken into the Turin 'hospitals' as part of the relief, they might continue to work as seamstresses and tailors from within the institution.[8] One suspects that female skills in lace-making became, under the dictates of fashion, an increasing part of the family economy from the seventeenth century; produced from home and requiring limited space, resources and equipment.

Women could enter presumed male preserves. Fifteenth-century Florentine women were in middle rank guilds, sometimes as masters, goldsmiths, painters, carpenters, butchers and cobblers; they were vintners, oil merchants, cheese dealers, and at least one was recorded as a blacksmith. Five women doctors and five apothecaries between 1345 and 1444 were registered by the guild of doctors and apothecaries.[9] In sixteenth-century Venice women are recorded as barbers and tooth-drawers; bakers, ironmongers, wallers and chimney-sweeps; glass and mirror makers, boat-makers, carpenters and coopers. In a 1569 list of eighty-five apothecaries (who dealt with not only medicines, but spices more generally, confectionery and wax), five were women; none of them was described as 'poor', while forty male apothecaries were in that category. In the Arsenal area women appear as sail-makers, blacksmiths, boatmen and sailors. The degree of up-front, public, physical involvement of the women in such 'male' enterprises – as opposed to behind-the-scenes management in place of deceased or absent husbands – is unclear. Partial censuses for Venice in the seventeenth century (from 1633, 1642 and 1670) record the occupations of more than 900 women, giving them 112 different occupational describers across the categories of craft women (mainly textiles), retailing and other services. Parish recorders were under-recording, since in some parishes no woman was allocated an occupation. In contrast, scribes in the Santa Croce district gave occupations not just to heads of household, but also wives and daughters.[10]

In retailing, women legally could not buy or sell without a husband or guardian's permission. But in practice women seemingly had a significant involvement in retailing, whether alongside men or alone; but no doubt usually with many handicaps. Bologna records in the late sixteenth and early seventeenth century showed that women were retailing on their own, but that male stall-holders were intent on keeping them out of the central city market areas, and confining them to the suburbs and rural areas. They used the police and magistrates to enforce this anti-competitive segregation.[11]

Female involvement in family businesses could be opposed by male guildmasters, who felt this could defraud the guilds of full dues. The 1446 rulebook of the Venetian mercers declared:

> Because in the Merceria, and at San Polo, and in many other parts of the city, there are men who employ their mothers or wives in their shops, and they themselves are there too, but do not pay dues to the Scuola, and because of this many men out of their malice and meanness enrol [only] the said women and the women are held responsible for everything, be it understood that from now on no one may under any cover or fraud refuse to join the Scuola. . . . Moreover . . . if the said women wish to join the Scuola for their devotions, we shall be obliged to accept and enrol them like the other women mercers who are established in the various districts of the city and who go to market at San Marco and San Polo and to the fairs.[12]

Female involvement was allowed, but with full responsibilities and obligations.

Women could find niches in the world of production and retailing, probably increasingly so away from home from the seventeenth century, if less well-paid and profitably than for men. The male–female balance in the servant world had more complex competitive fluctuations, as will be suggested below.

The professionals and officials

Italian cities, and some *contado* areas, had a whole range of professionals and male officials, of different reputations and prestige. Over the period there was an increase in professionalism and bureaucratisation: in formal organisation, training, the establishment of status and in social and organisational demarcations. Members at the top end of the legal, medical and educational professions could be part of the social–political elite, as could the secretaries, chancellors and humanist scholars who served princely courts, and staffed the major administrative and fiscal government agencies. Social prestige could produce intellectual ossification, especially in lesser universities, where professorial appointments might be confined to members of the local elite, ignoring talented outsiders. But the detrimental effects of this tendency, as of increased government regulation which some have seen as social control, have been exaggerated.[13] At the lower end of the professions many had a social prestige reputation little different from lowly artisans.

The major secular professions were those of law and medicine, whose prestige remained high throughout the period, and with those at the top end socially being seen increasingly as 'noble'. Brescia developed three Colleges of Judges, Notaries and Physicians from the sixteenth century that were involved in professional accreditation, in pathways to conciliar government and control of administration, and to social mobility and recognition of nobility. This was part of a fashionable tendency to stress a collegial structure and status for elite professionals. The universities produced many lawyers; an elite group went on to serve as leading advocates and judges, and gained elite status through Colleges, while others increasingly staffed bureaucracies at different financial and social levels. Medical graduates similarly scattered through social levels. Florence's Medical College had been founded in 1560 to differentiate a select group, primarily physicians, above the broader guild of physicians and apothecaries, who were not necessarily graduates.[14]

The medical profession, and medical practice, involved a range of people: the collegiate physicians and surgeons, guild barbers and apothecaries, midwives, specialists in making trusses and other supports for those suffering from hernias, *ciarlatani* peddling remedies both helpful and dubious, and 'cunning women' with herbal treatments and abortifacients. Through to the fifteenth century women have occasionally been traced as guild-recognised doctors and apothecaries, (as in Naples and Florence). Others practised by special licence, as in Rome and Venice. *Protomedici* and their deputies increasingly supervised the profession, probably to the detriment of women as doctors. Medical practice was improved by better biological and chemical knowledge, which printing publicised. Anatomy from the early sixteenth century was more openly and publicly practised (with church blessing). However conservative the official curriculum of the universities, in practice much new science was taught, and experiments made. The collegiate pursuit of status, and demarcation disputes over who should do what, could undermine good practice, and the learning process. The medical professions were sometimes too tied up with the magical sciences, and too supportive of magical and miracle cures. Medics and clergy supported the use of elixirs like the *Flos Coeli* (seemingly derived from alchemical secrets), while the charlatans employed elixirs sold in the *piazze*. Doctors and midwives might back some of the faith healers and 'living saints', and recommend their patients to resort to the curative powers of relics, while admitting they themselves did not have all the answers. Despite demarcation disputes, the different areas of medical practice shared common mentalities, and high and low culture comingled with both beneficial and adverse results.[15]

By the early seventeenth century there were fourteen medical Colleges, dominated by the physicians who saw themselves as professionally, culturally and socially superior to surgeons. They developed the networks of *protomedici*, and interlocked with them. The medical colleges varied in their exclusivity and inclusivity; and in the degree of control over other practitioners. Since Milan's limited itself to local patricians, many other physicians practiced outside this corporate body. Bologna normally only accepted citizens, and tended to encourage a family succession of physicians; but was ready to accept a prestigious outsider, such in 1691 with Marcello Malpighi, an outstanding anatomist and microscope user. Salerno was the most open, socially and geographically. These Colleges set up one kind of social demarcation. Below them surgeons battled to achieve a separate, higher status than mere barbers. They disputed with apothecaries, whose guilds in turn had disputes with grocers, since they dealt in similar goods at times. The fuzziness of status and practice kept the *protomedici* busy. University physicians might teach and practice surgery without social stigma, while elsewhere a physician found it demeaning to conduct a surgical operation. Surgeons could aspire to be physicians or be forced to administer physical remedies without consultation with a physician. In many communities a barber-surgeon played all roles as the only qualified medic available. Apothecaries, supposedly servants to physicians, might know far more about drugs, and again be the only person available to help a patient. Whatever the Colleges said, some apothecaries could achieve considerable social prestige in their community, as Malpighi's friend Lorenzo de Tomasi did in Messina, and then Rome; he was noted as also a physician and mathematician. Most apothecaries, however crucial to the life of small communities, were encouraged to keep a humble place, showing off neither in Latin nor in flamboyant carriages.

Midwifery in early modern Italy remained a female speciality that gave certain mature women a dominant role and influence in local society. It was largely an occupation for widows, experienced in childbirth themselves, who developed a reputation locally, and were possibly possessed of a specialist birthing-chair. They were there to help mother younger women giving birth; the common Italian words for the midwife, *comare*, *mammana*, derive from *madre*, mother. The baptismal records for the Roman parish of S.Giovanni dei Fiorentini 1586–90 show a Florentine widow (*donna* Catherina *obstetrix Florentina*) as regularly called upon for births; she enters the record because she also acted as godmother.[16] Post-tridentine church reform stressed the role of the midwife as responsible for baptism (by her) if the baby's life was in danger; and for having the child's birth and baptism recorded in the newly required parish records. She was also expected to report the parentage of illegitimate babies. Besides assisting with births, the midwife dealt with problems of conceiving and rearing, a range of female maladies, advised about sterility and became an expert witness in cases of infanticide or rape.[17] In the late medieval period a few women seemed well qualified in surgery. On the other side of law and morality, a midwife might be expected to use herbalist and chemical expertise to provide abortifacients, and contraceptive techniques. Slowly through our period registration was developed, more formal control instituted, and a kind of professionalism established, at least in the cities. Eighteenth-century registers indicate that midwives passed on their expertise to relatives who started as recognised apprentices. By then midwives in key areas like Venice were well trained, educated in new surgical knowledge, organised and licensed – by men of course. Grevembroch reported that Venice had about 100 recognised midwives (and some others). In Italy it was not until the late eighteenth or nineteenth century that gynaecological control and domination passed to university-trained male doctors.

Notaries and scribes were professionals at the heart of Italian culture, seldom granted the prestige they often deserved. Notaries and lesser scribes have been seriously understudied, though their voluminous records are the key to much historical investigation.[18] Notarial clerks were required for most serious contracts, and the preservation of their records crucial for resolving disputes. Skills were required in drawing up different kinds of documents in true form, that could withstand legal contestation. For the illiterate they have been seen as 'the priests of practical literacy, the professionals who had the reins of power over memory', and so wrote up 'memoirs' for a peasant.[19] Their roles ideally required trust and discretion for all parties involved in civil matters; but they also had to be aware of government and church wishes – as over testamentary dispositions in favour of hospitals or church establishments, or the need to ensure that transactions avoided usurious interest rates. Some notaries travelled considerably, and sometimes dangerously, to accompany judges and administrative officials, civilian and clerical. They took depositions, made enquiries for courts, wrote and rewrote testimonies, and in practice they probably ran many courts, as in much of the Veneto. They had to be multilingual, even in a city like Venice, which from the fifteenth century used Latin much less in the operations of government, administration and the law, for they might have to interpret a number of vernacular languages or dialects.[20] Since neither the notary nor the judge or presiding official might be from the same area, much interpreting must have gone on through to the surviving preserved written record. The implications for understanding the surviving evidence, and the power and social roles of the notaries, have not yet been fully faced by historians.

The training, organisation and status of the notary varied considerably geographically, and maybe through the period. In some areas a recognised notary was clearly distinguished, but in others little distinction between a licensed notary and a clerk or chaplain (as on Venetian ships)[21] able to notarise documents. Some notaries were part of the government elite, and from patrician families, others socially much inferior. Other scribes learned some notarial skills and earned some prestige. By the fifteenth century Perugian notaries had a powerful corporate identity in a consortium, putting them outside and above the normal (and powerful) city's guild structure, subject to the College of Judges. They could serve as judges in certain cases. They had prestige and privileges, some were rich and boastful of it. Giovanna Benadusi argued for a town like Poppi that through the early modern period the status of the notary declined; but here in the fifteenth and sixteenth centuries the leading families of the town were providing most notaries, which was not the case in, say, Perugia. Some notaries clearly wanted to be counted as gentlemen, while other professionals resented such pretensions. When Giovanni Borelli advised his fellow physician Malpighi how to behave when going to Messina as a professor, he told him to maintain a carriage to show his status: 'no physician would be without one'. He added that many notaries and apothecaries had them, so they could not be that expensive to keep.[22]

Notaries might move in and out of bureaucratic positions within cities, and even head the administration as chancellor. The Lapucci or Baldacci families of Poppi shifted from strict notarial careers into the wider Tuscan administration, earned added prestige and influence, and then withdrew from the notarial profession. In Venice the Ducal Chancellery's main officials often had a notarial background, and some were classified as *cittadini originari*, the second elite. In Rome the senior members of the papal notarial-chancellery structure, the participating protonotaries, could be very powerful and prestigious men, who ranked in ceremonial ahead of mere bishops; their elevation to this title may have come after an influential career through the papal clerical system. In Rome's civilian structure the top group of notaries forming the Thirty Capitoline Notaries had, at least in the seventeenth century, prestige, wide powers and influence. But many Milanese notaries came from artisan and lesser merchant families, who thought it helpful to have one son legally trained primarily for business purposes, and to provide an additional network of social contacts. Cities like Vicenza and Verona had colleges of notaries who were ranked alongside physicians and lawyers, above the guilds of artisans, which might put them on the path to nobility.[23]

Notaries and businessmen often worked closely together, as Marina Gazzini's study (1997) of the account books of Donato Ferrario da Pantigliate in early fifteenth-century Milan illuminates. Donato was at the centre of neighbourhood groups in the Porta Nuova area in particular, and later in Porta Romana, who were involved in a variety of investment enterprises within the city, in the *contado*, and in connecting city and countryside. At times a local hostelry, with its investing owner, was a focal point. But more significantly, merchants, notaries and officials were brought together by a charitable confraternity – the Scuola Della Divinita – which Donato helped launch in 1429. Donato's wife Antonia Menclozzi was an active business partner, bringing through the marriage a useful network of contacts in Milan for the relatively new man, Donato. Yet business could go on among retailers, artisans and small businessmen without notarial intervention, as a study of 17 local merchants in Prato in Donato's period has shown. They relied on their own ledgers, and a degree of trust (*fiducia*).[24]

Many offices required business expertise, so somebody like Donato Ferrario had official posts connecting with supervising money coiners and other metal workers (which may have got him established in the city), and later provisioning Milan – based on his experience in both transport and animal husbandry. Presumably serving as an official likewise benefited subsequent personal business. Many other 'officials' would have had legal training in civil and/or canon law at university, or were notaries. They served dynastic political courts, courts of law and policing systems, the guilds, bureaucratic offices dealing with food supplies, taxation, health regulations and so forth. Given the way Italian governments worked, with frequently changing councils, advisory bodies and short-term contracts as legal or financial officials to avoid corruption and favouritism, an 'official' might have many different jobs through a career, and be peripatetic. Historians have stressed the development of prestigious bureaucracies, with an increased professionalism and education derived from university legal and notarial studies, as notably in Tuscany from Cosimo I.[25]

Venice can usefully exemplify the world of officialdom. Through our period the Republic developed a complex system through the two main levels of elites, of patricians and *cittadini* (*originarii* or *de privilegio*). In 1440 there were 347 patrician offices for the city, 16 for the mainland supervision and 71 for overseas (*stato da mar*); for 1540 these figures were 551, 78 and 117. The city offices so counted ranged from the Doge, lawyers (*avvocati*) for various bodies, councillors for various councils, senators, the six heads (*capi*) of the *sestieri* districts, the three patrons of the Arsenal to officials (*savi* or *provveditori*) dealing with controls over wine, grains, salt and various taxes, and the six *signori di notte* who policed the city at night, and investigated criminal and moral activities. An individual official from such elites might move between the city, the mainland and colonial posts. As a sample we can take two Venetian officials, respectively from upper and middling patrician families. Leonardo di Zuane Emo (1475–15??) joined the council of Forty soon after he was twenty, was captain of a galley in 1510, had two years on the Senate, then various strategic posts for war activities 1512–14 in Bresciano, Padua and Friuli. From 1515 he had many city posts. Notably he served as a ducal councillor (1515, 1522, 1528, 1531), was a member of the council of Ten (1518, 1519, 1521) and then headed it as *Capo* 1524–31, while also being a *savio* of the council 1527–36. He had various military posts again in 1520–22. Secondly we have Vincenzo di Pietro Zen (from the Santa Sofia branch of the clan, *c.* 1467–1521); though on the Maggior Consiglio from 1487 he does not feature in known office lists until 1500 when he was elected as a minor judge. He joined the Forty, served as *podesta* (judge and administrator) in distant Caravaggio, returned to Venice to be a *signore di notte*, went off to be castellan of Faenza, was again a *signore di notte*, then was away once more as *podesta* at Antivari in Dalmatia. After over three years there he appealed to the Senate to be replaced, but had to wait another year as his scheduled replacement was detained in France. On return he was almost immediately dispatched to lead, at his expense, a troop to help defend Padua (1513); there was then a gap in his office-holding career, until he became a *provveditore* controlling firewood supplies, in which post he died.[26]

Most officials remain mere names, their real lives and duties often obscure. However we have recently been granted unusual insight into one man's career in the fifteenth century, that of Beltramino Casadri of Crema, who served as magistrate for the Gonzagas of Mantua and the D'Este of Ferrara. Particularly through his own letters to his political masters we learn what it was like to be a travelling magistrate in various posts trying to control crime, enforce justice against violent bandits and equally violent local lords, and cope with political and social pressures on all sides.[27]

From seventeenth-century Rome the life and personality of an urban lay official can be understood through the diary and other writings of Giacinto Gigli (1594–1671), and some other surviving documentation about him. From a well-established

Roman merchant family, he was a law graduate (after a Jesuit education), who considered himself noble. A fervent supporter of the papal Barberini family, he was proud to serve the city and its government based on the Capitol, especially as its district officer (*caporione* di Campitelli). He was involved in commercial affairs, taxation and processional ceremonials; ever anxious that the civic life of the city be properly conducted, and honour also paid to the papacy as appropriate. An active official life was conducted alongside his literary interests, and he engaged in some acute observation of Roman secular and religious life.[28]

As the 'modern state' evolved through the early modern period, whether with supposedly 'absolute' territorial Princes or with the few remaining enlarged oligarchic Republics, there was an increasing professionalism of senior bureaucratic officials, notably in the secretariat around the central government. Francesco Sansovino in his much-published *Del Secretario* (from 1564) propagated the view of some theologians that a secretary in his closeness to the prince was comparable with angels, close to God. The prestige of high-level secretaries, like that of chancellors or similar figures close to the ruler, was enhanced in the fifteenth century by their roles as writers and speakers of elegant Latin, producing formal documents and scholarly letters and conducting important discussions with other states and their orators. They could be useful humanist propagandists, and be chosen for their literary skills. Through the sixteenth century and beyond, other types of secretaries emerged, as in the Medicean Dukedom of Tuscany, more noted for their political skills and administrative abilities; firstly substituting for the prince in foreign relations, then taking on subsections of the burgeoning domestic administration. The Medici Grand Dukes had a cadre of twelve such secretaries in 1588, rising to twenty-one in 1609, though the numbers were reduced again by the mid seventeenth century. In place of frequently changing councils and officials of the old communal systems there were long-serving officials, like Bartolomeo and Giovanni Battista Concini or L. Usimbardi, who developed considerable expertise. These officials in Tuscany were largely drawn from those with legal training, while their Savoyard equivalents were more often chosen for their close loyalty to the ruler, and as part of a clientele system. Such men, with a degree of professionalism, become part of a secondary urban elite.[29]

Over the early modern period the professional, legal and bureaucratic sectors of urban society had thus become more prominent administratively and socially, as government became more complex, as amateurish local councils and petty tyrants and their entourages declined or disappeared. There was much scope for social competition, status rivalries, in a more genteel mode. But it must be stressed that families could provide representatives in different categories outlined above, and individuals alternate between 'professional' and 'official' roles, and move between major urban centres, and *contado* areas.

Servants

Many in urban society, male and female, were servants – whether in their main career, or more briefly in youth. Service was a very common occupation for both sexes, embracing domestic service, but also people (usually young), who worked in *botteghe* or on farms without being formally apprenticed, or being a paid labourer. The account book of the Venetian painter Lorenzo Lotto (unmarried) records a confusing variety of apprentices and servants, male and female, serving him in different ways as he travelled about.[30] Under the category of 'Servant' we can include upper-status children and youths of both sexes learning and serving in other aristocratic houses, older ladies-in-waiting and companions to the rich, lackeys and footmen, gondoliers in Venice, housekeepers for priests (who might be an elderly relative or mistress), down to skivvies and near-slaves 'below stairs' or in the attics. Figures are difficult to interpret, because some records only registered in-house servants, and sometimes only those serving nobles and leading citizens, as Dennis Romano found in studying various Venetian figures. Some patricians had many servants, but plenty of artisans had a servant, as did prostitutes we know about in Bologna, Rome or Venice. In Siena in 1560 about half the households headed by bakers and masons had at least one servant. In Parma in 1545 out of 1900 households, 293 had one servant, 160 had two or three, while 75 had four or more.[31]

For a significant number of urban Italians being a servant at some point was part of the life cycle, especially in their late teens and early 20s. In Verona in 1545 30 per cent of those aged 16–20, and 19 per cent of those aged 21–25 were servants; in Parma in the same year the figures were 34 per cent and 25 per cent. For females in particular domestic service was a way of earning a dowry, and then they left to marry, while males might move to artisan jobs. However various figures for Parma, Siena and Verona imply 10–20 per cent of all later age groups to the 50s were servants. The balance between male and female servants was on the male side, but not overwhelmingly so. It was probably the largest job category for girls and women. In Venice there were significantly more female than male servants: 8234 female and 4574 male in 1563, with 6554 to 3681 in 1642. But the patricians and *cittadini* tended to keep male servants for status as well as utilitarian reasons; females were more commonly servants in artisan families.[32]

There is an argument that the servant population shifted towards the male to the detriment of female job opportunities under the moralising impact of catholic reform. Living-in servants were sexually vulnerable, whether from the master and his sons, or other servants. While in the fourteenth and fifteenth centuries some of the resulting bastards might be absorbed into the household, this was to be less so in later stricter moral climates. Employing male servants might be less embarrassing than having to dismiss female servants, and send their offspring to the foundling hospitals. The arguments are complicated by the fact that in Florence Christiane Klapisch-Zuber has detected an earlier shift, through the fifteenth century, from young girls to older women, presumed widows; and other evidence indicates that the proportion of female servants in Florence *increased* through the sixteenth century. Rome tended to have a high proportion of male servants in the sixteenth to eighteenth centuries – as moralists would hope given the large servant-employing households headed supposedly by celibates – and female servants appear attached to female-led lesser households. Yet Hanns Gross's figures – admittedly for a very select group of parishes – show a significant rise in the percentage of female servants as the eighteenth century progressed.[33]

While doubtless conditions for the average servant could be grim, the job ill-paid, and the chances of sexual exploitation high, more positively the young girl could end up with a respectable dowry, saved from her payment (and supplemented by a gift from a satisfied employer), and a desirable marriage, and the longer-serving and older women might be remembered in the employer's will. Male servants in Venice also received such recognition. Government regulations tried to produce harmony, especially within patrician *palazzi*, and showed worry about disobedience, disloyalty and violence from servants; courts records indicate offences on both sides.

According to Klapisch-Zuber the most respected and rewarded servant (leaving aside the upper-crust lady-in-waiting) was likely to have been the nurse; the wetnurse who breast-fed the household babies, and stayed to cosset them into adolescence, and beyond. The wetnurse (*balia*) was a person who could be praised and rewarded, or reviled and persecuted. In the absence of any reliable substitute for breast-milk for infants, wetnurses were needed for babies in respectable conditions, when the mother died or was too ill to feed her own child, when the mother needed to continue her own work but did not wish to abandon the baby (if paying another was cheaper than sacrificing her income), when the wife had a social profile and role militating against her own active nursing and – probably most commonly in respectable families – when the husband did not want a long gap before he resumed sexual relations with his wife. Learned authority ruled that sexual intercourse while the mother still breast-fed was detrimental to all concerned. Wetnurses were also needed when babies were abandoned and taken up by nunneries, confraternities and hospitals.[34]

The opportunity to earn money as a wetnurse was largely, but not exclusively, the result of death. But it became increasingly organised, even professionalised, through the early modern period. Though it is medically possible for a woman to produce breast-milk without having been pregnant and giving birth, presumably very few if any in the period mastered the technique. Wetnurses were women who had produced their own child; that child might have died (from natural causes, deliberate neglect or infanticide[35]), leaving the mother with milk still to offer, but this was not (as used to be argued) always the case. The mother might wean her own child early, and take on another baby for pay before she dried up. She might breast-feed another child (or two) alongside her own; this was not liked by respectable families, or by some institutions, because of cross infection. Some poor bastard-bearing mothers (such as dismissed servants) were taken into foundling hospitals to have and rear their own child and feed others there as well. A mother might pass on her own child to another (within the family, or to a cheap wetnurse, particularly in a village), and then take her milk to offer for greater money to a respectable city family, or better-paying hospital.

Wetnurses operated in other people's homes at the top social level; otherwise in their own homes in cities as well as in the countryside, or within hospitals. The limited evidence suggests that Italians were more inclined to organise wetnursing within the household than, say, their French equivalents. If Italians wanted wet-nursing outside the family they tended to send babies to nurses in villages, where air was supposedly better and women more robust. Foundling hospitals used in-house wetnurses and outsiders in city or *contado*. Evidence from foundling institutions in cities like Rome, Perugia, Bologna and Milan reveals that some families took on a succession of foundlings for wetnursing (with the husband as the contractual organiser). Wetnursing could clearly be significant for the domestic economy of some families, and also for certain large villages or small *città*; Gorgonzola in the early modern period was more notable for wetnursing the babies from the great Ca Granda hospital of Milan than for its cheese. The wetnurses who came to serve in the larger households might end up as lifetime servants there, and confidantes of children and mothers.

In contrast there were nastier male servant companions, the *bravi* – defined in 1609 by the Venetian government as those 'who seek to earn their living by arms'.[36] As such they were a criminal element, escorting more elite figures, or coming into the city to carry out threatening activities and intimidation. Many were already outside the law as *banditi*, but others had been (or would return to being) more legitimate unarmed servants. Bodies of *bravi* were a major problem in rural areas, intimidating peasants on behalf of landowners. But they have shown to be a major nuisance in Venice, and the subject of much legislation and intermittent legal action. Clearly being a *bravo* for a patrician was a significant way of earning a living, having an exciting urban life for a short while at least. *Bravi* operated protection rackets for their masters and themselves, settled vendettas, were frequenters of gambling dens and brothels and facilitated the sexual escapades (often violent) of their employers. Garzoni's *Piazza Universale* portrayed them as brutal animals, whose gifts to a prostitute were 'bites on the breasts, and making her howl like a desperate bitch'.[37] Venetian legislation treated them all as dregs of society, unskilled and a menace. In practice they did have fighting skills with various weapons and may well have enjoyed a moderate social status at some point. While some violated prostitutes, others defended them. In 1609 rival courtesans Alba Albanesi and Cornelia Savioni both employed factions of *bravi* to protect themselves and their trade. Venetian legislation may to some extent have stereotyped and demonised them, but some *bravi* were undoubtedly involved in serious violent crimes, alongside violent renegade patricians like Michiel and Antonio de Silvestro Memmo, Alvise and Zuanne de Gabriel Zorzi and Lunardo Pesaro, who were accused of murder, rape, sodomy, extortion and so forth. In practice distinctions were not clear between unarmed and armed servants, soldiers, *sbirri* and outlaws, when healthy males unable or unwilling to have a peaceful way of earning money sought employment.

Service could thus be a respectable long-term career for both sexes, an apprenticeship, a pre-marital path to a respectable dowry and marriage, but also a dangerous transient expedient, that alternated with other casual labour and employment.

Casual work: labourers, pedlars, *sbirri*, messengers

Below the level of the organised artisans socially and often, though not invariably, economically were many occupations besides service for more casual and precarious employment allowing males, and fewer females, to survive. Some were legal and respectable, others verged on the criminal. Chapter 5 has already discussed the itinerant sellers, organised in guilds or not, who were a major part of the marketing systems; here some men and women could move in and out of a commercial activity as they faced difficulties, while for others such trading was their life career. Some occupations provided a precarious living for the unskilled or offered salvation for the more skilled who had fallen on hard times through general economic crises, through personal family and business misfortunes or through falling foul of legal proceedings, whether guilty or innocent.

Estimating the extent of a manual labour force outside the guild–artisan structure is very difficult, even for a well-documented and bureaucratic city like Venice, as R. T. Rapp admitted.[38] Guilds varied in what unskilled workers they incorporated, and who they left as an individual to seek work by the day, without protection or control. In Venice the ratio between those in guilds and those outside the structure was about 3:1, but with variations from 1:1 for the Arsenal, and 1:4 for the wool sector (in the 1590s). Rapp admits defeat in estimating the unincorporated and casual silk workers. The less controlled and protected labour force included porters, messengers, building-site workers, street-cleaners, lamp-carriers, gardeners and street vendors. Rome in the eighteenth century had about 260 kinds of street vendors (male and female), some in guilds others not, though all supposed to have licences and the quality of their wares checked.[39] Rome had considerable areas of vineyards, market gardens, and meadows within the walls, to provide casual labour for urban residents and *contadini* entering daily. Venice's Giudecca and other parts probably provided the same opportunities on a smaller scale. Building operations involved unskilled manual workers. In fifteenth-century Florence and Rome large numbers were hired and paid in cash as individuals on a daily basis. By the seventeenth century it seems that in Rome most building labourers were employed through the guild system, as in Venice or Milan.

The *sbirri* referred to were the messengers and police or prison officials who served the various legal and administrative bodies in all Italian cities and towns. Garzoni was as vituperative against their violence and corruption as against the *bravi*. His views were shared by later writers, such as Giovanni Rainaldo in the seventeenth century who judged the papal *sbirri* to be: 'ignorant, vile, haughty, voracious, miserly, insolent, lying, greedy, and fraudulent'.[40] In practice diverse lesser officials, messengers and servants were employed in running the urban community and linking with the hinterland. In Florence many were literate and reasonably honest serving the main policing system and magistracy, the Otto di Guardia, as they may have served commercial institutions and guilds. Others all too readily alternated between being messengers, prison guards, soldiers and prisoners themselves. Serving judicial and administrative officials, delivering warrants, collecting fines and debts, seeking to arrest accused, protecting the magistrates and so on were dangerous, life-threatening activities – more particularly if sent out of the city to the *contado*, as we know from accounts concerning Mantuan and Ferrarese magistrates and their officials in the fifteenth century,[41] or of forces of *sbirri* sent out from

Bergamo, Brescia, Padua or Verona to do battle with Venetian *bravi* and *banditi* in the sixteenth and seventeenth centuries. Given low pay, the temptations to do corrupt deals, free prisoners or avoid implementation of sentences were considerable. A Roman *sbirro* in 1629 was judged too poor to pay personal tax. Establishing how many people were involved in this type of activity seems impossible, given the considerable number of institutions and officials that needed *sbirri* of some kind, and that the more formal appointments were often on two- to six-month rotas, that there might be unofficial equivalents under a generic title of *sbirri*, as well as those officially called that. Scattered documentary scraps give momentary insights. In Florence the Otto di Guardia alone had a cross-bow guard of 200 for civic control; in the eighteenth century the captain of the Bargello commanded a force of 60. Andrea Zorzi reckoned that by the fifteenth century the Florentine police forces constituted 1 to 150 inhabitants or even 1 to 125.

In 1790 Rome had 163 official *sbirri* under 8 captains (*bargelli*), serving the various courts and tribunals, but notably the main Governor's court for both criminal civilians cases. Some of these would operate outside the city as mounted police; but in the province of Umbria and Duchy of Spoleto within the Papal State 31 communities had 96 *sbirri* and *bargelli* paid for by the central Roman government, and another 81 by the local communities. By this period the *sbirri* of the Papal State had an evil reputation for brutality and corruption; they were seen as being recruited from the dregs of society, as ready to extort money, rape women and to use violence indiscriminately against clergy and nobility (at least until the latter bought them off). Earlier, in the fifteenth and early sixteenth centuries, the motley forces in Rome of *marescalchi*, *bandaresi*, *turrieri* and *balestieri* etc., had been much more socially acceptable, and less worrying than this. The growth of the papal absolute state had produced a more feared force, but with no improvement in justice and law enforcement.[42]

Casual labour was available whatever the extent or otherwise of guild controls and incorporations. While some servants, female and male, were long-term careerists, others would have come from the pool of casuals available. Hawking and peddling of goods might be regulated within Venetian or Bolognese guilds, but was probably open and uncontrolled elsewhere; and in Venice incomers could start outside the *arti*, especially the *merzeria*, but be embraced by the system, and given more security. Women (and girls from about 7 years old, as in seventeenth-century Rome)[43] could pick up unskilled or limited skilled jobs in textiles industries or could earn money from lace-making at home. In crises – personal or general economic – girls and women resorted to prostitution as a temporary solution, until able to return to textile work or domestic service. Some women (and a few men) must have supplemented incomes by magical practices, though the Inquisition records do not help us much on the returns for such risky services.

The marginalised poor, if able-bodied, had casual employment opportunities – at least in sound economic times. In mortality crises some unemployed casuals could shift to grave-digging, which through both pay and theft might be lucrative should they survive the disease, and the professional grave-diggers' antipathy.[44] It is probable that artisans would at times also drift in and out of policing forces of various kinds, especially as they were expected in some cities like Rome to act in a civic militia as required. Poor, underemployed artisans from Venice voluntarily or under government pressure were employed in the state galleys.[45]

Prostitutes

Female prostitution was a major aspect of the urban economy and social life of the larger Italian cities, as was recognised at the time. Italian authorities, lay and clerical, had conflicting and changing attitudes and policies towards female prostitution.[46] In a panic over plague (as in Perugia in 1487 and 1493), food or political crises, with worries about law and order (as in the 1559 crisis in Rome on the death of Paul IV), the authorities might temporarily expel prostitutes along with vagabonds and alien beggars. They did not resort to the draconian measures of some Protestant northerners who closed down brothels and tried heavy punishments for all extra-marital sex. Catholic reformers did encourage prostitutes to reform, and sought to seclude them from further temptation in conservatories, but they recognised that vulnerable women might have to resort to the income of prostitution to survive, and needed philanthropic aid of shelter, food, clothing and even marriage dowries in substitution. Prostitution was generally tolerated and subject to limited control to avoid excessive public scandal. In the eyes of moralists sodomy and male prostitution were far greater sins and evils, and female prostitution was a less undesirable substitute for sexually frustrated, late-marrying males – as particularly in Florence. And the toleration of licensed prostitutes would save other innocent girls and women.

In some cities prostitutes were officially confined to set red-light areas and buildings: the Mercato Vecchio (old market) area of Florence; near the Rialto in Venice. In fifteenth-century Perugia prostitutes were allocated a zone between the two main squares and thoroughfares – called the *Malacucina*.[47] Laws were sometimes imposed to make prostitutes wear red or yellow badges, and to control their ostentatious dress. Florence between 1403 and 1680 had a major magistracy, the *Onestà*, designed to both control and protect prostitutes. Prostitutes and clients alike resented and evaded control in an atmosphere of inefficiency and corruption, not least because from the 1540s licenced users of the bordello were taxed to help pay for institutions for the 'reformed' prostitutes. When from 1633 harsher regulations essentially criminalised prostitutes, more sought to go underground – or operate as 'exempt' courtesans.

This leads to various points about the numbers of prostitutes, and classification. Extravagant, polemical, allegations were made at times that key cities, especially Rome, had thousands – or even 10,000 – prostitutes as part of their moral corruption. A census return for Rome in 1621 is more realistic in giving 718 prostitutes. That figure, and similar ones, derive from what parish priests reported to the Roman Vicariate or Vatican officials based on their *status animarum* returns. Priests were supposed to record those women who were active, unrepentant prostitutes who might be spiritually unfit to receive Easter communion. Studies of the actual registers suggest that the recording of such women was rather haphazard; that the end total did not always tally with the notifications of *meretrice* against names in the house-by-house register. Clearly some clergy were reluctant to count and classify prostitutes; the curates of Milan in 1610 merely counted eight, hardly an accurate tally of the activities in ill-reputed areas such as the piazza S.Marcellino, and around the Castello.[48] Probably these were the professionals, the full-time common prostitutes surviving – sometimes doing well – on this activity. Additionally there were more girls and women who entered prostitution intermittently according to personal and general economic circumstances; and there were 'higher class' courtesans who were likely to be treated differently as part of elite, cultured society. In a Florence census in 1569 the Onestà had 159 prostitutes registered in the red-light brothel areas; 77 other women, 'richer' and more highly taxed, were allowed to operate as non-registered practitioners – consorting with elite and in court circles. Bologna in 1598 registered 584 prostitutes for fining/taxing purposes, of whom at least 71 can be identified as non-Bolognese by birth or parentage. Given the dire economic conditions of this decade one would expect a high level of prostitution.[49]

An elite prostitute was often called *cortegiana*, rather than the more declassè *meretrice* or *putana*; but there were contentious borders between the classifications. At the top of the scale, courtesans could be highly accomplished, educated and cultured women, prized as ornaments of elite patrician society and courts, and having a lavish lifestyle. They might dress flamboyantly boasting the finest jewellery, and be painted nude or semi-nude by the greatest painters like Titian and Palma il Vecchio. They presided over their own salons, or ran salons and academies for their chosen lovers, picking their competing clients and patrons at will; and they could settle for a prestigious husband at the end. Such elite social figures were most famous, or notorious, in Rome in the first half of the sixteenth century, in Florence under the Medici Dukes, and especially in Venice through the sixteenth to eighteenth centuries. Possibly the best known, making a lasting cultural contribution, were Tullia d'Aragona, a leading contributor to the poetic and musical circles of Rome in the 1520s and 1530s and then in Florence, and Veronica Franco in Venice, one of the finest sixteenth-century poets.[50]

Some courtesans clearly enjoyed a fine lifestyle, without being too close to the most powerful, as the surviving inventory of the possessions of the Venetian Julia Lombardo and her sister demonstrate.[51] Those who attached themselves to respectable patricians and merchants could do well; but there was always the danger of becoming involved with rougher patricians (from the same family, as Veronica Franco herself found), to become involved with the *bravi* – both as victims and employers.

Prostitution concerned more than selling the body and simple sex in return for money and survival. If cultural services were provided by the tiny elite at the social peak, more dubious skills were offered by others at all levels. Professional prostitutes were experts in love, expected to be knowledgeable about love potions and magic, spells and incantations to bind or loose lovers and rivals. Extrapolating from this expertise they knew how to cure illnesses or find lost property. The trial records of ecclesiastical inquisitions and secular courts indicate that there was a perceived and real link between prostitutes and superstitious practices – on their own behalf (seeking to keep a lover/patron/ financial supporter stalwart), or that of others. In Venice in 1588 the courtesan Paolina de Rossi mixed sage (a recognised aphrodisiac) with her menstrual blood in the food and wine of a victim, to regain his affections.[52] Andriana Savorgnan, a higher-class Venetian courtesan, was accused (among other charges) of using superstitious practices to bind the nobleman Nicolo Corner to her. She had used olive branches issued to her in church, bound them together and dipped them in holy water; then said: 'As I bind this wood with this string, so too may be bound the phallus of Nicolo Corner so that he may not be able to go to any woman but me.' Then, having planted the wood in the ground: 'As this wood will not grow again or branch out again, so too Nicolo Corner may not be able to have relations with other women than me.'[53] She was not a great success as a magician; Nicolo's wife had a child about a year later. However, Andriana survived inquisitorial enquiry and the dangers of prostitution to become a patrician's wife.

In Rome the courtesan Lucrezia the Greek was investigated by the Governor's court in 1559 for her uses of love magic (involving candles, lamps, prayers) to seek the favours and support of various men; '. . . the courtesan Lucrezia the Greek makes alliances and uses magic to conduct the risky politics of love'.[54] From this investigation, and from another trial in which she also appears, Lucrezia was well enough off to have two or three servants; she was an acceptable part of a co-operative neighbourhood community. But she was also vulnerable to unwelcome threats to house and body from undesired or dissatisfied clients, and to the scourge of syphilis – as allegedly from her illustrious 'friend' Cardinal Strozzi.

Prostitution was a significant part of the female economy, a salvation for betrayed and deserted young women, sometimes a pathway to marriage and stability. It saved families in dire temporary economic conditions. With services and skills beyond the mere selling of sex, it empowered a significant number of women. It involved women from many levels of society, though probably most ended among the destitute.

The poor and destitute

These categories of the social order were even more fluctuating than in modern society. The concepts of the 'poor' and '*miserabili*' were varied at the theoretical level, with commentators, charitable institutions and tax organisers anxious to make discriminating sub-divisions of these categories. Social welfare was affected by such subtle categorisations. Many individuals from sectors of society discussed above in this chapter might be deemed 'poor' and even be destitute at crucial moments in their lives, through economic misfortunes, deaths of relatives or major illnesses. A merchant might be in dire circumstances through the loss of a ship and his cargo, especially if he had a large family of females to support, or even one daughter to dower when he was sick, as Francesco Bonaventura claimed (successfully) in petitioning for a grant from the Venetian confraternity of S.Maria dei Mercanti in 1553.[55]

This section briefly looks at those more obviously poor for long periods.[56] Various historians agree that in western Europe, including Italy, there was a category of structural poor of about 4–8 per cent of the population needing help for long periods or all their lives. Up to about 20 per cent constituted the conjunctural poor, meaning those who could expect to be dangerously poor at one or more points in their lives, given normal extraneous economic conditions. But 60 per cent or more of the population could be rendered destitute in a prolonged crisis induced by food shortages and very high prices. S. D'Amico (1994, 1995), using Milanese parochial records for the period 1580–1610, reckons that about 17 per cent of the city population consistently were counted as poor, on a basis with which modern assessors could concur. The financial and health crisis of 1619–21, especially affecting the silk industry, rendered 40 per cent of the working population unemployed. In 1661 the Venetian government treated 33 per cent of inhabitants of the city as poor, on the criteria of their living in charitable institutions (such as alms-houses), or in rented habitations for less than 12 ducats a year, which meant damp first level housing, or wooden shacks.[57]

The structural poor sector might include the very young and old without able-bodied relatives capable or willing to support them; the maimed and long-term sick; single women without skills or in cities where there were limited opportunities for textile production outside small family units; males with limited skills or physical ability to secure more than an intermittent casual job; those 'criminalised', under threat of arrest or being killed who could not secure open employment. Such people survived by begging on the streets, at church doors or even inside churches (though attempts were made to curb that from the later sixteenth century), by stealing and by prostitution. Parochial, monastic and confraternity poor-relief systems developed especially from the mid sixteenth century.

We have limited knowledge of how and where such people lived. Some lived and died on the streets, as found by confraternities (such as the Della Morte companies in Rome or Perugia), who were concerned with giving decent burial to the poor. Health board officials, as from Florence or Genoa, worried about plague, typhus and dysentery epidemics, testified to grim conditions of people existing in damp or flooded basements, with putrid mattresses or sordid straw, with alleys as open sewers polluting the air and infiltrating basement rooms. In 1630 Florentine gentlemen appointed to survey the plague threatened city were horrified by the living conditions of the poor: 'in many houses there are no beds and people sleep on scattered straw and some have palliasses that are filthy and fetid.'[58] Such existence in Bologna in the 1590s received publicity from the published poetic Laments of Giulio Cesare Croce, who emerged himself from poverty to read, write and publish.[59] Room renting was seemingly fairly cheap, and this could be made more so by single persons, male or female, cramming together however unhygienically. It is also surprising how many people lived alone, in richer or poor areas. At the most marginal levels of society people could drift in and out of habitations and hardly enter the records, especially if male. From the mid sixteenth century they were likely to be at times institutionalised as mendicants.

While Chapter 5 sought to outline the organisation and nature of the central core of the male urban population, the backbone of the economy, this chapter has categorised a number of other categories of society, female as well as male, that were part of the working community, at least in better times. At the top end, professional and bureaucratic society seems to have become more organised and professional over the period, and sometimes haughtily elitist – as will be later emphasised. At the lower end there were always many vulnerable persons. Problems of evidence make it difficult to tell whether the opportunities for casual employment became proportionately greater, though we will later note a probable increase in philanthropic help as an alternative or supplement for those poor deemed deserving. Opportunities of employment for women seem to have fluctuated over time and in different locations but, while the paucity of unveiled records may distort the trends, jobs for women in textile work, retailing and sometimes in domestic service seem to have grown through an increased level of material culture. Employment opportunities, social security status, the need to seek casual employment or resort to prostitution, depended much on the strengths and weaknesses of the family and household, to which we now turn.

7

THE FAMILY AND HOUSEHOLD

Different concepts and composition of the 'Family'

The nature of the 'family' and the relationships of members of a family have been much re-considered by social historians of Europe, more particularly with Britain and France than Italy. The concern in Italy has been more with family–clan and family–household inter-connections, than with affective relationships within the closer family. The composition of the household, whether it is a multi-generational group with unrelated servants and apprentices or a nuclear family of two parents and young children, affects the relationships and affections of key family members. So a discussion of household and family structure precedes a consideration of marital and parental relations.

The supposition for western Europe is that historically from the middle ages to the present various forms of composite or extended family and multi-generation households gave way to a norm of a family and household structure with two parents and their children (until those grow up and leave home in early adulthood). Increasingly, social historians detect greater variations and complexities in the composition of family–household structures, past and present, and in the meaning of 'family'.[1] Several relevant issues have already been raised, as in dealing with population figures, with rural tenancies or with the employment of servants, many of whom lived within a household or 'family', and some of whom might be illegitimate children with an ambiguous status.

A large family or household might be seen as a sign of prestige and object of pride. The humanist architect L. B. Alberti (who incidentally never married), wrote a Dialogue on the Family, in which one speaker defined the family as 'children, wife, other relatives, retainers, and servants', and another commented: 'we pay salaries over the years to various strangers and feed and clothe servants, not because we wish only to take advantage of their services, but because we want to have more people in our house'.[2]

This is an optimistic approach to a large establishment. The intrusion of servants, apprentices and other outsiders within the household has recognised negative aspects. A well-run, and lucky, household might have loyalty from its servants. But many owners were fearful of servants, worried by the possibility of thefts and about immoral behaviour between servants, and between servants and younger family members or the master. Servant problems could seriously disturb marital and child–parent relationships. Alternatively servants and apprentices might fear the discipline, wrath and violence of master and mistress, which could even lead to murders, as Venetian prosecution records show.[3]

Modern research has undermined past simplistic views that the Mediterranean world had a typical family–household model with multiple generations (sons not necessarily relocating on marriage), and with women marrying young (under 20). This family characterisation has been undermined, with commentators stressing complex diversities up and down Italy, and within narrower areas between urban and rural, and/or economic groups.[4] In rural regions of central and northern Italy the configurations of households became more complex from the fifteenth to the eighteenth centuries, while the female age of marriage rose. Piedmont, Lombardy and Liguria maintained the late marriage profile, and had multi-generational families. Other parts of the north-central regions, such as Umbria and the Marches, also had multiple households of a horizontal configuration, where married brothers lived in the same house or housing group with their offspring.

The south tended to see more families splitting into nuclear families in separate residences; but women were still marrying young in the eighteenth century. A delay in the age of marriage occurred in Puglia through the seventeenth to eighteenth century, but women were still marrying in their late teens. For the rural south G. Delille (1985) argues for a division between monocultural plain areas with large estates, where women married younger, and more mountainous areas of mixed-crop farming and smallholdings which encouraged later marrying. Some communities in the sixteenth and seventeenth centuries might have women marrying on average aged a mere 15.2 years, others at 26.4. In Venice by the eighteenth century, marriage for both women and men was delayed into the twenties, with many postponing to nearly thirty. In northern urban areas, and in Sardinia, late-marrying couples tended to move into their own residences, not staying with parents or siblings.

Before marriage many children and youths went to live outside the parental home, as farm-hands, servants or court attendants. Marzio Barbagli argues that in northern urban areas in the sixteenth century a third or even half the males, and a third of the females spent some years serving others; from the seventeenth century such male service declined considerably, leaving domestic service to women. In northern rural areas in the sixteenth century about 20 per cent males and 10 per cent females did a period of service, and this persisted in the following two centuries. In the Pisa *contado*, 30–40 per cent households included a farm-hand, with males aged ten to twenty. In the eighteenth century some started such work before their teens and served about eight years, and came from families headed by widowed or abandoned women. In southern Italy, however, few youngsters went into service with other families, in rural or urban areas.[5]

All kinds of peculiarities and interesting variations existed. This might be illustrated by consideration of two different areas, at the beginning and end of our period. The Florentine *Catasto* of 1427, the register of wealth of households/hearths as the basis for taxation, has provided the fullest information on households, families and resources for any area.[6] The bare statistics that the Tuscan population of 264,210 persons was divided into 59,770 households indicate that the average household size was 4.42 persons. This might suggest the prevalence of the conjugal family, but in fact a considerable number of small household units of one or two persons existed (especially in the towns), and a significant number of very large households. Nearly 44 per cent of the hearths contained fewer than four people; and 10.8 per cent of the population lived in substantial households of eleven to twenty-five persons. The large households could be those of the urban wealthy, with numerous servants and ready to house affines and cognate relatives in one substantial palazzo; but there were also large households of share-croppers under the *mezzadria* system; poor rural families not owning the land maintained multiple family households, and sons did not move out to another home on marriage. Multiple households could house the rich, and the poor.[7] Multiple households containing parent(s) with children and their spouses numbered 8104 households (13.4 per cent of all designated households), while multiple households with married brothers together (called a *frérèche*) were 3147 (5.24 per cent). In contrast 3980 'households' were of solitary women (6.66 per cent), and 3804 (6.36 per cent) were made up of widows with children.

Florentine law dictated that inheritance of the patrimony went to sons, and females did not share in the patrimony; a wife was brought into the husband's family, but it was rare for any of her relatives to be added to the multiple family structure. If widowed she might go back to her father or brothers. A son might bring his bride into his father's household to create a patrilineal multiple family, but a daughter would rarely bring her husband into such a structure.

The largest household found in the 1427 *catasto* record was the *frérèche* of Lorenzo di Iacopo, living in suburban Florence. It had forty-seven members from four generations, centred on Lorenzo and three brothers. There were ten conjugal families, eighteen unmarried children or nephews and eight grandchildren or grandnephews. Unfortunately there is no evidence about the physical living arrangements for this group.

The second instructive example selected comes from eighteenth-century southern Italy, where W. A. Douglass has studied the joint-family in Agnone and some neighbouring localities in Molise.[8] Agnone was the largest town in Molise in the seventeenth century, and remained an important regional centre for some time. In the eighteenth century two-thirds of the inhabitants were involved in agriculture, whether as labourers and share-croppers on property of local landlords (generally absentee), or having their own small plots of land. The town of Agnone (with 861 households in 1753) was 850 metres above sea level, on a border level between arable and pastoral agriculture, as was the dependent village of Pietrabbondante (133 households). Lower areas farmed wheat, grapes and olives; upper land meant pasturage. Douglass argues that the ideal household formation was the joint-family where sons married and stayed with father, though demographic realities made this hard to achieve on a full scale. A static figure in 1753 gives 63.2 per cent as nuclear, and only 10.5 per cent of households in Agnone as joint, but a long-term study of families in one major parish suggests more families aspired to this latter configuration, only to be impeded by marital plans and untimely deaths. The first married sons remained with their fathers, but later sons might leave a crowded household on marriage and start new households. There were few *frérèche* households in Agnone or dependent villages. The death of the father led married brothers to split up. Unlike the earlier Tuscan scene, this Molise region shows few solitary households, female or male (about 2.5 per cent of households).

Douglass looks to joint-family, multiple households governed by economic poverty in the central and northern Italy as a possible point of comparison, and finds interesting differences. In the north share-cropping arguably encouraged the continuation of joint-families, because the landlord saw greater efficiency in keeping a labour force together within the tenant family. If the active household became too limited the share-cropping agreement might not be renewed. But this factor hardly operated in the Agnone area which only had share-cropping on a limited scale. Here we have poor labourer families in largish joint-family households; Pescopennataro – situated at 1190 metres and reliant almost entirely on animal husbandry – had even more joint-family households. In this area, unlike in Emilia or rural Tuscany under the *mezzadria* systems, there was no tendency to stabilise the workforce by delaying marriage or encouraging male celibacy. Nearly all males married, on average aged 25.85 years. Most women also married, and were likely to be forced out of the natal home if they did not. The mean age for first female marriages was 22.88, which might be expected for mountainous areas according to Delille's verdicts on southern Italy generally. So we have a different version of the multiple household from a poor area, with different family implications.[9]

The 'family' of course extended beyond the household structure systems, even of the most complex kinds. We can usefully distinguish between (a) 'family': the nuclear or conjugal group of parents and children whether married or not; (b) 'lineage': a kin group of blood relations who recognise their relationship with each, and know it as stemming from a common ancestor; (c) 'clan': a kin group where the members have a sense of community and of relationship, but without clear and accurate knowledge of the precise relationship, lost way back in the family tree.[10] The extent to which this extension was recognised and played a role in family strategies, economic arrangements and political ploys was again variable. Kinship factors were not only important for patrician and noble families, when much might be at stake financially and politically, but also for some peasant families with smallholdings who used kinship relationships in planning marriages that would help keep properties together.

An 'ordinary' household (as opposed to large palaces of the elites), could include persons who were not blood-relatives, marriage partners or servants and apprentices; i.e. friends, business colleagues or apprentices who remained as adults. Examples have been noted in Altopascio. An interesting example that has been clarified is that of the household of the Florentine artist Agnolo Bronzino, who did not marry or have his own children. Bronzino had been caringly treated, as it were 'fathered', by his own painting master, Jacopo da Pontormo. Bronzino became close friends with Cristofano (Tofano) Allori, a sword-maker, and lived with him and his family; and when Tofano died young in 1541, Bronzino immediately took care of his widow and the young children, including five-year-old Alessandro. Bronzino and the Allori had previously shared expenses, but now Bronzino became the main financial support, paying for the funeral, liquidating old debts and helping provide a dowry for the daughter Alessandra. He also trained Alessandro to become a major painter, to whom he later left his artistic equipment and pictures. For years he essentially paid for the whole family as if his own. In the 1540s Bronzino brought into the Bronzino–Allori household his own mother and a niece, creating an extended family of seven for a while. After marriage, Alessandra and her husband remained close friends and visitors, and helped him look after and feed his old master Pontormo. After Bronzino's death (1572) Alessandro Allori signified his love for his master and surrogate father by having him commemorated on the Allori family monument. This example not only highlights the complex natures of households and families, but illustrates the place of friendship (coming to the rescue after untimely death) and hospitality, and the ties of artistic relationships.[11]

Economic factors of various kinds affected the size of households in both countryside and towns, and the work of Douglass and Delille emphasises that the relevant economic forces involved could vary within a short distance. A significant number of people occupied households containing several blood-relatives, but also living-in servants, apprentices and farm-hands. The complex mixture could affect the wealthy, living in large urban palaces or in villas, but also poor farming families. The household composition was likely to affect personal relationships, marital and parental. Parent–child relationships at most levels of society could be influenced by teenagers leaving home to work elsewhere, and – in better-off families – by having babies sent away to wetnurses.

Formation of the family: marriages and dowries

Marriage planning was one of the most crucial decision-making processes for the family, since much could be at stake. Marriage was seldom the decision of the couple alone, and they might be the least of the decision makers. While love and affection, sexual attraction and unwanted pregnancies might play their part, the more hard-headed financial and political considerations of parents, brothers and uncles were far more important. The family had to consider the suitability of the intended bride or groom in terms of social standing, the nature of the family relations who would thus be conjoined, the earning power of the male, the implications for land ownership or tenancy-control and the size and nature of the dowry to be given or received.

The major considerations for marriage hinged on inheritance laws and the dowry systems. The inheritance laws were not uniform throughout Italy, and on the fringes of succession – when direct patrilineal succession could not operate – could be very complex. There was, however, a great stress on the power of the will and that the testator's wishes should be upheld. Local social conditions and customs would affect the tendencies of will-making. Fundamentally, in non-feudal cases primogeniture did not operate; the patrimony was divided between the surviving sons, but not daughters. The principle of male partible inheritance not only affected upper ranks with significant property to pass on, but could affect peasants with tenancies. In the southern feudal areas if a nobleman died intestate then all feudal property went to the eldest son, but the non-feudal possessions were divisible between all sons and those daughters without dowries.[12] The essential protection for daughters was a dowry, whose value had to be guaranteed by her husband's family and was to be available to restore to her if widowed; it did not become part of the husband's patrimony. Under the social pressures of will-making the testator sought a balance where possible between preserving intact a family patrimony, and providing something for all offspring, male and female.

These conditions had considerable implications. To preserve basic family resources and the patrimony younger sons might be encouraged to delay marriage or not marry at all, and remain within the multiple household. Various ploys had to be used to prevent excessive subdivision of landholdings, whether noble or peasant. In the region of Biella in the north the remedy by the eighteenth century was for all sons to inherit the holdings jointly. On the other hand daughters would be encouraged to move out of the parental home, with a dowry for marriage or a convent. But the expense of dowries might space the marrying of daughters while resources were accumulated, so leading some to marry late – or not at all if family conditions worsened.

The bridal dowry was of great significance. In the past a married couple had received dowry and gift contributions from both families to resource the new family, often in near equal amounts. But by the fifteenth century, virtually all the contribution came formally from the bridal dowry and her trousseau. The dowry amount had to reflect her family's social standing, and her honour. A dowry remained attached to the woman until her death, to act as a resource and protection if she were widowed. A dowry was an indication of respectability, and was deemed a requirement for the honourable poor as much as the patricians. As Christiane Klapisch-Zuber put it, for the pre-tridentine period: 'From the top of Tuscan society to the bottom, families rushed to the notary to establish a dowry, and a marriage without a dowry seemed more blameworthy than a union unblessed by the Church. The dowry penetrated to the very heart of the social ideology of the time.'[13] In the fifteenth century, Florence in particular developed an elaborate dowry fund to enable the upper families notably to plan suitable family strategies, consolidate kinship networks and preserve honour and wealth.[14] The fund became an investment institution with wide political implications for the Republic. The problem of the dowry for others in society led philanthropic confraternities to provide dowries for poor virgins so that they could secure husbands, and not be forced into an evil life.

The early modern dowry system meant that daughters could be very expensive – and unwanted in some families. It encouraged fathers and brothers to send females into convents, whether they had a vocation or not. For entry into most convents an entrance dowry, and often some continuing contribution to maintenance, were required; but this was considerably less costly than the marriage dowry – possibly a tenth less for the patricians of Venice and Genoa, where marriage dowries were generally the highest in the sixteenth and seventeenth centuries. Rural families, lacking resources for dowries, might send their daughters into domestic service, through which they could accumulate resources for a later marriage.

The complexities of the dowry system were legion, and the implications were not always detrimental to women. Dowries could be made up of cash, jewellery, land, bonds, furniture or agricultural implements. Some part might be handed over on the signing of the marriage contract, or consummation; some might be allocated but not distributed until the couple set up a new home, or the wife died and the husband or his family claimed the remaining dowry for the children. If land was part of the dowry settlement the implications for the overall property management of both families could be considerable. The husband and his family had to protect the dowry and its value. They may have had the management of the new wife's dowry assets, but they needed to be able to restore its worth should she be widowed. The husband and his family may have expended considerable sums 'dressing the bride' and making gifts, to add to the honour and acceptability of the marriage, at least in Tuscany and Rome.

If a wife perceived that her dowry was being mismanaged and her position endangered, she could in some places and under some conditions resort to law – through her male relatives or a guardian such as the Florentine *mundualdus* – to protect it or gain control over it.[15] Since the dowry was the wife's and was not in her lifetime absorbed into the husband's patrimony (though as Gregorio Dati's diary shows, husbands could use dowries to fund business activities), she could be in a position to reallocate it in her will.

The dowry system made planning who married whom a wide family consideration, and the wishes of the couple concerned could be of minor concern. Negotiations might be conducted through family intermediaries, friendly go-betweens such as the Florentine *mezzani* or even officially recognised marriage-brokers as in Siena. At the upper levels of society, with considerable political implications in family and clan alliances, political leaders were often actively involved, like the fifteenth-century Lorenzo de' Medici who had weddings completed in his palace.[16] The couple concerned might not know each other or meet before a betrothal (and even that, especially with dynastic princely marriages could be undertaken by proxies at opposite ends of the peninsula). A very short period only might elapse between initial meeting and consummation of the marriage.

The degree of pressure on offspring to marry or not, to go into a convent or agree whom to marry is hard to assess. L. B. Alberti (unmarried), advised the young man to find out the character of his intended bride, and that of her relatives, before agreeing to a match. Florentine records imply considerable discussion of the intended or contemplated partners, and that the views at least of the groom-to-be were ascertained, even if the couple did not converse directly.[17] Arcangela Tarabotti in the seventeenth century famously attacked Venetian fathers for forcing daughters into convents, but Venetian patrician mothers often secured their daughters a choice in their fate. The bitter debates at the 1562–3 sessions of the Council of Trent about clandestine marriages suggest that many couples were perceived to be forming unions contrary to parental wishes. While Trent did not insist on parental consent for a marriage to be recognised, some secular governments, such as that of Piedmont-Savoy, did.

Given the cost of dowries, pressures were powerful to arrange marriages within kinship groups to keep the resources close to home. This tendency has been found among feudal families in the Kingdom of Naples such as the Carafa, Caracciolo, Ruffo di Scilla and Tocco, but also among Neapolitan rural families to preserve tenancies. In the north, in mountainous areas around Como, numerous petitions were made for dispensations to marry within normally prohibited degrees of kinship. This reflected a desire to keep property within a kin-focused society – as well as the problem of finding suitable partners within isolated inbred communities.[18]

Some marriages were triggered by pre-marital sexual relations. The extent of pre-marital sex and pregnancy is hard to establish, especially as through much of our period there was a battle to establish a common form of marriage, and then to enforce the Tridentine rules on marriage. It is possible in some areas to match marriage and baptismal records, and establish that a certain number of brides were pregnant. This still leaves open the question whether pregnancy had caused a shot-gun wedding that would not otherwise have been likely; or whether an agreed relationship had been established, with or without formal betrothal, and that marriage took place when pregnancy proved the desired fertility of the union; i.e. nobody was seriously embarrassed or shamed, even if the parish priest might be annoyed.

Rape, or an allegation of it, could lead to marriage. Rape of a very young virgin or of a nun was condemned as a very serious offence, but rape of an adult secular woman was treated as an assault, and as an offence against the honour and property of the father or husband as much as against the female victim. The attitude of courts and society tended to be that the couple should marry if both were unmarried, and so rescue her honour (and the family's). If the rapist was married and his victim not, then he was expected to compensate by paying what would amount to a dowry for her to marry another with some respect, or enter a nunnery. Though seemingly not a good foundation for a satisfactory marriage, for many women it must have been seen as a lesser evil than dishonour. Many rapes were probably resolved within the families without recourse to law. The record of the case initiated by Orazio Gentileschi accusing another painter Agostino Tassi of raping his daughter Artemisia Gentileschi in 1612, does strongly suggest that she was unwillingly deflowered (whatever the counter-charges of her attacker and some of his friends). Once this has happened she allowed further intercourse to take place: 'What I was doing with [Tassi] I only did so that, as he had dishonoured me, he would marry me.' It is when it becomes clear that marriage will not follow willingly, that her father goes to court on her behalf – though by then for punishment not an enforced marriage. Tassi received a sentence of exile, but before he set off he had the sentence cancelled as too harsh, and he was soon running a complex studio again, as we have already noted. Artemisia married another, though this relationship did not last long and she became an independent artist and mother. Her father again worked with Tassi.[19]

However in some cases 'rape' was part of a more complex scenario, as has been revealed by Elizabeth Cohen's study of some rape cases investigated by the Governor of Rome's court in the early seventeenth century. Virginity, as she argues it, was a 'negotiable commodity'. A premature and illicit deflowering could be by choice as well as force. A charge of rape could be used to secure a dowry and marriage; opportunists used the initial sexual episode and the law to secure a desired but ambivalent (about marriage) male, or to persuade the parents of a lover, or her parents, to agree to a marriage. The court transcripts show the females concerned as often remarkably adept at using the court to their advantage.[20]

The formation of the marriage was thus often a matter of economics, social status and legal strategies that we might find unseemly, and not conducive to a happy and stable marital scene, especially when the household could be large. However we need to look more closely at relations within the family.

Personal family relationships

The emotional content of family life and affections, especially for France and England, has been hotly debated. This can be connected with another debate on the extent of misogynist attitudes (and whether they grew or decreased over the period), which might have affected husbands' and fathers' attitudes to wives and daughters. New work on Italy further undermines old allegations of affectionless childhoods and marriages before the eighteenth century.[21] It is dangerous to assume a marriage to be loveless because arranged by others, with partners much different in age; or that the high mortality of infants froze emotions concerning children. The existence of multiple households, and/or households with resident servants and apprentices in buildings which might not allow much privacy, could have impeded the development of close relationships. The age difference may be more significant again in modern terms than it was in the past; though it was good copy for sixteenth-century plays, where old husbands are ridiculed while their young wives enjoy youthful lovers, as in Giovanni Maria Cecchi's *The Horned Owl* (*L'Assiuolo*, 1549), or Girolamo Bargagli's *The Female Pilgrim* (*La Pellegrina*, *c.* 1564–8).[22] The age gap probably encouraged a patriarchal mentality; but this need not necessarily have frozen out affection.

Much of the public literature of the period suggests a misogynist attitude that would have fostered a domineering patriarchal attitude within the family. A prevalent male attitude throughout our period towards women was that women were weaker physically and mentally, that they were vulnerable and in need of male protection – whether paternalistic protection against marauding males, or protection against their own weak and inferior natures. Women were also seen as dangerous to men, because of their supposed sexual insatiability once their sexual instincts were aroused (so beware in particular the young widow), or because they could wield magical powers over men (or other women), particularly through using their menstrual blood. Such attitudes are found in literary dialogues or sermons, or in trial records investigating women charged with superstitious and witchcraft practices. It is difficult to know how far the extreme views were shared by most males, or were even the 'real' views of the writing persona. There is currently some debate as to whether the misogynist attitudes towards women worsened through the period, and their social roles became more circumscribed – particularly as a result of the Counter-Reformation, whose reformers might stress the role of women as wives and mothers, or as enclosed nuns. However recently historians have highlighted males who wrote to defend and praise women, and women who counter-attacked in literary polemics and in playing an active role in society and cultural activity. On either side much was part of an exaggerated literary battle of the sexes.[23]

For male misogynist writing one can cite from Niccolò Machiavelli, diplomat, political theorist, historian and leading literary figure. Hanna Pitkin, has particularly stressed Machiavelli's concentration on the masculine world of politics, and how a feminine presence can be threatening to men of *virtù*. 'Women have caused much destruction, have done great harm to those who govern cities, and have occasioned many divisions in them.' (*Discourses*, Bk 3, ch. 26: 'How women (*femine*) can be the cause of the ruin of the state'.) He is seen as despising and fearing women and the effeminate (with *effeminato* as a major abusive epithet). Characters in his plays argue that 'all women lack brains, and are timorous'(*Mandragola*, Act 3); though once angered women are full of deceit and cruelty, pride and anger so unable to pardon, as he argues in *Clizia*. Relationships between the sexes involve battle and struggle, with men having to show mastery, to conquer, to make sure they take women, and are not taken by them. In his short story, *Belfagor*, a devil is released from hell to marry; he possesses a number of women, falls in love with a beautiful one, and makes the mistake of being besotted by her; in return she becomes arrogant and begins to lord it over him. His servants prefer to return to hell 'to live in fire rather than stay in the world under her rule' and he finally escapes 'to return to hell rather than again with such great annoyance, anxiety and danger put his neck under the marriage yoke'.[24]

Less well-known is the late fifteenth century Neapolitan short-story writer, Masuccio Salernitano (alias Tommaso Guardati), whose collection of stories, *Il Novellino*, attacked lusty women, along with immoral clerics and misers. Women belonged to a putrid, coarse and most imperfect sex, full of every kind of lasciviousness. The theme of part three of his collection is of insatiable female desire, such that for example a widow who seduces her son is called a most luxurious pig, an inhuman and most rapacious wild beast. Rarely do Masuccio's women receive favourable treatment and comment from him, and they are constantly treated as inferior to men. Women, in his eyes, exist to be admired: 'they universally hold that their whole reputation, honour and glory consists in nothing else, unless to be loved, gazed upon, and exalted for their beauty, and they would sooner be seen as beautiful and vicious, than be reputed very virtuous and ugly'. If not granted easy admiration they will use their wiles and skills to win it, and satisfy their lusts. One critic of Masuccio argues that this deep misogyny is heartfelt, and not just the product of literary conventions (unlike some of his anti-clericalism).[25]

The inferiority of women was based on legal codes and attitudes. They were not equal before the law. They could not act as a litigant in their own right, needing father, brother or guardian to pursue their causes. The extent to which they could fully inherit, control and dispose of property was variable between states and cities, and much debated by lawyers.[26] Domenico Bruni da Pistoia, one of the male defenders of women, argued (in his *Difese delle donne*, 1559) that until the legal discriminations against women were removed there would be no serious change in misogynist attitudes, such as those just quoted. Men treated women as inconsistent, licentious, vindictive, treacherous, mentally imperfect and so on, because their legal and economic restrictions rendered women weak; they could not hold public office, not judge or pass sentences, not accuse in a criminal trial, not make wills on their own, not adopt children, not provide collateral. If it was better recognised that women could be the equal of men economically – as when working as farmers, gardeners or tailors – then respect might grow towards women in each rank of society, and laws eventually be changed.[27]

None of the above was conducive to happy family life, breeding distrust and maltreatment – if and when it was believed. However there were counter attitudes. In the fifteenth century and beyond companionate marriage was advocated, as by the Venetian humanist Francesco Barbaro, celebrating (1415) the marriage of a Florentine friend, Lorenzo de' Medici (brother of the famous Cosimo), to Ginevra Cavalcanti:

> What greater pleasure, than to decide together all things, even while spared concerns of the household? Than to have a modest wife, a companion in good days and bad, a spouse and a friend? To whom you can confide your most private thoughts regarding your affairs? Whose sweetness and company soothe all your cares and woes? Whom you love so much that you think that a part of your own life depends on her well-being?[28]

Rudolf Bell (1999) has shown that printing generated a considerable literature as guidance for middling classes not just the elite, giving advice on family life and strategies, lively and mutually enjoyable sexual relations to produce healthy children, on household management and ensuring family harmony. While most emphasised a subservience of children to parents, wives to husbands, they did encourage mutual consideration, care and affection. Sermons spread such messages to the illiterate.

Italian women, especially in northern cities, were not always seen as restricted in behaviour or demeanour. Foreign visitors admired (or hypocritically disdained) the extravagance, flamboyance and freedom of upper-crust women as well as courtesans. The Welshman William Thomas in his 1549 *History of Italy* noted that 'in good ernest, the gentlewomen generally for gorgeous attire, apparel, and jewels exceed, I think, all other women of our known world. I mean as well the courtesans as the married women . . . specially where churchmen do reign'. While for Venice he noted the number of beautiful courtesans for the many men who did not marry, in Genoa – a city which could teach Ovid the arts of love – wives were very open:

'Truly the Genoese themselves deserve that their wives should be praised, because I saw in no place where women have so much liberty. For it is lawful there openly to talk of love with what wife soever she be . . .' The Genoese defend the liberty of talk and action of wives, 'thinking that their wives through this liberty of open speech are rid of the rage that maketh other women to travail so much in secret'. So 'the supreme court of love is nowhere to be sought out of Genoa'.[29]

In contrast, the early modern period perpetuated the attitude that female adultery was an offence to the honour of the husband, and others in the family; and that it might be punished by death of the woman and her lover. Masuccio Salernitano stressed this in his short stories. This attitude and the legal system evolved out of Roman law in the *lex Julia*, and medieval adaptations in communal law, with glosses on the Roman law. There was some debate whether – for such a reprisal killing to be justified and exonerated – the offenders had to be caught in the act, and in the house of the offended husband; whether evidence of kissing was enough to indicate adultery; whether the male lover had to be warned beforehand. It was not only argued that an offended husband could be excused for killing his adulterous wife, but also argued in Naples that a husband had a duty to kill or punish her, and would be seen as a 'pander' (*pro lenone*) if he spared her. A compliant husband would be socially disdained, alleged Antonius Matthaeus (though himself disparaging such an attitude in 1644). The Milanese argued that resorting to law over an adulterous wife – as opposed to taking the law into one's own hands – was mistaken, since it added to the shame and the publicity. Suspicion of adultery was enough to mitigate punishment for murder. In sixteenth-century Milan, Togninus Garmendus warned Menghinus Dentonus not to have dealings with his wife; Menghinus insulted Togninus in the street, called him a billy-goat, for which he was killed. The murderer was merely sentenced to three years in the galleys, because this was a homicide for the sake of honour. Apparently many Milanese senators deemed this sentence too harsh a punishment after such provocation.[30]

The marital relationship was often very unequal, with the wife encouraged to be subservient, if adoring, but many husband–wife relations in the upper orders of society produced considerable consultation about family and business matters. When husbands were away on business, political-diplomatic careers or on military service wives were as likely to be left with some control as another male relative or paid manager. And when political exile was involved in the fifteenth and sixteenth centuries wives appear as the stalwart family organisers and co-ordinators as with the Strozzi in Florence or the Baglioni in Perugia.[31] Widows could and did take over affairs on the death of husbands. In the case of the Caracciolo di Brienza clan a succession of young widows from the sixteenth to the eighteenth century beneficially used their extensive dowries and organisational skills to foster the clan's interests, preserve patrimonies and re-establish their sons, nephews and nieces. They usually earned male gratitude for their efforts.[32]

The assumption that the family in the period was patriarchal and that all key decisions were made by the father/husband when present, and that wives and mothers had limited say, needs qualification. Stanley Chojnacki's studies of the

Venetian patriciate up to the early sixteenth century show how and when females could make a major impact on family affairs, especially for their daughters.[33] The age at which patrician daughters were betrothed and married rose generally through the fifteenth century, from child bridehood at 12–13 years to more mature adolescence of 15–16, or later. This may be attributed to the growing influence of the mothers, who also were more inclined to allow daughters to choose freely between marriage and the convent (and more occasionally continuing spinsterhood). A patrician female's only claim on the patrimony was her dowry. But in Venice this tended to be substantial, and she was freer than her husband to distribute in her will to the wider lineage or clan relations, and to remember her female relatives more. Women could thus (and in other ways) accumulate their own non-dowry property, and use this with some freedom. As the patrician dowries increased in relative value, so did the economic use of it by the women, who could happily get involved in capital investment, lending and business enterprise – usually in connection with their kinsmen. Ingoldise Morosini even entered as a partner in a soap-manufacturing business in 1420. In the political arena female relatives were involved surprisingly frequently in sponsoring the young patrician men in the Balla d'Oro process whereby they were judged eligible as patricians to enter the Grand Council, and so the political offices that stemmed from this. While the male's testament is usually seen as manipulative over wives and daughters, Venetian women could use their wills to influence the behaviour of their male kin, or offer greater freedom to daughters. Maria Bembo, married to Girolamo Zane, in her will of 1479 so disposed that her three daughters would have financial resources to choose between marriage, the convent or life-long spinsterhood whether living with their brothers or separately. Studies of wills of women in places like Florence, Genoa or Tivoli, also show them – for the beginning of our period – in control of much money and property, and as shrewd business women.[34]

With children, all those who married expected and wanted to have male issue to perpetuate the family, and would struggle to that end – and manuals advised how to conceive a male. The surviving eldest male was likely to be the child to receive most attention and physical care. As already indicated girls might be deemed a financial liability. That there was some 'family planning' should probably be accepted, through (in ascending order of importance or efficacy) contraception, sexual practices, abandonment of babies and timing of marriage in the first place. Condoms were available in a primitive form from the sixteenth century; but they were probably reserved for protection from infection from syphilis. While John Riddle (1994) argues that the classical and medieval knowledge of partly efficacious herbal contraceptive and abortifacient concoctions had declined by the late Renaissance (as tested by surviving manuscripts and printed books), it is difficult to believe that such knowledge did not persist among both midwives and cunning women. Techniques of *coitus interruptus* and anal intercourse were used to some extent to limit conceptions, judging by church and court condemnations. Infanticide, especially of female babies, was part of family control, explaining notable differences in sex ratios revealed by the Tuscan *catasto* records of the 1420s. The spacing between children was undoubtedly affected by whether babies were breast-fed by the mother, or given to wetnurses. Upper-rank women who more regularly used wetnurses became pregnant again more quickly. Breast-feeding in itself may delay conception; and parents were advised to avoid sexual intercourse as long as a baby was being breast-fed, in case the milk was contaminated or weakened by intercourse. The merits and demerits of employing wetnurses, and their selection and treatment, were seriously debated.[35]

The abandonment of babies rose through the period and reached a horrendous peak in the nineteenth century. The apparent increase of abandonment from the later fifteenth century can be explained partly, as Richard Trexler (1973) in particular has argued, through a reduction under religious and civic pressure in infanticide of unwanted babies; by a rise in population, followed by war and dearth crises of the early sixteenth century; and by the greater provision of foundling hospitals and other institutions, especially following the model of the Innocents' hospital (designed by Brunelleschi), which finally opened in Florence in 1445. An airy and healthy hospital designed to save and bring up abandoned babies (*esposti*) safely, it was soon swamped by excessive numbers. This was to be a pattern; the more facilities there were to rescue abandoned babies, the more were abandoned. The death rate was high, given normal childhood ailments and the lack of hygiene, exacerbated if the babies stayed in a hospital facility, the weaknesses of babies brought in from a distance, then often sent back out to country wetnurses and the lack of care and fraudulent intent of some wetnursing families. By the late eighteenth century, exposure of babies virtually amounted to a death sentence.[36]

While many of the abandoned babies were bastards, many others were clearly not. Through the sixteenth to nineteenth centuries poor Italian families abandoned their later babies and children when they felt they could not cope economically – as a temporary or permanent measure. Clearly some of the abandoned children had been wanted and loved, but parents could not cope and thought institutions would help. Some left notes, talismans and tokens to help later identification, expressing an intention to reclaim the child if family conditions improved; some families did make such attempts to bring back their offspring, and some found them alive. Many of course made no such attempt, and their initial expression of intention may have been merely to calm their conscience. Whatever the intentions, by the end of our period child exposure was an effective if callous family limitation practice. It is difficult to know how aware parents were of the likely death rate for abandoned children.

The major family controls over the size of a family were from controlling the age of marriage, and who married. By and large the later the marriage the fewer children for the child-bearing mother; with breast-feeding or wetnursing having some effect on the periodicity of pregnancy through the childbearing years. It is not clear that there is much change in the mother's mortality rate through our period. The other family planning factor could be a conscious decision-making that only certain males would marry with a view to establishing new generations. Certain patrician clans, for example in Venice and Milan, deliberately limited inheriting heirs to preserve the patrimony intact. Unmarried younger sons were maintained as part of extended households (along with spinster daughters), or established in bachelor households.

These 'bachelors' might of course have courtesans, mistresses or non-noble wives, provided their offspring had no claim on the main family estate. Patricians might select their concubines from the city, or from their country estates – as with Maddalena di Moscaglia or Lucia Coradina, revealed in Avogaria di Comun records. Some ended marrying their concubines, and getting formal recognition of their offspring by this vetting committee.[37]

From the late seventeenth century the Milan patricate managed to control and limit their families; child mortality decreased (especially for the later children), but fertility of the mothers was reduced (no longer producing ten or more live or dead children as in the early seventeenth century) and there was more control over who did or did not marry.[38]

Parent–child relationships in the early years are hard to fathom. The high mortality rate for most families until the end of our period may have, as often argued, discouraged a heavy investment of emotion in babies. But arguments for lack of concern based on the cryptic and unemotional entries in chronicles, family journals or surviving letters may be misleading, while effusive emotions are certainly found in Florentine writings, from Boccaccio and Petrarch among others.[39] Births were celebrated with ceremonial trays and cups and a party spirit. When we do find some outpouring of joy about a birth, and deep grief about a child's death – as in the case of Giovanni Morelli in early fifteenth-century Florence – it is difficult to know whether his emotion is unusual, or just his willingness to record it. Giovanni Morelli's *Ricordi* expressed his joy over the conception, quickening and birth of his healthy firstborn Alberto; then ten years later the deep shock at the painful and tragic death of that son, which clearly affected his emotions ever after. But Giovanni recognised that his own father (Pagolo) had had a grim childhood: banished to a country nurse until ten or twelve, beaten by successive schoolmasters on his return to the city, and suffering from resentful older brothers out to deprive him of a share in the estate. The revered Pagolo's own early death had clearly adversely affected Giovanni; and his mother had deserted him to marry again. Giovanni wanted Alberto to have the happy and secure childhood he had not had; and wanted to ensure mothers who outlived early dying fathers should not similarly desert and deprive them of care. And he agonised that he had not made Alberto happier, and paid more attention to him.[40]

When Valerio the eight-year-old son of the Venetian patrician and military leader Jacopo Antonio Marcello died in 1461, the father went into deep shock. His grief generated a collection of consolatory humanist writings for him (notably by the humanist-architect Francesco Filelfo and Isotta Nogarola of Verona, the leading female humanist), which he collected and preserved. It is clear that father and son for the last few years were devoted to each other, the intelligent and precocious son adoring to hear of his father's military exploits.

> He grew in years with such force of love towards me, his father, that this was the infant's most amazing quality. . . . If ever I was agitated with anxiety or perturbation . . . he acted as if he thought of nothing other than me . . . [Later, on hearing of his father's and Venice's military successes] he wanted

> to know by what art, by what genius those ships had been dragged from hill to hill, across dangerous chasms and paths, and lowered into the Lago di Garda. . . . I could forsee that he would accumulate in himself by his acute mind the virtue of my ancestors, so that our whole posterity would be enriched by the glory of deeds well done.

The consoling literature, though drawing on classical formulae, suggests that Jacopo Marcello was not alone in this deep affection and grief. Filelfo had similarly lost an eight-year-old son. 'A companion stricken with the same disease, it should be recognized that I myself must be consoled as much as I console you. For what counsel can he give who cannot advise himself?'[41]

The increase in the age before marriage suggests a teenage and adolescent period before full adulthood in marriage. For many it was a period of service in another family, whether court or large household, or apprenticeship in small artisan workshop. For a few there would be schooling (often with harsh discipline), based in the family household for boys, but in a convent for many girls. Some males had an adolescent period of licence and liberty, semi-licit or illicit: the world of homosexuality before most settled into respectable heterosexual family life (as in Florence and Venice), gang rapes of prostitutes or virgins, *charivari* (festivals where social roles were inverted and authorities mocked), of rough sports (the *palio*, jousts, the battle of the stones in Perugia until the sixteenth century, the battle of the fists (*pugni*) in Venice). There were youth confraternities, especially in Florence and Genoa, designed to be more moral and respectable, and sometimes to absorb energies in musical and theatrical activities, though likewise part of male-bonding operations.[42]

Insights into childhood, family relations and the concept of service come from Annibal Guasco's published instructions to his daughter Lavinia, originally written when he (then in Pavia) sent her off (aged nine) to the Turin court to be one of the 'women' serving the Infanta Caterina, marrying the Duke of Savoy. Lavinia (born 1574), in an introductory letter to the printed edition in 1586, apologizes for the delay in securing its publication, requested by her father! The eighty-page discourse is long-winded, at times pompous, but shows affection and concern for Lavinia, and for the great step she is taking in going to court at this tender age. With God's help, with her strong beliefs, and with this parental guide written with love ever to hand, worth more than any jewel, to rule her life she will survive and prosper. Lavinia has clearly been well educated already in the liberal arts, with her father very proud of his role in fostering this, and Christian doctrine. She is musically accomplished, especially in the viola da gamba (to accompany her singing) and clavichord, which should serve her well at court. The father's instructions emphasise the virtues of honour, chastity and reverence for parents and offer advice on how to treat her patroness/employer, other court girls and ladies, and her own servants, to avoid or cope with the envy prevalent at court. She should read Castiglione's *Book of the Courtier* and Della Casa's *Galateo*, as guides to courtly behaviour, and adapt to Spanish courtly customs (which he clearly admires), learning Castilian Spanish in order to converse with the right courtiers. Here is parental affection for a daughter, an intense education, but a short childhood, and much early career planning (presumably with a view to a court marriage, though this is not specifically stated). He had a concern for Honour that would have echoed by many concerned fathers of daughters:

> I understand honour to be chastity. If chastity is respected then a woman however poor or ugly may become rich and handsome (*formosa*); and if without chastity, the rich and beautiful woman is reputed a liar and deformed. Chastity is worn like a garment which, if stained has that stain for evermore, because it cannot be washed or hidden from a good eye; and, worse, the stain remains even when this garment of chastity is ripped up and burned – for not only in life, but even after death, the woman remains stained by dishonour.[43]

It is dangerous to assume from certain types of records that fathers had limited concerns for their daughters, especially after marriage when they were usually transferred to another household. As Renata Ago warned, we should not deduce from the absence of females in some family genealogies, or from some family record books, that fathers or brothers were remote from the females. Genealogies were not 'innocent' or necessarily designed to be a full record, but to serve as reminders for certain inheritance strategies. In seventeenth century Rome, Orazio Spada's domestic memorials may become silent about his daughters on marrying, but surviving correspondence reveals regular affectionate concern with their daily lives, whether married or in nunneries.[44]

Older children could become 'unwanted' when one parent died and the other remarried, as Giovanni Morelli lamented. Some households absorbed, with whatever tensions, step-children; and suddenly large households emerged with widow and widower entering second marriages with a number of children each, and producing more. But especially when sizable dowries and inheritances were involved some children were rejected. A youngish widow might have to abandon *her* children in the care of her late husband's family; but take on step-children of her new husband. There was considerable room for emotions of abandonment, rejection, the 'cruel' mother and step-mother.

The fate of the widow could be fraught, but there is no easy pattern. The obvious sufferers were the poor old or middle-aged widows, from already disjointed – possibly migrant – families, without economic resources or extended family support, and maybe burdened still with children and other dependants. They might receive some assistance from charitable organisations. In more well-established families (whether from a solid economic point of view, or from the coherence of poorer extended household systems), the widow with or without children might be well-absorbed. For the younger widow remarriage was a complicated problem, since she faced conflicting pressures from relatives who wanted her to marry and those who did not. She probably had more freedom of choice if she had daughters and no sons. Increasingly in Tuscany the Court of Wards (*Magistrato dei Puppili*), listened to mothers, awarded them custody of children (though this might debar them from remarrying) or acted when they reported abuse of their children by other relatives.[45] It had to be considered what would happen to her existing children, and to dowries, legacies and 'gifts' if she remarried. Many wills and conditions of dowry payments sought to control remarriage and the possible alienation of resources from one family to another. There were also social taboos against second marriages, especially if a youngish, experienced woman was seen to be enticing eligible bachelors. Such a remarriage might be punished by *charivari* extravagances, fines, rides on donkeys backwards, the removal of house-roofs unless compensation was paid to the local community, through Youth Abbey groups (organisations, in Piedmont in particular, that had festivals where normal hierarchies and social relations were temporarily inverted or subverted), religious fraternities and so forth.

The complexity of the situation when a woman faced widowhood – and a number of other aspects of family and gender relationships – can be illustrated from the different experiences of a noble Florentine woman, Maddalena Nerli, as relayed through her journal, and her second husband's. In 1583 Maddalena aged twenty-one married Francesco Giordano Martelli, and they had a son and two daughters before he died in early 1588. She was denied custody of these children, who remained with the Martelli family, and forced to return to her brother's house. She then married Cosimo Tornabuoni in November 1589, after one meeting. Cosimo had already lost two wives in childbirth; Maddalena became step-mother to two surviving daughters. Maddalena and Cosimo then had eight children by 1599; Cosimo died in 1605. This time Maddalena was left fully in charge as guardian of the surviving family and the family home. While her husband had had an active political-diplomatic career she had developed considerable expertise in managing his properties and promoting agricultural improvements. She continued this activity as a widow, while she also organised marriage alliances for her daughters and launched the two surviving sons into military and diplomatic careers. By 1625 she was given guardianship of her grandchildren, and briefly in 1638 of three great-grandsons. She worked well with her sons, and with one daughter, Caterina, who had developed psychological problems. Her husband turned to Maddalena for help; to them, their children and grandchildren she was very supportive. But Maddalena had twenty years of bitter conflict with her other two daughters (Cassandra and Virginia) and their husbands, primarily over dowries. The last two years before she died in 1641 seem to have been quiet and peaceful. Maddalena's story shows distrust and rejection by one husband at death (causing her to sever links with her young children), but the opposite reactions from her second; shows how the widow could be the solid foundation and great organiser of an extended family; and how battles between families over expensive dowries could produce bitter emotions. There was no affection in the first marriage, plenty in the second. Though less well documented other women clearly faced similar mixed reactions, and developed strategies to survive and compete.[46]

This section has sought to give some flavour of the attitudes and postures within the inner family, with a few individual examples that tend to emphasise personal concern and consideration. They are designed to suggest that family relationships might not have been as formal and economically determined as some past accounts have assumed and implied, and to indicate some new researches and approaches to personal family relationships.

The extended family

Households and families (especially involving remarriages and step-children), already discussed, could be complex enough. But family relationships extended to wider kinships and clans, and had to accommodate spiritual relationships through god-parents. Various concepts of the clan, kinship or family and of who mattered existed, under different names and legal recognition. In Florence *consorteria* was often used to indicate the widest linkage of the family, assuming for the most part patrilineal descent; other names used, however, included *stirpe*, *nazione*, *casa*, *schiatta*, *progenia* and *famiglia*. But some contemporaries talked about more than one *consorteria* within the same house, and some admitted non-lineal relatives or outsiders into the *consorteria* to be favoured. In Genoa *alberghi* were similar, though the recognised kin links might be narrower. Here, as in Venice, with legally recognised, closed political systems, it was especially important to be assured of lineal descent in upper-rank families, to determine eligibility for office; though this did not mean that all members of the same Genoese *albergo* or Venetian *casa* would cooperate. Outside the specifically political there was undoubtedly an awareness of kin relationships, and a will to record them, as demonstrated by family chronicles, diaries (for example of the fifteenth-century Florentine Gregorio Dati, who paid particular attention to all the god-parents of his twenty-odd children), compilation of genealogies, and so forth.[47]

Fifteenth- and sixteenth-century Florentine family documents show considerable conscious concern for kin, and what duties were involved. Giovanni Rucellai in his *Zibaldone* – a family record for the benefit of his heirs – showed the most concern for his relatives, including many entering the relationship through marriages. It was important to know from whom he might thus receive support and favours, and to whom he had a duty and obligation. He was inordinately proud of the extensive *consorteria*, and of the large households in extensive palazzi on which it was based. He supported the attitude of L. B. Alberti, that when the richer members of the clan, like himself, were approached by kinsmen: 'Duty requires helping them, not even so much with money, as with sweat and with blood, and by any means one can, even to giving your life for the honour of the house and its members.'[48]

In a large system numerous tensions appeared over conflicting loyalties, and *consorteria* could generate both loyalty and tension, as F. W. Kent's study of 194 households that made up the Florentine *consorteria* of the Capponi, Ginori and Rucellai in the fifteenth century revealed. Pressures to focus wealth on the narrower family might here be resisted for sake of wider kin. But this may have diminished in later generations of the elites. Matteo Palmieri recognised orders of priority in his *Della vita civile* (written about 1430): love first went to sons, then 'grandsons, and anyone else born of our blood; among these I include first of all everybody in the household (*casa*) and the stocks (*le schiatte*), lineages (*le consorterie*), and huge families (*copiose famiglie*) which must develop as its numbers overflow'. The wider kin would often be preferentially selected in forming business partnerships, in lending or borrowing money, arranging marriage alliances, in operating political and administrative appointments or in establishing contacts in other cities like Venice and Rome. Large sacrifices might be made in the interest of kinship relationship; Lorenzo de' Medici (*Il Magnifico*) asked Giovanni Rucellai to sell him his villa at Poggio a Caiano; Giovanni – loving his property – was upset at the idea, but allowed his son Bernardo to tell Lorenzo (Bernardo's brother-in-law) that he would agree for 'we are dealing with inlaws and relations, not with outsiders'.[49]

Kinship relationships criss-crossed. They might lubricate the wheels of politics and commerce – but create great tensions. Kin had to select those to work with, and those to ignore, reject and distrust. If the love of kin was thwarted, a connection betrayed or ignored, then the feelings were embittered. The counterblast to the anthropological stress on the positive workings of kinship can come from historians showing the breakdown of kinship, and internecine family warfare.

A clan that illustrates the breakdown of extended family relations and their political repercussions is that of the Baglioni, whose members dominated the affairs of Perugia and surrounding parts of the Papal State in the fifteenth and early sixteenth century, and which provided some notable military commanders or *condottieri*. The family is notorious for its murderous infighting, publicised in the nineteenth century by Jacob Burckhardt, but the fertility of the family and the co-operation of some households facilitated leadership of the wider oligarchy.[50] The Baglioni were most numerous in terms of households, with twenty-eight registered as separately taxable in 1511, and twenty of them with enough property to qualify for all offices. The nearest rivals were the Armanni della Staffa with twelve separate households and the Montesperelli with ten. Some of these Baglioni taxable-households lived in inter-connecting buildings, or possibly in the same building. But other branches of the clan were remote in lineage, living well away from the main political households, with signs of political or social contact not readily detectable. Great tension, conflict and murder characterised the lives of the dominant households. Braccio Baglioni murdered his cousins when they took over the town of Spello in 1460, and then effectively dominated Perugia. The leading Baglioni co-operated enough to expel the rival Oddi in 1488, but the history of their influence in the city until 1540 (when the Papacy took back full control, and razed Baglioni houses to create a great fortress), is characterised by bloody conflicts between legitimate and bastard offspring of key households.

The most gory family dispute erupted in 1500 at the end of the wedding celebrations for Astorre's marriage to Lavinia Colonna of the famous Roman clan – the Red Wedding. Poorer or bastard members of the Baglioni (led by Grifonetto and Filippo di Braccio, bastard) turned on the leading clique, killing some of them including Guido and Astorre, whose heart was cut out and symbolically bitten by Filippo. In all about 200 died before Giampaolo regained control and chased out the assassins. Later Giampaolo was to be assaulted or murderously plotted against by at least three different Baglioni challengers.

Leading Baglioni were married to members of the Oddi, Arcipreti, Della Corgna, Armanni, Baldeschi and Ranieri clans; all of whom were to provide key enemies as well as some supporters. It meant that the leading challengers who lost in the 1488–89 struggle, the Oddi, were never a totally coherent opposition; and an offshoot started to distance itself, and reclassify itself as the Oddi Novelli. Bernardino Ranieri, though married to Drufolina di Braccio Baglioni, backed the main Oddi in a conflict in 1482, but kept out of the way in 1488. He was soon back in the city, and a member of a dominant emergency council, but by 1491 had to flee when his son Costantino led an attack on the city on behalf of the Oddi. His fief at Schifanoia was sacked in revenge. In 1491 Penelope di Guido Baglioni, having remained in the city, deserted her father to join her exiled husband Giulio Cesare Armanni.

That different kinship considerations could divide families is highlighted by the following supposed conversation, reported by a very knowledgeable chronicler, between Girolamo and Agamennone Arcipreti, brothers:

AGAMENNONE: Girolamo, I would like to know from you your intention, for I wish to help the house (*casa*) of Oddi, my relatives (*parenti*).

GIROLAMO: . . . and I wish to help the Baglioni, because they are my aunts (*zeie*), and the Baglioni are closer to me than the Oddi to you.

AGAMENNONE: there is time to think and to decide within the space of an hour.[51]

The Arcipreti family was split, though there seem to have been more key players on the Oddi side, or on that of lesser Baglioni against the dominant ones.

Marriage strategies were clearly used in attempts to build alliances and reconcile differences, but with very mixed success, and with some tragedies. Braccio II Baglioni married a Donna Marsilia de Bellis, the wealthiest private landowner in the 1511 tax assessment, which might have been a valuable strategic move. However in 1534 he killed her, and her lover Annibale Baldeschi, following this with a vendetta against the Baldeschi as a whole. This hardly helped his wider campaign to dominate Perugia.

An attempt to consolidate branches of the Baglioni clan was the marriage of Atalanta di Galeotto Baglioni to Grifone di Braccio Baglioni. Unfortunately they produced a jealous or ambitious son who played a murderous part in the 1500 Red Wedding, only to be killed in the revenge assault by Giampaolo, dying in the arms of his mother whom he had chosen to see rather than flee. Atalanta went on to commission from Raphael the famous *Entombment* for the Baglioni chapel in San Francesco al Prato, Perugia [1507, Galleria Borghese, Rome]. In another marital bid for reconciliation, Atalanta's sister-in-law (Grifone's sister) Leandra had married Simone di Guido degli Oddi (d.1496/8), who was officially exiled in 1488. She ended up commissioning for the same church, but for the Oddi chapel (founded by Simone's sister Maddalena), Raphael's *Coronation of the Virgin* [*c.* 1503, the Vatican]. At least culturally there was some common cause and family co-operation through the females.[52]

Social historians can establish genealogies, and deduce that 'family' relationships were the key to political power, social advancement or business dealing; but detailed study of Perugia indicates that the family factor was only one of many in the battles for power and control. These Perugian details will also serve to illustrate a number of other general points made elsewhere in this book; about the nature of elites, the causes of violence and roles for women in a male-dominated society.

This chapter has aimed to show the wide ramifications of what it meant for an individual to be part of a 'family', to indicate some of the values attached to that social concept at the time and to give an idea of how social historians have differently approached the family. Juxtaposed with some broad generalisations, extended examples have been provided to highlight the complexity of the concept of family. The extent to which the inner family was enmeshed in a larger household was affected by economic needs of land-holding or urban businesses. The household might include many non-blood members for economic reasons, and distant blood-relatives through accidents of marriages and deaths. An extended family-household could protect vulnerable individuals. The wider kinship networks might facilitate economic and political advancement, though kinship games could readily get out of control, and obstruct progress, as the lengthy Baglioni example illustrates. Should family solidarity fail, the individual could seek support from guilds, confraternities, neighbourhood groups or un-related members of a social elite in class or order solidarity – though without guarantee that they would be tension free.

8

THE SOCIAL ELITES

Attitudes to nobility and status

The study of elites has attracted considerable scholarship in Italy. Arguably Italy had a greater range of social and ruling elites, with more fluidity between them, than in most parts of Europe.[1] They were based on power and prestige in the *contado* or in the city, or in both. As elsewhere they were affected by concepts of nobility, and increasingly so. Before differentiating between Italian elites it should help to consider the attitudes to nobility and status that complicated the groupings.

Concepts of honour, nobility and status were undoubtedly significant in the mentality of the early modern period, especially for the middling and upper ranks of society.[2] Some concepts were very varied and changing in use and meaning in the period. Most historians would probably agree that from the early sixteenth century Italians of the elites were more conscious of the concept of nobility and were keener on preserving the exclusiveness of the 'noble'.[3]

The supposed increasing concern with nobility and its associated virtues within Italy has been linked to various factors. Post-unification Italian nationalists blamed the influence of the Spanish in the peninsula from the early sixteenth century, mostly notably in the Kingdom of Naples, but with knock-on effects in other states. The alleged economic decline in terms of international trade and manufacturing reduced the merchant class or classes, and shifted investment to the land. This encouraged 'refeudalisation', whereby large portions of the *contado* were granted as feuds with jurisdictional rights to leading families, who had often been troublesome oligarchs in the larger cities. Adding an honorific title increased the prestige of such feuds. Regionalisation of the economy and the development of regional states (to the detriment of the small city states), led by a ruling elite and bureaucracy centred on a more absolutist court, encouraged the reward of courtiers with status symbols as their political functions were curtailed. For some commentators, past and present, the presupposition was that nobility dictated who should or should not be admitted into the ruling elite or class (*ceto dirigente*).

Before the sixteenth century some penalties were attached to being 'noble', especially in north-central Italy. Struggles between and within city communes had sometimes brought the expulsion of the rural-based aristocracies, dubbed *Nobili* or *Magnati*, and the confinement of executive and advisory councils to representatives of the *Popolo*. i.e. the middling classes of merchants, professionals and artisans. Subsequently some of the socially elite needed to emphasise the virtues of 'nobles', their right and duty to lead society and government, and to argue that those deemed ignoble by birth or occupation should be excluded from government.

Nobility could derive from birth or behaviour. Distinctions between noble and gentleman (*gentilhuomo*), and associated attributes, were debated. *Gentilhuomo* was not necessarily seen in the simple terms of Giovanni Botero in the early seventeenth century, as a man who had sufficient property to support himself from its revenue.[4] Nobles were not necessarily titled, or with a landed power base. Italy had urban-based families, deriving wealth from business, banking and industry, who were classified as a noble elite, but titleless. While these may be designated 'patrician', as for the elites of Venice, Genoa, Florence or Milan, the members concerned and their literary propagandists were usually intent on stressing their noble virtues, status and exclusiveness.

'Patrician' (*patrizio*) was rarely used in the period, though in Venice *patritio* and *nobele*, *patritia* and *nobiltà* were used by and about the closed group of families eligible to provide members of the Grand Council.[5] Pompeo Rocchi (*Il Gentilhuomo*, Lucca, 1568) used it as the Roman equivalent of his *gentilhuomo*, a man 'who has had in his lineage many excellent men in desirable matters'. For him patrician could cover honourable men who were not senators, i.e. not part of the current magisterial class. The theologian Giovanni Antonio Delfino (1507–61), however, equated patrician with senator. The modern usage of patrician for those Venetians eligible (through the closed Golden Book of noble families) to sit on the Grand Council, from which derived most key offices and councils, is in line with this concept. Rocchi's concept of patrician/gentleman/noble implied that virtue and wealth were part of the 'desirable'. Where patrician wealth came from worried some. In 1593 the Milan College of Lawyers (*Giureconsulti*) excluded from the patrician category those directly involved in commerce, and by 1663 appeared to rule out intermediaries:

> One must consider as patricians (*patrizi*) only those who derive their origin from an ancient (*antica*) family and one of ancient nobility; a family is considered ancient if it is over a hundred years (both of nobility and residence in Milan), and if furthermore it has abstained from trading (*mercatura*), from business (*affari*), and from sordid profits (*lucri sordidi*) of all kinds, whether exercised personally or through intermediaries; only to be admitted are those profits (*guadagni*) – according to Cicero's definition in his second Book of *De Officiis* – by which a family patrimony is formed by activities immune from any immorality.[6]

This anti-commerce attitude was not however shared by all elites as will be indicated later.

The speakers in Girolamo Muzio's well-known dialogue, *Il gentilhuomo* (first published in 1571), generally imply that wealth and virtue are necessary to maintain the noble or gentlemanly status. Muzio tried to distinguish two nobilities:

> There are two kinds of nobility (*nobiltà*), the one natural and the other civil. The first is that which comes from the perfection of nature, which is virtue (*virtù*). And the civil, that of the families called noble, for which come the magistracies and honours, which are normally distributed by princes and cities. That nobility of virtue is universal; that the virtuous man (*virtuoso*) is noble in the view of all those men who in all areas have the intellect of men. And the civil nobility is particular; such as a Venetian gentleman (*gentilhuomo*), a Neapolitan, a Florentine, or one from another city.[7]

A southern writer in the early seventeenth century, F. Imperato (in his *Discorso politico intorno al regimento delle piazze della città di Napoli*, Naples, 1604), distinguished four kinds of nobility: (1) that derived from virtue or *animo*; (2) that from the blood line; (3) *nobiltà politica o civile*; civil or political nobility which is a quality conferred by a prince, and is recognised in military, equestrian and doctoral dignities; (4) mixed nobility, mixing blood and virtue. This was part of the campaign to buttress a civil, urban-based nobility- or *ceto civile*, civil class – against the old blood nobility of the feudal territories. Other writers, like Camillo Tutini, maintained more conservatively like Dante that nobility came from virtue, but this was shown in the distinction of the family line, and in the preservation of riches – so that the family would not have to descend to unworthy activities to besmirch the family honour.[8]

The interconnection of nobility through birth origins and through virtues was confusingly debated. The humanist scholar Platina (Bartolomeo Sacchi, 1421–81) in his *De vera nobilitate* (*On True Nobility*) argued that

> Only virtue confers nobility and gives the title of nobility to descendants. Nobility . . . allied to and companion of virtue conquered by our efforts and not others', is absolutely incompatible with vice. We can pride ourselves in drawing from illustrious ancestors blood and guts not nobility; that depends solely on our own spirit (*animo*).[9]

In reality of course the closed political nobilities of Venice or Genoa, registering only certain families as eligible by nobility for high offices and councils, neither tested the next generation for virtuous behaviour (though they might exclude for criminal behaviour), nor readily admitted new families because they had shown themselves virtuous and noble – unless they had saved the Republic from major military defeat. However, in some parts of Italy individuals were seen as betraying their nobility, and so right to political and administrative high office, if they participated in lowly artisan, mechanical or manual activity, industry or merchandising.

Gentilhuomo might have more readily been associated with merchant than *nobile*. G. Politi's study of Cremona found *gentilhuomo e mercante* as a frequent phrase in the documents. In Perugia *gentilhuomo* became increasingly attached from the early sixteenth century to those representatives on the main city councils who came from the top guilds (especially the merchant and banking guilds). While increasingly some such representatives were inactive in business and trade (and simply used the guild system to get into politics and administration), others – as from the Alfani family – were both at the heart of business and part of the socio-political elite.[10]

In practice in some cities and states nobles remained active merchants without derogation of noble status, or apparent loss of social prestige. Many Alessandria nobles lived off trade in the early seventeenth century. A Venetian ambassador and member of one of the top patrician families of Venice, Tomasso Contarini, commented in 1588 that 'the wealth of the Florentines is dependent on crafts and mercantile activity: the mercantile activity of the *nobili* and the craft of the *popolo*. However, the *nobili* are not only superintendents but also with their own hands are involved in the crafts.'[11]

A mercantile republican elite could readily maintain its commercial and craft activity in a new climate of aristocratisation under a recognised princedom, but it might be harder to break into an old aristocratic system from a mercantile background. A leading merchant could reach the titled nobility; as most famously the early seventeenth century merchant Bartolomeo d'Aquino who came to dominate, as a tax farmer especially, the finances of the Kingdom of Naples. He became Prince of Caramanico. However when he wanted to marry the sister of the Count of Conversano, of ancient lineage, other old baronial families objected on the grounds of his ignoble origins. The Litta family of Milan made its fortunes in commerce and financial speculation, then in 1574 seemingly without any trouble – and with the approval of Philip II – became enrolled in the nobility as marchese di Gambolò and conte di Valle, with full access to government positions. The brothers continued to create many commercial companies and control numerous ports on the Po.[12]

Changing concepts of nobility, and the partial disparagement of commerce and industry, contributed to changing attitudes towards the land and agriculture. From the mid sixteenth century there was a proliferation of books about agriculture aimed at the noble and middle-class elites, encouraging them to invest in land and make it more productive. It was accompanied by a further idealisation of the countryside and villa life, following in particular the earlier practices and beliefs of Lorenzo de' Medici and his true friends, and then humanist Cardinals and their friends who revived the villa life of ancient Rome. Many of the villas from the sixteenth century, particularly in the Veneto owned by noble families from Venice, Verona and Vicenza, were at the centre of active farming, (as well as being locations for high culture, entertainment and airy relaxation). So noble values could lead to entrepreneurial activity in the countryside. A noble disdain for active business and commercial activity could lead to economic progressivism elsewhere, and was not entirely negative.[13]

These varied Italian attitudes to nobility both derived from the diversity of political, social and economic elites, and enabled the social co-mingling of elites with different power bases.

Varieties of social elites

The high urban density of northern and central Italy, and the past roles of the city-states, had formed urban elites of considerable power and influence, increasingly designated as noble, which had varying kinds or relationships (depending on city or territorial state) with rural or land-based elites. This section will now seek to elucidate the different kinds of elites, their power and their limitations.

It is usually too simplistic to see a straight split between landed nobility and middle class/bourgeoisie, or to view the period from the fifteenth to eighteenth centuries as a transition from a vital economy based on a fluid set of elites, largely urban based, to a refeudalised, landed aristocracy and court nobility allowing the economy to stagnate and decline; though this is how the social developments of these centuries have often been explained.

In some states the Court might be seen as indicating a social elite, if not coinciding with the political elite. In his *Il Cortegiano* (*The Book of the Courtier*, 1528) Baldesar Castiglione boosted the concept and role of the courtier and courtly values. He assumed the good courtier would be from a 'noble' family, but he saw that nobility deriving as much from virtues, military and cultural, as from birth. The book's dialogue recommends that the courtier play an astute advisory role beside a prince, but much of the advocacy is cultural enhancement, with the female courtiers (*gentildonne*) providing a civilising ambience to counteract masculine military tendencies. This book had as much a role in enhancing civility in European society away from courts as in buttressing the court itself. Some governments paid more attention to courtly values than others. Courts around the rulers of Florence, Piedmont, the Viceroys of Naples and Sicily and the Pope in the Vatican contained the powerful social and political figures of the moment, but they could come from ancient landed aristocracies, families of merchant financiers or the liberal professions. The courts also contained writers, musicians and artists of much humbler origins. Women at court had varied social origins, from famous lineage to humbler courtesan skills, but might exercise political influence directly or through roles in the marriage game. 'Courts' existed outside the political centres under princes, cardinals or republican patrician families. They constituted sectors of the social and cultural elites. The lesser courts of Neapolitan, Genoese, Venetian or Milanese patrician noble families, or of Cardinal families like the Farnese, Del Monte, Barberini or Pamphili, became part of intense political and social competition. Any court would have members of social elites defined by other terms, but an active presence in court did not necessarily confer a lasting social status. Nor was dependence on, and involvement with, Italian courts necessarily as ruinous or debilitating for Italian nobles as Norbert Elias' model, based on Louis XIV's court at Versailles, would suggest – though some rulers did try to emasculate noble families by useless routine at court.[14]

Along with the growing stress on nobility discussed above came the increased award of titles. From the sixteenth century thc Spaniards expanded the numbers of titled nobility, primarily in the Viceroyalty of Naples, Sicily and the Duchy of Milan-Lombardy; and laid down the hierarchy of titles: *duchi*, *marchesi*, *conti*, *visconti* and *baroni* (with female equivalents). The Spaniards also encouraged the recognition of untitled nobles who would have more or less exclusive access to key advisory or executive councils and magistracies. Urban elites, which had been closely linked to trade, banking, textile industries and even skilled craftwork up to the fifteenth century, tended to become aristocratised, narrower and divorced from direct commercial and industrial activity. Both officially recognised at the time, and under modern analysis, there were secondary elites, whether focused on commerce, bureaucracy or professions.

Mentalities of nobility, backed by chivalric literature, meant that many nobles or would-be nobles, pursued careers in the Italian and European-wide armies throughout our period. The courts, as in Turin, Naples, Parma, Piacenza and Florence under the Grand Dukes, fostered military virtues, created military orders and encouraged chivalric tournaments. From the sixteenth century the adventurous sons of feudal and patrician families, (including from Venice and Genoa), served well in organised armies – possibly reducing their nuisance value in the localities and cities. On return to civilian and court life they sought, and received, noble titles and sometimes feudal powers, which they would hopefully exercise with more maturity. An astute ruler inflated the titles to massage egos, but restricted the actual 'feudal' power. The danger was that with war experience, but still frustrated, noble soldiers could be a menace for central governments and local peasants.[15]

In Italy, unlike in France, duelling was not particularly a mark of the noble, soldier or civilian. Books on duelling techniques were popular in the later sixteenth century, with some stress on noble attributes, but soon it seems the skills and attitudes permeated through many levels of society, especially as many non-nobles were licensed to carry swords and guns. Many could match the noble soldier, and duelling skills and codes seem not to have marked out an elite. Serious military experience may have encouraged nobles to treat the small handgun, lavishly decorated, as the 'noble' weapon, practical and showy.[16]

Titled nobilities were helpful in designating an elite, governed by prestige and instant recognition by nomenclature. Such titles came from non-Italian royal powers of the Holy Roman Empire, France, Spain and later the Austrian Habsburg rulers; or from the Popes within Italy itself. From the mid sixteenth century smaller Italian states were adding to their titled nobilities, as in Mantua, Parma and Modena. Some but not all titles were connected with landed territorial power, and with varying degrees of jurisdictional power over towns and villages. In 1645 Giuseppe Caracciolo fictitiously sold one of his fiefs (Sasso) to his close friend and neighbour in Naples, Achille Capece Minutolo, so that the latter could have a ducal title. No jurisdictional powers changed hands.[17] Knightly Orders were fostered to designate certain people as part of a courtly elite, such as the Order of the Knights of Santo Stephano under the Grand Dukes Medici of Tuscany. Cities like Genoa and Venice had closed patrician elites, with record books of those families deemed eligible for the top government system and its councils. Though titleless from their own state, they could receive noble titles – with or without feudal territory and rights – from foreign powers, as with Genoese patricians dominating the finances of the Spanish Empire from the mid sixteenth century.

The major princely states witnessed a considerable inflation of titled families, and often untitled holders of feudal jurisdictions of some kind to dominate the countryside, most obviously publicised in the Kingdom of Naples. Under Philip II there were about 245 different surnamed feudal nobles – who had civil and criminal jurisdictional powers over their estates, towns and villages in the provinces (though they themselves might reside mainly in Naples itself). The noble titled families (extended, as opposed to individual households) increased to 446 by 1672. But untitled barons as feudal nobles with lesser estates brought the number of the feudal nobility to 937 families, meaning about 15,000 persons, or just less than 1 per cent of the population.[18] Politically the noble patrician elite in Naples and the main provincial cities belonged to the five noble *Seggi*. Six *Seggi*, five noble and one non-noble, were the key divisions for the administration of the city. Membership was passed on in the direct line of the family only, and from 1553 it was closed to new families. From 1629 to 1703 between 126 and 132 families belonged to these *Seggi*, including most of the major titled feudal nobility. There was also a *nobiltà fuori piazza*, of local nobles not admitted to the *Seggi*, plus incoming nobles from abroad and some merchants and financiers who had been allowed to buy feudal fiefs. Donati calculates that in all there were about 2500 noble household-families of all kinds (though the membership of the 'family' might vary from one active male to 50); and that they controlled 70–80 per cent of the 2,850,000 population in the mid seventeenth century. An inner core of about seventeen old and new titled noble clans, home-developed or brought in from other parts of the Empire – regularly intermarrying and reintegrating – dominated both Naples and the provinces. They included famous old names like the Caracciolo, Carafa, Pignatelli and Sanseverino, and incomers like d'Avalos, de Lannoy, Gonzaga and Piccolomini.

Lombardy saw a similar emphasis on feudal title-holders. The Spanish Kings granted 276 titles of nobility (*conti* and *marchesi*) linked to fiefs between 1554 and 1706, to which the Austrian rulers added 124 more from 1707 to 1740. These, and untitled patricians of Milan or other cities, could also secure titles from rulers elsewhere. From 1769–70 there was a complicated revision of noble titles in Lombardy; from then to 1796 the official register recorded 284 lineages with 195 different names. In Piedmont under the House of Savoy there was a rising feudal nobility with titles (*marchesi*, *conti*, *baroni*), involving about 800 families in the early seventeenth century, and 1246 in 1724. A *Camera dei Conti* in Turin recorded and vetted the entitlements as granted by the sovereign. But other cities and areas in Piedmont recognised their own local nobles as a traditional elite.

As an emblematic example of both the inflation of titles and of the social mobility in the Piedmontese elite, with international connections we have the man sent by Grand Duke Cosimo III of Tuscany as *his* plenipotentiary to Milan in 1709 to deal with the imperial representative and Prince Eugenio of Savoy (the military leader) over war taxation. He chose somebody who was dependent on the House of Savoy, but who might favour the Medici – the marchese Ercole Turinetti, of Priè, Pancalieri and Cimena. Ercole was also Count of Pertengo, Castiglione, Cordua and Ostero, baron of Bonavalle and Castereinero in Piedmont, Count and captain of Pisino in Istria, *signore* of Fridau and Rabenstein in Austria, Grandee first class in Spain, magnate in Hungary, *marchese* of the Holy Roman Empire, and Knight of the Supreme Order of the Nunziata from the Pope. His father Giorgio had been a Turin banker, and then general of finances (and so made a Count), and his grandfather a grammar teacher in Chieri. The rise to prominence was common in the Piedmontese elite, but something that the Medici would have rarely allowed within their own government. Giorgio Turinetti's marriage to Maria Violante Valperga di Rivera linked him with one of the most prestigious of noble families, and a leading court lady.[19]

The major Republics had their own patrician elites, whose nobility, without formal titles, was increasingly stressed through the period. There were closed elites, whereby certain families only were recognised as constituting an aristocracy suitable for filling the leading republican offices and councils. Once these patrician families were recorded there were procedures to allow the legitimate offspring claiming entry to be vetted and registered; and with rare exceptions the elite did not admit new families. Venice had led the way by establishing between 1297 and 1323 a hereditary closed elite of families eligible to provide members of the Grand (or Great) Council (and hence most councils and offices derived from this), who would be deemed to be nobles; a Golden Book recorded such families from 1506. Although formally a closed elite some Venetian families were (contrary to some assertions) admitted to the Grand Council list (the Donà in 1430, the Savorgnan in the early sixteenth century), before the 1646 decision to 'open' the lists more publicly. Some foreign families were also admitted as honorary members and entered in the Golden Book, including papal families and even Henri III of France in 1574, but they played no active role in the city.[20]

The elite of the Republic of Genoa closed itself and its Golden Book in 1528 (when the elites were reorganised into 28 recognised confederated clans, or *alberghi*). Lucca moved towards a similar position, though only formally declaring a closure in 1628. Brescia (1488), Vicenza (1567) and Padua (1623) also had Golden Books recording patricians eligible for offices. Closure meant declining numbers of Republican 'nobles' in contrast to the rising number of feudal and court-based nobles in princely states. Families died out, or failed to produce legitimate male offspring in the direct line. Individuals or branches were excluded by marrying women too inferior socially or by entering ignoble occupations. The politically active pool was further diminished when members of eligible families emigrated or spent long periods abroad – especially from Genoa and Lucca. Lucca in 1628 registered 211 families, but only had 88 (with about 200 male nobles) in 1787. Genoa had 289 noble families in 1621 and about 2500 noblemen (with only about 1500 in the city) to draw on for political service; only 128 families in 1797. Venice itself had about 2500 male nobles eligible for the Grand Council in the mid sixteenth century; only 1660 after the plague of 1630–31. The Golden Book was opened in 1646 to replenish the stock, and 127 new families were added till the mid eighteenth century; but attrition by mortality still operated and there were only 1090 eligible patricians in 1797. The dependent cities on the Venetian mainland all had their own patricians and 'nobles' (though not eligible to serve on the Venetian Grand council). Donati suggests that the major cities (Belluno, Bergamo, Brescia, Crema, Feltre, Padua, Treviso, Udine, Verona, Vicenza) had about 9000 male nobles in 1766, when the mainland population was about 2,250,000; but lesser towns also had individuals recognised as noble and elite for social and/or political purposes.

To be noble, under whatever definition, was not necessarily to be part of a ruling class. As E. Stumpo argued: 'One could not be patrician without having offices while one could be noble without any public role.'[21] Nobles were not necessarily persons effectively running the state; and those in the leading administrative and technical offices were not necessarily accorded noble or patrician status.

The implications and privileges of being recognised officially as noble, or belonging to a professional elite, varied across Italy; but generally they were less than in other European states. Fiscal immunities were granted for some but not all feudal estates in the Kingdom of Naples, and for noble property in Naples – where notaries also gained some concessions in the eighteenth century. There were also tax exemptions for some noble estates in Piedmont, but not simply for noble status. Piedmontese lawyers, Vicenza lawyers, notaries and doctors attached to their respective Colleges also had privileged tax treatment, but nobles in Venice or Florence did not. The judicial privileges for nobles were limited in Italy – though in practice nobles might manipulate the courts in their favour. The jurisdictional powers granted to fief holders in Italy (notably in Tuscany) were generally less than in other countries, though the areas under seigniorial justice were extended in Naples and Sicily from the sixteenth century – even if in practice barons and their *bravi* exercised brutal rough justice. Noble status of some kinds might provide the passport for office-holding (or inversely the office confer noble status), but some nobles (e.g. Genoese and Lombard territorial nobles) might be excluded from offices.[22]

If one considers which elites exercised political, social and economic power, one finds a number of variations. Fairly clear distinctions existed between elites (titled and untitled) who dominated in and around central government (as for Naples, Rome or Venice), and a feudal elite entrenched in more remote provincial areas of the Kingdom of Naples, the Papal State and the Veneto. But in most cases power and influence was spread through various elites. As the power of certain patrician elites diminished, families were mollified by titles, and some semblance of power in feuds.

The political art of rulers was to balance elites, to boost the semblance of power, but create a small loyal power elite. The previously mentioned inflation of feudal titles in Piedmont enhanced the prestige of both the old aristocracy and rising bureaucrats and military officers, but did not mean much alienation of power from the House of Savoy. The amount of land and population under feudal control did not increase. Instead jurisdictions were subdivided between vassals, and the incomes for each title-holder remained limited. Real power and income (as opposed to impressive titles) continued with the elite members who remained close to the court, with the urban bureaucracies and military careerists. The old citizen patriciate in Turin had had to transform itself into a court nobility, with many noble and feudal titles. Deprived of serious power at the centre, it was given a little power in the localities. Emanuele Filiberto after returning to the Piedmontese part of his inheritance in 1560 established a new elite, focused on the Turin Senate, derived from legal expertise – a *borghesia del diritto*, or legal bourgeoisie. This then ran the financial-military complex that was at the heart of the new state. To supplement local talent he and his successors brought in foreigners, like the Genoese financier Negron di Negro and the urban planner Ascanio Vitozzi. While some key contributors came from the old nobility, like the Valperga, new bourgeois families like the Carrone, Claretti and Pasero headed the bureaucratic elite. While some moved up to the nobility by the eighteenth century, new middle range families came in from the bottom, providing a degree of social mobility not normally found in Tuscany, the provincial cities of the Papal State or Lombardy. However the House of Savoy controlled the Piedmontese provinces by appointing military commanders from the old noble families as Governors. The Piedmontese bureaucratic elite (unlike the Tuscan) had limited access to land and alternative incomes, so loyalty to the state was encouraged.[23]

Florence-Tuscany and the Papal State had their noble and patrician elites, which evolved differently. In the fifteenth century the Tuscan city states, and many cities in the Papal State were decidedly republican, and excluded (certainly for political purposes) feudal, land-based nobles or *magnati*. Of course in practice recognised elite patrician families (like the Medici, Strozzi and Rucellai of Florence, the Baglioni or Oddi of Perugia), dominated urban politics, and had land-based wealth, as well as banking or commercial sources. But even the Medici insisted on their 'republican' citizen status and credentials. However, through the sixteenth century and beyond nobility became more acceptable and more emphasised. Honorifics were added, then formal feudal titles and fiefs, or membership of chivalric Orders. The Medici encouraged this when they became Dukes after 1530 (especially with Cosimo I). Similarly the Papacy practised social ennoblement by feudal compensation with small towns and villages, while it eroded patrician political power in key cities like Bologna, Perugia, Orvieto or Viterbo. Tuscany had no formal nobility until 1750. Essentially the elites (informally recognised) emerged from securing regular service of family members on key committees and councils – and thereby securing renomination, election, co-option, etc. In the fifteenth century Florence probably had an inner elite of 150 families providing the key committee and council memberships, but with a wider pool of 1000 families. By the later seventeenth century about 385 families were recognised as the political and social elite, worthy of being called noble, with or without titles. The surviving families among those were essentially the ones entered in the Golden Book of 1750, when they were officials and courtiers of the Grand Duke, feudal lords in Tuscany, or Knights of St Stephen. Each city of Tuscany from Siena to Borgo San Sepolcro, Pisa to Prato, Pistoia to Pescia, had its own locally recognised government-service based aristocracy or nobility, ready to keep out the unworthy and ignoble.

When the Medici after 1537 consolidated a dynasty as Dukes of Tuscany, and Cosimo I developed a territorial state that some have seen as close to 'absolutism', the nature of the ruling class changed. Cosimo initially developed a court nobility to run a new governmental system, and to counter-balance the power and influence of the old patrician families. The court nobility included many people who had been part of the patrician elites of other cities in Tuscany, which helped compensate for a loss of some local power. But the old Florentine patricians (like the Alberti or Guicciardini) soon adapted to the new court group, joined the Order of St Stephen, or ran the new bureaucracy. The old patricians provided a high profile bureaucracy, using it to defend their interests, to maintain their commercial and banking interests and survive the economic crises of the seventeenth century. Only with the Lorraine-Habsburg rulers of the eighteenth century was the bureaucracy handed over to new middling classes.

The Medici Ducal court set new standards and concepts of nobility, so the patricians and aspiring citizens adapted. From the 1560s families increasingly sought to have their clan recognised as noble, and they adopted the noble style. Gino Ginori might still stalwartly call himself *cittadino fiorentino* when he married in 1583; but his son was designated *nobile fiorentino* in his marriage document in 1618.[24] The number of urban patricians who became feudal fiefholders rose considerably from the early seventeenth century; for example Lorenzo Guicciardini bought the marquisate of Montegiovi in 1639, Vincenzo Salviati that of Montieri, south of Siena, in 1621. But this feudalisation of Tuscany was on a much smaller scale than in Lombardy or Piedmont; the territories involved were often minor, and the administrative powers devolved to the holders by the Grand Dukes limited. The prime importance was for the urban patricians to look and sound noble-like and be attractive as courtiers; then they would secure the significantly powerful positions within the city and protect their overall financial interests.

The Papal State combined the urban-based patrician systems, evolving from 'republican' council service to untitled nobility as found in the Venetian Republic or Grand Duchy of Tuscany, with a feudal baronage like the Neapolitan. The former predominated in the large urban areas of Bologna, Perugia and Ancona, but also in lesser towns or cities of the Marches. From the mid or later sixteenth century many were effectively closed elites, recognising traditionally serving families, and rarely allowing new entrants. Bologna had a patrician elite of about 300 families from the later sixteenth century, Perugia about 50. In other parts of the Papal State, especially in Lazio, the feudal aristocracy ruled; the old medieval families like the Caetani, Colonna, Orsini or Savelli survived, though sometimes having to give way to feudal families established by papal relatives, notably the Farnese, Borghese, Barberini and Pamphili. Many of these families also had a social, political and cultural base in Rome, overlapping with, and competing with, other elites (drawn from all over Italy, and sometimes from the rest of Catholic Europe like the Borgias or Altemps) based on the Vatican.[25]

For Rome the composition and operation of the social and political elites was affected by the quick succession of Popes in comparison with secular princes, which meant a more rapid turnover of personnel at the centre. The palaces of the old and new families provided social, cultural and patronage leadership across Rome as small courts, linked to or rivalling the Vatican itself. Besides the famous named families above, many others provided legal, administrative and diplomatic officials for the Papacy, like the Spada and Santacroce in the seventeenth century. All these provided network systems that brought people from different levels of society and geographical areas to pursue careers in the church, secular administration or the arts and sciences. Then many pathways led to a more settled place in the Roman elites. While the key roles were played by male celibates, it is becoming clearer that elite women were very important in Roman society and politics. Leaving aside the odd concubine, the leading clerics brought in mothers, sisters, nieces and cousins who became part of marital policies and networking, as with other elites. These women also were valued in the seventeenth and early eighteenth century at least as power brokers, unofficial diplomats and arbitrators. The Roman elites had the most diverse and fluid clientele system dependent on them.[26]

The elites based in some way on noble status, whatever their derivations, were formally recognised in several ways, including through vetting committees or councils, followed by entry into registers and Golden Books. Very useful for recognition were the knightly Orders, all of which had procedures for investigating the background, birth and behaviour of candidates. This further encouraged a mania for compiling family genealogies, often imaginatively. The most notable Order was that of the Knights of Malta, with elaborate and supposedly thorough investigative procedures. Recognition by this international organisation was likely to ensure social acceptance internationally, and facilitate entry into court and top administrative circles in the home state. Second in prestige to this Order in Italy, though localised, was the Order of St Stephen, created by Duke Cosimo I of Tuscany in 1562, based in Pisa. It was designed to create a noble elite based on the court, to enhance the prestige and legitimacy of the Medici as rulers over Tuscany, and to control a fleet to defend Tuscany against the Moslem Turks. Petitioners for admission supposedly had to prove sixteen quarterings of noble lineage (with much room for definition there!). The Grand Duke could ennoble others by conferment; and others could secure entry by purchasing a *Commenda*, a benefice that would support the knights. Thus new blood entered the noble elite, and notably families from other Tuscan cities, and faithful bureaucrats and courtiers were integrated. The Order stipulated:

> [A Knight] himself, his father, mother, grandfathers and grandmothers on the paternal and maternal side should be descended from noble houses (*casate*) . . . should enjoy in the homeland (*patria*) those major dignities and grades that the most noble gentlemen are accustomed to have . . . be born of legitimate marriage, not have exercised any craft (*arte*), but lived as gentlemen . . .[27]

Italian concepts of nobility and elitism did not necessarily share the antipathy to commerce and industry found in some other parts of Europe. The Knights of Malta, representing landed aristocracy values across Europe, normally banned involvement in trade – except for nobles of Genoa, Florence, Lucca and Siena. While the Order of St Stephen ruled out personal involvement in a craft or trade, and required members to live like gentlemen, they clearly did not veto the management of banks and commercial operations, or earning money through investment in them.

The foundation in the fourteenth and fifteenth centuries of many of the families who became central to the recognised nobilities of the sixteenth century and beyond had been based on combinations of commercial and industrial activity, investment in lands and service on communal councils. The entry to political and administrative bodies had often been through membership of the trade and artisan guilds. In the major commercial cities there was a reluctance to gainsay this commercial or industrial background entirely. But while some of the old patrician families might continue in central commercial and industrial enterprises, and new families who had made money in these areas were admitted to the recognised nobility with a view to political and administrative power, the tendency was away from this foundation of the elites. Replacements into the social and political elites were more likely to come from those with land-based wealth and power, those playing a crucial role for the princely governments as tax-farmers and financial backers, those serving at court, in the bureaucratic offices of state or those rising through the learned professions of doctors and lawyers or the learned academies and universities. Some of these might constitute secondary elites, as bureaucrats, lawyers or academicians, operating below and separate from the courtly nobility; and proud of remaining both separate and powerful.

The tendency of the commercial-based elites of the fifteenth to mid sixteenth century to shift their investment and interest to landed property, rents and government loans and bonds has been recognised, especially for Venice. The leading Venetian families withdrew from long-distance trade, especially the spice trade through the eastern Mediterranean, and reinvested in land on the mainland, and in some urban property. Many of them like the Barbaro, Barbarigo, Contarini and Michiel families proved entrepreneurial, and made major improvements in land management, to the benefit of family wealth and public welfare. Others were more ruthless exploiters of common land, or passive investors, obtaining adequate but safe returns on investment. However not all of the elite withdrew from trade and commercial enterprises. Members of the Bragadin, Dolfin, Priuli and Paruta families continued to trade with places like Istanbul, Alexandria and Syria. The Foscarini remained involved in the timber and oil businesses, even if mainly using non-noble agents.[28]

The famous Florentine patrician families happily continued with commercial enterprises, with rapid movements of capital from enterprise to enterprise, and some members of the clans became involved in crafts, but without losing social prestige, political and court recognition – as the Venetian ambassador in Florence, Tomasso Contarini, reported in 1588. Major investors locally and internationally in the 1570s–1600s included members of the Capponi, Corsi, Gondi (with one branch trading from Lyon and also obtaining a French barony), Guicciardini (e.g. in Florentine goldworks) and Strozzi (especially merchandising in Sicily through Palermo). The Mercanzia records also show that at the same time a Capponi was a dyer, a Corsini a goldsmith, a Gondi a wool-shearer. Simone Corsi (1508–87) was a dominant merchant, recorded openly in 1560 as 'cittadino et mercante fiorentino'; but in 1556 he had been admitted to the Senate – the heart of the patriciate. Succeeding Corsi bought a fief (Cajazzo) in the Kingdom of Naples in 1617, and were top investors in the Florentine silk business in 1650. Corsini were heavy investors in merchant companies in Naples, Palermo and Messina in the early seventeenth century, and secured the Tuscan marquisate of Laiatico in 1644. A later Corsini, Lorenzo, was to be the last Florentine Pope, Clement XII in 1730, and his relatives became Roman nobles.[29]

Such Florentine or Tuscan positions and attitudes are partly explained by an inclination of some writers close to, or from, the leading old families (like Benedetto Varchi, Alessandro Piccolomini and Vincenzo Borghini) to stress at the same time the mercantile origins of the current patrician families, the duty to serve the state in office as an aristocracy, focused on the prince (Cosimo I) who was producing peace and quiet, to create and protect a truly free city (*città libera*) and to avoid the factionalism of the past. The land-based magnates of old had betrayed Florence and not been public spirited; a new noble elite must be. Florence was noble (like Venice in the eyes of some of the Florentine writers) because served by men made noble though a combination of service through the pen, the sword and merchant activity.[30]

Many Tuscan elite families who had based their wealth on commerce and banking, and especially the wool industry, shifted to become dominant land owners and fief holders, not only in Tuscany but also in the Kingdom of Naples and the Papal State; notably the Albizzi, Capponi, Guicciardini, Ricasoli, Riccardi, Ridolfi and Salviati. However, some noble houses, such as the Riccardi, were ready to head commercial companies through the seventeenth and eighteenth centuries. The old patrician families from Lucca (Arnolfini, Buonvisi and Burlamacchi), or Genoa (Pallavicini, Doria), were more intent on preserving the commercial, capitalist basis of their wealth and power through the darker economic days of the seventeenth and early eighteenth century, though not ignoring the attractions of land investment and feudal estates (as notably with the Doria in the Kingdom of Naples). In the case of the Salviati from Florence some branches based in Tuscany remained fairly aggressively commercial until at least the early seventeenth century; others looked to the land in Tuscany; more important branches built ecclesiastical and courtly careers in Rome, and invested in land, benefices and bonds.[31]

The old Milanese commercial patricians – from families like the Arese, Crivelli, Litta or Melzi – faced with the economic crises of the seventeenth century rapidly shifted their investments into fiefs and landed property. Already in 1593 the College of *Giureconsulti* (which essentially created an untitled urban elite, separate from the titled nobility nominated by the Spaniards), excluded from this body families seriously involved in commerce, and in 1663 made clear that even the use of intermediaries was not allowed.[32] However, the Austrian rulers reversed this attitude, and in 1713 declared that mercantile and mechanical activities should not impede noble dignity. Before then the noble Adda and Borromeo families had been successfully involved in mines; and Gian Pietro Carcano had accumulated a sizable patrimony from 'vile' merchant activities, and secured entry into the nobility.[33]

A final example of a mixture of urban elites, old and new, can come from Verona, one of the richest dependent cities of the Venetian Republic.[34] The twenty-nine elite families (spread across 201 households in 1653) comprised medieval families of distinction, fairly recent immigrants and some old residents recently arisen to prestige. The old communal families associated with the Scaligeri and Visconti rulers maintained their political and administrative domination. From the mid sixteenth century this established elite was rigid, trying to exclude new rich and resisting their attempts to use central Venetian support to infiltrate the main councils. The old families stressed their genealogies and family histories, while ambitious new families attempted the same. But some distinctions remained between the old knightly noble class (*classe*), and the governing power elite (*ceto*). The Zenobio and Ottolini families who were respectively *spezieri* (spice dealers, apothecaries and/or grocers) and goldsmiths in the sixteenth century, rose to be titled counts and huge landowners by the eighteenth. But they did not enter the main Council. On the other hand Ottolino Ottolini was a dominant figure in Veronese cultural life in the eighteenth century, with European-wide correspondence, and a magnificent library.

The Veronese old elite, the nobles, might have been conservative and restrictive in terms of political power, but they were leading figures in entrepreneurial, capitalist agriculture in the Veronese plain, especially with rice production. A branch of one of the grandest and oldest noble families, the Bevilacqua Lazise, was at the forefront of this; as was the almost equally prestigious Spolverini, which provided in *marchese* Giambattista (1695–1763) not only a leading gentleman farmer, but a noted literary, sometimes poetic, advocate of rice production and active noble involvement.

Venice had a closed elite of families eligible to serve through the Grand Council, and another severely restricted citizen elite (*cittadini originari*). But there have been doubts whether the whole of the Golden Book families constitute the patrician ruling class. There were select groups with the real power within that body; they operated a clientele network involving less active and poorer councillors. Alex Cowan has argued there were important interconnections between the *nobeli* and *cittadini*.[35]

The ruling group was much narrower than the eligible men from the Grand Council, whether 2500 in the mid sixteenth century or 1500 in the seventeenth. The decline of this pool was worrying, and hence the opening to new families in 1646 and intermittently later. Talented men were less willing to serve in top positions (such as supervising the Terraferma, or serving as ambassadors), since they cost family money, rather than earned it. An increasing number of patricians had important ecclesiastical careers, which removed them from central politics and administration. Gaetano Cozzi suggests there were 80-odd patrician ecclesiasts through the early seventeenth century, 123 in 1706, 166 in 1760.[36] The narrowing of the pool could of course be advantageous to the ambitious. About 300 men were seriously active in making decisions, administering, debating in the Senate (dealing with foreign policy and war matters) and lobbying. Within that group fifty to sixty might be the real power brokers. They would include key members of the Collegio – a committee of twenty-five headed by the Doge, and including five *savi* who had major responsibility for the Terraferma, and three judges as heads of the *Quarantia* – and the Council of Ten (Consiglio dei Dieci). Once an emergency committee, the Ten was the major power body, dealing with crime and security, but also the Mint, or the top rank of confraternities, the *Scuole Grandi*, which were central to religious, philanthropic and much cultural life in Venice. The innermost active elite included the leading ambassadors abroad, and those governing or supervising the dependent territories, notably the *podestà* and *capitano* of Padua (dealing respectively with civil and military affairs), the *rettori* of Vicenza or Verona and the *provveditore generale* of Palma (Friuli). Leading figures move back and forth between home conciliar service and service abroad as ambassadors or governors, or as military and naval commanders. The ruling elite's dominant men were versatile. Somebody like Antonio Priuli commanded a galley, was *capitano* of Padua, ambassador to France, a member of the Ten. He ended as Doge (1618–23) , as did similarly versatile figures such as Lionardo Donà (Doge 1606–12), or Francesco Erizzo (1631–46).

The concentration of power at any given moment in the hands of an inner group or groups of 50 or 300 (the *grandi* or *vecchi* (old)), left most *nobeli* seemingly out in the cold; but this can be misleading. Some were younger men who would later enter the inner groups; others were 'poor' nobles who never did. The latter were given a role, and an income (or access to less legal funds) through numerous council and office positions – sinecures or of limited activity where the *cittadini* bureaucrats did the serious work. Most councils, committees and offices changed personnel frequently, renewed every three, four, six or twelve months. Medieval Italian cities created highly complex electoral systems, sometimes with rounds of voting and balloting before a final team was formed. Venice continued to have one of the most complex – designed to prevent favouritism and corruption. But, despite the myth of an uncorrupt patrician class dedicated to public service, this was not the case; there was a considerable degree of manipulation, bribery and favouritism (though probably less than in most governmental systems), known as *broglio*.[37] Arguably this produced a degree of harmony most of the time. Lesser nobles (and related *cittadini*) were given roles, influence and income while they kept the experienced *grandi* in power. The latter established networks of patronage and favour to maintain their position.

The inner and outer Venetian elites seriously clashed at times. In 1582 excluded elements, generally younger (the so-called *Giovani*), challenged the *grandi* or *vecchi* in the Ten, and reduced its power over the Mint and foreign policy. There was another clash when Giovanni (or Zuan) Corner was elected Doge (1625–9). He used his power and influence to secure key posts in church and state for his sons and other relatives, and looked like establishing a dynastic rule – in the eyes of opponents like Renier Zen. The exclusion of poor nobles from the Ten was again resented. Zen had limited success with his 1628 confrontation, and only minor changes followed, though the Corners and their allies may have become more cautious and emollient. Zen (who was not a 'poor' noble anyway) may have overplayed his hand by too radical speech (for a pretty conservative broad elite). The old guard may also have been rescued by the operation of a clientele network down through the ranks of the poor nobles (who did not have ambitions to serve on the Ten or Collegio, or the money to serve as ambassadors, bishops or governors) and secretariat (whom Zen also denounced as part of the conspiracy). So inner and outer patrician elites intermingled and colluded, even when they were in conflict.

The *cittadini originari* (citizens by birth), have received less analysis as a secondary elite.[38] The eligible families were entered in a Silver Book, that was equally subject to scrutiny and attribution of status. This elite provided the secretariat that ran the bureaucracy behind the ever-changing noble councils. It culminated in the highly prestigious position of the Grand Chancellor. The origins, nature and development of this special kind of citizenship, and the number of persons involved, are all subject to debate and some confusion. It insisted on being native-born and was contrasted to citizenship granted to foreigners by 'privilege', or to others with mixed background. Recognition of being a *cittadino originario* meant full commercial rights, as for patricians – who might be called 'noble citizens'. The class was not apparently restricted until the end of the fifteenth century, when a standard of education and quality seems to have been applied. By 1569 with a codifying law, this kind of full citizenship was for native-born Venetians, legitimate over three generations and not involved in mechanical arts. An illegitimate son of a noble might be recognised as a *cittadino originario*. A provisional study of about 3500 people who obtained recognition as *cittadini originari* from the vetting authority, the Avogaria di Comun, between 1569 and 1700, indicates that in up to 30 per cent of applications fathers had been in the public sector (i.e. largely the bureaucracy serving the noble councils), 20 per cent came from the liberal professions, 25 per cent from commerce or artisan activities, and up to 25 per cent lived off property incomes.[39] About 20 per cent of those recognised as citizens up to 1640 were bastard nobles; then few appear.

The citizen class and its profile, whatever commercial privileges might be attached, in practice become linked to the bureaucratic elite. Andrea Zannini argues that there was a considerable turnover in this citizen class, people moving in and out, with the main objective being to secure recognition for public service posts: notably for the chancellery which had 80 to 100 officials, and for which (since 1478) the status of *cittadino originario* was essential. From at least 1517, and until 1636, this status was theoretically also required for another section of the bureaucracy, that controlled by the Quarantia Criminale, involving over 400 posts in the 1630s. In the case of the chancellery posts, citizen applicants were further subjected to tests of suitability, then to some balloting, and then training in the chancellery school. In final selection it helped to have noble support. Unlike in most office-holding systems, no substitutes were allowed. By the seventeenth century there was clearly a discrimination in favour of chancellery families as a kind of closed elite. The Quarantia-controlled offices had a different trend. In the sixteenth century they were more subject to concessions 'by grace' and political manipulation, to allow appointees to maintain the post when there was meant to be a new appointment, and to pass it on to son or nephew; or the noble councillors ignored the Quarantia's supported control of the bureaucrats, and made their own direct nominations. Then in 1636, under the financial pressures of war, the Senate moved over to the general Italian and European practice of selling the intermediate bureaucratic offices. Though the Senate had a right of veto over the results of the auction, controls weakened, the use of substitutes became common, and the qualification of being a *cittadino originario* was often ignored. Applications for recognition as a *cittadino* diminished.

So the Venetian citizen class had a golden age in the sixteenth century, but shrank to a narrower closed elite of ducal chancellery families, working closely with the patrician families in the elite above. Some of the *cittadini* families were active in the privileged Levant trade; others bought property on the mainland, and rivalled the upper elite in villa building. Alvise Garzoni commissioned from Jacopo Sansovino a considerable one at Pontecasale; Giulio Maffetti built one at Ciuran in the 1630s. The Freschi family from the fifteenth century is a choice example of those with lavish lifestyles to rival the *nobeli*, as in some spectacular wedding celebrations. For her wedding in 1506 Giustina Freschi wore crimson velvet and elaborate jewels, her father provided several banquets with dancing in a house full of extravagant furnishings, and ensured the family coat of arms was prominent, like a nobleman.[40]

Across Italy the position of the professions in relation to the elites varied. In general, intellectual prowess was ennobling, so that leading university professors were expected to socialise with educated patricians in the academies, and the already well-born were favoured for professorships in universities like Perugia by the later sixteenth century. The attitude to practising lawyers, judges and notaries was more ambiguous. The political elite of some cities like Lucca, Treviso and Venice distrusted lawyers and distanced them from power, though Venetian patricians with limited legal knowledge might head powerful legal tribunals. In Florence and Vicenza in contrast jurists and notaries were much more incorporated into the elite. In Vicenza the Colleges of Jurists and of Notaries both became part of the local elite, playing important roles in the ennobling and enclosing of the patricians and building from the later fifteenth century their own barriers against entry into their professions from humbler backgrounds.[41]

The relationship between noble-based and bureaucratic elites takes on other interesting aspects when considering the Kingdom of Naples and urban power from the later seventeenth century. Three secular elites might be differentiated, marginally interlocking, but also competing – and causing a degree of political instability and economic stagnation. First came the *ceto nobiliare*, the old feudal nobility (with some newcomers who had come in through tax farming and financial manipulation of the Spanish government); this feudal elite dominated the land and most of the economy, and was probably the most active political element. Second, a bureaucratic class (*classe burocratica*), of functionaries, tax officials and tax farmers, rich *borghesi*, was wedded to, but subordinate politically to, the baronial elite. Third, a legal and intellectual elite, *ceto civile*, emerged from the mid seventeenth century, and articulated its ideas and an identity through the Accademia Palatina. This elite group became the centre of opposition to the papacy and clerical influence, promoting the concept of an independent secular Naples. It accepted other modern ideas like Cartesian rationalism. In the later seventeenth century there was insufficient overlap between this intellectual elite and the bureaucratic one to provide a dynamic new force in politics and the economy. However, arguably by the mid eighteenth century, interaction between the intellectuals, lawyers, administrators and some enlightened baronial nobles produced an elite leadership for reform and revival.[42]

Two important cities within the Kingdom of Naples involved in international trade, Bari and Salerno, had their own interesting elites. Salerno's fair in the sixteenth century was a major commercial distribution centre for the Kingdom; Bari linked in with Puglia's agricultural production, and with the export of olive oil, surviving the crises of the seventeenth century, and maintaining strong international links with Venetians, Florentines and Milanese. Until the mid sixteenth century these cities had been the centre of seigniorial courts (the Duke of Salerno, and Isabella and Bona Sforza). The Salerno elite was then split between a governing class, and a nobility without involvement in local power; but it proceeded to witness the influx of bureaucrats and leading lawyers, of lesser provincial nobles linked to the Sanseverino clan, and foreigners. In effect Salerno was ruled by a combination of nobles, businessmen and bureaucrats. In part they treated Salerno as a stepping-stone to the ruling circles of the nearby capital of Naples. Bari, more remote from central government, witnessed a tightening of the urban, aristocratising elite, and in the seventeenth century crisis this buttressed itself by forming links with the feudal aristocracy of Puglia. It retreated from this dependence when its commercial position improved after the 1650s.[43]

The Italian social elites may have become more elitist in mentality, more aristocratic and noble through the early modern period, and made it harder for newcomers to rise into a particular elite (whether office-based, professional or landed), but they were not necessarily castes without links with the lower social orders. Many elite 'families' in practice had rich and poor branches, or individual members. One might move in court circles, another in the academies and universities, another be a travelling merchant, another a humbler craftsmen, another part of the church hierarchy; they would thus have different networks of contacts, different economic resources.

There were networks of dependence that stemmed from the elite families, with duties and obligations working up and down a hierarchy. Many elite families had large numbers of living-in servants, with their dependants. Leading princes of church and state had extensive palaces in which lived secretaries, librarians, chaplains, painters or musicians. Such palaces in Rome, Venice or Naples could have workshops and shops on the ground floor that inevitably produced close contact between high nobility and lowly craftsmen. Some of the elite structured their social and political domination on neighbourhood groupings within a city, or encouraged confraternities and guilds in which the elite met with social and economic inferiors.

Some nobles distanced themselves from ignoble money-making, but others not only invested in long-distance commerce, industry and mining, where their contacts might be remote, organised through a trusted agent of some status, but they also invested in the lowly city neighbours. When in Florence a Guicciardini invested in a man who operated a kiln, a Rucellai invested in a local haberdasher, or a Strozzi in a feed dealer just outside a city gate, one might deduce a more direct relationship and interest in the outcome of the work.[44]

This chapter has emphasised that through the period from the sixteenth century nobility and status was increasingly stressed, by the inflation of titles and honorifics, and allocations of feuds. Much of this was image-making more than a real transfer of power to a new nobility. The ennobling and refeudalisation policies were less detrimental to commercial and entrepreneurial activities than in many other European areas. Elites of old patrician families, rising new urban ones, or old and new rural landowners, interlocked and changed places. Astute political leaders took advantage of elitist competition, and the desires for status with or without power. Somewhat less prestigious elites of professionals, academics and bureaucrats worked in the shadows of the more aristocratic in some cities, but created their own identity and power. In the case of Naples this helped undermine early modern structures and attitudes in the Enlightenment.

9

SOCIAL GROUPINGS AND LOYALTIES

Individuals had associations with and loyalties to family and kin; they might have them with an elite social group disassociating itself from other sectors of society, though this is less clear-cut in Italy than in some other European areas where nobility was more clearly defined. Between these groupings and belonging to a village or city, other groupings and partial loyalties existed. Particularly in cities, physical area groupings such as districts and parishes subdivided the large environment. Areas were dominated by an elite family with patronage networking below. Institutional organisations such as guilds, confraternities, universities, colleges and religious houses could variously group people. This chapter will selectively illustrate some such groupings, showing the loyalties and tensions involved. An obvious subdivision and grouping would seem to be the parish; this, however, has many complexities and variations within Italy in the first part of our period, but becomes more standard and significant under Catholic reform policies, and will be discussed separately in Chapter 10. In the earlier period other neighbourhood organisations were sometimes more important, and will be discussed below. The creation of the ghettos for Jews is an extreme form of zonal and loyalty control within some cities, and merits specific attention. We have encountered the guilds as economic organisations, but they could have wider significance, overlapping with the lay confraternities which may have grouped, for religious and non-religious purposes, up to a third of the population, rural as well as urban.

The discussion here challenges two major theories about the early modern period; first that the Italian Renaissance feeding into our period was characterised by a growing 'individualism'of self-expression and identity, and men (if not women) broke free of corporate identities, familiar destinies and group activities. Second, it tests the idea that as cities expanded – or at least a few great cities developed – a growing degree of anonymity led to alienation in the pre-industrial city; (though the philosopher Descartes in the seventeenth century happily lauded Amsterdam for the anonymity it provided). Several modern studies demonstrate that individuals could be part of networks of loyalties and associations, structured laterally or hierarchically, with room for various forms of neighbourliness; group loyalty through common activity might still reign supreme over individualism or 'the family'.

Neighbourhood loyalties and urban spatial subdivisions

Cities, towns and larger villages might have formal subdivisions imposed by secular and/or religious authorities: the parish, the administrative district, the electoral district, the local defence and policing sub-unit. Less formal neighbourhood zones might develop over time, based on industrial trade and artisan groupings, or on a major monastery. A leading family clan might develop a neighbourhood patronage network, permeating down through the orders of society.[1]

For an individual, locating himself spatially within a city might be of considerable importance, and he might use various reference points. The Florentine painter Neri di Bicci stated in his account book (*Ricordanze*) in 1475: 'a painter, from the parish of San Friano, the district of the Drago, and the quarter of Santo Spirito'; while in his 1427 tax return Salvestro di Ciecho di Lenzo called himself: 'shoemaker, popolano and citizen of the city of Florence, and the parish of San Pier Maggiore and of the district of the Chiavi [Keys]'.[2]

Some city administrations encouraged parochial subdivisions for secular purposes within the larger organisational districts – though, confusingly, secular and ecclesiastical parish boundaries could diverge, as in Perugia and Verona. For administrative purposes cities were often subdivided into various larger districts: in the fifteenth and sixteenth centuries Rome had thirteen *rioni*; Venice six *sestieri*; Florence four *quartieri* (after 1340, being reduced from sixths); Naples twenty-nine *ottone*; Siena seventeen *contrade*; Brescia four *quadri*, Perugia five *porte*, Verona forty-seven *contrade*, and so on. Such subdivisions were variously used for allocating places on municipal councils or guild committees and for organising tax collecting or civic guards. In some cases, maybe most, such subdivisions remained administrative and book-keeping units. But in others, particularly Perugia and Siena, they had wider sociological significance.

Perugia had five districts, named after the five main gates (Porte) of the city; Porta Sant'Angelo, Porta Sole, Porta Eburnea, Porta Santa Susanna, and Porta San Pietro. These persisted as the organisational units for all purposes; major councils, emergency committees, guild boards would have so many representatives per Porta. The dependent countryside with its lesser towns and villages, the *contado*, was subdivided as similar extensions of these city Porte. The parishes (forty in 1564 for a population of probably just under 20,000) were largely fractions of these Porte, but some inconveniently cut across Porta boundaries and caused confusion. The five Porte were and have remained the key social divisions, as I found in the 1960s when my elderly neighbours in Porta San Pietro still used them as reference points. Perugia's centre, of Etruscan origin, is on the top of a high hill; the Porte districts meet there, and stretch out and down the five fingers of the city's structure to the main exit gates of the walled city. In the early modern period chroniclers gave references in their narrative to these Porte. The violent and often murderous 'Battle of the Stones' – a contest like a local football match that should have side-tracked the violent energies of youth in a politically violent city – which survived up to the later fifteenth century, was organised on the basis of Porte. The leading oligarchic families tried to establish their power bases within a Porta, as the obvious political unit, but also might organise neighbourhood parties – as for a wedding – on the same basis. The main Baglioni households were concentrated in San Pietro, the Oddi and Della Corgna in Santa Susanna, the Ranieri in P.Sole, and Arcipreti in Sant'Angelo. Other foci for loyalty, such as confraternities, or leading monasteries, cut across the Porta groupings, or subdivided them; the rival monasteries of San Pietro (Benedictine) and San Domenico (Dominican) were both within Porta San Pietro. But for Perugia the Porta unit was socially and culturally significant.[3]

The Sienese *contrade* have been seen as the key to that city's society. These seventeen *contrade* still have publicity because of the horse-race, Palio, run two or three times a year in the main square – though only ten *contrade* compete in any one race. These *contrade* have been the subject of modern sociological analysis, with some historical background research. The Palio is not a folklorist revival, but a more or less continuous activity since the 1560s or 1570s. The current seventeen *contrade* with their emblems were established by the 1540s (though there may have been others in the sixteenth century as well). The *contrade* had and have their own officials, their own property, and act as corporate bodies. Each had its own church and priest, separate from the normal parish church, its own patron saint as well as symbol (e.g. the Giraffe). Their officials organised services, processions, games as well as the horse-races, celebrations with tableaux and feasts involving the district. In the sixteenth century when the Medici Dukes gained full control over Siena they curbed some political aspects of *contrada* organisation but encouraged them to be involved in non-political activities, such as the pawn-broking system of the Monte dei Paschi (founded in 1472, it has evolved into one of Italy's major banks). When Grand Duke Peter Leopold in 1784 as part of his enlightenment programme seized a certain amount of ecclesiastical property, he handed over some to the *contrade* corporations. For Siena the *contrade* were neighbourhood associations linking all levels of society in a loyalty network.[4]

Florence had complex organisational and loyalty structures. After 1343 it had four administrative quarters, divided into four *Gonfaloni* each, with parochial divisions used for secular as well as religious purposes criss-crossing these new administrative boundaries The *Gonfaloni* districts were named after their flag emblem (The Red, Black, White or Gold Lion, The Unicorn, The Keys, The Green or Black Dragon, etc.), and were led by a standard-bearer, the *gonfaloniere*. Originally these were defence systems for the *popolani* (middling classes) against the nobles; but they came to serve wider political and social purposes. The *Gonfaloni* elected representatives to the *Signoria*, the main legislative councils, and various committees. The *gonfaloniere* and his organisation was 'to give aid, counsel and support to any member of that society, so that none should suffer any offence against his person or his property from anyone', according to a 1415 statute. During the 1494–5 crises of the Republic, with Fra Savonarola leading the anti-Medici campaigns 'the men of the *gonfaloni* gathered in the churches and held many councils' (according to the diarist Luca Landucci), and says another diarist Bartolomeo Masi, 'the company *gonfalonieri* overran the city in the name of the people and its freedom'.[5]

The districts of the Red Lion and of the Green Dragon have received detailed study.[6] The Red Lion district covered two main parishes, San Pancrazio and San Paolo, and contained the major properties of two dominant clan families, the Rucellai and the Strozzi, who provided leading opponents of the Medici. For years the district leader was the Abbot Benedetto Toschi of the Vallombrosan convent, who protected the interests of the exiles. The Medici in turn used the Golden Lion district as a neighbourhood power-base, but sought to operate within the Red Lion as well to undermine the opposition. The Green Dragon district was in a poor quarter with many cloth workers, based on the parish of San Frediano and the Carmelite church of S.Maria del Carmine. The Soderini and Brancacci families provided patrician leadership and patronage. The parish church was a focal point of loyalty, backed by two confraternities in Sant'Agnese and San Frediano. They developed strong neighbourhood loyalties, and sought to keep out 'foreigners', but the Medici made strenuous efforts to create a patronage network there and to undermine the Soderini, by joining confraternities (and becoming officials) and distributing alms. These districts served many purposes of political organisation (for manipulating elections and councils), for patronage over jobs and contracts and for helping the poor, as through local confraternities. There was a hierarchical structure of neighbourhood allegiances for the mutual benefit of leading families and those ready to serve them. That these neighbourhood districts could not be exclusive to any one clan meant that they were not entirely self-contained or harmonious. The considerable use of the *gonfaloni* during the period of Fra Savonarola's domination, 1494–8, meant that when the Medici were fully restored to power in 1531 they finally abolished the *gonfaloni*. Thereafter other ways of organising social relationships within the city, especially the parishes or confraternities, had to be devised.[7]

Some Venetian neighbourhoods have also been studied, especially those of the Nicolotti and the Arsenal (Map 5). In the West Dorsoduro area of the main lagoon area of Venice is the parish church of San Nicolò dei Mendicoli, around which in the fifteenth and sixteenth centuries there developed a fairly well-defined social community.[8] It was a community of fishermen and artisans in the parish of San Nicolò, but also including the smaller parish of Sant'Angelo Raffaele. St Nicholas is the patron saint of fishermen, and the twelfth-century church dedicated to him (with a prominent bell tower and open space, *campo*, around it) was the social centre for the Nicolotti. The community earned an officially recognised independent status, led by a top official, the Gastaldò, who was often called a Doge, and who – along with other local officials – was elected by the local community. At an annual ceremony the Doge of the Nicolotti met the Doge of Venice to show allegiance, and receive authority. In 1586 this community had a population of 3992 inhabitants in 981 families; 355 heads of households were given as fishermen. The Nicolotti gained various privileges for fishing in the local waters, both freshwater and salt; though from the later sixteenth century State officials (notably the Savii dell'acqua) sought to impose controls and restrictions on methods of fishing and on the diversion of waters. The Nicolotti comprised a fairly self-contained working-class community; they developed their own confraternities, and alms-houses for their own poor. In 1721 the Nicolotti established their Fraternity for the Poor (*Fraterna dei Poveri*) to control the distribution of assistance to the poor, and to find work for the unemployed and vagabonds. There was some outside investment in houses and shops – from the Tron and Barbarigo families of the San Polo parish, and from the major city-wide confraternities, the Scuole Grandi of San Marco and San Rocco especially; and, by the seventeenth century, from the Procurators for state-assisted housing.[9] This may be seen as some outside attempt at social control and social welfare. The neighbourhood identity of the Nicolotti was seen particularly in rivalry against the Castellani, the inhabitants of the Castello and Arsenal district of the city.

The Arsenalotti comprised a coherent neighbourhood community in the parishes of Santa Trinità, San Martino, San Biagio and San Pietro di Castello (the Cathedral parish of the Patriarch) on the extremities of the city.[10] In 1642 there were about 3200 members of the Arsenalotti families, with 855 working men over eighteen. A consolidated number of families lived and worked in the Arsenal area, with many now owning their own houses. A management enclave existed near the Arsenal (Campo dell'Arsenale) with state-provided housing large enough to include resident servants. Parish records suggest much intermarrying within the area, and within the street or *campo* area, suggesting a close-knit community. The focal point of worship and society was the chapel of the Beata Madonna, with a miracle-working image to offer good luck to those on the way to work; it was situated on the *fondamenta* of the canal giving access to the Campo dell'Arsenale. The Arsenal area was not fully self-contained, lacking a broad range of shops and non-shipbuilding crafts in the area, though a shopping street along the Rio di Castello (sixty-eight shops in 1661) provided limited goods and services, while itinerant sellers paraded the streets. Women played significant roles. They headed about 21 per cent of households, not just because they were widows having lost their men at sea. A number were of foreign origin, often prostitutes. Women worked as canvas cutters for sails, but they could be sailors and blacksmiths; and more obviously midwives, wetnurses. Plenty acted as healers and cunning-women, to the concern of the Inquisition authorities.

The Arsenalotti or Castellani gained a reputation among the rest of Venice as tough, violent and arrogant. Their community solidarity was most clearly expressed in the Battle of the Bridges; as an extension of ancient sports (like Perugia's Battle of the Stones, above) and Carnival celebrations at various stages in the year, youths of given areas had massed struggles to control particular bridges, to show off local neighbourhood prowess.[11] Some such battles were unplanned gang-fights, but major planned events could become major spectator events, with accompanying gambling and feasting. A great show was provided for Henry III of France's visit to Venice in July 1574. Often the struggles came down to a battle between the Nicolotti and Castellani; the fishermen of San Nicolò and the arsenal workers of the Castello would provide the leadership and hard core of the teams, but would absorb other youths from contiguous areas. In 1639, 30,000 people from far and near witnessed a series of battles for the Ponte dei Gesuati, a wide bridge on the Zattere, which allowed spectators to see from boats on the Giudecca Canal.

These inter-neighbourhood struggles could be violent and costly. Over forty people were killed in the 1639 series of battles, and city life could be disrupted as shops were closed and production ceased for days. But such struggles could accentuate group solidarity, and allow youthful frustrations and violence to be dissipated in partly organised and controlled circumstances, diminishing the chances of totally uncontrolled urban riot.

The neighbourhood loyalties of few cities have yet been analysed. Much depended on geographical configurations, administrative structures and the placing and relocation of powerful families. In sixteenth–seventeenth century Brescia the administrative districts did not match the five-gate spatial structure, or the locations of elite clans, who dominated more by brute force than the mutually helpful social relationships found in Florence, Genoa or Siena.[12] The neighbourhood divisions and loyalties of Rome would repay close study. Knowledge of the confraternities, guilds and hospitals of the Trastevere district (until recently a poor artisan area), suggests that this had a degree of social cohesion. The Piazza Navona was to a large extent taken over by the Pamphili family immediately on the election of Cardinal G. B. Pamphili as Pope Innocent X in 1644; dramatic celebrations with fireworks and architectural decorations were focused there, then palaces and churches were elaborated to enhance the family prestige. Both artistic and political patronage seem to have created networks of supporters in this district.[13]

The examples have shown urban neighbourhood subdivisions that were formed through a combination of geography and initially fairly arbitrary administrative arrangements, but which were fostered by political and social leaders. Neighbourhood loyalties could exist and be welcomed for purposes of political patronage, economic solidarity, charitable purposes and entertainment. The formation of these networks and loyalties were to a large extent voluntary. The next neighbourhoods to be discussed were formed under some compulsion.

The Jewish ghettos

The most obvious neighbourhood groups, confined in delimited locations in some cities, were the Jews in ghettos.[14] 'Ghetto' derives from the first official segregated area established in Venice in 1516 (Map 5). This was on a former foundry area on the edge of the Cannaregio district, and the name ghetto probably derived from a word for casting metal. Segregation of Jews from Christians in cities had been practised earlier, and was desired by many Jews to develop their own culture, and as protection against intermittent anti-Semitism. In the fifteenth century some cities like Bologna (1417) or Turin (1425) banned cohabitation of Jews and Christians. Major Jewish contributions to biblical scholarship and to medicine were appreciated in cultural circles, but some Franciscans led attacks on the supposed excessive profiteering of Jewish moneylenders, and established from 1462 onwards Christian pawnbroking institutions – Monte di Pietà – to replace them. Franciscan propaganda was often misleading, as Jews had in fact been invited to cities like Verona and Brescia to be cheaper lenders than usurious Christians. However, the creation of the Monti made it easier for preachers, governments or local communities to ban Jewish moneylenders or expel all Jews. The creation of the Venetian *Ghetto Nuovo* (New Ghetto) followed debates on whether Jews should be expelled from the city. The Republic decided not to have a Monte in Venice itself, but use Jewish lenders, under strict government control. All Jews were, however, required to move to a restricted residential area, from where they could do business and trade, and be locked in at night. This New Ghetto held about 700 persons. It established precedents for similar *ghetti* in Italy and further afield. The policy for Catholic Europe of either banning Jews altogether (as Iberia had done from the late fifteenth century), or having them firmly segregated, was reinforced by Pope Paul IV's Bull *Cum nimis absurdum* of 1556, which was coupled with a policy of banning Jews from the Papal State, except for ghetto areas created in Rome (1556) and then Ancona. Other Italian states followed suit, with ghettos created in places like Florence (1570), Siena (1571), Verona (1599), and a range in the next century – Bologna, Cremona, Ferrara, Modena, Padua, Reggio and Rovigo. Some small Jewish communities survived, or re-created themselves in the later sixteenth century onwards, without a formal Ghetto being created; this could happen quietly and precariously even in the Papal State (with Perugia), or more obviously across the Veneto, such as San Daniele, San Vito, Portogruaro and Spilimbergo. The counts of Spilimbergo allowed the Jews there to do everything the Christian merchants and artisans could.[15]

The *ghetti* gave advantages and disadvantages on both sides. They varied considerably in size and conditions. A recognised area gave the Jews more security than being caught between changing policies of bans and readmission, and they could retain their own religious practices and culture. It might protect them from the kind of anti-Semitic accusations of ritual murder of children that led to the cruel persecution in Trent in 1475, when the body of a two-year old was discovered in the cellar of a Jewish house on Easter Sunday, and attempts to have baby Martyr Simon canonised.[16] Governments that recognised the economic merits of Jews as traders, bankers and moneylenders but also as doctors and scholars could more readily defend their presence against religious zealots who wanted to exclude Jews from Europe. Under Catholic Reform pressures, Jews were at times subject to harassment or temptation to convert. Those in the Roman Ghetto were forced to hear conversion sermons, and males might be subject to ignominious nude racing competitions. Some confraternities attempted conversions, and offered money to poor Jews who succumbed. Venetian Inquisition records show Jews converting a number of times to secure funds (returning to the Ghetto when fortunes improved); they were seldom severely punished. The states or cities most favourable to the Jews in the sixteenth century and beyond were the Venetian Republic, Piedmont under Emanuele Filiberto from the 1560s, Ferrara and Modena under the D'Este and later Livorno under the Medici. They gathered in Jews expelled from Spain (1492), Portugal (1498), some coming via the Netherlands, others from parts of German, from the Levant, from other Italian states (as when Ferrara rescued Jews from Ancona at the height of Pius V's papal threats). The resulting communities became very diverse and vital. Under Medici encouragement, Livorno's Sephardic population grew from 134 in 1601 to 1250 in 1645, while under the Austrian Peter Leopold the community expanded to 4327 in 1784.

As a result of tolerated immigrations the Venetian ghetto complex was expanded with the addition of the Ghetto Vecchio (1541), and the Ghetto Novissimo (1633). It reached a peak of about 5000 inhabitants then but soon declined. Restricted by canals, the housing became dense and high rise, as can be seen by the modern visitor. Within this Ghetto considerable self-government was granted, and the community could develop a number of synagogues, schools and Jewish confraternities. Once the gates were closed at night a sense of freedom might prevail, to be celebrated with lively entertainment, including dancing frowned on by some rabbis (as also in Mantua). There was a mix of rich and poor throughout its existence (while Rome had few rich Jews). Numerous shops and warehouses served the Jewish residents, and non-Jews who could enter by day to trade or borrow. Jews could similarly exit to the rest of Venice. They were allowed storehouses elsewhere in Venice, and Jewish second-hand dealers competed or co-operated with the Christian *arte degli strazzaruoli*, and could serve Senators and foreign ambassadors as well as the poor. Major Jewish merchants traded with the Ottoman Empire, notably through Salonica and Alexandria, to the benefit of the Republic, as the Muslim world tolerated Jews more than Christians.

This links with serious issues of identity and loyalty. Ghettos were meant for Jews, who had never been baptised. Once baptised, the convert to Christianity (*converso*) was meant to live as a Christian with Christians, and was liable to Inquisition jurisdiction if he or she deviated. Many Jews, especially in Iberia had been forcibly converted (and so could stay), but many had later fled. If they reached Venice (and later Tuscany and Livorno), Venetian authorities might not hold the forcible conversion against the *converso*, and gave the choice of reverting to a Jewish life (and so live in the Ghetto), or re-affirming a Christian identity. This created a fluid and complex situation that presented both the Inquisition and state officials with many problems. Peripatetic families divided, some reverting to Judaism, others saying they were true Christian converts, as in the case of Gaspare Ribeiro and his children in a famous case in 1580. Gaspare himself moved between the two religions, whether because of genuine uncertainty, fear or dissimulation. A number of merchants like him found it convenient to be Christian in Italy, and Jewish in places like Salonica (Thessaloniki). A Jewish leader, Chaim Baruch, consul to the Levantine Jews, likened such men to a ship with two rudders, sailing with different winds according to convenience.[17] He was no happier with such behaviour than were the Inquisitors. But the Venetian system, as to some extent the Ferrara, Modena and Livorno ones, allowed some fluidity of body and soul between the Christian and Jewish environments. Inquisition records testify to social interactions, active sex lives, love-magic practices and sorcery across the religious and physical divides, despite the creation of *ghetti* being designed to prevent this. For example in 1587 Valeria Brugnaleschi (widow of a physician) and her daughter Splandiana Mariano were investigated for using sorcerous incantations, diabolic objects and a flask of holy water to conjure devils, seeking to find stolen property, and using semen in love concoctions. Some of their activities took place with Jews in and outside the Ghetto. Valeria had lived in the Ghetto for two years, where she taught Jewish girls reading and writing. According to a witness (a 'good Christian'), she believed 'the faith of the Jews is better than ours and that it pleases her more because they observe it better'. The two women were sentenced to be whipped publicly, pilloried and exiled for five years 'for love magic, witchcraft and bean-casting', as a placard was to declare – not for consorting with Jews.[18] The Venetian Ghetto was a neighbourhood community (or group of communities when separate synagogues were fully established), but in practice Jews and Christians could cross physical and social borders.

Guilds and confraternities

Guilds and confraternities provided institutions that offered social cohesion and networking opportunities, which could generate loyalty as well as serving their main economic and religious purposes, respectively. The economic roles of guilds have been discussed in Chapter 5. More can be said here about their wider social aspects, and their relationship with lay confraternities.[19] In some examples the organisation grouped together a narrow band of people within a social hierarchy, while others attempted to unite rich and poor, or high, middle and lower orders.

In Perugia the top-ranking guilds lost their primary economic functions, and became elite social and political networking groups between the sixteenth and eighteenth centuries. Through the sixteenth century, and especially after the Papacy reasserted control over the city in 1540, the aristocratising top families concentrated more and more on the Mercanzia and Cambio guilds, and clearly their membership had nothing to do with relevant commerce and banking activity, and everything to do with council electoral politics – even if the papal Governor had the real power. These top guilds in Perugia, as elsewhere, were inclined to become exclusive political-social clubs for those whose power base was landed and/or professional (in law and the University), to the detriment of local economic activity. Eventually membership of the Mercanzia and Cambio guilds in Perugia was confined to those deemed noble. It was this uneconomic social elitism, as in places like Milan, that partly explains the attack on the guilds by eighteenth-century enlightened writers.[20]

Most Italian guilds or trade and craft corporations had many functions. Besides the economic roles and the regulation of working conditions, and the connections with wider urban politics and administration alluded to above, the guilds could be a centre of religious activity, entertainment and social welfare for members and their families. As a result they could be important social and loyalty groups outside the strict working world. Most guilds had an oratory (as Perugia's Cambio had), or a chapel within a church that was special to them. They would at least have an annual patronal feast-day celebration of solemn mass, which might involve all members parading with lighted candles (as for the barbers of Naples). In Milan the ribbon-makers (*bindellari*) had a weekly Mass; the Cremona smiths a monthly one. Guilds might be responsible for maintaining a chapel within the Cathedral, a parish or other church, providing a priest and ensuring its decent upkeep. Such connections should have led to more regular religious commitments by guildsmen and the fostering of community loyalties – as apparently with most guilds in Florence, Verona, Milan, Turin and Ferrara. In Florence the famous Baptistry was entrusted to the Calimala wool-merchants' guild by 1592. In Rome the barbers in 1508 commissioned Raphael to design a new church of Sant'Eligio. In Catanzaro the Silk Guild from 1401 had a chapel in the Cathedral, and in 1569 funded a new chapel in San Domenico. The Venetian mercers through their own guild-confraternity and through the Scuola di San Teodoro, which they dominated, came to control the major feast of San Tedoro (9 November) and major public celebrations.[21]

In Rome the economic guild was based on a church or chapel where meetings could take place; this seems to be mandatory by the eighteenth century. In a dispute (1785–6) between the wool-workers (*Lanari*, or *Giovani Lavoranti* of the Arte Della Lana) and the Merchants and Masters (*Padroni*) of the Collegio di Mercanti Lanari, the former challenged the right of the latter to make or reform statutes for the former; the Masters had no chapel of their own. The Cardinal Protector agreed:

> The first requirement needed to obtain the approval of any statute whatsoever is to have a Church, Oratory, or at least Chapel where it is possible to meet collegially, and without such a requisite one cannot concede to anyone the faculty to form or reform statutes.[22]

The wool-workers were based on the chapel of San Biagio in the parish church of Santa Lucia de' Ginnasi; they alone maintained it and recognised the acts of visitation from the Cardinal. The Masters had no role in this, therefore they were not a proper corporation, and could not issue a statute banning the wool-workers from working in their houses. The archival documentation indicates that for the wool-workers the chapel was both their legal basis, and the foundation of their loyalty; they wanted to preserve it against interference from the bosses.

Guild group activity might be public, in city processions, especially for Corpus Christi. Such occasions could become unseemly in that rival guilds (and confraternities) vied with each for precedence, and for display, in the interests of communal social prestige, and possibly sometimes economic advertising. Special public celebrations brought out the different guilds in group presentations, such as the celebrations in Venice of the naval victory of Lepanto against the Turks in 1571, the visit of French King Henri III in 1574 or the Roman thanksgiving processions at the end of the plague in 1632.

Public Roman guild celebrations may not have been that common. The 1632 events partly connected with the fact that during the plague, as at other times, the guilds had been required to provide groups of guards to protect the city from plague-bearing outsiders. Roman guilds were sometimes involved in organising Carnival celebrations. In Florence public group activity by guilds tended to be discouraged, following the labour unrest of the Ciompi revolts back in the fourteenth century.

Guilds were involved in various aspects of social welfare; such as assisting with the payment for funerals in fifteenth-century Florence, and providing dowries for guildsmen's daughters, or relief for widows. The possibilities of such relief could encourage guild loyalties and commitment that would go beyond pure economic necessity. Such welfare activity overlapped with that of the confraternities.

Lay confraternities were and are associations of people who come together to promote their religious life in common, according to certain agreed rules.[23] Confraternities still exist in small numbers, but they played their main role in religious-social life from the thirteenth to the eighteenth centuries. Though often primarily concerned with preparing for the afterlife, and praying for souls, the confraternities could be fully involved in the social, political, charitable and cultural life of communities. Though predominantly for lay men, they could also involve clergy, women and children – as members or as recipients of philanthropy.

Lay confraternities and guilds developed side by side from the fourteenth century in urban communities, and inevitably some overlap and confusion existed between them. Some trade guilds formed confraternities as more or less separate organisations instead of just having religious and welfare activities within the trading/artisan corporation. This was particularly so in Venice, where most trade guilds (*arti*) created separate religious fraternities, usually called *scuole*. The two units might share leading officials. The *scuola* was for the religious and social welfare aspects of community life. A guild member might be compelled to enrol in the related *scuola*, unless he or she was a member of another *scuola dell'arte*, guild-linked *scuola*. Alternatively a group of people in a particular trade or craft might start a confraternity, and then try to turn it into an economic guild. In Venice immigrant Germans working as assistants to master-bakers were allowed to start a *scuola* in 1422 'for the sole purposes of looking after their souls and of correcting the errors to which they are prone';[24] but by 1543 the master-bakers were complaining that these assistants were trying to use this *scuola* as a threat to the economic and religious organisations of the master-bakers. In Florence the wool-trimmers (*cimatori*) created a religious confraternity in 1494, which by 1508 was allegedly conspiring to fix prices and organise strikes. Similarly in late sixteenth-century Naples artisan-based confraternities were accused of using their corporate solidarity to ensure fixed minimum wages.

Membership of religious brotherhoods or confraternities, with or without economic or political overtones, could constitute one of the most meaningful social relationships of medieval and early modern Italian society. Confraternities became more widespread, more diverse in their activities and more socially significant from the late fifteenth century in Italy. They are important for the social historian for the way they grouped people in society, and affected social conditions and behaviour – whether in the narrow religious context, or in social welfare schemes.

Lay confraternities are documented from the early Christian centuries, but fully developed from the thirteenth century under the impact of new Marian cults, flagellant movements, hospital expansion and the diversification of some trade guilds. Further variety and growth came with Catholic Reform in the later fifteenth and early sixteenth centuries, in promoting more outward-looking philanthropy, new Marian cults, more respectful adoration of the Host and more frequent communion for the laity. Medieval fraternities had offered some welfare help to members of the fraternity, and close relatives. From the late fifteenth century some increasingly assisted poorer members of society outside the fraternity. After precedents from fraternities in Brescia and Ferrara the Companies of Divine Love (initiated by Ettore Vernazza in Genoa in 1497) notably spread new charitable and devotional ideas, and fostered hospital practice. The effects were felt both within the confraternity movements, and on the new Religious Orders like the Oratorians and Theatines.[25] The promotion of the Rosary by the Dominicans led to the growth of confraternities dedicated to it, initially in Germany, then France and Italy (from Florence's San Marco Rosary confraternity of 1481, then Venice's San Domenico in Castello in particular). The Rosary confraternities became especially important for the spiritual life and social roles of women.[26]

The reforming Catholic hierarchy's attitudes to confraternities were ambivalent; while bishop Giberti of Verona early on valued new Corpus Christi fraternities for the veneration of the Host, other clergy were suspicious of lay confraternities because they were dominated by laymen and allowed laymen to preach, or discuss the Bible and doctrine, because they were often very secretive or because they had unseemly feasts. The suspicions encouraged the Council of Trent to rule in 1563 that confraternities, hospitals and similar pious places should be subject to episcopal control, especially through the scrutiny of their statutes and accounts. Subsequently fraternities came under fuller clerical supervision, not without lay protests. Following the lead of archbishop Carlo Borromeo of Milan, reforming bishops tended to encourage Rosary, Sacrament and Christian Doctrine confraternities based on the parish church and under the priest's supervision, and to discourage societies that existed independently in their own oratories. The new and reformed Orders, especially the Capuchins and Jesuits, fostered more as part of their mission campaigns in city slums or remote rural hills. The Jesuits particularly provided a whole network of religious-social relationships across Italy and other parts of Europe, in bids to combat heresy.[27]

By *c.*1600 fraternities had a considerable variety of devotional and philanthropic preoccupations. So people were grouped together for diverse purposes, and could satisfy many different needs by being members. The welfare that many fraternities offered provided incentives for association, as co-operative providers of help as well as potential beneficiaries in times of trouble. Socially it interconnected rich and poor, for mutual benefit of soul and body.

Membership in any individual fraternity varied from a handful to many thousands. Naples' company Dei Bianchi had about 6000 in 1563. This organisation ran a range of welfare activities, in which active members probably operated in more manageable sub-groups. The top group of Venetian fraternities, the Scuole Grande, officially had 500 to 600 members; the Perugian Name of God (*Nome di Dio*) confraternity had at least 824 male and female members in 1613. At the other end of the scale, village Rosary or Holy Sacrament societies might only have half-a-dozen members. The more usual membership was probably between 20 and 50.

A city might have over a hundred confraternities. Venice had 120 in the early sixteenth century, 387 in the eighteenth; Genoa had at least 134 operating between 1480 and 1582, though some came and went rapidly. Rome in 1601, according to Camillo Fanucci's 1601 guide to Rome's religious and charitable institutions, had 49 confraternities based on guilds or national groups of foreigners in the city, 52 'universal' fraternities, and 11 confraternities based on or running hospitals.[28] Perugia city, with about 19,000 people, had over 40 confraternities in the early seventeenth century; and there were 139 confraternities in eighty-eight smaller towns and villages in the rest of the diocese. In the south, Lecce and surrounding Puglia were prolific in confraternities by the seventeenth century; a local historian cited 27 in 1634. Terra d'Otranto (which included Lecce) in the eighteenth century saw the fullest expansion of confraternities; when a third or more of the Otrantine communities had a Sacrament fraternity, a third had a Rosary one, and 29 per cent one dedicated to the Immaculate Conception (*Immacolata*). Research on Puglia and other southern provinces is revealing ever more confraternities being founded in more rural areas through to the late eighteenth century, and decorating chapels, though evidence on what else they did is limited. Many of these remoter ones appear to have been parish-based devotional confraternities, but some ran hospitals or hospices, had cheap loan systems or provided dowries for poor girls. The diocese of Benevento had 94 confraternities in 1590 (population about 136,000), and 352 in 1737 (population 124,924).[29]

In the later part of our period, when new catholic-reform fraternities were added to older medieval institutions that were reinvigorated, up to a third of families might have some contact with a confraternity. In some areas like Milan, Genoa and Bologna the proportion was probably much higher. Thus we are dealing with potentially very significant social groupings.

Confraternities were primarily male societies. Some were exclusively male or, occasionally, female (often dedicated to the Rosary or Saints Ursula (Orsola) and Anne); others were sexually mixed, though men dominated the offices that organised them. This factor helps explain our difficulties in detecting female participation, which has been under-recorded, (Mackenney 1997). Male exclusiveness was based on a number of attitudes besides prevalent views about female inferiority, and the need to keep women tied to the home. The economic-guild origins of some societies usually dictated male membership. Many fraternities were flagellant in theory, and often in regular practice up to the early fifteenth century and again from the later sixteenth, which discouraged female participation. Flagellation involved the whipping of one's own bared back, or that of a another brother, as penitential mortification in memory of Christ's whippings. This was a popular devotion in central Italy in the fourteenth century, and one major type of confraternity had incorporated it into its rituals. The scene could be bloody especially when whips with sharp metal barbs were used; though some fraternities instead used silken cords symbolically. Such a group session was not usually deemed suitable for women – as participants or witnesses. However some flagellant confraternities did have women members, some with their own communal flagellation sessions. Women were often seen as gossips, as a Corpus Domini fraternity in San Frediano, Florence, made clear in its 1573 statutes,[30] so their presence was discouraged in societies that might have political overtones, be suspect to some outside lay or clerical authorities, or which mixed socially diverse men who would not want such close co-operation to be known in the public domain. Some confraternities should obviously be seen as male-bonding societies, as in Florence, which could lead to charges that they promoted homosexual relationships.

However, over our period female participation in confraternities, whether along-side men or in separate institutions, received some encouragement. As a Sacrament fraternity at Ponte a Greve near Florence argued in 1564, God created woman to help man, so the fraternity should now admit women and allow them to share all the benefits alongside men, though not be office-holders. The Barnabite Order and other reformers, especially in Rome and Lombardy, encouraged family membership and sharing in the same confraternities. The creation of Christian Doctrine confraternities to help teach in Sunday schools encouraged the involvement of women, especially when the schools set out to teach girls as well as boys. The development of women-only sororities in the sixteenth century was probably accelerated by the negative factor of male exclusiveness in existing fraternities, and by a more positive feminist movement to enhance women's spiritual well-being. The growth of the Rosary cult, which had a particular appeal to women, led to many Rosary sororities, which gave women a group loyalty outside the home and immediate family. Some expressed themselves by commissioning their own chapels and paintings to their taste; the sorority of Our Lady in Sant'Antonio Abate, Perugia, commissioned a Nativity from Lo Spagno, and other panels from Mariano di Ser Austerio (1510–19).[31]

For the individual man or woman, confraternity activity might be occasional and limited, or very full: involving regular communion, singing lauds and offices of the Virgin, flagellation, public processions, annual general meetings, business meetings of officials to allocate alms and dowries, or helping equip and decorate the parish church. It is very difficult to establish the degree of active membership, the numbers for whom being part of a fraternity was a major experience and commitment – as opposed to those who enrolled to ensure a decent burial and subsequent regular prayers for their soul, or as an insurance policy for hard times when alms, cheap or free housing, marriage dowries might be provided. Ronald Weissman's studies of some Florentine fraternities, especially San Paolo in the fifteenth century, suggests that active/passive involvement varied considerably thorough a life-span. My own investigations of attendance or voting show some societies with high turn-out of enrolled members for meetings, others where real activity was confined to office-holders. In some confraternities, notably in Bologna, Modena and Milan, there was a formal distinction between an inner active elite (*stretta*), and a wider (*larga*), more irregular membership. On the evidence of Perugian fraternities like San Martino and San Girolamo, it would seem that it was difficult to get a member dismissed for irregular participation – or even for immoral and troublesome behaviour. Brothers were clearly unhappy to break a relationship once a loyal commitment to the group had been made; as for example with a Francesco di Fabri, brother of Bologna's Santa Maria della Vita, who was reinstated – on the promise of better behaviour – after being suspended for disobedience over speaking improperly at meetings, not carrying a torch at a woman's funeral when ordered, threatening the Prior and so forth.[32]

Group solidarity through the confraternity was ideally designed to end disharmony and enmity, encourage humility, foster brotherhood and reduce social inequalities. Much might be achieved through a fraternal Holy Communion, as the Florentine humanist Cristoforo Landino stressed to the Magi company in 1476; it was a symbolic act of fraternity that 'purged . . . the old condition of malice and iniquity' and made brothers 'new unleavened dough of sincerity and purity'. In the same year another lay preacher, Giovanni Nesi, in his Holy Thursday sermon to the Florentine Nativity fraternity, on Humility, urged them to:

> become one group in which the rich man befriends the poor man, the great befriends the lowly, the powerful befriends the powerless, and the lord befriends his servant. And having put aside honours and human dignities, let each (as is the precept of the Lord) not love his neighbour less than he loves himself . . . Pythagoras certainly understood this when he said that friendship is one composed of many, and knowing that all things are held in common among friends.[33]

Group activity was for many probably fullest and most meaningful when brothers foregathered for a group penitential flagellation session in a darkened chapel or meeting room, and followed it with ritual cleansing, singing, Vespers or a Mass; for the annual patronal festival, involving both a general business meeting, and a feast of food and wine; for great processions – whether celebratory for a feast-day or victory in war; or for pleading for God to stop incessant rains or an epidemic. Processions could involve the donning of coloured cloaks and hoods, carrying of torches, painted banners, playing of musical instruments and singing, and might end with refreshments of food and wine. Group activity and social involvement would be enhanced if such processional celebrations involved putting on full plays or mounting illustrative tableaux on carts pulled through the streets. The Florentine fraternity, the Company of the Magi, was notable for its plays in the fifteenth century; Roman confraternities performed in the Colosseum. In the 1590s in Rieti a number of confraternities put on plays about Christ's Passion, Ascension and Resurrection, or about Saints Barbara, Biagio, George and John the Baptist.

Confraternity pilgrimage journeys took members to a distant holy place – to the well-known Virgin's House in Loreto or Santa Maria degli Angeli below Assisi, to a more locally advertised sanctuary like the Madonna della Ghiara at Reggio Emilia (after an association with a miracle there in 1596) – or particularly to Rome for the Great Jubilees or Holy Years every 25 years from 1550. These Jubilees involved hundreds of thousands of pilgrims, many of whom went as confraternity groups. The extensive surviving record of the Perugian Company of Death (*Della Morte*) pilgrimage to Rome in 1600 indicates how elaborate and significant such an enterprise could be. It involved disciplined walking from Perugia to Rome and back; with singing, lavish entertainment – food, wine and music – by other confraternities, visits to the great Roman basilicas, and a Mass in the new St Peter's (still under construction) celebrated by Pope Clement VIII.[34]

Some fraternities had no fixed location; most were based on an altar or chapel in a parish church; others had modest oratories or rooms of their own, while a few had spectacular premises – especially the top Venetian group of discipline fraternities, the *Scuole Grandi*, which made significant contributions to religious art and music. It was probably where a confraternity had its own premises that the social grouping, cohesion and loyalty was most significant. A fraternity might have a long, tortuous and emotional struggle to move from a Cathedral or parish church into its own self-contained premises, as Perugia's Sodalizio di San Martino eventually succeeded in doing in 1585.[35]

Confraternities could be agents of social cohesion, or social tension and divisiveness. Loyalty to the single confraternity produced major conflicts with rival confraternities. There could be regular disputes, even full-scale battles, for precedence in processions that would reflect social prestige and historical longevity. Such conflicts were regular in Venice, and of some concern to state authorities through the period, as the competing *scuole* tried to negotiate the narrow bridges over canals, and side alleys. Good Friday 1512 was marred by serious jostling in the large St Mark's square. In the 1620s, two communities outside Naples expressed their views about the status and division of parish boundaries by confraternity parades under suitable banners. Major disputes could fester, as in Bologna through the sixteenth century between Buon Gesú, Santa Maria della Vita (Life) and Santa Maria della Morte (Death) over the right to bury certain people or organise the funeral procession in a given order.

Some confraternities were socially exclusive – for nobles, or particular craftsmen; others deliberately mixed social ranks, rich and poor, in the interests of social harmony – or to group the most religiously committed of a parish.. Confraternities might group together members of a number of artisans from different trades and crafts, as a lower middling solidarity group; such as Santa Maria dell'Orto in the Trastevere district of Rome, which ran a notable hospital for members of thirteen local guilds – from millers, poulterers and fruiterers to local gardeners, vermicelli-sellers and river-bank traders. Jesuits sometimes encouraged social segregation; in Lecce they had five different fraternities for nobles, students, scholars, youths and artisans – and there was another fraternity for peasants not sponsored by the Jesuits. In Perugia the Jesuits divided their sponsored fraternities between nobles, artisans and *contadini*. From the sixteenth century the increased stress on noble and gentlemanly values and status encouraged the creation of some noble-only confraternities. Naples, as one might expect, took this path – as with the creation of the Venerazione del Santissimo Sacramento for noble men (under Jesuit leadership), and the Devote di Gesù for noble women (1554). In Perugia Bishop Bossio in 1565 started the Annunziata for nobles only. One should stress, however, that while the noble-exclusiveness gave social solidarity for their common worship or administrative roles, in these cases the noblemen concerned themselves charitably with outsiders; abandoned girls and converted prostitutes in Naples, poor girls needing dowries in Perugia.

Many confraternities, in contrast, sought social cohesion and class co-operation within their societies. Genoese nobles chose mixed rather than exclusive associations. Perugian records that indicate membership show that the leading fraternities in the sixteenth and seventeenth centuries mixed members of leading aristocratic families, notaries and lowly artisans. Venice's *Scuole Grandi* and *scuole delle arti* mixed rich and poor, masters and journeymen, high and low born. As the Counter-Reformation progressed, and more parish-based fraternities and sororities emerged, more devotional associations linked different orders of society in a common cause and loyalty. In such socially mixed fraternities the nobles or other upper orders tended to dominate the official positions – as a deliberate policy of social control in Florence under the Medici Grand Dukes. Noble leadership might more innocently be justified in that nobles had more time than working craftsmen to be fully active organisers of funerals or charity; but it could be resented as in Vicenza's Crocefisso fraternity, which ruled in 1602 that offices should be allocated equally, and not be reserved for nobles.

Immigrants into some cities could find a social grouping, and focus of loyalty through 'national' fraternities.[36] In the larger cities there were 'national' fraternities exclusively or predominantly for foreign groups. These might be non-Italian groups like the French, Flemings, Germans (which might include northern Netherlanders, Bohemians or Hungarians, as in Perugia), Slavs, Greeks or Albanians; they might also be people from another part of Italy away from home-base: Lombards, Bolognesi, Florentines. The configurations depended on the city and the type of immigrant. The national confraternity would be run by long-term alien residents in the city, but offer a welcome to more temporary visitors – students, pilgrims, legal petitioners from the same locality. They had their own churches or chapels, and ran hospices or alms-houses. Venice, with numerous immigrant workers, had national guild groups, such as the fraternity for German cobblers and shoemakers as well as the aforementioned *scuola* for German assistant bakers. This meant that a traveller or potential immigrant could arrive in a large city like Rome or Venice, lesser ones like Perugia, Verona, Siena and Bologna, and find a religious-based community that understood the home language and customs, and which offered temporary help with accommodation, with illnesses – and in the end, funerals. This might be the path for gainful employment and permanent residency. Those who stayed, but did not prosper too well, could receive alms or – as with the Bolognesi and Spaniards in Rome – help with dowries for their daughters.

Thus the national confraternities helped overcome the anonymity and dangers of the big city. The extent to which they maintained alien loyalties and sub-groups over a long period is hard to gauge, though there was pressure from the Spanish establishment, through the late sixteenth and early seventeenth century to maintain and foster 'la natione spagnuola' in Rome, involving all levels of society through its confraternity of the Holy Resurrection. In fifteenth-century Siena, German artisans centred on the confraternity of St Barbara in the Dominican church, and expressed their pride and identity in commissioning an altarpiece from Matteo di Giovanni (1478), with various Germanic characteristics. At this point they had Sienese supporters, but subsequent relations are not yet clear. In Venice the German and Greek Orthodox communities did largely maintain separate identities and loyalties; in the case of the Germans this was encouraged or enforced by suspicious government authorities worried about Lutheran influences. Roman parish records for the later sixteenth and early seventeenth century suggest impressionistically that the immigrant populations from outside Italy as well as within were soon scattered as far as housing is concerned; and that Flemings, French as well as Neapolitans, Romagnoli, Lombards and Piedmontese did not predominantly seek marriage partners or godparents from the same nation.[37] Presumably most who stayed in Rome soon amalgamated into local parish and district networks, and the national confraternity and its church ceased to be dominant. The latter served a major, but short-term, role.

This chapter has illustrated a number of social groupings that were open to the individual (notably in cities), should family and clan fail him or her, and should additional social solidarity be needed. Some groupings were extensions of the workplace or work-organisation – guilds and some confraternities – and likely to be combining social equals. Neighbourhood organisations, and other types of fraternities following Giovanni Nesi's ideal, consolidated some social hierarchical relationships, buttressing patronage networks, and possibly mutual political interests. Over the period the importance of the neighbourhood and district organisations may have declined (certainly noted in Perugia and Florence, if not Venice and Siena), though there are few studies to provide suitable evidence. The growing emphasis on status through the period may have weakened neighbourhood solidarities and some confraternity attempts to link most ranks of society, rich and poor, in one group. Parish groupings and loyalties, as we shall see next, became more important from the mid sixteenth century. As with families and clans, many tensions could develop – within neighbourhoods, guilds and confraternities. What can be emphasised is that the individual within a city could find a number of social networks to help promote his interests, protect him or her when vulnerable or to offer consolation. This applied to immigrants who broke ties with family and clan, which remained the mainstay (if anything) in rural society, at least until in some areas the parish and parish-linked confraternities also offered welfare and support.

10

PAROCHIAL SOCIETY

The parish systems and parish priests

For the social-religious historian the parish would seem an obvious unit of social organisation, and a manageable category for an analysis of society in hierarchies. In a developed Christian society the parish might be expected to be the centre of social as well as strictly religious activity and organisation. In practice the situation in Italy during our period was variable in time and place. Generally the 'parish' became a more significant social unit through the period, particularly as and when Catholic reformers made an impact from the sixteenth century; and the parish church physically became more important in the lives of individuals – even if some social activities of a dubious religious nature were barred from the church interior.[1]

The parish, as we conceive of it now, was not necessarily in the fifteenth century a significant social unit, though it could surprisingly be so in mountainous areas of the Florentine state.[2] Often monastic churches, confraternity oratories or local chapels associated with an icon image might have more significance. A shift of loyalty from these other places to the parish church was the concern of leading sixteenth-century church reformers from Gian Matteo Giberti or St Carlo Borromeo onwards, and the extent to which this happened has been of increasing interest to church historians.

Previously there was no unitary concept of the parish, but a number of parochial systems. The modern Catholic concept of the parish is of an ecclesiastical unit, a subdivision of a diocese, based on a church possessing a baptismal font, entrusted to a priest who exercised cure of souls. This system existed by the fifteenth–sixteenth century particularly in central Italy and the south, but was unrecognisable in other areas, notably in the north, and in Puglia. In the north, under Lombard influences, a collegiate system had developed under a larger baptismal district. Baptismal churches called *plebes* (Latin), *pievi* (Italian), were the centre of a network of lesser churches or chapels. Priests resided at the *pieve* mother church (where they preserved exclusive baptismal rights, and often burials rights), and went out from there to serve other churches for certain services and pastoral care, though the subordinate churches and chapels might also have curates. In the cities the Cathedral often retained the sole font, and thus technically was the only *parish* church, though this did not prevent most inhabitants from paying more attention to closer churches and chapels, with their vicars and curates. By the sixteenth century much of the *pieve* system had in practice been eroded, as lesser churches in north and central Italy claimed and exercised independence. Fonts or confessors were inconveniently placed in distant Cathedrals or baptismal churches. Relics and cult pictures might encourage loyalty and pride in the neighbourhood church.

In parts of southern Italy another collegiate system for Cathedral chapters and churches, called *ricettizie* prevailed. This is less well known than the *pieve* system.[3] Likewise a college of clerics exercised the cure of souls collectively and had a common ownership of property but, unlike the *pievi*, the collegiate bodies were normally recruited from local people, with the bishop having very limited jurisdictional rights. In the later sixteenth century about a third of southern 'parishes' were part of the *ricettizie* system, as high as 70 per cent in Terra d'Otranto.

While Catholic reformers and Tridentine legislators succeeded in further eroding the *pieve* system, they were less successful with the *chiese ricettizie* in the light of greater jurisdictional problems. This lessened episcopal-led reform of the church in the south, with implications for the degree of social control over the laity, the diminution of 'superstitious practices' and the Christian and moral education of southerners.

The Council of Trent finally (1563) envisaged a uniform parochial system, with manageable-sized parishes with a resident parish priest exercising full cure of souls, who would know all his parishioners. The Tridentine legislation and episcopal supplementation from reformers placed the parish church at the centre of the lay person's life from infancy to the grave, even if baptism was sometimes conducted elsewhere. The reformers tried to ensure that through parishes the flock should be properly led and controlled. Better-educated priests would be resident, offering public Mass every Sunday and major feast days, with a sermon, homily or improving reading. They would control marriage and funerals, organise religious education of children and the ignorant, enumerate the populace, investigate their moral and economic conditions, help provide assistance for the deserving poor and chastise the major sinners. In practice of course many impediments hampered these plans and ideals.[4]

Reformers failed to erode the *pieve* and *ricettizie* systems entirely, which could produce major jurisdictional problems and impede reform. In practice though, for weekly purposes, dependent churches often came close to being parochial, and we can from the late sixteenth century loosely talk of a parochial society through the peninsula. The ambition of having equal-sized parochial units, with a fairer distribution of funds, largely failed, though there were some successful rationalisations in Rome, Reggio Calabria and Lecce. Over-populated urban parishes could often cope by using a collegiate group of lesser priests and vicars. Under-sized and under-funded rural parishes and *pieve* were more of a problem, especially if the unit comprised several scattered hamlets through the Tuscan or Bolognese Apennines. Rich resources remained with monastic houses, large Chapters and secular patrons who appointed low-paid vicars, or sent out monks on cheap annual contracts. Some of the deficiencies in the parochial cure of souls were made good by the new Religious Orders – Jesuits, Barnabites, Theatines, Capuchins especially – as well as some old Benedictine, Dominican or Augustinian houses, and confraternities not dependent on the parish.

Despite the problems, the parochial clergy of whatever level came to have greater control of society from the late sixteenth century. The Council ordered parish priests to keep orderly records of baptisms and marriages. Such registers had been recommended by previous church councils, the Justinian Code and pre-Tridentine local reformers, and were sometimes produced. These records were deemed essential because the Church now claimed exclusive powers over the validation of marriages, and sought to control Christian baptism and the role of godparents. Subsequently the Papacy added requirements for the orderly registration of parishioners, and codified the norms in the Roman Ritual of 1614, adding the need for records of deaths, and of the *status animarum* (state of souls). The *status animarum* registers were primarily designed to list those old enough to receive communion, those who made the obligatory annual confession and communion (normally at Easter), those who contumaciously did not and those who were barred from receiving communion – because, for example, they were concubinous, or were unrepentant prostitutes. In practice the properly produced *status animarum* registers tried to record all the population of the parish, including young children. People were listed by households (which might be all in one room or hovel of course, as well as in a *palazzo*), with ages; a family name, where it existed, occupation and place of origin if not native to the city, might all be added to the Christian name of adults; widowhood, extended family relationship, status as servant or apprentice, or as prostitute, might also be appended. The responsible cleric was expected to provide summary statistics, to be handed on to the bishop or his vicar.[5]

The fact that these registers became normal by the seventeenth century indicates that the parish was a control centre for society. A sampling of Roman parish-based registers shows that where parish priests and their assistants were assiduous (and standards varied considerably) they could find out quite a lot about their parishioners, and be in a position to control, regulate or advise them. Some were more preoccupied than others about who were prostitutes and who were concubinous (which normally in this period meant a reasonably stable relationship, but not one recognised as a real marriage under Tridentine rules). Some death registers (for example for the Roman parishes of San Sebastiano in the 1560s and Santa Maria in Aquiro in the early 1600s) show that the priests were well aware of illnesses, poverty and misfortune. A register of marriages and baptisms for San Giovanni dei Fiorentini shows that in the 1570s a young priest called Cesare Baronio was assiduous in interrogating couples prior to marriage, testing their Christian knowledge and trying to ensure they would live up to the ideals of Christian marriage. Baronio went on to be a leading Oratorian, Cardinal (with great reluctance) and major church historian; arguably the best Catholic reforming Pope the Church nearly had – he was vetoed by pro-Spanish Cardinals when his historical writing challenged Spanish jurisdictional claims in Sicily.[6]

The role of the parish priest as registrar of the population, along with his position as the provider of a weekly Mass supposedly for all parishioners, led secular authorities to use the parish priest for various communicative and regulatory purposes; for the communication of edicts and declarations, or for the registering of the poor. This might thus contribute to wider social control.[7]

The control of marriage is the second major change after Trent that re-emphasised the centrality of the parish.[8] Before the Council of Trent the processes of betrothal and marriage were variable: public cohabitation by common consent without benefit of lawyers or clergy; marriages through a notarial contract; or betrothals and marriages conducted in church, with nuptial masses and blessings. After heated debate, especially over clandestine marriages, the Council laid claim to regulate all marriages and to rule on their validity. The church in implementing the claim was producing a social revolution. Despite the allowance of some dispensations, it was reinforcing the central position of parish priest and parish church. All Italian states, in accepting the Trent decrees, accepted this changed position of marriage; though some added rules, such as the need for parental consent for a wedding to be valid in civil law in Piedmont. However, the church had a long battle to educate the populace about the new rules, and to enforce them.

Enforcing the social revolution proved difficult, and levels of success were very variable. Much depended on the quality and enthusiasm of bishops, and whether they secured the co-operation of the secular rulers, or even the Papacy. The quality of episcopal leadership in the 287-odd Italian dioceses was obviously very diverse. Even the best of post-Tridentine reforming bishops were impeded in their task of improving parish leadership by limitations on their appointments. Control over benefices was widely spread, sometimes fiercely contested. Bishops had to compete with continuing papal rights of presentation, with rights and precedents that allowed monastic houses, collegiate churches, military Orders, private families or even local communities to nominate to the parish.[9] This last occurrence is best known in the Venetian parishes, where usually in sixty out of the seventy-two parishes householders elected the parish priest (called *piovan(o)*). He did not operate alone but headed a parish chapter, with up to eight assistants (*titolati*) – who were themselves elected by the chapter, not the householders. Even with this supposedly democratic local electoral situation, other pressures operated. For example patrician women, without voting rights as such, 'patronised' many Venetian parishes. Community elections of priests can be found elsewhere, as in Pisa where householders (but also institutions) could chose candidates to be approved by the archbishop, in five parishes. The bishop had a right of veto, but could find it difficult to enforce, as in Venetian cases, when the community or patrons proved obstinate. A bishop might secure a proper competition or *concorso* to find a parish priest; but even when this was considered the norm, he could find himself frustrated by procedures and manoeuvres whereby the incumbent could engineer a chosen successor before resignation.[10]

The extent to which bishops could directly control parochial appointments (free collation) varied considerably from diocese to diocese, and the overall picture is unclear. By the time Grand Duke Peter Leopold sought to reform his Tuscan state and its church in the eighteenth century it was calculated that Tuscan bishops only had 37 per cent of parishes under free collation. In the Abruzzi diocese of Teramo in the 1590s, reforming bishop Montesanto could only freely appoint to 40 out of 140 benefices; others were under Curial patronage, or that of the feudal families such as the Acquaviva.[11]

There was no lack of secular clergy; the problem for reformers was securing the right kind in the right places, for the right reasons. From the sixteenth to the eighteenth century the proportion of clergy (priests or deacons) to the whole adult population increased through most of Italy. The presumed reasons were manifold, and throw interesting light on Italian society and economics. In 1592 Rome the ratio of secular priests per head of population was 1:81, in 1760 1:55; Venice had 1:277 in 1586, and 1:164 in 1642; the diocese of Milan 1:124 in 1766. From southern examples one can cite Reggio Calabria where the ratio was 1:250 in 1595, and 1:144 in 1636. In Naples there were about 1000 priests for about 200,000 people in 1574; by 1706 the figures were 3849 priests for 337,075 residents (1:88). Of course the very high proportion of clergy in Rome was uniquely conditioned by the needs of the clerical bureaucracy running the central institutions of the whole Catholic Church, and of the Papal State; and the *palazzi* of the Cardinals included a fair number of men in orders, hoping they were on a beneficial career path. Various studies suggest that in general the increase of those in both minor and major orders was most extensive in the south. Lombardy at times slowed its increase, partly because of the effects of war – both through male casualties, and the alternative careers in various armies.

Some increases can be taken as genuinely vocational as existing reformers stimulated others, and as seminaries or colleges run by Orders like the Jesuits offered educational opportunities to young boys, and then oriented some of them to the lay priesthood. Economic pressures also encouraged an increase. Economic stagnation or depression in town or country pushed some sons to seek careers in or through the church; patricians aimed at canonries and sees, while peasants sought a minor role as a mass priest. The clerical state offered fiscal advantages. As Alessandro Bicchi, bishop of Isola and papal nuncio in Naples, wrote to Cardinal Francesco Barberini in 1630 there were too many who 'did not wish to be ordained, except for exemptions from tax burdens'.[12] Family strategies – at all levels of society – to avoid the splintering of property (owned, leased or share-cropped) pushed males into the celibacy of the lay clerical state or the monastery, just as girls were encouraged or forced into nunneries.

The ratio of the lay clergy increased; but it meant not only more competition (possibly beneficial) for parish positions, but also many low-level clerics eking out meagre livings. What an increasingly Catholicised population wanted was more masses for departed souls and more splendid funerals; so they paid for clergy who would say those masses and accompany funerals. This was not necessarily beneficial for services for the living; nor for adequate incomes for those chaplains who failed to secure the more lucrative benefices. Some priests did prefer to be 'mass priests' because they could earn more than in poorly funded parishes. By the later sixteenth century in the Siena diocese it was not uncommon for testators, male and female, to require a 1000 masses to be said soon after their death. In some cases this involved elaborate sung masses on special days; and the clergy there did not offer discount rates for such a large order.[13]

Inadequate fixed parochial incomes could mean a reliance on parishioners' goodwill – which might undermine the priest's authority and discipline; or on strong-arm tactics to secure extra incomes, causing fear and opposition; or on the pursuit of more lucrative incomes from private masses. There was also a resort to outside jobs, whether accepted occupations like school-mastering, or other less compatible economic enterprises. In Pisa in the 1630s only ten out of forty-three parish priests lived off the parochial income or an allocated salary, and in only two cases was this substantial. The rest relied on incomes from other benefices without cure. Paduan Visitation records from 1560 to 1594 show incumbents cultivating the fields or acting as businessmen. In the 1570s the parish priest of San Pantalon in Venice worked as a merchant on the Rialto. In southern Italy there were complaints that priests acted as merchants, especially in the olive-oil trade, to the detriment of pastoral care. Some were licensed to earn by bishops and vicars general who recognised the inadequacy of the parochial incomes. One could of course argue that such priests might have a closer understanding of their parishioners' daily needs; but generally the supposition is that this situation diminished services, religious and social, for the lay community.[14] So by the eighteenth century Italian society had an over-abundance of proletarian clergy – of limited dedication and of dubious morality, seen by enlightened reformers as a major drain on the economy whether as unproductive labour or tax-dodgers.

A key ambition at Trent and of later episcopal reformers like Carlo and Federico Borromeo (Lombardy), Gabriele Paleotti (Bologna) and Paolo Burali (Piacenza) was to ensure properly trained parish priests, who would subsequently be better watched and instructed, in order to lead and teach their flock. The ideal was to create priests dedicated to the cure of souls, to be pastors as well as administrators. It envisaged the institution of a seminary in every diocese (where there was no better institution such as a university or college training potential clergy), to train suitable ordinands. The seminary has been seen as one of the major achievements of the Council of Trent, but disappointments and limitations were soon evident. Lack of leadership, money and cooperation from richer diocesan institutions, and jurisdictional tussles, all impeded the establishment and maintenance of seminaries. By about 1630 and the end of the first wave of reform activity – and before war and economic setbacks increased the problems – only about a third of dioceses had established seminaries; the eighteenth century saw another spurt of foundations. Certain areas like Umbria, Lombardy, the archdioceses of Ravenna and Reggio Calabria were soon reasonably well served by seminaries – though that in Reggio was destroyed in the Turkish raid of 1594. Tuscany and the Roman provincial and suburbican dioceses were slow to provide seminaries. The situation in the south generally improved from the 1580s. The size and quality of the seminaries varied considerably – from the very elementary (for about 12 boys/youths starting at age 12) to those of university standard by the end of the course, as in Milan, Perugia or Santa Severina, where philosophy, classical rhetoric, Latin, Greek, music and law were added to higher-level theology courses. It should be noted that seminaries might take in fee-paying pupils using the institution for a secondary education, without intending becoming priests.[15]

The efficacy of such seminary training for those about to serve in ordinary parishes can be doubted.[16] Seminarians reaching high educational levels might be far removed from their flock, adding to tensions between elite and popular culture. If a seminary functioned properly as recommended by the Theatine archbishop Burali, taking boys aged 12 into strictly disciplined monastic boarding schools, then the product might be hardly fitted to deal with the wider community of parishioners, family life and broad socio-religious attitudes. If they were not properly supervised the seminaries might contribute to troubles – as was argued by Archbishop D.G. Caracciolo in the early seventeenth century in complaining of his Bari clergy:

> with little spirituality, badly disciplined and without letters, which instead of pursuing the path of virtue heads for that of vices; whence is maintained a seminary of persons, delinquent and totally contrary to the clerical profession, from which derives the unquiet and scandalous life of the city.

Faenza's bishops argued that a record of good conduct and frequency at the sacraments were better preparations for parish service than formal education.[17]

We know too little about most clergy and their background. Most parish priests until the late eighteenth century at least were not seminarians, but trained by the local parish clergy, learning on the job through minor orders, receiving additional education from local grammar masters and canons giving theological teaching in Cathedral or collegiate churches and monasteries – as has been clearly shown for the Novara diocese. There were also the schools and colleges run by the Orders, notably by the Jesuits, and the universities – though these last were, in Italy, not particularly suitable for training parish priests or theologians as opposed to lawyers. The rigour – or otherwise – of testing suitability for the priesthood and a parish appointment, is little known. However, G. Pelliccia's major study of Roman ordinations after Trent suggested that procedures were improved, and that the quality of ordinands rose, thanks to seminaries, colleges and the work of Jesuits generally.[18]

The background of priests is usually hazy. Most Venetian parish priests came from the city and the Veneto, and were of the middling sort likely to be in harmony with the effective electors from the parish, and not always to the liking of the Patriarch; especially when a parish insisted on electing (and re-electing after patriarchal veto) the son of the previous incumbent. Novara, though not subject to the same local electoral system, similarly recruited priests locally in the early seventeenth century: about 90 per cent were natives of the diocese, and from reasonably wealthy families. Elsewhere visitation and other records suggest that lesser clerics and priests moved about, and that cures were not filled by local men, unless they were the southern *chiese ricettizie*, or attached to richer collegiate churches, or when the patronage system for local influential families might operate, as in Pisa or parts of the diocese of Trent.

After Trent the parish priest was not left alone to carry the burden of educating his flock, or ensuring its spiritual and social well-being. Under all but the most negligent bishops and vicars general he was likely to be assaulted by instructions, recommendations and investigations – even if he could ignore some with impunity. Bishops and apostolic Visitors reminded the clergy to have and use copies of the Tridentine decrees, and a catechism to help them teach the basics of Christian belief and instruction. Reformers like Carlo Borromeo, Paleotti and Panigarola bombarded their clergy with instructions, commentaries, homilies and letters – some of which helped them deal with parishioners. The calling of a diocesan synod might lead parish priests to meet their bishop, vicars general and other priests, or at least would involve telling a vicar general about parochial problems, with a view to formulating new legislation and instructions.[19]

The parish was expected to establish a library of usable books. Bishops and apostolic Visitors were known to check on library resources. Our knowledge of actual libraries before the late eighteenth century is limited. In the Rimini diocese in the 1570s and 1580s more than half the urban parishes definitely had a collection of books – from 22 to 225 in number. Monastic and conventual libraries served rural priests. What was read and used may have been very different, but facilities and opportunities for wide reading and well-founded instruction existed. The post-Tridentine production of missals, breviaries, catechisms and calendars should have led to a better performance of church ceremonies and instruction of parishioners than before. The standard of literacy seems to have improved, and priests were under more pressure to perform properly.

The moral position of many clergy remained subject to criticism, and anti-clerical critics past and present have fun with the sexual sins of parish priests and curates. Bishops and vicars general lamented the defects of the clergy as they toured around on their Visitations, noting the absentees, the concubinous and the sodomitic. But it is worth reflecting on the problems of 'the poor parish priest', giving 'poor' its economic and its emotive meanings. Poverty could be found in rich cities, but the priest serving a remoter parish, or part of a *pieve* or collegiate system, was likely to have a much more difficult time economically and socially. Loneliness and isolation was the lot for many, made worse by any strict application of reforming zeal.

The Church as part of an eleventh-century 'renaissance' or reform had insisted on clerical celibacy; an ideal that took, and in Rome still takes, little account of natural worldly instincts and temptations. Vows of poverty and chastity were and are an ideal that can bring their own satisfaction in this world as well as in contemplation of the hereafter. But many, male and female, took such vows, or put themselves on the path to such vows, at an early age, before puberty or full sexual awareness, and often before any full experience of the adult world and sexuality. Many males through the middle ages sought education, advancement, even survival, through a clerical career, without the prospect of marriage. For long after the official Roman call for celibacy, the injunction might be ignored. Well-established clergy might have liaisons, and bastards – including Cardinals who might become Pope like Alexander VI (1492–1503). Lower clergy might have house-keeper companions, mothering priest and children, with little local opposition, even with local acclaim, since an active heterosexual priest was more likely to understand the problems of lay families and female penitents – and less likely to molest either them or vulnerable male youths.

The imposition of reform measures in the sixteenth century created as many problems as it solved. The cost, human and social, of a better-educated clergy could be high. A new parish priest educated through seminaries or colleges run by the religious orders, was de-racinated, and educated beyond his station if sent back into a rural or poor urban parish. His removal from family life, and female society, at an early age was likely to affect his relations with lay families once given cure of souls. If well educated, even just literate, he might be placed well above the level of education of virtually all his parishioners and so intellectually isolated. Archbishops and vicars in the Bologna archdiocese recognised the physical and intellectual isolation of priests in remoter parishes, with some understanding.[20] Pievanal priests, and collegiate clergy sent out from monasteries that controlled parishes, might have no roots in a parish (though some friendship through a central collegiate congregation). Confessors were peripatetic and lonely – and so subject to temptation, and vulnerable to the charge of 'solicitation'. The only access to comforting female society might be through the confessional; and if that situation was the only opportunity for a frustrated spinster, or more likely an unhappily married woman, to discuss intimate matters (as confessional manuals suggested), there might be sinful encouragement for the priest from the other side.

There were dangers and temptations for the celibate priest. Encouraged to fear and avoid close relations with women, he might readily succumb to the temptations of boys whom he would more commonly encounter. Temptations would be there in the sacristy. A priest out in the world with a young boy as 'page' was a more likely sight than a priest with a female escort. Bologna records detail the lengthy investigation of Francesco Finetti, a priest originally from Milan, seemingly lonely, without an established abode, who was accused of 'picking up' a ten-year-old boy begging outside a college, taking him off to a rented room next to an inn, providing the boy, Antonio Grain (German in origin, but arriving as an orphan from Siena), with food and drink and of sodomising him numerous times over four to five days.[21] A lonely priest, without domestic support, might be tempted to eat, drink and have company in a tavern or inn, even just to keep warm at others' expense; there to be tempted by free women, or simply have the accusation of impropriety thrown against him, if other behaviour offended a neighbour. A priest seen visiting a woman after dark might readily find the *sbirri* banging at the door; it being dubious whether, as in the case of Juliano Ruggeri, because he was genuinely reported as lecherous, or because he was an innocent framed by nuns in contention with the widow he was helping.[22] Whatever the protestations of innocence coming from Finetti and Ruggieri, it is tempting to assume they were guilty when we do not know the outcome. Even if, as Finetti repeated, *sbirri* were notoriously corrupt and malicious, the circumstances were compromising, and in the case of the accusing Antonio, the accuser held to his charges under torture. Priests were vulnerable to temptations, and open to false charges – as probably with the *piovano* of S.Simone, Venice in 1594, when a husband, jealous of his young bride's confession sessions, made her denounce the priest to the Patriarch's court for having repeated sexual relations with her. She later withdrew the charges (fearing her own seclusion as an adulteress in the Casa del Soccorso, a house for vulnerable women), and the priest was publicly exonerated, having had other parishioners testify to his goodness.[23]

A fully established and resident priest might laxly fit into local society. As pre-Trent, his parishioners might encourage him to have an accommodating housekeeper – not a sister or an elderly widow – and might not inform Visitors of the concubinous relationship. The diplomatic priest, with the tactful 'housekeeper', could provide mutually suitable – if 'immoral' – pastoral care. But as work on the Sienese diocese has shown, the situation was very vulnerable if the priest were too intent on family and household, or the *compagna* was too domineering and influential and flaunted her position.[24] If, as happened in a Venetian urban parish, the friendly local (voting) householders, wanted the son of the parish priest to succeed, it might occasion the wrath of the Ordinary.[25] Ordinaries did not want priests to be too close to parishioners; it would be bad for discipline and authority. But then the isolated moral priest might not understand family problems or command respect. This might not worry the godly elite or superior clergy, who could indulge their own social life in many different, moral and immoral, satisfying ways. Not only the morally weak were vulnerable; so was a highly dedicated parish priest, and licensed confessor. Intent on dealing with faithful laity, tertiaries and professed nuns, he might find himself enthralled by the sanctity of a woman, and then be accused of fostering her 'false sanctity', as those involved with Angela Mellini of Bologna found in the 1690s. This poor seamstress, who was able to write a diary, had ecstatic religious experiences with visions of Christ: 'my Jesus exposed my breast and opened my ribs and took my heart and in place of it he put all the instruments of the sacred passion'. Eventually she was treated as a spiritual mother and confessor by one admiring priest – which was too much for higher authority, who charged her with 'affected sanctity'. She was released after penances, and the most affected priest sent away from Bologna – for discussing problems of his own chastity with a woman.[26]

Some reformers showed compassion for loneliness and poverty of existence and opportunities. They sought to remedy the economic problems, to make serving the clergy and the flock easier, and ultimately (in this world at least), more beneficial for the laity as well. I have stressed the moral problems of the priest in a reforming Catholic society, as an often misunderstood and under-estimated aspect of relations between local society and the church.

Church religious–social life

The parish church, like other churches – collegiate, monastic, confraternal – served numerous social as well as religious purposes. It became busier and more important for narrower religious reasons, and less important for the fringe social purposes. A largish church (including porticoes, cloisters and frontal squares) had often the one available public space in a village: as neutral ground for business negotiations, for arranging betrothals and dowries, for secret trysts of lovers, for settling disputes and making peace, for entertainment. Some of the problems and tensions can be deduced from a surviving diary of a parish priest, Giorgio Franchi, at Berceto near Parma in the 1550s. It was a troublesome time. He reported the church and its sacristy in use for local representative assemblies, as a meeting place for soldiers and as an arena for legal and illegal disputes. Some remedies were sought, and he reported some brutal public punishments for those profaning the church, especially in cursing and swearing. But he revealed that he shared some varied superstitious beliefs with his parishioners.[27] Once reformers acted in the sixteenth century there were pressures to eliminate or reduce the more secular uses of the church and sacred space, and instead to have the churches better used for sermons, religious instruction, more major Masses, funerals and weddings.[28]

By Tridentine norms and by more consistent practice – as judged by Visitation reports – on Sundays and major feasts there would be a parochial Mass, with a sermon, or at least a reading from an improving spiritual work. Increasingly parishioners were encouraged (by religious orders and confraternities, if not their parish priest) to confess and communicate more than the stipulated once a year – which meant more often making peace with the community and individuals, as well as with conscience, confessor and Maker.[29] Baptisms and marriages were to be more a parish church event, with fewer extraneous ceremonies and celebrations.

Baptism as a rite in the parish or *pieve* church was probably more standard than rites of matrimony or death before the Catholic reforms. Baptism was increasingly stressed as a prerequisite for salvation, which affected attitudes and procedures over dying or dead babies. As before, Trent allowed for an adult (usually the midwife) to baptise a baby whose life was in danger; but there were pressures to reduce abuses of such procedures, and discount claims (in northern Italy) of temporary 'resurrection' of a moribund baby while it was baptised. All abnormal, non-church, baptisms had to be registered with the parish priest as well. Limited studies of baptismal registers indicate that they were fairly uniformly kept; they often omitted the still-born, those dying soon after birth, and in some cases illegitimate births (as in Lucania [now Basilicata] until 1765) – though elsewhere the formula 'ex damnato coitu' is sometimes used for those obviously conceived out of wedlock. The number of registered god-parents was reduced after Trent. This had various social implications. Creating a network of god-parent relationships could be important as part of family strategies for political and social power, as has been noted for fifteenth-century Florentine patrician families. At lower social levels in remoter communities even a limited god-parent system created spiritual affinities that then impeded the choice of marriage partners, unless dispensations were obtained.[30]

Betrothal and wedding were the major planned aspects of family life, hedged around with economic and socio-political considerations. In the early part of our period the church's involvement could be negligible, but the Council of Trent sought to standardise procedures on betrothal and the marriage sacrament. This was an attempt at major social change that involved much campaigning and conflict. The issue of marriage appears to be the single most repeated topic in the post-Tridentine synodal legislation, pastoral letter writing and probably in homilies or sermons.

Before Trent, priests and the church might play little or no role in the marital process. In Perugia in 1487 a professor of civil law, Baldo Baldini, performed the words of marriage in a private house, for the much celebrated patrician wedding of Vincenzo Baldeschi and Richabella Arcipreti; it involved a horse-drawn carriage, lavishly decorated, followed by a feast in the square, with a wooded scene constructed, with nymphs, singing and recitations.[31] Florentine diaries might stress a betrothal (promises *de futuro*) negotiated in church – a neutral public place – where relatives and lawyers negotiating dowries were more prominent than the affiancing couple; later, leading the bride to her new home and bedding her would be more noted than any marital promises (*de presenti*) or priestly blessings.

In Florence and other areas the ring-giving ceremony between the couple was often the key social ritual. Priests played little part in patrician marriages, though they may have been more used, as witnesses rather than blessers, for marriages of artisans and *contadini*. The Church's main role might have been to grant dispensations to allow marriages within the normally prohibited bands of consanguinity and affinity. The path to a fully negotiated marriage might be multi-staged, lengthy and confused. As the 1517 Florence synod admitted: there were many 'ignorant people who fail to understand the force of the words they speak; often thinking they are becoming engaged, they speak the words of marriage'. Marco Antonio Altieri (1450–1532), a Roman noble, in his *Li Nuptiali* (written *c.* 1506–13) outlined the procedures and customs supposedly practised by better-off contemporary Romans, or ones he wanted them to use in his campaign against social decadence and money-grubbing in Rome. The church was often a location for encounters and agreements, but not for elaborate ceremonial. The final stage – up to a year after betrothal and notarised agreement – was escorting the bride to church to meet the groom, hear Mass inside, be blessed by a priest – accompanied by much noise, jollity and irreligious ceremonies with bread, wine and water performed by the entourage; and the couple were then escorted to the marital home, and bedded. In other parts of Italy formal ceremonies were diverse. In Bologna up to the sixteenth century marriages were celebrated before witnesses, with or without a notary; only later was a church blessing sought, if at all. For many couples public cohabitation was deemed sufficient without a Mass or blessing. Though church-announced banns were required by the 1216 Lateran Council, and by local councils and synods (as in Florence in 1517), there is little evidence of their use before Trent.[32]

Trent sought exclusive control over the sacrament of marriage, laying down norms of procedure to create validity.[33] Since matrimony was deemed to be a sacrament performed by the couple themselves, a couple *freely* making promises in the present (*de presenti*) could create a marriage valid in the eyes of God, and therefore preventing any other marriage while one of them lived. But if the Tridentine rules were not followed, the marriage was illegal in the eyes of the church; the couple were to be separated, and possibly punished, unless and until they completed church marriage procedures in due form. The Church wanted the marital sacrament publicly recognised and validated in church – normally the local *parish* church – and blessed by a priest. It also wanted solemnity within the church, and public jollity elsewhere – seemly and without excessive expense.

Priests repeat endlessly the rules about no clandestine marriages. Public banns were required as well as a church ceremony before at least two witnesses and the parish priest (though he need not consent or fully participate). Couples were not to cohabit before the final blessing – if, because of Advent or Lent, such a blessing had to be separated from the marital promises. Opposition, and the weight of local custom, was considerable. Guidance was very necessary and was provided by leading reformers. Bishop G. Paleotti of Bologna in 1577 provided an oft-printed guide for use by his parish priests. He stressed the desirability of parental consent (though not its necessity under church law), that the couple should at least know the Our Father, the Ave Maria and the Ten Commandments. The wedding was to consist of the Mass, the blessing of the ring, a sermon and the linking of the couple under a veil. This might be followed by the final blessing on the marriage before leaving the church; or it could be a separate ceremony; or not be given at all for a second marriage. Paleotti provided 24 sermons of various lengths and styles to be used by the priest as appropriate. Unlike Carlo Borromeo, for example, Paleotti was less inclined to treat marriage as an inferior state to celibacy, and there was less emphasis on marriage being a remedy against sin and fornication. Paleotti also provided an exhortation to be delivered to the bride and female attendants for seemly and unostentatious dressing, with warnings against dance music being played to and from the church, against 'ridiculous spectacles' in the streets and against excessive feasting – though he did not wish to prohibit nuptial hilarity. Borromeo stressed the importance of a good Christian marriage for the moral upbringing of children and preventing social disorder.[34]

The parish priest's presence was required when promises were made, but not his consent. The Congregation of the Council (the arbiter for the Pope of queries about Tridentine rules) in 1581 ruled that a marriage was still valid even if the priest was under some compulsion to be present, provided there were two other witnesses. Events in Alessandro Manzoni's great nineteenth-century historical novel *The Betrothed* (*I Promessi Sposi*) about seventeenth-century Lombardy are triggered by a loving couple's attempt (unsuccessful) to trick the very unwilling parish priest to *hear* them make promises before two witnesses. Don Abbondio threw a tablecloth over Lucia before she completed saying 'and this is my husband'. This novel, based on historical records, provides valuable insights into many aspects of seventeenth-century Lombard society, including under plague conditions, and into the pressures of 'feudal' society. Baronial threats, including using *bravi*, against the priest and the couple's marital hopes in the novel were probably realistic. In the eighteenth century Pope Benedict XIV indicated that ploys to evade priestly opposition to marriages were a serious menace.[35]

The most intimate involvement between parishioner and parish priest or curate should have been through confession. The elites might have their own specialist confessors, and richer urban parishes employed special licensed confessors, but the majority probably confessed to the local priest. In the fifteenth century Archbishop Antonino of Florence, Fra Savonarola and some lay fraternities advocated that the laity confess more frequently than the obligatory annual Easter confession. In the Catholic reform period enthusiastic bishops like Agostino Valier of Verona, religious Orders like the Jesuits, lay confraternities and writers like Buonsignore Cacciaguerra added their advocacy. Pressures built up to make confession more searching and private; though the introduction of partitions and then the confessional box into churches (especially advocated by Carlo Borromeo to give a degree of anonymity for the penitent, and physical protection for women) seems to have been a rather slow process. Priests were provided with ever more sophisticated manuals for effective confession, designed to produce a more moral and socially aware society. Borromeo was anxious that the examination should be rigorous; though Bartolomeo Fumo in his *Summa* (1554) had argued that the confessor should not interrogate, but encourage the penitent to confess voluntarily; also (possibly aware of disharmonious social consequences) that confessors should not seek specific details when the penitent's sins concerned others. The Roman Ritual of 1614 and archbishops of Naples warned against inciting people to sin through excessively detailed quizzing. Resentment did surface in Italy against inquisitive confession sessions, as from some Venetian Arsenal workers in 1562 (possibly being quizzed about heterodox views), who argued that confession should only be to God. Known complaints against priests, and general episcopal warnings, suggest that intimacy was a worry and danger in other senses – especially in the fondling of young women by confessors.[36]

Under reform campaigns the parochial communal Mass was meant to become more important, and the Eucharist better venerated. A main Mass on Sunday and major feast days, with a sermon and with the Host well displayed, was intended to be central to the life of the community. Reformers sought to ensure that churches were better kept and furnished, and that space was cleared (by removing intrusive tombs, screens or altars) for a major congregation to hear sermons within the church, and see the celebration of the Mass at the high altar. However, certain factors impeded the regular masses from become a significant religious-social event. No dramatic liturgical reform produced active congregational participation, through singing or vocal prayer. Seating was limited. Many services must have been badly performed, little comprehended by an inattentive audience which wandered about making social contacts. Attempts were made – and carried out with varying enthusiasm according to visitation reports – to segregate men and women to avoid distractions, and to remove intrusive beggars seeking alms.[37]

However, the Italian Tridentine church succeeded in emphasising the Eucharist, and providing some dramatic Masses for special occasions. Increasing numbers of Sacrament and other confraternities assisted the priest in ensuring better respect for the Eucharist, protecting the sacramental bread and having the Host on display in chapels lit by oil lamps and candles. They accompanied the priest when taking the Host and holy oil to the sick. Church architecture, furnishings and decoration added to the sense of display. The Host as symbol and magic had widespread appeal – to be used and abused in the community for healing purposes. Celebrations of the Mass were impressive and commanded attention when conducted in well-run Cathedrals and Chapters, in Jesuit churches, in some parish churches and confraternities' oratories. This was particularly so for major feast days, notably for Easter and Corpus Christi, and local patronal feast days; churches were elaborately decorated with hangings, with branches and flowers. Spectacular parades wound through the streets and around the whole church, with confraternity members dressed in their special robes, carrying painted banners or movable altar-paintings and torches, sometimes with musical instruments to accompany singing.

Also notable from the later sixteenth century onwards, were the Forty-Hour (*Quarantore*) celebrations, when the Host was on display either continuously for forty hours including through the night, or for successive periods of daylight and early evening. Elaborate instructive scenic effects behind and around the altar emphasised the importance of Christ's sacrifice and the symbol of the Host. Further effects were created by numerous candles and reflective mirrors. Confraternities and members of religious Orders organised successive processions of parishioners (usually segregating male and female) to parade into the church and special chapel, to pray, hear a short sermon, admire and depart. Though infrequent, such occasions had social significance for the organisers – especially lay confraternity members – and beneficially reinforced through the sense of spectacle some church teachings.[38]

Religious and social life could be enlivened by various kinds of very elaborate festival celebrations, especially in the large cities. These ranged from the scurrilous and lewd Carnival celebrations in the lead-up to Lent, to performances of religious plays, processions with carts carrying scenic tableaux, elaborate processions of relics involving numerous confraternities, Orders, musical groups and refreshments of wine and food. While attempts were made to curb the secular excesses of Carnival in the mid sixteenth century, from the mid seventeenth century onwards Rome and Venice in particular were notable for Carnival activities to attract touring foreigners as well as locals. Religious plays and tableaux were well known in Tuscany and Umbria up to the sixteenth century, most famously in Florence – with Epiphany plays put on by the fraternal Company of the Magi in which members of the Medici family played roles. Rome had its Mysteries of the Passion with elaborate scenery and machinery on Good Friday in the Colosseum. Puritanical reforming authorities sought to ban or discourage religious play-acting – with some effect. But elaborate processions with costly scenery, costumed (if silent) human representations of biblical characters and saints, huge statues of saints, etc. took place intermittently through our period, as with the Holy Thursday *Carro di Battaglino* procession in Naples.[39]

Social excesses, in the eyes and minds of purists, were a natural accompaniment of 'religious' festivals great and small. Authorities tried to restrict churches themselves to proper religious practices, eliminating feasting, drinking, dancing, trading and the like as far as possible. They also, as the Bishop of Tropea warned Rome in 1620, had to curb the use of churches as refuges and sanctuary for bandits and other criminals. The struggle against church feasting and dancing was long running; through the seventeenth century Piedmontese bishops complained of the Youth Abbeys that continued to organise such celebrations; and the Bologna synod of 1698 was still condemning dancing in the churches. Eating and drinking as part of Vigils were regularly frowned upon or banned (theoretically), along with the excessive noises made to drive away evil spirits, especially early in the morning through Holy Week, and during the very vulnerable hours of Holy Saturday. The celebration of John the Baptist's day – and the vigil before (23–24 June) – had long been recognised as a popular festival, welcomed or feared for its licentiousness: involving the collection and study of special herbs for therapeutic and prognostic purposes (for love and future spouses), bell-ringing through the night and ritual bathing for purification and renewal. Southern Italy had similar activities at Christmas as well. Such activities persisted through to the eighteenth century and beyond, with apparently some pale reflections in the present.[40]

Feast days, as condemned by puritanical reformers, sound an enjoyable relief for many city and rural dwellers from drudgery and meagre living. But there were economic disadvantages as well, if feast days were multiplied. The increase in days of obligation, requiring church attendance, also meant abstinence from work. Those working for a landlord might find that most working days were committed to his farm, leaving no time legally to work for themselves. The number of days involved varied considerably from place to place, depending on the relevant calendar of saints, and the extent of episcopal insistence on abstinence. In rural Castel del Piano in Sienese territory for very nearly a third of the year peasants were not supposed to work. In nearby Santa Fiora, a more artisan area, there were meant to be ninety days of rest; here the threat of trouble might have encouraged church authorities to licence work on certain lesser feast days. Much depended on the extent of supervision and enforcement, but clearly the excess of feasts occasioned protests against priests and landlords – as shown in the 1560s in certain Venetian heresy trials. So some bishops periodically pruned the calendar of days of obligation, and/or granted licences for individuals to work on their own holdings on the lesser feast days without punishment.[41]

Sixteenth-century reformers wanted more parochial control over the dying and dead. While Trent wanted a priest involved in the burial process – and abolished funerals conducted by laymen only (as had been common in Tuscany and Piedmont) – the officiating priest was by no means necessarily the parish priest, or the chief organiser. He was in competition with both religious Orders and confraternities. The ideal of a funeral involving all three contingents in a large processional display risked unseemly rivalries over precedence and overall control. It helped if confraternities were based in the parish church, and/or if the parish priest was the normal priest for confraternities involved in accompanying the dead to burial, whether confraternity members or parishioners. A common task of the active parish priest was taking the sacrament to the sick and dying, accompanied in many cases by members of confraternities carrying candles and crosses to provide a seemly procession.[42]

Funerals and memorialisation probably became more elaborate and costly for the wealthier families through our period. They were aided and abetted by confraternities, whether based in the parish church or in separate chapels and churches; whether part of the general remit of a Sacrament fraternity or the prime speciality of a Company of Death (*Della Morte*). For the more famous deceased, churches and chapels might be festooned with black drapes, with elaborate catafalques, with scenic displays commissioned from good artists. Lengthy processions involved priests, members of Orders and confraternities, with the poor paid to swell the ranks to render respect and assist the powers of prayer for the departed soul. The funeral of a leading citizen or cleric became a major social occasion. From the sixteenth century certain fraternities were also ready to ensure that the known poor and even abandoned bodies lying in streets and fields should receive a decent burial.

All the major rites of passage had been accompanied by unorthodox rituals and abuses that church leaders eventually sought to curb through episcopal legislation. It is impossible to know the extent of the practices condemned. Constant reiteration suggests an inability to eradicate abuse (though some bishops just copied attacks from their predecessors). Nineteenth-century anthropological studies confirmed some practices. Inquisition records also help confirm the abuse of sacraments and sacramentals as part of magical practices, the appropriation of blessed wafers and oil and the use of baptismally blessed umbilical cords, talismans, magical writings and playing cards (for gambling luck). Efforts were made to prevent the consummation of a marriage between betrothal and a final church wedding, or delaying it too long after for superstitious reasons; 'on the pretext of avoiding witchcraft which will impede copulation', as the synod of Rimini said in 1624. Death rituals also were difficult to control, such as eating and drinking in the presence of the dead, or excessive wailing and groaning in mourning (especially if this involved paid performers), and the particularly southern custom of wives and mothers cutting off their hair and placing it in the grave.

For priests and bishops it was difficult getting the balance right between strict religious dedication and customary lax behaviour, between perceived religious requirements for the salvation of souls and the economic requirements of the body (not to mention the temptations of the flesh). Many seem to have ignored the stricter dictates of the rule books, compromising in order to secure some church attendance and observance from the average parishioners. Godly archbishops like Carlo Borromeo or Burali might fulminate against old 'pagan' practices and demand instant results, but tactful education to create a more godly society was the safer path for the parish priests and curates.

Church instruction and education

The early modern period witnessed an expansion in the religious and social instruction offered to the average parishioner, especially in urban areas, and in the north and central zones of Italy. The instruction came from more regular sermons and homilies, from schools of Christian Doctrine, from schools run by the Orders, or from secular masters who were increasingly subject to some kind of clerical supervision and pressurised to include religious and moral education even if they were specialists in the classics or the abacus. The expansion and cheapening of printing in the sixteenth century assisted the instructional campaigns of religious reformers.[43]

Instruction from the pulpit was supposed to be more regular, and probably was. Up to the sixteenth century, sermons from parish priests or even bishops were infrequent. Irregular, but possibly spectacular, sermons were preached by specialist preachers from the Orders, with sermon series in Lent, and sometimes Advent, often organised and paid for by civic authorities and held before huge crowds in the main squares. In the fifteenth century, star preachers like San Bernardino of Siena, Savonarola or Bernardino da Feltre had a wide impact as they attacked the social ills of usury, greed, pornography and sodomy. The two Bernardinos also attacked Jewish money-lenders and stimulated anti-semitism. Bernardino da Feltre's onslaught, however, helped launch Christian pawn-broking institutions, the *Monti di Pietà*, to assist the poor. Such dramatic preaching continued through the next centuries, with the Jesuits and the Capuchins becoming the star performers, conducting major missions to Christianise remoter rural areas (the Indies of Italy), or the slum parishes of great cities like Naples or Genoa. The Capuchins were leading practitioners of dramatic and scenographic preaching, armed with large crucifixes, images of the Madonna and other props. Sermon cycles remained ecclesiastical highlights of the year.[44]

From the mid sixteenth century there was more mundane preaching and instruction on Sundays and major feast days as enjoined by Trent. Priests risked losing their benefices if they did not preach regularly. If incapable of composing their own they could read from sermon collections, or read out from improving books sanctioned by the local bishop, such as Landolfo's *Life of Christ* in the Cesena diocese. Carlo Borromeo's Milan seminary paid special attention to training pupils how to preach, and Federico Borromeo continued this emphasis. Archbishop S. Gesualdo at the Conza synod of 1597 stressed that preachers should teach clearly, offer nothing disapproved of by the Church, not narrate from the Apocryphal biblical writings or miracles not approved by recognised church writers, and not tell inappropriate, ridiculous, useless, fruitless tales. The parish priests were also required to read out instructions and homilies from bishops and vicars general and to reiterate major Tridentine rules – as about marriage or paying tithes; they might also be message-bearers for local civilian authorities.[45]

Religious education increased through various kinds of catechism or Christian Doctrine schools, with some knock-on effects on general literacy and education. The idea developed that on Sundays and major feast days children – and later sometimes adults found to be defective in basic Christian knowledge when they proposed to get married – should be taught the rudiments of the faith and morals. From 1417 some Bologna churches had such feast-day schools, and from 1433 there was a confraternity to develop such teaching. From the 1530s Castellino da Castello and others launched a similar movement in Milan, leading to the creation of the Company of Christian Doctrine, which soon had offshoots in other cities. This partly influenced the 1563 Tridentine decree that parish priests should organise the teaching of Christian doctrine to children on Sundays and other feast days. Some priests operated alone; others were assisted by lay men and women, who created confraternities both as organising units and to help their own religious life, or by members of Orders.

Such schooling basically involved learning – and ideally understanding – the Creed, Ten Commandments, Our Father and Hail Mary and learning about the sacraments and basic Christian tenets. Teachers were expected to rely on the major catechisms, notably the Roman Catechism. Jesuits treated these catechism schools as also elementary schools for wider learning. Confraternities of Christian Doctrine in their schools in key areas such as Rome, Venice, Turin, Milan, Como and other Lombard places taught reading; a few also taught writing. Those in Rome and Bologna, where different levels of classes were organised in certain parts of the cities, organised disputations and competitions. Prizes were awarded for good conduct, as in Rimini. Various manuals stressed that the schools should be enlivened with singing, processions and competitions. Such were the carrots, to offset the sticks and whips that in some places like Bologna were used to ensure that recalcitrant children attended and behaved while undergoing instruction.

Instruction in Christian Doctrine schools thus could embrace basic Christian doctrinal teachings, and elementary literary skills, but also social and moral teaching, good neighbourliness and the practice of good works. The schooling probably encouraged social conformity and reduced juvenile secular playfulness on feast-days, and benefited general literacy, at least in north-central cities. In such areas also, especially in Rome, schools involved girls equally with boys. This broadened the educational opportunities for females, and took them out of the household into a wider community – which was sometimes resented and feared by more elite families.

The extent of the Christian Doctrine schooling is hard to gauge. Bologna, the archdiocese of Milan and Rome were probably the major success areas; in the 1580s Bologna had about forty different schools with about 600 adults teaching 4000 children; Milan in 1599 claimed to have 20,504 children enrolled in Christian Doctrine schools in the city and neighbouring areas; Rome in 1611–12 claimed seventy-eight schools with 5800 boys and 5090 girls being taught by 529 confraternity brothers and 519 sisters. This, however, may have been near the peak, with a decline in enthusiasm and activity coming from the 1630s, though by the end of the century a whole range of district (*rionali*) elementary schools – free public or private – catered for girls as well as boys. Rome had benefited from the size and efficiency of the Archconfraternity of Christian Doctrine, backed by the illustrious Cardinal Roberto Bellarmino and his various catechisms. A study of the archconfraternity archives, however, warns that even in Rome there were considerable problems in maintaining the schools. Many, especially for the girls, changed locations frequently. Children going to the schools might be molested and endangered by the irreligious and immoral. Considerable tensions could exist between the archconfraternity and local parish priests.[46]

Religious reform motives enhanced broader education in other ways, and added religious-moral dimensions to secular education. After Trent, attempts were made to ensure that all those who taught in any kind of public schooling should be checked for religious competence and conformity. The survival of records of attestation has allowed Paul Grendler (1989) to provide an invaluable snapshot of the range of schooling and teachers in Venice in 1587. About 4625 pupils were enrolled in formal schools, under 258 teachers, in independent or church schools, whether teaching grammar and the classics, vernacular literature or the *abbaco* (mathematics, business concerns, etc.). Additionally there were the Venetian catechism schools. The extent to which bishops and vicars throughout Italy did check on the religious and moral dimensions in formal schooling, and accredited teachers is hard to gauge.[47]

New religious Orders expanded the educational horizons at all levels. In Naples the Jesuits had opened their first school in 1552, and by 1558 claimed to be teaching 300 boys Italian literature, Greek and Latin, with Christian Doctrine on Fridays and Saturdays. The boys were exhorted to confess and communicate regularly – still a dangerous novelty. From 1586 the Oratorians organised public instruction in poorer districts of Naples (the Mercato, Lavinaro and Borgo dei Vergini). In 1626 the Scolopians opened their first Naples school in the Duchessa district, notorious for its prostitutes – and so their offspring. According to José Calasanz (or Calasanzio) they lacked the resources to answer many requests for more such schools. Earlier, Calasanzio and his Scolopians had made their mark in Rome by launching a school for 100 pupils in the poor parish of S.Dorotea in Trastevere, for elementary education and the catechism. When they soon moved to the more central area of S.Andrea della Valle they claimed to have about a 1000 pupils.[48]

While it is argued that Protestantism fostered literacy more than Catholicism did, current knowledge suggests that in Italy for at least the major cities, and some other parts of north-central dioceses, lay learning and literacy was significantly encouraged. Though the *whole* Bible was not readily available in Italian (after an adventurous period of publication and dissemination in the first half of the sixteenth century), religious vernacular literature at all levels was plentiful for those who could read at all: catechisms, lives of Christ, the Virgin and Saints, and manuals for religious devotion. A personal approach to religion, rather than just through the parish priest or spiritual adviser, was encouraged by some church leaders. Even the highly dictatorial Carlo Borromeo was not averse to family prayers, and the Barnabites among others encouraged a family domestic approach to religious life. Some confraternities, especially of the Sacrament, the Rosary and Christian Doctrine acted primarily as agents of the parish priest, and might be seen as perpetrators of a narrow authoritarian, unthinking mentality. But other confraternities encouraged a lay independence, vitality and debate.[49]

This chapter has focused on parochial society, primarily looking at attempts to create a fuller and more uniform parochial society through Catholic Reform. More Italians became better informed about Christian beliefs and values. Bishops attacked and probably curtailed pagan and dubious popular practices attached to Christian rituals. The parish unit was better defined, the parish church a more recognised centre. The parish priest or his vicar was more dominant and effective, as an agent of social control through the parish, or as a facilitator of social amelioration. Where the parochial systems worked well, literacy and educational standards rose, affecting both Christian orthodoxy and more sceptical criticism, as well as the wider uses of secular literacy. Visitation reports suggest that from the later sixteenth century the physical conditions of churches and chapels, and their accoutrements, improved, and the churches were more fit places for worship. This was probably best when parish clergy and confraternities worked in some harmony; but there could be plenty of tension between them as well.[50] Many tensions and failures have already been indicated, when the laity resisted limitations on some past practices. Stricter moral, sexual codes were resisted both by clergy and parishioners, and in many parishes a blind eye was turned to clerical and lay concubinage. The difficult and ambiguous position of the celibate clergy in early modern society has been highlighted as an under-discussed and misunderstood topic of significance for social harmony in villages or urban parishes. The Inquisition might take a harsher line on certain moral as well as theological matters, often alerted through denunciations by both disgruntled neighbours and worried priests. Some such adverse and beneficial aspects of changing parochial relationships are further explored in the next chapter.

11

SOCIAL TENSIONS, CONTROL AND AMELIORATION

Social disharmony, violence and social control

Modern Italy has had an image as a particularly violent society, by western European standards, since the late 1960s. This fits the image of the Italian Renaissance, as conceived by Jacob Burckhardt in the nineteenth century, or fostered by the eminently readable *Autobiography* of the goldsmith-sculptor Benvenuto Cellini (1500–71), that features violence and bisexuality as well as great artistic and political tensions in Rome and Florence.[1] Previous chapters have already exemplified tensions, strife and problems of control. This chapter will explore some causes and examples further, consider the extent to which conflicts were modified if not controlled, and note areas where social control, by governments, elites and the reformed church, increased.[2]

Italian sources suggest a violent society through the fifteenth to seventeenth centuries, fostered by communal political struggle and baronial lawlessness. As indicated in Chapter 1, the post-1559 situation helped diminish violent political trouble, rendering urban areas more stable. Courtly and gentlemanly codes may have encouraged social-political struggles to be conducted in less overtly violent ways, as Edward Muir argues for the Friuli region after the murderous 1511 Carnival scene in Udine. The Counter-Reformation ethos fostered peace-making and loving your enemy, what John Bossy sees as a 'moral tradition'. Rural violence, especially with waves of banditry, may not have lessened much, though Jesuits and other peace-makers even made inroads into remote southern fastnesses.[3]

Various factors encouraged lawlessness in Italian society, including geography. The ruggedness and remoteness of much terrain provided bases for fugitives from the law and (temporary) political losers. They could chose when and where to harry and raid. Forces of law and order or of the main political authority were at a considerable disadvantage. A multiplicity of hilltop communities and towns allowed dissident barons or communes to defy central authority. Where there were many small competing 'states', as in late fifteenth-century Romagna, disorder and violence would be encouraged, unless a lord (*signore*) was particularly strong.[4] The high density of many Italian cities – on hilltops, or climbing up in the cliff-side as in Genoa – made the problem of keeping order within cities very difficult.

Violence is not necessarily a test of levels of social dislocation and disharmony. As has long been argued for England, bread riots or political 'mob' activity may have had some basic rules, orderly procedures and limitations on excess (by both rioters and governing authorities), that suggest a process of social adjustment and bargaining, not a breakdown in the structures of society. The cruelty and violence behind feuding and vendetta (allegedly an Italian speciality), may be interpreted – as in Angelo Torre's study (1994) of an eighteenth-century Piedmontese vendetta – as part of fairly coherent procedures for altering and settling several different social relationships and power struggles. Insights into physical and verbal violence in Roman society in Cellini's life-time suggest that much of the physical violence against persons and property, and a whole range of verbal abuse (often connected to the violence, and with strong sexual language), conformed to well-recognised patterns of behaviour, with recognised meanings for the recipients, and for the legal authorities who took cognisance of such cases, and often reacted appropriately according to the codes of honour and dishonour involved. Distinctions can be made between the violent brawling of (maybe drunken) youths, and violence conducted more rationally according to recognised responses to invasions of home and body (especially the female body), of affronts to and betrayal of personal and family honour or friendship.[5]

Brigandage and banditry – seen as major scourges through the early modern period – were sometimes part of strategies of political conflict, landlord–peasant relations, or governments' law-and-order policies, not just products of personal greed, dire necessity or original sin. Bandits were much feared, and were mythologised. Not all *banditi* should be seen as 'bandits' in normal English usage, meaning armed gangsters creating mayhem in the countryside. Governments lacked the resources to imprison criminals for long. Declaring somebody a *bandito* was a common sentence, applied when death or the galleys were deemed too severe, or politically unwise and a fine was considered impractical. But additionally somebody could be declared *bandito*, without trial, if contumaciously not appearing when summoned to court to face accusations and charges. Given problems of communication, the innocent or guilty, unaware of an initial summons, might be thus *banditi* before they knew it. Others did not risk the vagaries of a court, and fled. *Banditi* thus disappeared from major urban areas – where authorities and their police (*sbirri*) or soldiers might readily capture them – to remoter villages or towns.

Some *banditi* tried to settle unnoticed into a new environment to live peaceably and law-abidingly, as Bologna court records suggested. Others of course sought safety and income by joining a band of *banditi* to pursue a criminal career. Banishment could be rescinded and the accused receive grace, by making peace with the original victim, by paying a fine to the court or another state institution – the Grand Dukes Medici had this as a major element in their punishment and fiscal policies – or by securing the intervention of a confraternity or guild given the privilege of releasing prisoners and the condemned. A *bandito* could secure his own pardon by killing or securing the capture of another, notorious, *bandito*. Prospero Lapino, sometime miller of Montalera, prosecuted 1595–6 in Perugia, then in the Roman Governor's court for 'excesses' (murder, knifings, sexual molestation, pigeon stealing, fraud), had earlier been pardoned for armed violence when he helped kill a notorious bandit leader, Count Cesare Montemelini.[6] Different states made conditions about what kind of bandit could be killed to secure remission for the killer. Such procedures encouraged violence through the countryside. Governments hoped real trouble-makers would eliminate each other. It added to the unrest of some *contado* areas – but that was of less concern usually to central authorities, until banditry became too rampant – as it did in the Papal State, Tuscany and the Kingdom of Naples in the late sixteenth century.[7]

Some bandit groups were formed by evil, criminal men (occasionally women) intent on stealing, pillaging and raping to survive and enjoy life, while others fitted Eric Hobsbawm's 'social bandit' model, the Robin Hood who stole from the rich to help the poor, with selective targeting of victims and rules of what might be seized and redistributed. Marco Sciarra's great band caused havoc in the Abruzzi region, then the Papal State, Tuscany and the Veneto between 1584 and 1593. In Rosario Villari's view, Sciarra led 'a genuine guerrilla force' whose main members 'scrupulously followed norms of behaviour which conformed to Sciarra's social ideal'.[8] However, many bandit bands in the fifteenth and sixteenth centuries were geared to feuds and vendettas among leading families. Those running a vendetta could take advantage of criminal bandits, exiles and soldiers, as in the west Friuli in the 1560s–70s. 'For some, military service, crime and membership of an armed band were interchangeable or alternative forms of employment.'[9]

In the Val Fontanabuona of Liguria more than 200 bandits active between 1564 and 1635 have been identified. Few were professional or career criminals, or simple peasants. Many came a distance, from families of tavern-keepers and millers or workers with silk and velvet – all occupations that could involve, or easily lead to charges of, fraud. Taverns were ideal meeting places for those involved in illicit activities. Bands formed and dissolved quickly. They worked along the trade routes between Rapallo, Chiavari and Genoa or the Po valley, attacking mule trains carrying olive oil, grains and chestnuts. Powerful local figures, nobles in the sixteenth century, more often merchants in the mid seventeenth backed them. Banditry connected thereby with both local feuding and business activity, licit and contraband.[10]

The worst period of banditry was probably from the mid sixteenth century to the early decades of the seventeenth, generated by the ending of the major European conflicts by 1559, and the fall of the Republic of Montalcino, or 'commonwealth of exiles' (1555–9), resisting the Emperor, the Medici of Florence and their supporters in captured Siena. The survivors infested the remoter parts of Tuscany, and backed Alfonso Piccolomini, Duke of Montemarciano, as the major bandit leader.[11] Other nobles in the Papal State, Tuscany, Venetia and the Kingdom of Naples under threat from central governments, affected by shifts from arable farming to pasturage acted as leaders or, like the Caetani, protectors with safe castles. Religious wars in France and the Netherlands encouraged soldiers to move between transalpine soldiering and home brigandage, like Prospero Lapino. State cooperation finally tamed the worst excesses of this cumulative banditry, including the break-up of the Marco

Sciarra bands. However, the food crises of the 1590s added to violent protest, desperate criminality, punishments by banishments. From the seventeenth century the brigandage problem seemingly lost some vendetta and noble-feuding elements for at least north-central Italy. The combinations of contrabanding, profiteering, localised feuding, social protest against landowners and tax collectors and self-protection of *banditi* still generated violent troubles, especially in areas remote from judicial control. Typically we find this in Friuli in the late eighteenth century, when tobacco had become a major focus of theft and smuggling over the Venetian–Austrian borders; this overlapped with social-protest brigandage as rural conditions declined. Forceful use of *sbirri* by the authorities based in Udine, Cividale and Pordenone encouraged resentful support for brigands and smugglers, to liberate whom whole villages – men, women and children, backed by priests and some local nobles (like Count Giuseppe di Prampero at Gemona in 1779) – were prepared to attack and kill officials and their police. Worse violence was to follow with the French invasions and the fall of the Venetian Republic.[12]

In southern Italy the infestation of the countryside with bandits was even harder to eradicate, especially when some noblemen willingly offered protection, used bandits for their own disputes and hampered government action. Sometimes, however, Viceroys did organise a major purge, as over Marco Sciarra's allies in the 1590s, or again in the 1680s. The Viceroy G. de Haro y Guzman, Marchese del Carpio, ensured that leading noble protectors of bandits were harshly imprisoned for some years – including the Dukes of Termoli (who died in prison), of Acerenza and of Ardore (who was, unusually for a nobleman, severely tortured) – while armed forces were deployed in strength, especially in the Abruzzi and Campagna. Eventually hundreds of bandit leaders were decapitated, and a thousand sent to the galleys. Brutal resolution could work, but few Viceroys had the determination or the available forces to keep up the pressure against lowly criminals and criminal aristocrats.[13]

Riots and revolts

Selfish criminal activity, clan or personal vendettas and anti-government protests by high or low born usually made common cause. This generally counteracts concepts of 'class war' in the countryside. The interlocking of urban and rural society means that it is hard to distinguish between 'peasant' revolts and urban riots, though Tuscan mountain villages staged a largely successful peasant revolution against Florentine tax exploitation in the early fifteenth century.[14] The troubles centred on the Carnival massacre in Udine in 1511 combined an urban revolt of lower orders against the elite, elitist factional fighting and rural conflicts where 'peasants' under one clan, the Savorgnan, fared better than those under other landowners – such that peasants fought peasants, often as well-organised village communities.[15] The Naples and Palermo revolts of 1647–8 (and continuing longer in parts of the Kingdom of Naples) show the co-mingling of all levels of society at key points of the revolt – against foreign occupation, taxation policies or food shortages. The key events were in the two great cities, but there were many ripple effects for months after in smaller towns and *università*, where local issues produced different configurations

The key periods when there was seething rural discontent and violence over a wide area, such that peasant revolt might be seen as a dominant factor, were probably in the late 1490s to 1520s in the south and in the Veneto, especially Friuli (during the Italian War period); in parts of the Papal States and neighbouring areas of Naples and Tuscany in the 1570s–90s, overlapping with connected and separate brigandage problems; and in the late 1640s and early 1650s following the Masaniello revolt in Naples. None of these appear to be as extensive as the French peasant revolts of the sixteenth and seventeenth centuries. Urban riots over rising grain prices or food controls did take place, though there seems no easy pattern. Naples may have been more vulnerable than other large cities, as in 1505, 1508, 1585–6 and 1647. As in 1647 some riots had significant consequences. A Faenza riot over corn prices in 1477 brought down leading Manfredi *signori*, though the rioters allowed other family members to take over. Trouble over food in Venice in 1527–9 led to positive government policies to ensure food supplies, and help for the poorest. Other cities learned similar lessons that rendered rioting less likely.[16]

Sixteenth-century revolts in the Kingdom of Naples are not easily seen as simply anti-feudal. Revolts against changes in feudal lordship might be connected with wider political policies of the government (notably with the Spanish–French conflicts in the early sixteenth century), with known or feared characteristics of the new baron and his family. Revolts might be against obvious excesses of power, but also over any innovations by a more active baron or over ambivalent views about forest rights, pasturage and the use of common lands. The rioters might be lowly peasants, or lesser nobles, civic officials of the *università* and substantial farmers. Leading nobles were readily killed by vassals, especially in 1513–14, including the rising merchant Count G. C. Tramontano at Matera, whose lavish lifestyle incurred wrath. (Even in the twentieth century thousands lived in curious cave dwellings in the ravines there.) Matera successfully secured the recognition of communal privileges by 1518. Other Basilicata communes successfully revolted against unwelcome new feudatories. Among those who seem to have been killed for seeking to raise feudal exactions were Duke Belisario Acquaviva at Nardò, and a poet, Galeazzo di Tarsia, *signore* of Belmonte (Calabria), in 1553.[17]

The most famous and spectacular Italian revolt in our period was that in Naples in 1647. The background factors included bad harvests and food shortages, rising taxes by the Spanish authorities to pay for their world-wide war struggles, increasing exactions imposed on peasants from some landowners to pay for their conspicuous consumption, inflated dowries, and declining incomes from other sources. An influx of peasants into Naples made the situation more volatile when taxes were raised on flour, vegetables and fruit to pay for the Spanish armies. News of a revolt in Palermo (in May), which prompted the cancelling of a tax on fruit, encouraged the initial attack on the tax office in the Piazza del Mercato on Ascension Day (6 June). Two leaders soon emerged: a fisherman, Masaniello (Tommaso Aniello of Amalfi), and a lawyer, Giulio Genoino, who had long argued for the political equality of middling classes (*popolo*) with the nobles. Masaniello was initially a popular hero (having support from recent peasant incomers as well as long-term residents, whether artisans or professionals), especially in the light of early assassination attempts by nobles and financiers anxious to save their palaces from attack and looting. Two Carafa brothers and some alleged assassins were killed with certain ritualistic gestures, and echoes of popular justice meted out to Giovanni Starace in the 1585 Naples revolt. Masaniello was praised as 'a man sent from God', who sought social justice and economic benefits, then allegedly became somewhat megalomaniac and 'mad', so was called a 'tyrant' by erstwhile supporters. He was then assassinated (16 July) by a baker (Salvatore Cataneo), the man in charge of corn supplies (Michelangelo Ardizzone) and others; his head was carried around the city on a pike, while children dragged his body through the streets. Who lay behind the plot is unclear; the Viceroy (the Duke of Arcos) or Genoino were the chief suspects, in collusion but from different motives (as Rosario Villari believes). When the authorities then reduced the size of the official bread loaf – sold at controlled prices – the dead Masaniello became a folk hero again, and was given a spectacular funeral. Soon talk started of miracles resulting from relics, such as his hair. Public agitation continued spasmodically into the next year in Naples itself – with major riots or demonstrations by weavers or armed students. Genoino (until banished by the Viceroy) and others pursued a more intellectual and subtle republican cause. With the involvement of some dissident aristocrats a Republic was declared, the rule of Spain rejected and appeals made for French support. The Masaniello revolt turned into an international episode in the Spanish–French struggle for hegemony. After a mismanaged French intervention Naples returned to Spanish allegiance in April 1648.

Meanwhile the revolt had been taken into the countryside, and peasants killed landowners who failed to show sympathy. Giuseppe Galasso (1977) pointed to 'revolutionary' provincial leaders like Matteo Cristiano in Puglia and Lucania, or Ippolitano Pastena in the Salernitano region. According to the Medici agent, in Calabria there was no hamlet (*casaluccio*) that had not made a revolution with burning, murdering and theft. Francesco d'Andrea, a leading lawyer-administrator and part of the intellectual/professional elite (*ceto civile*) was involved in the protest movements in the Abruzzi, and ready to justify this in his memoirs much later. Baronial excesses and aristocratic arrogance or worse had become intolerable for many in most levels of society.[19]

On the Masaniello urban revolt there were many contemporary accounts, from conflicting viewpoints, that have allowed for varied interpretations of motivations and actions. The events highlight the major political, financial, economic and social tensions in a Kingdom where the strains of the Spanish imperial wars had worsened conditions for most people. However, the cult of Masaniello was fostered by propaganda writings, elitist and popular, by prints and paintings (by Micco Spadaro especially), by medals (including ones showing Masaniello on one side, Oliver Cromwell on the other) and by oral communications. He remained a figure who could be invoked as revolutionary martyr and popular hero – to inspire protest against government tyranny, excessive taxation and greedy landowners – through to the French Revolution and the declaration of the Neapolitan Republic in 1799.

The Masaniello revolt in Naples itself was clearly multi-layered and multi-causal, as many sectors of society vented their anger against Spanish authority and economic conditions in general, but diverse and more personal targets in particular. The social diversity of those involved, and their conflicting aims, made a dramatic result unlikely, short of strong French involvement – but Paris had its own crises. The wider arena of revolt in the Kingdom, while less clear in details, seems to have been a more widespread and interlocked series of anti-feudal revolts than encountered before or later until the early eighteenth century. The unprecedented publicity, with popular religious overtones, of the Naples revolt probably encouraged more people to act through the Kingdom on endemic local grievances.

Problems of keeping control

Controlling Italian society, whether through judicial proceedings or policing activity, was extremely difficult in the early modern period. Communication difficulties through hostile terrain inhibited knowledge of crime through much of the *contado*, and the policing of any legal response. Let bandits eliminate bandits. A multiplicity of states and semi-independent jurisdictions competed or colluded depending on temporary political circumstances. The legal structures were complex. The strong theoretical foundations of Roman Law, civil and criminal, competed with Canon Law for anything that might pertain to the Church, and fundamental communal statutes drawn up over the centuries to govern local procedures, policies and targets – supplemented by edicts and decrees on a more temporary basis. Italian universities specialised in training men to take full advantage of legal conflicts. There were grey areas between Civil and Canon Law; local edicts might supplement Canon law, say, over marriage procedures. Some states like Venice paid little attention to Roman Law, relying more on their own law creation and procedures, while the Papal State was more wedded to Roman law. For those with money and power, there were endless opportunities to dispute jurisdictions and competence procedures. However, at a serious criminal level justice might be quick and arbitrary even over powerful nobles who got caught.

State and cities had numerous courts and tribunals, with varying degrees of investigative, judicial and punishing powers, using their own officials and 'police' to apprehend, investigate and punish. Councils and committees that were primarily deliberative, administrative and executive might have certain judging, punishing and policing roles attached. Florence in the 1560s had about twenty-eight courts and tribunals that could issue criminal condemnations – though Cosimo I had made one, the Eight on Public Safety (Otto di Guardia a Balià), the most powerful and wide-ranging criminal court, and central to his policies. This controlled the main police force at the Bargello prison, but there was also the more notorious prison of the Stinche, with other police. The Abbondanza tribunal primarily controlled food supplies, but was competent to try and punish those involved in smuggling and fraud. The office of the Capitano della Parte Guelfa mixed civil and criminal cases in dealing with property conflicts. The Sanità was the chief public health body, which (as in other cities like Bologna) could dominate the scene during plague and other epidemic crises. Specialist 'moral' courts existed, such as the Onestà to deal with licensed brothels and illegal prostitution, and the Ufficiale di Notte, which from 1432 to 1502 specialised in sodomy cases. The latter became the competence also of the Conservatori delle Leggi, whose major remit concerned banditry and altering banishment orders.

Other large cities similarly had numerous courts, if not so many. In Venice the most powerful executive council, the Council of Ten, could turn itself into a court for 'political' offences, and was responsible for some secret executions. The Avogadari di Comun was the chief criminal court and policing establishment; but the deliberative Council of Forty (*Quaranta*), partly dependent on it, could handle assault cases including rape. In Rome the Governor's Court, based in the Tor di Nona prison till the seventeenth century, then in the model New Prisons (*Carcere Nuove*, built 1652–7), was more obviously the dominant criminal court. It was headed by a leading ecclesiastic, as was the Vicariate court, which dealt with spiritual cases which included marital offences, midwifery, morals, exorcism and licences for school-masters. Some of these problems and offences could also be investigated by the Holy Inquisition. The Senator's court, based on the Capitol (*Campidoglio*) was the leading municipal court, dealing with both criminal and civil cases, which sometimes challenged Papal powers.[20]

Policing power was variable in competence and riddled with corruption. Forces were ill-paid and untrained, employing former prisoners and soldiers. Joining briefly secured weapons for private use later. Being a court or tribunal official must have opened up opportunities for wheeling and dealing, accepting bribes and fees. The use of informers seemed crucial in helping unmask crimes, especially in the country-side. Military garrisons were used to help keep order, and soldiers accompanied city-based authorities appointed to control the *contado* and prevent serious trouble. The Venetians from the early fifteenth century established local military forces, *cernide*, to police and discipline their mainland territories. By the seventeenth century these were well and diversely armed (keeping the Brescia armaments industry occupied), but the costs of maintaining them upset local cities and communities who were made to pay for them, and who resented interference in their traditional smuggling activities. In the early seventeenth century Venice hired Corsicans, or Turks and Venetians from the Balkans, to police the Friuli and Polesine especially, because they had no local ties, allegiances or interests.[21] Venetian officials supervising the Terraferma in the sixteenth and seventeenth centuries frequently complained to the Republican Senate that they lacked enough soldiers to tame the armed *bravi* of local noble landowners, exploiting their peasants.

In Bologna the Torrone was the major magisterial court covering city and *contado*, and had its own *sbirri*. Its copious surviving records of denunciations and reports surprisingly show how a police official or small group might appear in remote areas, and catch trouble-makers; or might be summoned for alleged acts of violence and intimidation. Men guarding sheep on the hills, having words, coming to blows, were reported and imprisoned at least overnight. Arrogant youths of the middling sort were arraigned with insulting and threatening social inferiors, though the *sbirri* might on other occasions have trouble asserting their authority and protecting the weak. As Ottavia Niccoli (1995) using Torrone files stresses, there was much youth crime, with young children as perpetrators and victims. In the late sixteenth and seventeenth century groups of children (pre-teens or early teens), without parental control, were some menace to society. That we know of such activities indicates efforts to maintain some law and order. At least in Bologna and some of its *contado*, *sbirri* working for both secular and ecclesiastical authority might appear at house doors, in hostelries and rented rooms hunting for priests sodomising boys, wenching and gambling, or for laymen who were too openly adulterous. Some appearances by the *sbirri* suggest tip-offs from the public. At least in the city they pursued those suspected of evading plague regulations, whether by immorality or seeking to work in closed-up workshops.[22]

Excessive *sbirri* activity might be resented by a local community. Letters sent from Castel Bolognese by its vice-podestà to the central Bologna government in the 1660s and 1670s expressed unhappiness about the size and cost of the *sbirri* attached to the Bargello court. They wanted the Legate to reduce the squad to the least possible, so money could be spent on repairs to walls, mills, houses and public streets. The Bargello court did all sorts of deals with bandits from Romagna, (also part of the Papal State, but separately administered). But Bologna failed to protect the smugglers (*contrabbandieri*) from Castel Bolognese – involved in traditional wine and wheat smuggling – when they sought to defend themselves and their goods by resort to archebuses against officials from the courts of Romagna and Imola. Such smugglers should not be harshly punished. Thanks were offered when central Bologna authorities released Domenico Camersini, 'our inveterate smuggler', who might otherwise have suffered unduly. Within a 'state', or subsection of it, jurisdictions and officials clashed, lacking a common purpose. Economics demanded that some traditional illegal pursuits should continue (even if to the detriment of the central exchequer).[23]

Prisons were not primarily for punishment of criminals, at least until the eighteenth century, when qualms about capital punishment and the wish to curb bandits in rural society, suggested prisons be more used for correction and control. Prison rooms and cells were used to detain those arrested until they could be produced in a court, or have evidence recorded. Pre-trial investigations might necessitate a longish period in the prison. Cost-effectiveness suggested quick punishments not needing imprisonment: death, galleys, floggings, penances, fines, exile. Prison as a sentence was for the clergy, for 'political prisoners', for opponents of the state or city, feudal lord or church authority, where execution or exile might be more troublesome. Graffiti visible and recorded in prisons in Venice, Ferrara or Palermo give evidence of longer-term prisoners, some of whom faced execution. Otherwise prisons were for alleged or convicted debtors who could or would not pay and for beggars and other troublesome poor cleared from the streets.

Prisons varied from a small tower room or cellar to a major building complex. Large prison complexes, as in Florence, Milan, Rome and Naples, had different rooms and sections to combine the various functions – from court room, torture chambers and single cells for the dangerous, to large rooms for male and female prisoners who might move about freely within the complex, and even leave and return. Since it was desirable to have food and drink provided from outside by family, friends or creditors there could be considerable contact with the outside world; and opportunities for escape. John Brackett has well described the old Florentine Stinche prison, while visitors to Venice can join excellent guided tours of the prisons in and attached to the Doge's Palace.[24] They show very mixed conditions in terms of space and light (and their absence), if not the filth, damp and rats. For many prisoners there was a social community within the complex, with discourse and intercourse. Religious reformers from the mid-sixteenth century provided spiritual comfort, education and books, as well as food and medicines. Venetian Inquisition records show that prisoners charged with serious heretical offences and beliefs freely discoursed with other prisoners, and received visitors. Sometimes they talked too freely – and provided evidence against themselves.[24]

Crime and morality

Grey areas between crime and morality existed then as now if sometimes differently, as over rape, prostitution, sodomy, verbal assaults, blasphemy, superstitious practices, inappropriate begging or wandering about at night. Offences were handled in different courts in various ways: criminal, civil, mixed, ecclesiastical. Sometimes special offices and courts were created to deal with specific problems; Venice from 1537 had a Bestemmia magistracy primarily to curb blasphemy, but also handling cases of verbal abuse, and even of sedition (if the Council of Ten did not itself take these). But Florentine sodomy and prostitution cases might appear in other courts besides the specialist Ufficiali di Notte and Onestà courts, so even here historians have trouble tracking down the incidence of offences, and the extent of punishment. The harsh statutory punishments for offences like sodomy or rape (including the death penalty), sometimes contrasted with the actual punishments meted out. Confusion can be caused by the way moral and religious accusations were made, openly or in secret denunciation boxes, when the accused might have offended with other crimes (theft and fraud), or non-criminal political or social offences and insults.

Rape, as already mentioned, was treated primarily as a violent assault, and an offence against the honour of the father and the family, more than against the girl or woman herself. Since a sexual crime involving a mature woman was likely to involve passion and even love (which Venetian courts apparently took more cognisance of from the mid fifteenth century), the court might punish less harshly than for a 'rational' crime like housebreaking. Rape against children or nuns was treated more seriously than against other women, and could lead to serious punishment; as could gang rapes. But in many cases a rape charge was resolved by marriage to the perpetrator (if unwed), or a dowry payment that would allow her to marry another, so restoring her (and the family's) honour. It was hard for a female to prove rape against a totally uncompromising male, especially if she was pregnant, since her (at least partial) cooperation in the act was often assumed. Awareness that a 'rape' charge could be a complex marital strategy (as already discussed), must have made it even harder to persuade a court to convict and punish a seriously violent rapist.[26]

Adultery was punishable by death in some law codes; in Ferrara the guilty woman was to be burned alive, but not the man. In practice the courts often took a much more lenient view, as in sixteenth-century Venice, though the honour of offended aristocratic families might encourage the murder of both male and female offenders, with little consequence for the murdering cuckold or his supporters.

Sodomy was one of the sex crimes that occasioned the most extreme statutory penalties, and excited the most lurid pulpit and other condemnations. The concern stemmed primarily from the Old Testament and the Church's opposition to any sexual act that could not be productive. The word *sodomia* was given various meanings, though it usually covered sexual acts between males; it could include anal intercourse between heterosexuals, lesbianism, oral sex and masturbation. 'Sodomy' could constitute a form of birth control within marriage, even if few were prepared to admit it. Confusion can thus be caused in trying to decide what took place when courts or chronicles made brief references. In practice the courts dealt mainly with male homosexuality, and reserved the extreme punishments for cases where young boys were involved, and/or leading clergy. The punishment procedures were often erratic, and seemingly became more lenient over time. Renaissance classical interests might have made male friendship, love and sexual activity more acceptable – and prevalent. We know most about homosexuality in Florence and Venice, cities that were denounced as being the most vilely sodomitic, and where authorities at times might have been the most tolerant. Michael Rocke (1996) has seen sodomy as prevalent through all levels of society, and as being part of the male life cycle of both the elites and the artisan classes. Youths between thirteen and eighteen appear in the records as 'passive' partners, often serving many 'actives', who were generally aged from about nineteen to thirty, then demonstrating their virility and indulging in male bonding through group sodomy sessions. Clearly many then entered married heterosexual lives, with very few older men appearing before the courts. There are doubts whether actual homosexuality then ended when past practitioners now had a female partner; just as some of the extrapolations from the figures for the extent of youth homosexuality have been challenged. Florence's Europe-wide reputation for sodomy was one reason why its special court was abolished in 1502 – for highlighting the crime. It was then dealt with by a variety of courts, and officials may have deliberately curtailed prosecutions in the interests of the city's image. Late marriage and celibacy among the upper ranks of Venetian society may have similarly encouraged male homosexuality there. The continued insistence on clerical celibacy risked encouraging homosexuality. Rocke judges the incidence in Florence of clerical sodomy as low, and lower than in Venice – as indicated by known accusations and charges; but ecclesiastical court records, difficult of access, need more study. Indiscreet clerical buggery of very young boys did risk a death sentence, but much might have been discreetly covered up.[27]

'Sodomy' could be a useful charge or libel to throw at enemies to secure their arrest, or to make them desist from certain activities. Like charges of 'atheism' it can mislead as to the orientation of those so accused. The charge was used against the major baroque poet Giambattista Marino as part of a literary duel, when his arrest in 1598 had probably been for seducing a rich merchant's daughter in Naples. Some poems imply that he at least viewed homosexuality with favour. Benvenuto Cellini had charges of sodomy thrown at him, including by his arch rival Bandinelli, though he was almost certainly actively bisexual. There were cases where religious and sexual deviancy probably genuinely went together. When the priest Francesco Calcagno was charged in 1550 by the Venetian Inquisition with atheism, blasphemy and sodomy, he advocated under questioning the superiority of homosexuality over heterosexuality, which was 'a matter for plebeians'. In the early seventeenth century philosopher-libertines like Antonio Rocco, who popularised the heretical ideas of Galileo's friend Cesare Cremonini about the immortality of the soul, had allegations of homosexuality and writing obscene poetry thrown at them (in the Council of Ten rather than the Inquisition), though they were not condemned – Rocco at least had powerful political supporters.[28]

Prostitution received ambiguous treatment by Italian authorities. Basically it was considered a necessary part of social life, to be tolerated but controlled, and taxed. Prostitutes might appear in denunciations and trials for other reasons, since their real and alleged skills could include love magic, healing powers and prognostication. Courts were not necessarily hostile to prostitutes. Prostitutes were afforded legal protection by the Roman Governor's court against physical assaults from clients, would-be clients, rejected lovers and pimps; they were given their say in pre-trial and trial proceedings and listened to with considerable openness and tolerance. Their own physical and verbal assaults often met with lenient and understanding treatment – as long as any 'magical' arts used were not too extreme or threatening.[29]

Religious control and the Inquisitions

The establishment of the Holy Office of the Inquisition in Rome in 1542, and the subsequent creation (or re-creation) of local tribunals in the different states, was a turning point for the control of society, but this needs cautious treatment The public images of 'the Inquisition' are generally hostile, and almost invariably misleading. The 'Italian' versions are tainted by the (again usually exaggerated) criticisms of the Spanish version, created from 1478 and under royal control rather than papal. The Roman Holy Office, its creation influenced by the Spanish, developed a permanent bureaucratic structure under the leadership of a Congregation of Cardinals headed by the Pope. This linked with tribunals elsewhere. It could never exercise within Italy the kind of central leadership that the Suprema central body did in Spain and its empire. The existence of local tribunals and their exact form and local operation had to be negotiated with the rulers of each state.[30]

At present our best knowledge concerns Venice and the Veneto. The Inquisition in Venice was a joint operation between church and state, and its archives ended up as part of the State Archive and so readily consulted. Once under way the inquisition tribunals operated very legalistically, under rule books and guidelines in the hands of well-trained lawyers, with theological advisers. Prior investigations and subsequent trial proceedings were more thorough than in other ecclesiastical or secular courts. Physical torture was used sparingly, and under fairly strict regulation – though there could be significantly effective psychological torture through the lengthy investigations carried on while many accused remained in prison, and the nature of the accusation and the accusers often remained unrevealed. Death sentences were rare and usually reserved for heretics deemed to have lapsed, and to be a threat to others. The Friulian miller, Menocchio Scandela, made famous by Carlo Ginzburg (1980), was only put to death after a second trial, for repeatedly propagating his strange views on the origins of the universe, angels and men (as worms from moulding moving cheese); for being a repeat heresiarch. This was at the insistence of Rome, when local inquisition officials favoured leniency. Some booksellers were executed – but only when they had too frequently been caught printing and selling far afield books prohibited by the Index. The inquisitors were mainly intent on re-educating the ignorant and misguided, and emphasising the importance of Church authority in teaching, rather than with serious punishment and retribution.

The tribunals were under-staffed, and the Italian ones – unlike the Iberian – did not have 'familiars' paid to assist with snooping and denunciations. Records for Venice, Bologna and Florence suggested a lot of voluntary denunciation of neighbours and self-confession (as well as some appearances under pressure from parish priests and confessors). Some denunciations followed inquisitors' requests that parish priests warn their congregation about the dangers of certain beliefs and practices. Denunciation and confessions often remained uninvestigated because the tribunal thought the matter too trivial, reckoned witnesses would be hard to find, had no resources to pursue the matter further or judged the issue to be one of neighbourly dispute, with a possibility of false accusations. Only a few denunciations and confessions were taken to a lengthy investigation and trial. The tribunals kept files open in case further allegations were made against the person. Since enough business came their way from outside, Inquisition officials in Italy seem seldom proactive, confining their initiatives to checking on those already convicted of significant heresy, and members of their family; as for example with the anabaptist Bernardin Barbano of Vicenza in 1573, or Marco Cerdoni and his sons from Dignano, as deniers of Purgatory.[31]

From the 1540s to 1570s or so the inquisitors (along with active bishops) were primarily intent on curbing the more serious errors of faith; with 'Lutheranism', a loose term that could embrace Valdesian and Calvinist versions of Protestantism, with anabaptism and with the dissemination of books banned by the various versions of the Index of Prohibited Books from 1559. Venice had the problem of Jewish converts and Jewish–Christian relations, while Naples had worries about the real conversion of Muslims. Increasingly the inquisitors took on a much wider range of issues, connected with sexual morality, the misuse of sacraments and sacramentals, magical practices and superstitions (love magic and magical practices for healing, for finding lost property or treasure), with fasting. With the Council of Trent reinforcing that marriage is a sacrament, any sexual misconduct or deviancy outwith a proper marital relationship could become a concern for the inquisition, as possible heresy. Table 11.1 gives some idea of the pattern of interest in the best documented tribunals of Venice and the Friuli.

These figures are of accusations, denunciations and self-denunciations, not trials. Classification is based on the main aspect seized on by the compilers of different inventories, who used various definitions. The Venetian inventories used Lutheranism vaguely to cover a variety of non-Catholic beliefs, while the Friulian

Table 11.1 Accusations and denunciations before Venice and Friuli Inquisition tribunals, 1547–1720

Major charge	*Venice*			*Friuli*		
	1547–85	*1586–1630*	*1631–1720*	*1557–95*	*1596–1610*	*1611–70*
Lutheranism	717	109	77	0	5	56
Anabaptism	37	0	1			
Heresy in general	68	27	5	200	64	37
Judaizing	34	16	28	1	0	3
Mohammedanism	10	27	42	0	4	30
Calvinism	13	18	29	0	1	31
Greek Orthodoxy	3	8	11	0	0	26
Other conversions						2
Atheism/Materialism	1	4	14	0	0	0
Apostasy	15	17	12	0	0	3
Heretical propositions	62	26	107	34	45	89
Prohibited books	93	48	40	7	46	127
Prohibited meats	23	12	16	66	153	40
Blasphemy	17	41	61	4	11	31
Abuse of Sacraments	9	12	106			
Bigamy	3	7	12	1	0	12
Concubinage	7	5	4	2	1	0
Adultery	3	7	0			
Sodomy	5	5	5			
Solicitation	3	22	72	1	1	47
Magical arts	59	319	641	45	256	317
Offending Holy Office	10	8	6	1	13	8
Pseudo-sainthood	0	1	5	0	0	8
Illegal Mass	2	4	14	0	0	1
False testimony	14	7	4	0	0	2
Miscellaneous	21	66	31	11	5	13
Totals	1229	816	1334	374	609	895
Annual average	32	35	15	10	43	15

Source: Monter and Tedeschi (1991), Appendices 2 and 3.

general heresy cases could include the close following of Lutheran beliefs. 'Abuse of sacraments' in Friuli was inventoried as a secondary charge, (probably included with magical arts). Headings used in Venetian nineteenth-century inventories can be misleading. That said, these figures give some indication of what inquisitors, parish priests and denouncing neighbours found alarming, and when. A shift in both areas from doctrinal heresy and confessional heterodoxy to moral heresy and magic is clear.

In the campaigns to enforce good Christian practices and morality the Inquisition tribunals and the ecclesiastical courts of the Patriarch of Venice and the archbishops of Bologna, Florence and Siena worked together. In Venice the Patriarch or his substitute sat on the Inquisition tribunal, and denunciators clearly had an option whether to take an issue to the Inquisition or the Patriarchal court. In the Bologna and some Tuscan dioceses the archbishops could be more pro-active and intrusive over sexual immorality by clergy and laity, and called on the secular police (*sbirri*) as well as their own employees, which gave them more useable manpower than the Inquisitors.

Venetian records show that clerical authority had considerable difficulty through to the later seventeenth century at least in enforcing the rules of fasting, in curbing attempts to use 'superstitious practices' (casting ropes or beans, looking into glass carafes, etc.) to affect love relations or health, and find lost or stolen property. Venetian women as well as men were vocal about the justification – especially in terms of biblical teaching, or silence – for fasting rules, the efficacy of the cult of the Virgin and saints, and the doctrine of Purgatory. In some cases, artisans and prostitutes (home-bred or foreign) were almost certainly reading gospel texts in the vernacular, as well as questioning what was heard in sermons.[32] The apparent openness of discussions in hostelries, in the streets, on balconies or at mainland mills, implies that ecclesiastical curbs and fear of the inquisitors were limited. Accused and witnesses could boldly reply to the tribunal or recording notary with seemingly limited fear of the consequences.

The laity could readily use the inquisition for their own advantage, to seek revenge on enemies or punish a practitioner of magic who failed to deliver what was required by denouncing her as whore and witch. A suspected thief or cheat might more readily be curbed by accusing him of blasphemy, as with G. P. Sorattini in Vicenza in 1646. In 1653 the vice-chancellor to the Venetian Patriarch, Francesco Mattei, was denounced as a blasphemer; but it was indicated that his accusers were the target of legal cases he was trying to enforce.[33] An approach to the Inquisition could forestall a troublesome accusation from another, and consciences about past misdeeds could be cleared in return for a few minor penances. For outsiders the Inquisition could help secure integration into society. In 1638 Emanuele Lobo approached the Florentine inquisitor; he was a circumcised Jew from a Lisbon family who wanted to be assured he could live now unmolested as a Christian in Tuscany; he claimed he had been forcibly circumcised by his father as a youth, when he had fallen ill. In 1639 two Saxon Lutherans, shoemakers, re-educated by Jesuits, sought absolution from the Venetian Inquisition to live freely in this city; as did two

Calvinists (a French soldier, and an Italian who had fought in France), who had been converted to the Catholic faith by Capuchins, who attested to their contrition.[34]

The Italian inquisitions and other ecclesiastical courts, backed by episcopal decrees and legislation, campaigned against many superstitious practices, and 'witchcraft', which were seriously attempted by men and women. Plenty believed they had the ability and knowledge to use incantations, blessed objects from talismans to umbilical cords, holy oil and sacrament bread, special concoctions (that could involve menstrual blood or semen as well as herbs) – to affect for good or ill the lives, health and love lives of others. Such beliefs and practices were fairly common currency in the countryside, but also in a great city like Venice. Neighbours reported the incidents and failures; inquisitors and bishops varied in how seriously they responded, but generally they sought to educate, to curb, but to impose only minor penances. The harsh sentences tended to be reserved for those, especially priests and friars, who seriously misused the sacraments. Even if the alleged or actual practices involved invoking the Devil or devils, the inquisitors seldom panicked or over-reacted – unlike in other areas of Europe. There was little in Italy that could be called a witch-craze. Italy, at Todi in the early fifteenth-century, may have produced the stereotypical witch image (sex with the Devil, flying, etc.), that was fostered by the Dominican *Malleus Maleficarum* from the 1480s, with grim results in certain parts of Europe. But Italian society was not seriously afflicted by witch-hunting; thanks largely to the due legal processes of well-trained inquisitors, the limited use of torture, a healthy scepticism about mass conspiracies, a less fervid misogyny, an acceptance in all levels of society of beneficial healing and love-magic in the hands of women and maybe a healthy scepticism about the power of the Devil. Several of those accused probably believed in their magical arts, in sabbats, in devilish pacts and even that they could fly by night, and had lurid sexual fantasies. It is probable that some *benandanti* in Friuli genuinely thought they had flown out in spirit to do good, to save the harvests, against evil forces. It is interestingly debatable how far such people were affected by malnutrition, dangerously adulterated food, herbs and ointments used for contraception and abortion that might also induce hallucinations (belladonna, henbane, *Datura* with atropine).[35] A Dominican theologian, Jordanes de Bergamo in the 1470s claimed that 'the vulgar believe, and the witches confess, that on certain days or nights they anoint a staff and ride on it to the appointed place or anoint themselves under the arms and in other hairy places.'[36] Italian clerical and secular judges tended to be sceptical about the more fanciful and devilish accusations and claims.

The Inquisition was potentially the most powerful and efficient institution to control beliefs and behaviour, and its remit under 'heresy' was very wide. In practice it was less intrusive and feared than usually imagined, and its judicial procedures were probably fairer than those of most secular and other ecclesiastical courts. It impinged seriously on few people. It was as much a weapon for lay society as against it. Its denunciations and cases reveal much about social tensions. It was a control mechanism, but in its own terms it offered amelioration through re-education and the chance of salvation.

Controlling the poor

In Chapter 6 it was noted that among many who might be 'poor' permanently or for part of their life, there were some deemed to be dangerous for society and needing to be controlled. Especially from the early sixteenth century some authorities and writers worried about an urban underclass that preferred to live from begging, stealing and fraud.[37] In the countryside there were similar people (some hitherto urban dwellers driven out or fleeing as *banditi*), who created gangs to threaten honest peasants and travellers. These groups were seen as permanent problems. Additionally there were fears of what would happen under food and economic crises leading to very high food prices, starvation and unemployment. In such circumstances the poor needing help within the city might rise from 10 per cent to 40 per cent or more. But such crises tended to attract incomers from smaller towns and villages, seeking food supplies and philanthropic help.

Many poor were seen as menacing and undeserving of assistance, especially in cities where they might cause riots and be criminal. Begging threatened the respectable in the streets, and even worshippers in church during Mass. As already indicated, at the sign of economic crisis alien beggars and prostitutes were expelled; as in Florence in 1498, Lucca in 1527 and 1539–40, Bologna through the 1560s, Rome in 1561 and Mantua or Bologna in the 1590s. Governments banned public begging, except possibly for strictly licensed groups like the blind and crippled. Policies were adopted to institutionalise the resident able-bodied poor in 'hospitals' to protect society generally, make them work and save their souls by curbing their sinfulness. Girls and vulnerable women (orphans, ex-prostitutes, battered and abandoned wives) were helped and protected in institutions, to save them from male depredations or their own sexuality. These policies were affected by ideas that the poor were especially sinful, as the Jesuit Paolo Segneri, adviser to the Grand Dukes of Florence, argued in the seventeenth century.

Civic authorities accepted some obligations to assist long-term resident poor, even if they simultaneously punished them. Occasionally the real needs of innocent, and starving, *contadini* would be recognised, as by the Farnese rulers of Parma in the great 1591 crisis; they were given a little help in food or money, but sent out of the city after a night. The same family did somewhat unusually recognise that involuntary unemployment could result from food-price crises, and had some job creation schemes.[38]

In line with European-wide attitudes from the early sixteenth century, some Italian authorities considered confining the dangerous and undeserving poor, or the vulnerable. The confining might be in prison, in sections of hospitals, in special conservatories or in hostels. Welfare and control went together; civic rulers, church leaders and lay confraternities co-operated. The combination of attitudes and forces was possibly most successfully seen in the development in Bologna from 1563 (effectively), of the *Opera dei Mendicanti* (Beggars' Institution). Trying to take beggars off the streets, it helped with shelter, food, clothing, medicines and spiritual comfort; it provided work opportunities, compulsory for the able-bodied, and punished the recalcitrant and immoral. Holding up to about 1400 male and female persons (as in 1590), it provided some solutions, whether the perspective was that of policing, moral reform or the relief of starvation. Hospital and confinement policies and practices in other cities followed. Papal imitations for Rome itself provided unfortunate examples of failure. Sixtus V's S.Sisto hospital (planned for 400 inmates), of 1587, designed to clear virtually all beggars off the streets, soon was left to the blind, poor girls and disabled widows. His successors were unable or unwilling to fund it, and some religious reformers as well as beggars objected to strict confinement and no-begging procedures. Innocent XII's similar effort (1692) had a like opposition and failure. In the later seventeenth and eighteenth century the secular rulers of Turin possibly had better policies and institutions to control the poor, provide welfare and foster a work ethic. But getting the institutionalised poor to produce cloth and clothing brought protests from free guild workers about unfair competition.[39]

For many Italians harsh confinement and control policies did not work economically in this world, and were unsatisfactory in the religious economy of saving souls hereafter. Social amelioration, combining philanthropy, control and manipulation, was more satisfactory.

Social amelioration

It was recognised that some poor deserved assistance, and that even those normally well off could come to need temporary ills ameliorated from outside the family. Contemporary attitudes until the eighteenth century encouraged social amelioration.[40] Poverty was a blessed state, if voluntarily sought, and it could ease the path through Purgatory to Heaven. Riches impeded that path, but if honestly earned and morally dispersed they had virtue and a beneficial social function, as was stressed by San Bernardino of Siena in the fifteenth century: 'The rich are necessary for republics, and the poor are necessary for the rich'.[41] Alessandro Sperelli echoed this in 1666, when he argued that the rich could help the poor materially, and the poor pray for the rich in return. Giving to the poor brought the giver closer to God. Using modern 'capitalist' arguments a Sicilian priest in Rome, P. De Angelis, shortly before had advocated alms-giving by the rich to the poor:

> Such is the debt of charity, the more a man gives, the more he becomes a creditor; whatever you give in alms here on earth, you deposit in heaven, and whatever you give to your brother, you keep for yourself, so it is with alms, by answering to the needs of another, you yourself acquire merit, and by helping others you yourself profit.[42]

Debates took place through the period on who constituted the poor, who should be helped at what point, and what priorities should operate if the resources for assistance were limited. In famine crises governments, confraternities and hospitals recognised the need to help all they could without too elaborate discrimination (other than between those who belonged to the city or district and those who did not). In more normal conditions discrimination and preferences appeared, simple or very elaborate, workable or not. San Bernardino had a very long list of categories for those giving alms; the donor should think first of his family, then saints, the honest, friends, Christians (not infidels), nobles where poverty was not their responsibility and they were ashamed to beg, and then other poor.[43] Other poor were then categorised, though not prioritised, as the imprisoned (by implication for debt), those afflicted by age, sickness, blindness and other disabilities, girls of marriageable age whose honesty is endangered unless quickly married, young wives whose poverty might entice them into sin – prostitution. Philanthropic confraternities might concentrate their help for their own poor – old and sick brothers and sisters, and vulnerable female relatives. Some spent considerable time judging individual cases by perceived need, while others elected to specialise in one category of poor – prisoners, the hospitalised, poor girls. The single most popular category was that of the poor girl or woman in need of a dowry to secure a suitable marriage, to guarantee her honour and respectability.

Philanthropic activity expanded from the later fifteenth century, embracing more in society than had been catered for by medieval confraternities and guilds, or the hospices-cum-hospitals promoted by them or city governments. By the mid eighteenth century, enlightened reformers campaigned against charitable activities generally, especially by confraternities or alms-givers, on the grounds that they simply encouraged further idleness, undermined a productive economy and discouraged the able from supporting their needy families.

In policies, intellectual argument and in institutional development many parts of Italy moved towards a modern welfare system; notably Venice, as the French prophet Guillaume Postel praised in 1546.[44] This involved an awareness of needs, as well as some rational analysis of how they might be met, and of how to allocate limited resources, when amelioration was possible and control necessary. Through the period state and civic authorities generally shifted to a greater control of palliatives. The voluntary sector – largely in the hands of lay confraternities and some new religious Orders like the Jesuits, Barnabites, Capuchins and the hospital Order of Camillians – was more controlled, but attempts to remove it from the picture were soon abandoned (as with Sixtus V in 1587). Bishops and parish priests remained involved. The Council of Trent demanded episcopal involvement, at least in ensuring testamentary dispositions were fulfilled, and parochial reforms encouraged the role of parish priests in recording the poor, and who deserved support.

Much amelioration was potentially on offer, though real assistance could be diminished by the maladministration, corruption and empty hostels as revealed by some records. Physical assistance, in food or money, was often woefully inadequate, even deliberately mean. In practical terms the means to tax society to help the vulnerable did not exist, nor did the mentality concerning taxation. Early modern donors and policy makers saw spiritual salvation, the salvation of the soul, as more important than physical help; and the fate of the donor's as significant as that of the receiver's in the amelioration process. Much charity was fostered by other-worldly religious figures, and those with guilty consciences, seeking the salvation of souls hereafter. But a charitable institution such as Milan's Scuola della Dottrina could derive benefits from worldly entrepreneurs who founded it in 1429, such as Donato Ferrario and his associates in business, legal activities, and the affairs of churches.[45]

The worst conditions for the largest numbers in society came when bad weather and poor harvests produced very high food prices, near starvation and unemployment. Epidemics, especially if it was decided that 'plague' was the cause (requiring stringent quarantines, so curbing economic life), also increased the chance of starvation for the living. Through the period the governments developed policies and procedures to protect the major cities at least, where social unrest was most dangerous. Grain supplies were secured from better-off areas – as far away as the Baltic in the 1590s crises – and distributed at controlled prices or free according to need. Efforts were made to standardise the production of loaves, and to prevent adulteration and fraud. Rome and Venice tried to stockpile grain supplies from good harvests in preparation for dearth. In seeking to commandeer supplies for a major city, a surrounding territory might suffer, as Umbria did for Rome in the 1580s, leading to a riot in Perugia in 1586. But Italy's major cities had fewer food riots than one might have expected, through palliative actions as much as rigorous policing. We know that in Naples and Modena controlled selling prices could not be kept that much below a market level, so free or further subsidised provision was crucial for many poor. There were variations in the extent to which the distribution of food to the poor was handled by government agencies, or by confraternities and private hospitals. A balanced combination, as in cities like Lucca, Genoa, Venice or Prato, seemingly worked best. Up to a third or quarter of a city population might be receiving some food assistance, as in Bologna in the 1590s, or Prato in 1621–2. The governments of Bologna and Bergamo were unusual in making efforts also to help their *contadini*. A succession of Venetian officials dealing with the Bergamo region were very aware of poverty problems, given an agriculturally poor region, and many fluctuations in the fortunes of the mines or silk mills. They encouraged food storage for emergencies, and the charitable work of Misericordia confraternities that existed in about half the communities.[46]

Hospitals and confraternities were central to this welfare in normal times. 'Hospital' is a misleading word, because in our period it could cover anything from a major medical institution to a small room used to shelter pilgrims, sick travellers, a pregnant woman or old person without family support. In the medieval period many such little 'hospices' were founded, and a few famous major hospitals such as Florence's S.Maria Nuova or Prato's Misericordia, with competent medical facilities, a reasonable recovery rate and provision to shelter the indigent poor or receive abandoned babies. From the fifteenth century, governments increasingly reorganised the hospital systems to create large, multi-purpose hospital complexes. The Milanese Ca' Granda hospital (from 1459, with Filarete as architect) was the most spectacular project at this stage, though it had been preceded by Cuneo (1437), Casale and Turin (1440). In the 1450s Ospedali Maggiori were created in Mantua, Cremona, Reggio Emilia, Bergamo and Lodi; in the 1470s Genoa, Parma, Ferrara, with Modena, Novara and Imola in the 1480s. Some of the development was based on criticisms of the clerical and confraternal inefficiency in small hospitals/hostels, and on the assertion of princely or civic pride. But in most cases princes, municipalities, church leaders and confraternities co-operated in the running, servicing and fund-raising for such institutions. Amalgamated efforts bore fruit in the development and redevelopment of the great hospital complexes of the sixteenth and seventeenth centuries – such as Rome's S.Spirito in Sassia, and S.Giacomo degli Incurabili, Naples' Spirito Santo and Annunziata, Perugia's Misericordia, or even Turin's S.Giovanni in the eighteenth century, despite a strong princely secularisation policy. Other cities, including Venice, maintained an array of decentralised hospitals, while the above cities might also have specialist hospitals. Florence provided the model hospital for foundlings, the Innocenti. Rome's S.Giacomo was an initial specialist in treating syphilis, though later it broadened its coverage, and Rome's confraternity hospital of S.Maria della Pietà dei Pazzarelli from the 1560s pioneered a humane approach in treating the insane.

Some general institutions cared for people from cradle to (not necessarily early) grave; receiving abandoned babies and wet-nursing them, providing medical and surgical care for all ages, and shelter and nursing for the poor old infirm. Conditions fluctuated considerably, with limited concepts of hygiene, and a two-per-bed practice till the late seventeenth century or later. Rome's S.Spirito and Naples' Annunziata became very rich institutions, served the rich as well as poor, trained and used famous surgeons and utilised the best apothecaries. Nursing and food provision relied heavily on the family, confraternity members and some of the religious Orders. The moves under Catholic Reform to enforce the enclosure of nuns and curb female Tertiaries forestalled the development of dedicated female nursing.

From the 1490s a new spirit of philanthropy was promoted by various religious reform movements, and stimulated by the disasters or war, disease and famine. The Company of Divine Love, spreading from Genoa, was the most significant initial promoter of social welfare (including trying to tackle the syphilis epidemic). The better-off were urged to help others by organising and working in hospitals, orphanages and conservatories, or at least raising money for them. The founder of the Oratorians, St Philip Neri, tested his would-be followers by sending them to the Roman hospitals to clean wounds and sores, and comfort the sick. Other social religious leaders like Bartolomeo Stella, Girolamo Miani and Countess Laura Gambara reacted to the horrors of war, and civilian casualties, by creating special institutions (often called conservatories), that would rescue orphans and vulnerable women. Northern and central Italy at least soon had a significant number of such institutions, particularly for vulnerable girls and women. Some institutions started by including the really poor, but studies of Perugian and Bolognese institutions, for example, suggest that by the later sixteenth century the protected girls and women were from families that had some resources.

For economic reasons these conservatories could only cope with very limited numbers of the vulnerable females; Naples' conservatory attached to S.Spirito had about 400 girls in 1587, the Perugia Casa delle Derelitte about 40–50 through the later sixteenth century. To forestall some social problems, confraternities and other pious institutions provided welfare on a much wider scale by allocating dowries to poor girls and women, so they could marry with respect, or enter a nunnery. A fair number of confraternities might allocate them at the rate of one to three a year; a few might provide ten or more. Rome by the late seventeenth century was providing about 3000 dowries a year, most through the specialist S.Annunziata confraternity, which organised major ceremonial processions for the recipients, as a propaganda exercise. Competition to obtain dowries, especially if open to non-confraternity applicants, could be intense. The sums involved were not necessarily that large, but possibly enough to improve marriage prospects, or allow entry to a better-class nunnery.

Though begging and alms-giving were often attacked, in practice the sixteenth and seventeenth centuries saw a development of organised relief in money or kind for those deemed to need and deserve help. In real crises people turned up at the door of fraternity buildings, or at convents, and received help indiscriminately. But in more normal circumstances needy individuals and families could get a little help from fraternities, parish priests and their committees, hospitals or municipal governments' agencies. This involved list keeping, scrutiny, house visiting, certificates from doctors or parish priests and maybe the issue of official licences. A few might be sustained this way for a while, through an illness crisis or pregnancy, but surviving lists and accounts indicate that the sums involved were meagre, enough to buy food or wood for heating for a few days rather than months. But such a sum might have made a real difference in allowing somebody to secure a blanket or cloak to protect from cold. A successful petition to a confraternity might secure a single sum that was enough to get a breadwinner out of a debtor's prison and back to earning.

There were some confraternities, as in Bologna, Florence, Lecce, Milan, Naples, Rome and Venice, that specialised in helping indebted prisoners secure release so they could work and support families again. Others, along with religious orders such as Jesuits and Capuchins, provided help with food, drink, clothing, spiritual welfare, even education, for those in prison – whether for criminal or civil offences, or pending trial. Others comforted the condemned from confession to execution, and gave some assistance to the family. Some confraternities and (at least in Rome) trade guilds had the privilege to secure a pardon for certain persons condemned to death or the galleys.

Conforming with the injunction to house the poor, some fraternities – best studied and known in Venice – provided rooms and houses free or at reduced rents 'Amore Dio'. The Venetian Scuole Grandi offered between forty and seventy almshouses, while a lesser *scuola* like the Santissima Trinita (near S.Maria della Salute) in the seventeenth century had about ten on offer – advertised on public notices at the Rialto and San Marco. Efforts were made to ensure inhabitants maintained proper moral standards. Competition for such housing could be considerable. Most went to confraternity members and their relatives, but some could be for outsiders. We know of a certain amount of corruption in some Scuole Grandi housing, with the less than poor securing such housing.[47]

Increasingly through our period the poor, and not so poor, could ameliorate their situation by resorting to pawn-broking systems, notably the Monti di Pietà (or dei Poveri). These institutions developed out of Perugia and other Umbrian cities in the 1460s, under the influence of Franciscan preaching, advocating a Christian non-profit, cheap lending system to replace the allegedly extortionate Jewish lenders. Loans were to be given on the basis of pledged goods, which could be redeemed either with no additional charge, or a minor percentage to cover administrative costs, if those were not covered by the municipality or a charitable fraternity. Central and northern Italy cities took up the idea for their poor, (sometimes accompanied by some virulent anti-semitism, especially when the dynamic preacher Bernardino da Feltre was involved), though it was not till the 1530s that Rome and Naples followed. Venice itself decided not to have a Monte di Pietà, but to use the Jewish money lenders (under strict control over interest rates) instead. Cities in the Terraferma like Brescia, Padua and Chioggia did develop them. Monti were started through southern Italy in the sixteenth and seventeenth centuries, under civic or confraternal influence. Some, like that in Bitonto, added other charitable facilities and actions (hospitals, dowry funds, orphanages). Monti di Frumentari helped peasants by lending seed or money to start a new crop, especially useful in preventing one bad harvest having a major knock-on effect for the next. The ideal of the Monti was to help the poor; however, from the mid sixteenth century many provided investment and lending facilities for the better-off, with some – as in Siena and Naples – being the foundation of major modern financial institutions.

Italy developed many ways of alleviating the suffering of the poor and disadvantaged. Assessment of the degree of help really provided is difficult through want of evidence. Many institutions – like the Monti, the conservatories for girls and women at risk, the alms-houses – started with ideals of helping the lowest levels of the poor, but tended from the later sixteenth century to target middling respectable poor, and leave the lowest strata to casual assistance, mutual help (legal or criminal) – or none; with prison-like confinement as a likely outcome if not earlier death. Money left to aid the poor could too readily be diverted into building operations; the goldsmith and poet Alessandro Caravia so complained about the competitive extravagance of the Venetian Scuole Grandi, especially San Rocco and the Misericordia (which could not complete its new premises).[48] Impressive Monti buildings, as in Vicenza or Naples, might face similar criticisms. But the Italian urban poor still probably had more, and more diverse, opportunities to obtain some physical and spiritual assistance than most Europeans.

This chapter started by emphasising the violence and lawlessness in much of Italian society, and the difficulties of control, especially in rural areas. Government institutions were weak, and all levels of society were ready to take advantage of this fact, often co-operating in local circumstances, in some unlikely alliances. Straightforward class conflicts, or town–country battles are not found. Italians in conflict with lay or clerical authority could often find support and protection somewhere, just as those in need of amelioration of their living conditions had some chance of obtaining a little relief.

12

EPILOGUE

Events in the mid eighteenth century mark in some ways the end of the period, provide verdicts on progress through the early modern period and trigger some conclusions about the nature of Italian society.

From the summer of 1763 famine conditions developed through most of the Kingdom of Naples and afflicted others parts of Italy, notably the southern Papal State and Tuscany, through to 1767; a reasonable harvest in 1764 was followed by bad ones in 1765 and 1766. Varied adverse weather conditions through the previous winter and spring had severely affected all foods, not just cereals; and unlike a similar mainland crisis in 1759, Sicilian or Middle Eastern supplies could not come to the rescue. The situation tested the resources and abilities of a reforming government in Naples under Bernardo Tanucci, and the systems that had been developed to cope with food shortages over the past two centuries. 'We have begged at all the gates of Europe', declared Tanucci in April 1764, before getting some help from Piedmont. Naples was known to be better organised over food supplies, and helping the poor, so huge numbers initially headed there from around the Kingdom. Rebellious conditions developed in the city, though a total revolt was possibly avoided by the popular belief that the wrath of God was more to blame than government incompetence. Troops remained loyal enough to keep some control. Tanucci reported on major tumults in cities like Altamura, Crotone, Rossone and Taranto. Villages rose against feudal lords and pillaged their castles. Charitable resources could not cope. In bitterly cold December 1764, English ambassador William Hamilton reported seeing 2000 sick in a Neapolitan hospital 'crowded together with no other covering but a shirt which they have worn four months', having no bread for twenty-four hours 'owing to the failure of the charitable subscriptions that have hitherto supported them'. He also commented on 'the numberless emaciated objects that present themselves in every street'.[1]

Maybe 40,000 inhabitants of Naples, and 200,000 from the Kingdom died of starvation and disease before the crisis was over. Rome and southern parts of the Papal State as well as Tuscany (especially Pistoia, San Miniato and Lucca) were badly hit, but the casualties seemed fewer, even if reports came in of people dying on their feet from hunger. Rome in early 1764 was invaded by the poor from the surrounding state seeking relief, and troops were needed for control. Papal Romagna or the

Ferrarese, and Tuscan areas around Livorno, Pisa and Empoli could cope with actual food supplies and high prices. The Roman Annona and Florentine Abbondanza food-organising offices had more resources; in comparison with Naples the governments could raise more money and secure more supplies (as from France) through the ports of Civitavecchia and Livorno, and charitable resources appeared greater. This did not prevent some riotous conditions, as in Perugia, Fara or Ferentino – which threatened to establish a separate Republic.

These famine years indicate an historical turning point, and mark the beginning of the end of the early modern period. They tested governments and society which, in the case of Naples and Tuscany, were already reforming under the impact of intellectuals and writers. The failures to cope properly with the crises, and the lessons drawn about fundamental flaws in Italian society and mentalities, produced more reform campaigning, led from Lombardy and Tuscany, under internationally famous writers, ministers and advisers like Cesare Beccaria, Pietro and Alessandro Verri and Pompeo Neri. Tanucci and Antonio Genovesi renewed their reform efforts, and were followed by Gaetano Filangieri, Ferdinando Galiani, Domenico Grimaldi, Giuseppe Palmieri and many others.

The writers and reform campaigns reflected on the weaknesses of the society and politics of early modern Italy, but also on some strengths and 'progress' since the mid sixteenth century or earlier. From the late seventeenth century an educational and intellectual climate fostered new thinking. The Italians drew on the writings of key thinkers from France, England and Scotland – Descartes, Newton, John Cary, Montesquieu and David Hume; later Rousseau and Helvetius. Some of the Italians, like Genovesi, Beccaria and Filangieri, were to contribute economic and legal ideas to the cosmopolitan enlightenment, and reform policies in France, Russia and America.[2] Many leading figures came from patrician and noble elite groups, many were part of the church, like abbot-professor Genovesi or the pioneering historian Ludovico Muratori (who for years served as a parish priest as well as archivist-librarian to the Duke of Modena), and educated by Jesuits (like Beccaria). The old ambience of the elite academies changed, and new academies were formed, notably Celestino Galiani's in Naples in 1732, which triggered major discussions of economic problems or law as well as natural philosophy and mathematics. This provided a background for practical advice for reform, involving his nephew Ferdinando Galiani. Giam Battista Vico and Genovese rejuvenated Naples university in various disciplines, and that produced many reforming graduates and professors.

Out of the supposedly backward Kingdom of Naples came a major reform ethos and programme. A civic, legal section of the elite, concentrating on legal theory and some anti-clericalism, had persisted through the seventeenth century and was then stimulated by the fall of Spanish rule from 1700 and by a degree of political chaos to analyse and seek to mend society. They realised that the South had many riches and potential for wealth, but also many impediments. Too much land was owned and controlled by uncaring lazy landowners, secular and clerical; the peasants were grossly ignorant and incompetent farmers; peasants and their communities were massively in debt to landowners (and the famine had made this even worse);

commerce and the handling of key products like silk, wool and olive oil were in the hands of foreigners (whether English, Tuscan or Venetian). The 'feudal' systems inhibited not only good land-management, but sound administration and due legal process. Open critical analysis had limits; when Pietro Giannone in his *Istoria Civile* (Civil History of the Kingdom of Naples, 1723) blamed southern problems on the feudal dependence on the Papacy, with excessive papal influence over true religion and society, and called for complete separation of church and state, he was not only excommunicated, but suffered popular attacks – and had to go into exile. He continued his anti-clerical attacks, and criticism of the detrimental effects of monasticism and church landholding, from Geneva, where he became a Calvinist. Seemingly under papal pressure he was tricked, arrested in Geneva and smuggled to Piedmont in 1734 – to die in a Turin jail in 1748.

The 1730s and 1740s, as Franco Venturi strongly emphasised, saw the first major stage of Italian-wide critical analysis and some reform attempts, with an emphasis on economic and legal problems, and historical analyses of Italy's social and legal realities – led by Muratori. The problems of war helped generate major campaigns in many states to improve road and water communications, and land analysis for tax purposes. From 1763–4 came fresh impetus, initially focused on Beccaria's very influential *Dei delitti e delle pene* (On Crimes and Punishment), and a Milan periodical *Il Caffe* (1764–6), involving him with the Verri brothers. Beccaria notably attacked the practice of torture and capital punishment, but – influenced by Alessandro Verri's experience as a lawyer dealing with Milan prisoners – his work was an indictment of much else in law and society. Law and punishment should be divorced from social hierarchy and from moral concepts, and proportionately linked to damage to society. Society, laws and their effects must be analysed with a geometric spirit, rationally, from self-evident principles, and the overall aim should be 'the greatest happiness [*felicità*] being spread among the greatest number'. This egalitarian and utilitarian philosophy had him criticised as a *socialista* by the Venetian Ferdinando Facchinei, ex-monk, satirist, agricultural reformer and author of a life of Isaac Newton.[3] That Beccaria, like Giannone, was too radical for many other elite reformers, rendered their campaigns more difficult. *Felicità* is often translated as 'happiness', but 'well-being' might be better, since its use implied physical satisfactions as well as psychological, as Pietro Verri's slightly earlier *Discorso sulla felicità* (1763) makes clear.

The periodical *Il Caffe* under the Verri brothers was influenced by the English *The Spectator* journal for style, literary approach and lightness of touch in many articles, and by the French *Encyclopédie* for its willingness to analyse and comment on all manner of subjects, using a significant number of contributors. Most contributors to this, and much reform literature and work, came from sectors of the noble elite, often poorer and more vulnerable members. Aware of the conservative nature of their social order, and the ignorance of the middling sort, they aimed at gently educating and cajoling the elites to reform agriculture, commerce, the law and morals. Ideally or practically change would best be produced by the enlightened few advising and educating princely rulers to put political force and law behind some changes. Policies needed to be tailored to existing states, princely or republican; there were no serious campaigns for democracy or Italian-wide nationalism. Understandably, much of the best work came out of Lombardy, now directly ruled by the Habsburgs from Vienna (where a leading minister Kaunitz much favoured the Verri circle), and Tuscany, ruled by Peter Leopold, younger brother and successor of the Emperor Joseph II.

After the 1760s crisis, much discussion focused on grain supplies, the merits and disadvantages of free or freer trade, in foodstuffs and then other commercial activities. Tanucci, Genovesi and others realised that where free trade might help northern Italian states, and more so Britain, Neapolitan commerce and industry needed some protection until reformed from within. Tuscany abolished food control in 1766, and by 1775 promoted free trade between states. By the 1780s Naples had abolished or loosened many internal tariffs and trade controls. A considerable literature aimed at landowners, and even literate smallholders and artisans, was published to improve agriculture production, drain and terrace the land, improve implements and machinery for treating soil and crops, processing olive oil, spinning and weaving cloth. Some capital went into practices and education. There were erosions into the less productive land-holding systems outlined earlier in this book. 'Feudalism' was heavily attacked, and in the Kingdom of Naples about 150 major towns were brought back under direct government jurisdiction and control by 1789. The guilds, key aspects of corporate society, came under increasing attack as too restrictive and anti-enterprise; they were gradually abolished in Lombardy 1769–74 (with Pietro Verri and Beccaria as activists), and in Tuscany 1770–9. Confraternities and philanthropic procedures similarly were targeted. Muratori had led an attack on charity, for failing to help the real poor, encouraging the idle and diverting money from beneficial investment in land improvements. Confraternities were part of this detrimental activity in the eyes of some; but also they were seen as undermining proper parochial religion. Peter Leopold in 1785 accepted such arguments and abolished virtually all of them in Tuscany. One of his advisers, Lorenzo Mehus, had written a book that aimed 'to show that they [confraternities] are contrary to sacred laws, harmful to parish jurisdiction, and offensive to that status which, by right of divine decree, is held among their flock by rectors of churches, who in our day reside in them enjoying no respect and nearly insult'.[4]

Thus key institutions of early modern society were attacked and depleted. Anti-clericalism grew more rampant in some quarters, and in published works. Carlantonio Pilati, professor of civil law at Trent, in his 1767 *Di una riforma d'Italia* produced one of the most swingeing attacks on the economic, religious, charitable and legal situations; and included a diatribe against the Inquisition, which had condemned his earlier writings on natural law. The Jesuits were the target internationally, from scandals in South America, alleged influences on royal courts, excessive show or ostentatious wealth and (in the eyes of Jansensists and Dominicans as well as Protestants), gross moral equivocation. Finally Pope Clement XIV was pressurised to abolish the Order in 1773. In Italy this was a significant educational loss, though Jesuit teachers could find roles in other institutions. The Jesuits had honed the sharp minds of many who came to demolish their colleges.[5]

The visions and assessments of Italian society in the mid and late eighteenth century, by natives and non-Italian visitors, were ambivalent and misleading. They depicted joys and miseries, *felicità* and immoral indolence. Ex-Jesuit Abbot Saverio Bettinelli echoes Machiavelli's attack on foreign encroachment on Italy:

> Italy the first innovator of almost all the arts, no longer sees any of them flourish in glory; she once taught and overlorded all peoples, now she follows as adulator, and tribute payer to all; with varied commerce, but bloodless and constrained; with many governments, but little regulation; with fertile lands but poor; with a thousand studies, but few learned men recognised and rewarded, all united and enclosed by the Alps and Sea, but very diverse, and discordant in languages, in genius, in usages, money, measures, laws and the customs of the people.[6]

This Preface, from 1775, has a rhetorical exaggeration and deprecation of Italian talents. But many others noted the rich potential, the natural abundance of Italy, and the poor use of it. An indifference to using resources properly, whether by complacent landowners or ineffectual governments, was commented on by visitors. The 'many governments' of different types complicated the improvement of economies, and an ability to fend off British and French competition. But Republican, papal and secular governments may arguably have been too similar, as Giorgio Chittolini has suggested; the political and social networking of the elites and the executive body had blurred the distinctions between public and private in all cases, to the detriment of effective change, and the incorporation of new elements into government, administration and the economy.[7]

Several eighteenth-century visitors echoed the 'bloodless' accusation in a slightly different way, seeing Italian society as effeminate and lacking in moral constraint. They seized on the phenomenon of the *cecisbei*, the unrelated escorts of married women absent from compliant husbands. Before marriage upper society women were enclosed at home or taught in nunneries with no say over marriage partners; on marriage they could parade with escorts, presumed lovers. As Thomas Watkins wrote in 1792:

> Before marriage their women are nuns, and after it libertines. At twelve years they are immured in a convent, from which there is no return, but upon the hard condition of receiving from their parents a husband whom they have never seen. If dissatisfied with him (as it generally happens) they are at liberty (from universal custom) to chuse their *Cavalieri Serventi*, or *Cecisbei*, who attend them in all public places, for their husbands dare not, assist at their toilette, and, in a word, do every thing they are ordered; for which the ladies sacrifice their own virtue, and their husband's honour.[8]

Doubtless this applied to few women, but it marked a change from the more restrained central centuries of our period. Many women had had more say over marriage than this implies, had better relations with husbands but had not been able to move so freely in public.

In selecting social snapshots in this concluding chapter, I have offset this foreign verdict of immorality and dishonour among the elite, with pertinent social criticism from others in the elite, and the misery and mortality of the poor in famine conditions. The events of the 1760s were taken as an indictment of our 'early modern society'. Some of the corporate structures and institutions described in various chapters, and seen as sometimes evolving beneficially – guilds, neighbourhoods and network structures, confraternities, hospitals and parishes – were found wanting, in the social reality of selfish turmoil in and around Naples, Rome and lesser cities; and in the writings of critics. Through to the French Revolution and an ultimately disastrous French occupation of the peninsula, social reforms were attempted, with some successes, in virtually all states, princely or republican. Gains were made in legal practice, in education from universities to practical manuals for agriculture and industry, in freedom of speech and writing. There were winners among adventurous landowners and smallholders, especially in Tuscany and the Veneto. But a more efficient agricultural scene in the same areas could mean more landless underemployed *contadini*, with less common land as a safety valve, fewer charitable institutions and handouts, and attempts to rationalise Christianity as in Tuscany took away the psychological consolations of 'superstitious' religion. There might be more job opportunities for displaced peasants in re-industrialising Bologna or Piedmont – especially in the silk industry where Beccaria played a beneficial role, and sought higher wage-rates – but in most areas there were probably more vulnerable poor. The social scene was set for the chaos and misery of the early nineteenth century, out of which a more integrated Italy slowly emerged.

Our early modern period ends with a combination of disasters in the 1760s and 1790s, and in between partially successful attacks on early modern institutions and attitudes that had once been social strengths, but were now apparently atrophied. Finally it is worth emphasising some aspects of continuity and change, and some paradoxes. Fundamental geographical factors remained as impediments to communication, dictators of economic wealth and causes of disasters. However, people and nature changed some features with new crops, losses of forests and alteration of waterways. Against natural barriers there was throughout much physical movement, between country and town, between south, centre and north. Printing by the mid sixteenth century accelerated the transference of ideas and attitudes. Concepts of honour and status became more prominent at the same time, but in reality hardly rendered society more rigid and stratified in a class or caste system. Italian elites were varied, fluid and alternated between conflict and co-operation. Local hierarchies of society – noble, official, artisan in towns, or landlord, factor, tenant and bandit in the *contado* – worked together whether in common cause against a common enemy, or for business interests and political patronage concerns. Jurisdictions became more 'feudal' until the excesses were attacked in the eighteenth century. But in most of Italy this meant less transference of power from central government than in other European states, and the anti-feudal attacks were more against economic inefficiency and lassitude than against brutal exploitation of peasants. Part of the re-feudalisation was governed by shifts of investments from some international trade, textile industries, later shipping to the land in the mid sixteenth century onwards. Eventually the different Italian economies were overtaken in world significance by various non-Italian economies, notably in the Netherlands, parts of France and Britain. But within Italy there were very complex shifts and balances or gains and losses between cities, between rural and urban areas and between trades and commodities. The starting points by the fifteenth century of a high proportion of the Italian population living in urban communities, considerable interconnection between city and *contado*, strong corporate institutions or social networks in many cities, and a mentality that favoured conspicuous consumption and display, meant that much of Italian society could weather economic storms and competition through to the eighteenth century.

Changes in household, clan and family structures followed no easy pattern, and they were often governed by local economic conditions. Family affections in a modern sense probably developed through the period. Though renaissance attitudes emphasising individual *virtu* may have had an impact at the beginning of our period, the corporateness of Italian society rather than any individualism is what remains striking. Corporate loyalties and identities outside the family have been stressed in discussing urban districts and neighbourhoods, guilds and confraternities, parish identities and organisation. All may have lost their vitality and broader purposes when the enlightenment attacks were launched. In the resulting long transition to a fully modern society the Italian extended family or clan remained the only hope for those in trouble and need.

APPENDIX

Table A1 Population figures for countries/regions (in millions)

	1500	*1550*	*1600*	*1650*	*1700*	*1750*
Europe	81		100		120	
England/Wales	3.75		4.25		5.75	
France	15.0		19.0		22.0	25.0
Spain	6.5		8.5		11.0	
N. Netherlands	0.9		1.5		1.5	
Italy	10.0	11.0	12.0	11.0		15.7
Piedmont		0.6			0.9	
Lombardy		0.5			1.0	
Tuscany		0.8			0.9	
Papal State		1.6			2.0	
Naples/Sicily		3.6			4.0	

Table A2 Population figures for cities (precise figures and dates in Italy where acceptably accurate figures are available)

	1500	*1600*	*1700*
Amsterdam	14,000	65,000	200,000
London	40,000	200,000	575,000
Madrid		49,000	110,000
Paris	100,000	220,000	510,000

	1500	*1550*		*1600*		*1650*	*1700*	*1750*
Ancona						*[1656]* 9,556	*[1701]* 8,644	
Bari	8,000	8,000		15,000		15,000	13,000	18,000
Bergamo			*[1586]* 17,707	27,000			25,000	*[1764]* 24,468
Bologna	55,000		*[1581]* 70,661	62,844	*[1624]* 61,691	58,000	*[1701]* 63,346	69,000

Table A2 (continued)

	1500	*1550*		*1600*		*1650*		*1700*		*1750*
Brescia	*[1493]* 56,060		*[1586]* 42,660	36,000	*[1624]* 43,235	*[1642]* 25,063		35,000		*[1764]* 38,889
Catanzaro		11,500		12,000						
Cosenza		8,700		12,000						
Ferrara		42,000		*[1601]* 32,860		25,000		*[1701]* 29,129		*[1736]* 26,654
Florence	70,000	*[1551]* 60,773		70,000	*[1622]* 76,023	*[1642]* 69,495		72,000		*[1766]* 78,635
Genoa	60,000	65,000		*[1597]* 62,396		*[1660]* 38,360	*[1662]* 47,668			*[1788]* 77,563
Lecce		26,000		32,000		16,000				
Livorno		*[1562]* 563		*[1601]* 3,958		*[1642]* 12,302		16,000		*[1785]* 49,424
Lucca		24,000		24,000		25,000		23,000		*[1744]* 20,770
Mantua	28,000	38,000		31,000		14,000		21,000		24,000
Milan	100,000			108,000		100,000		*[1688]* 125,829		*[1773]* 128,473
Modena	18,000	16,000	*[1590]* 19,911	*[1591]* 16,695	*[1620]* 20,505	15,000		19,000		18,000
Naples	150,000	212,000	*[1596]* 237,784	*[1606]* 280,746		300,000		315,000	*[1743]* 294,241	*[1765]* 337,095
Padua	27,000	*[1557]* 35,852	*[1586]* 34,075	36,000		*[1648]* 32,714		30,000		*[1764]* 31,319
Parma	*[1509]* 19,034	25,000		33,000		19,000		35,000		*[1787]* 34,219
Perugia	25,000	*[1551]* 19,876	*[1582]* 19,581		*[1618]* 19,722	*[1656]* 17,385		*[1701]* 16,045		*[1736]* 13,997
Poppi		1,450			*[1632]* 704			*[1745]* 1,329		
Prato		*[1562]* 5,996				5,600	*[1672]* 6,623			
Reggio Calabria		12,000		17,000						
Rome	55,000	45,000	*[1591]* 116,695	*[1602]* 99,312		*[1652]* 118,047		149,447		157,881
Siena		*[1560]* 13,679		*[1610]* 18,659	*[1640]* 5,998		*[1670]* 16,544			*[1745]* 14,645

Table A2 (continued)

	1500	*1550*	*1600*	*1650*	*1700*	*1750*
Turin		14,000	24,000	37,000	42,000	*[1770]* 81,848
Udine		*[1586]* 14,579				*[1764]* 14,339
Venice	100,000	*[1563]* 168,627 *[1581]* 134,877	*[1624]* 142,804	*[1633]* 98,244 *[1655]* 158,772		*[1760]* 149,476
Verona		*[1586]* 52,109				*[1764]* 39,789
Vicenza		*[1586]* 21,268	37,000	25,000	26,000	*[1764]* 27,307

Sources: Black (1989), Appendix1, quoting sources; nowsupplemented and emended, especially byBeloch (1959); Beltrami (1959). Though some precise figures are given from state and ecclesiastical counts made at the time, there are various problems as to who was included: young babies, people in suburbs, monks and nuns, garrison troops, Jews, etc. The same criteria might not apply in successive counts for the same city.

NOTES

1 DISUNITED ITALY

1 For the problems of studying the history of Italy through the middle ages and early modern period, and for a sense of 'Italian' identity: Larner 1980, ch. 1; Hay and Law 1989, chs 1–2; Hay 1977a, ch. 3; Sestan 1950; AA.VV. 1972–, I, 949–1022. On languages and dialects: Maiden 1995; Maiden and Parry 1997. General history of this period: Hay and Law 1989; Cochrane 1988b; Sella 1997; Carpanetto and Ricuperati 1987. Space precludes fuller referencing for this chapter, but these works will lead to much.
2 Astarita 1999, valuably confronts the problems of scribal records and languages, esp. xxi–xxiii.
3 D. Laven 1995, an historian's short, balanced, introduction to the Machiavellian issue.
4 Croce 1970; Nicolini 1934; Villari 1993.
5 Braudel 1991; Black and others 1993.
6 See textbooks mentioned in note 1 for framework. AA.VV. 1972–, I–III.
7 Strocchia 1992, 79–82.
8 Ferraro 1993, 14 (map).
9 Abulafia 1995; Black and others 1993, 77 (map of invasion route and Italian Wars).
10 Arrizabalaga and others 1997; Henderson 1998; Wills 1997.
11 Chubb 1967; Labalme 1982; Cairns 1985.
12 Dandelet 1997.
13 Chittolini 1989 and esp. 1995; Lanaro 1999.
14 Clark 1985; D'Amico 2000.
15 Hibbert 1975, 307–11.
16 Venturi 1969–90, I, II, V: 1/2; Venturi 1972; Robertson 1992, 1997.

2 GEOGRAPHY AND DEMOGRAPHY

1 D. S. Walker 1967 (my main geographical reference); B. King 1985; Braudel 1972, I; Cohn 1999a, esp. ch.1 on mountain communications; Larner 1990; Maczak 1995. AA.VV. 1972– has much, esp. vol. 1 *I Caratteri originali* 1972, Haussmann, 'Il suolo d'Italia nella storia', Sereni, 'Agricoltura rurale'; vol. 5* *I Documenti* 1973: Day, 'Strade e vie di communicazione', Tucci, 'Credenze geografiche e cartografia'; *Annali* 8 1985, Pratesi, 'Gli ambienti naturale e l'equilibrio ecologico'.
2 Maczak 1995.
3 Black and others 1993, 77 (colour map showing invasion route and some passes).
4 Cohn 1996a, 1999a, esp. 8, 24–8 on Braudelian thesis.
5 Ginzburg 1980, 1983; cf. Ruggiero 1993, Del Col 1996 for Menocchio, 1998 for other Friuli cases.

6 Vaussard 1962, 32.
7 Ruffo 1916.
8 Kennet and Young 1990, 33–4.
9 Guiton 1977, 4.
10 Cited D. S. Walker 1967, 36; cf. Chard 1999, 92–3, 105.
11 Bellettini 1978; Beloch 1937–1961; Black 1989, Appendix 1; Cipolla 1974, 1992a; Del Panta 1996; Livi Bacci 1976, 1990.
12 A. L. Martin 1996 and Wills 1997 raise the major queries, and I am indebted to my colleague Sam Cohn, currently analysing the Black Death interpretations with due scepticism. Corradi 1973 charts a huge range of reported epidemics through the centuries, with indexes in vol. V. See also: Calvi 1989; Carmichael 1991; Cipolla 1976, 1977, 1979, 1981, 1992a; Pastore 1991.
13 Galasso 1982, I, 46–7; Black 1989, 151–3 with sources; Piva 1991; Preto 1984.
14 Wills 1997, 133–5.
15 Black 1989, 153–4.
16 Braudel 1984, I esp.; D'Ambrosio and Spedicato 1998; Basini 1970; Cognasso 1965, II, part 5; La Roncière 1983; Livi Bacci 1990; Montanari 1994; Musgrave 1992; Revel 1975; Sereni 1961, 1997.
17 Braudel 1972, esp. 594–606.
18 Chorley 1965.
19 R. C. Davis 1997, 85 (quote).
20 Crispolti 1648, 1974.
21 Pagano de Divitiis 1997, 157–66.
22 D'Ambrosio and Spedicato 1998; Arch.Patr.Ven., Curia Patriarcale – Sezione Antica, Atti patriarcale riguardanti le monache, vols. for 1591–9 and 1620–30.
23 Arch. di San Pietro, Perugia Mazzo xxxvi.
24 Camporesi 1980, 1993; Black 1989, 136, 158; Rouch 1982, with selection of Croce's poems.

3 THE CHANGING RURAL AND URBAN ECONOMIES

1 Koenigsberger 1960. See above Chapter 1, esp. notes 1 and 6. On European scene, and some major theories: Braudel 1972, 1984, 1991/1994; Wallerstein 1974, 1980. Goldthwaite 1993, esp. 11–67 is a valuable overview. On recent views and evidence for the 17th century: Sella 1997; Pagano De Divitiis 1997; D'Amico 2000. Also: Cattola 1988; Belfanti 1993; Van der Wee 1988; Ciriacono 1988; Malanima 1996; Mazzei 1979.
2 Braudel 1994, 223; and his chapter 'Is Italian decadence a discernible process?'.
3 Montaigne 1955, 1983.
4 Epstein 1993; Fasano Guarini 1986; R. K. Marshall 1999.
5 Ciriacono in AA.VV. 1992–7, V, 548–9, 565–7.
6 Epstein 1994; Sakellariou 1995.
7 Rapp 1976, 505–11; Pagano de Divitiis 1997, 172–4; McCray 1999.
8 Sella 1979; Faccini 1988; Pagano de Divitiis 1997; against e.g. Cipolla 1968. On Milan's crises 1570–1610, and some gains elsewhere: D'Amico 2000.
9 Belfanti 1993, 261.
10 Pagano de Divitiis 1997.
11 Pagano de Divitiis 1997, 136–8.
12 Fairchilds 1993; Stearns 1997; Ciriacono 1988.
13 Palumbo-Fossati 1984; Pavanini 1981.
14 ASB Tribunale del Torrone 5758 1629–30; Tribunale della Plebe Mazzo I 1579–1692.
15 Pullan 1999a.
16 Camporesi 1992; Sereni 1997, with some illustrations of the changing agriculture scene as

perceived in paintings and prints of period. See also AA.VV. *Storia d'Italia* Einaudi: Vol. 6 *Atlante*, F. Zeri 'La percezione visive dell'Italia e degli Italiani nella storia della pittura', and, by various authors, 'La campagna, gli uomini, la terra e le sue rappresentazioni visive', all with illustrations or maps; *Annali* 5 1982, De Seta, 'L'Italia nello specchio del Grand Tour'.

17 Ago 1980.

18 Gazzini 1997.

19 Ginzburg 1983.

20 P. A. Allerston has kindly given me access to her notes on Archivio di Stato, Florence, Archivio delle Arti, Università del linaioli, n.1, with *Statuto de'linaioli con approvazioni 1549–52*, fols. xvi^{r}-xviii^{v}.

21 Malanima 1990.

22 Fontaine 1996; Viazzo 1989; Niccoli 1990, esp. 12–19 on *cantastorie*.

23 Gentilcore 1995b, 299 (quote); cf. Garzoni, 1996, 1188–1197.

24 Gentilcore 1998, 98.

4 THE LAND AND RURAL SOCIETY

1 Jones 1966, Sereni 1997 on Italy, and Abel 1980, Slicher van Bath 1963 for the European context. See also Hay and Law 1989, esp. ch. 4; Carpanetto and Ricuperati 1987, esp. ch. 2; Sella 1979, esp. ch. VI. Regional studies in English worth highlighting: Cosgrove 1993; Herlihy and Klapisch-Zuber 1985, esp. 115–22; McArdle 1978; Marino 1988; Musgrave 1992. In Italian in general: Sereni 1961; Jones 1964, a version of Jones 1966; De Maddalena 1964. There is much in the many volumes of AA.VV. *Storia d'Italia* 1972–, esp. Vol. 1 *I Caratteri originali*: Sereni, 'Agricoltura e mondo rurale', 136–252, Vol. 5/1 *I Documenti*: Klapisch-Zuber 'Villaggi abandonati ed emigrazione interne', 311–64; Giorgetti, 'Contratti agrari a rapporti sociali nelle campagne', 701–58; vol. 6 *Atlante*: part 4: 'La campagna: gli uomini, la terra e le sue rappresentazioni visive', 425–664; vol.1 of *Annali Dal feudalismo al capitalismo*, esp.: Ugolini, 'Tecnologia ed economia agrarie dal feudalismo al capitalismo', 375–452, and *idem* 'Il podere nell'economia rurale italiana', 713–807; Aymard, 'La transizione dal feudalismo al capitalismo', 1131–92; vol. 8 of *Annali*: *Insediamenti e territorio*: Delille, 'L'ordine dei villaggi e l'ordine dei campi. Per uno studio antropologico del paesaggio agrario nel Regno di Napoli secoli xv–xviii', 502–60, linking geography, types of agriculture, villages and families. Berengo 1965, ch. v; Beltrami 1955, 1962, Ventura 1964.

2 Grohmann 1981, I, 72–4, II, 785, and 769–78.

3 ASP, Fondo Notarile, Notary 129, Pietro Paulo di Giovanni, vol. 676, f.42v, 10 Sept. 1527; Grohmann 1981, II921.

4 See note 1; Jones 1968; Brown 1982; Malanima 1979; Conti 1965.

5 Balestracci 1999.

6 ASPerugia, Fondo Notarile, Notary 141, Pietro Paulo di Ludovico, vol. 825, ff.22r–3r, 20 Jan. 1525. 'Ser' in Umbria usually indicates a notary. Grohmann 1981 II esp. 893–913, 1099–1147; Petrocchi 1972; Chiacchella 1974, esp. 134–46.

7 Balestracci 1999, esp. 52–61.

8 Sereni 1997, 232–5; Carpanetto and Ricuperati 1987, 213–15.

9 Finzi 1979; cf. Musgrave 1992, 132–4.

10 McArdle 1978; Dué 1994, Table 24.

11 McArdle 1978, 26, Fig. 10.

12 Mazzei 1977, esp. 61, 117–24, 134, 144; Dué 1994, Tables 23, 24.

13 Astarita 1992; Gross 1990, ch. 6; Giorgetti 1973.

14 Delille, 1990, 79–126.

15 Astarita 1992; Delille 1990.

16 Gentilcore 1992, 23; Visceglia 1988b, esp. 21–32, 115–141.
17 Astarita 1992, 111; Astarita 1999 for an excellent study of a feudal community at Pentidattilo, and jurisdictional roles.
18 Astarita 1992.
19 Marino 1988. See also Delille 1990; Gross 1990, 168–71.
20 Marino 1988, 90; AA.VV. 1972–, VI, 615, pl. 83, reproduces an interesting 1687 map of sheep locations, *Poste*, around Foggia.
21 Marino 1988, 41 and 316, note 3.
22 Luise 1983, 304, Table 2.
23 Villone 1983; Delille 1985, esp. 107, 129–39, 186, 328–9; Coniglio 1978, 127–9.
24 Woolf 1979, 45–6.
25 Masi 1957; cf. Nicolini, 1934, 309; Pepe, 1952, 215; Gentilcore 1992, 25–6, 49–51 for partial support, from a different perspective. On Jesuits, Masella, 1979 esp. 38–40.
26 Louise Bross, University of Chicago, paper given at the Sixteenth Century Studies Conference, Toronto October 1994, 'Architectural projects in the lands of Santo Spirito in Sassia', and in an interesting subsequent discussion.
27 Marino 1988, 138, 179, 220. On San Pietro: Black 1984, 447–8; Montanari 1966, 129–60; Guerrieri 1967; Chiacchella 1974, 136–46; Archivio di S.Pietro, Perugia, Diverse 38, 'Libro di Ricordi da 1527 al 1616'; Mazzo xxxvi.
28 Chiacchella 1974, 134.
29 Malanima 1977, 76–85, 1979, esp. Tables IV–VI for figures.
30 Astarita 1999, 88–110.
31 Bush 1988, 161–2; Black 1981, esp. 529–30, 537–8; Fasano Guarini 1978, esp. her 'Introduzione'; Ferraro 1993; Polverini Fosi 1985; Wright, 1980; Muir 1993, 1998; Pullan 1999a.
32 Black 1981; Coffin 1988; Ginori 1977; Logan 1972; Muraro and Marton 1986; Sereni 1997.
33 Romby and Tarassi 1992, exhibition catalogue with many illustrations of rural society, living and working conditions; AA.VV. 1972– *Storia d'Italia*, vol. 6, *Atlante* 1976, photos of different kinds of peasant housing, supporting Lucio Gambi, 'La casa contadina', 479–505; see also Sereni 1961, 1997, with some useful b. and w. illustrations from paintings. Bonelli Conenna 1980, 225–37, including reproductions of contemporary drawings of buildings; Gambi 1964; Balestracci 1999, 29–32, 110–14.
34 Belli, 1983, 346.

5 THE URBAN ENVIRONMENT

1 Cowan 1998, 4–12 with Table 1.1.
2 Hughes 1975; Burke 1997, ch. 7; Concina 1998, 192–3.
3 Gianighian and Pavanini 1984 and Trincanato 1995 on Venice; D'Amico 1994 on Milan.
4 *De Re Aedificatoria* VII: 1, cited Miller 1989, 105.
5 D'Amico 1994; Giusberti 1986; Calabi 1993; McCray 1999 notably on Murano glass-making.
6 Thornton 1991, 11.
7 Goldthwaite 1980, 89.
8 D'Amico 1994, esp. 34, 40–41.
9 Thornton 1991; Davanzo Poli 1997, for clothing, shoes, wall coverings; Pazzi 1996a and 1996b for gold, silver, jewellery; Dorigato 1986 and McCray 1999 for glass; Malanima 1990.
10 Waddy 1990.
11 Thornton 1997, splendidly illustrated: Fig. 21 reproduces the Vision of St Ursula, Fig. 24 has Lorenzo Lotto's delightfully informal drawing of *An Ecclesiast in his* [well-lived in!] *Study-Bedroom*, [British Museum]; Santore 1988.

12 Cipolla 1992a, 23, and 1981, 15–17; Black 1989, 156–7.
13 Key works: Adams and Nussdorfer 1994; Argan 1969; Braunfels 1990; Calabi 1993; For Bologna: Miller 1989; Florence: Fei and others 1995; Naples: Hersey 1969; De Seta 1994; Rome: Burroughs 1990; Delumeau 1957–59; Krautheimer 1985; Partner 1976; Turin: Pollak 1991; Venice: Bellavitis and Romanelli 1989; Calabi and Morachiello 1987; Concina 1994 and 1998; Crouzet-Pavan 1992; Goy 1989; Howard 1980 and 1990; Huse and Wolters 1990; Maretto 1992; Trincanato 1995; Zucconi 1995.
14 Mack 1987; Ackerman and Rosenfeld 1989, with plans.
15 Metzger Habel 1990; Krautheimer 1985; Morton 1966; Vertova 1995.
16 Goy 1989, Part 1; Crouzet-Pavan 1992; Concina 1998, 104–6 on Ca' Foscari.
17 Miller 1989; Montaigne 1955, 81, 1983, 62 for Bologna [it is misleading to translate as colonnades] and 61, 66, 169.
18 Cipolla 1992, 52–3.
19 Vanzan Marchini 1995a, 1995b.
20 Cipolla 1973, 1976, 1977, 1981, 1992a; Wills 1997; Calvi 1989; Vanzan Marchini 1995a, esp. 13–38, 65–102; Pastore 1991; Palmer 1982, 1999.
21 Farr 1997; Mackenney 1987; Gross 1990, esp 91; Guenzi and others 1998, esp. Fanfani largely exonerating guilds; D'Amico 2000.
22 *Primum {-quartum} volumen statutorum Perusie*, Perugia 1523–8.
23 ASP, Iura Diversa, vol. 190, folder dated 14 gennaio 1535, Ars Capellarum: cases 1535–7; Giudiziari, 1522 volume for taverners and mainly notaries; cf. Briganti 1910, esp. 167–95, 210–14.
24 On welfare aspects: Spicciani 1984; Mackenney 1987; various contributions in Guenzi and others 1998, Part III. There is overlap in this area between guilds and confraternities. See below 159.
25 Fanfani 1959, 176–7, 206–7; Delumeau 1957–59, 369–70. ASR, Camerale II. Arti e Mestieri, Buste 6, 19, 25, 33, for eighteenth-century sub-divisions, and competition between guilds.
26 Rapp 1976, 171–5.
27 On Milan Moioli 1998; on Brescia Belfanti 1998.
28 Fanfani 1959, 176–7, 179.
29 Chambers and Pullan 1992, 287–9.
30 De Roover 1966.
31 Cavazzini 1997, with extracts in Italian from incest trials; Garrard 1989, whose Appendix gives a translated transcript of the 1612 rape trial.
32 Fanfani 1959, 213–15; Marshall 1999, 7–9.
33 Black 1967b; Rapp 1976, 22–5.
34 ASB Tribunale della Plebe Mazzo I; ASR Arti e Mestieri, Buste 6, 19, 25, 33; Cerutti 1991; Poni 1989, 1991; Guenzi and others 1998, esp. articles by Travaglini on Rome, Guenzi on Bologna hatmakers.
35 Concina 1988, with many illustrations; Davis 1991, 1993, 1997; Lane 1987, 1992; Rapp 1976; Tucci 1980.
36 Davis 1991, Table 1.1.
37 Davis 1997.
38 Notes kindly provided by Allerston from ASV Sant'Uffizio, b.94, proc. Marietta Battaglia Rubini, 21 April, 18 Nov. 1639.
39 Trincanato 1995, 56 for drawing; Lane 1992, ch. VI on private shipyards.
40 Pagano de Divitiis 1997; Cipolla 1992b, ch. 2; analysis and illustrations in the catalogue *Livorno: progetto e storia di una città tra il 1500 e il 1600* Pisa, 1980.
41 Pagano de Divitiis 1997, 120–1.
42 Black 1984, 451–2.
43 Battara 1937; Mackenney 1987, 15, 92, Table 3:1; Giusberti 1986.
44 Ginori 1977, Fig. 1.

45 Allerston 1999, 53, where she also uses a *c.*1650 print to illustrate a mercer's shop with bolts of cloth; and a two-storey shop-house in the background.
46 Illustrated in Davanzo Poli 1997, 116, no. 180.
47 Coloured illustrations from his work in Museo Correr, Venice reproduced in Marangoni 1974.
48 Allerston 1996, 179–81; Fanfani 1959, 108–9; Fontaine 1991, 1996; Vianello 1993, 95–105; Zompini 1980. Pignatti 1969, for Pietro Longhi's paintings, pls. 88 *Woman Selling Doughnuts*, Ca' Rezzonico, 89 *Man Selling Salad*, Longleat, England, 164 *The Perfume-seller*, Ca' Rezzonico; see two drawings reproduced in Calabi and Morachiello 1987, pls. 11 and 12.
49 Allerston 1996, 179–81, 185–96.
50 Allerston 1996, pp 234–52; see also Majarelli and Nicolini 1962; ASP Monti di Pietà, Debitori e Creditori, vol. 1.
51 Thornton 1997, 24–6.
52 Martin 1993, 170–1.
53 Martin 1993, 171; Wilton and Bignamini 1996, 118, no. 75.
54 Allerston 1996.
55 Walker 1998a, ch. 7, 235, and 1999a, 33.
56 Martin 1993, 170; cf. Martin 1996b.
57 Maczak 1995, 63.
58 Wilton and Bignamini 1996, 107, no. 59 *An Inn at Barletta 1778* with quotation in Lamers' catalogue entry.
59 Marangoni 1974; ASR Camerale II. Arti e Mestieri, Busta 6, Caffetieri; Giusberti 1986; Wilton and Bignamini 1996 no. 72, David Allan 1744–96, *A Roman Coffee House*, *c.* 1775; no. 71, Allan's *The Arrival of a Young Traveller and his Suite during the Carnival in the Piazza di Spagna*, Rome, *c.* 1775. Pignatti 1969, pls. 452 *The Coffee-House* attributed to De Gobbis rather than Longhi, 490, print of *The Coffee-House* by P. Wagner, from lost Longhi painting.
60 Walker 1998a, ch. 7, and 1999. The quotation is from ASV Esecutori contra la Bestemmia, Busta 54, 31 Dec. 1598; courtesy of J. Walker. He uses Antonino Collurafi, *L'idea del gentil'huomo di republica nel governo politico, ethico, ed economico* (Venice, 1633); the work of a noted tutor to patrician families.

6 URBAN SOCIETY

1 Martin 1996a; Garzoni 1617 originally consulted, but also subsequently the 1996 edition; the length of the work, over 800 pages in the 1617 edition, is largely explained by the prolixity of classical and later historical references; Gnavi 1990.
2 Grubb 1996, esp. 175, 107–32.
3 Parker 1996. See also Lowry 1979; Masetti Zannini 1980.
4 For the general European context, with varying detail on Italy, Davis and Farge 1993; Hannawalt 1986; King 1991; Wiesner 1987, 1993; in Italian: De Maio 1987. Some key studies: Brown 1986a, Brown and Goodman 1980, Herlihy 1990, Herlihy and Klapisch-Zuber 1985, Klapisch-Zuber 1985; Burke 1987 esp. 35–39 on the problems of recording women; Brown and Davis 1998, esp. Cohn on the fifteenth century. In Italian: Barbagli 1988.
5 Herlihy 1990, Table 7.1; Herlihy and Klapisch-Zuber 1985, 124, 300 and Table 10.3.
6 Fabretti 1885; *Primum (-quartum) volumen statutorum Perusie* Perugia, 1523–8, vol. IV Rubric 109.
7 Mackenney 1987, 23.
8 Cavallo 1991, 173–5.
9 Cohn 1998; Park 1985.
10 See e.g. Burke 1987, 35–9; Davis 1991; Mackenney 1987; Rapp 1976.
11 ASB Tribunale della Plebe, Querele, Mazzo I 1573–88.
12 Chambers and Pullan 1992, 283, trans. R. Mackenney.
13 Dooley 1989.

14 Ferraro 1993, 63–5, 96–8.
15 Gentilcore 1994b, 1995a, 1995b, 1997, 1998; Ghisalberti 1985; Park 1985; Pomata 1994, esp. ch 3; Troncarelli 1985.
16 ArchVicR, Libri Parocchiali. 14: S. Giovanni dei Fiorentini, vol. 2 Battesimi II 1571–90, fols. 65r–93r, *passim*. Filippini 1993.
17 Astarita 1999, 155–6, 190–7.
18 Abbondanza 1973; Musgrave 1992, 16 notes both the roles of court notaries, and how little we know of their extended powers and duties. Astarita 1999 now notably highlights the roles of scribes in a remote feudal enclave in Calabria, esp. xxi–xxiii.
19 Balestracci 1999, xiv (introduction by Muir).
20 Gentilcore 1995b, 123–4.
21 Lane 1987, 343.
22 Gentilcore, seminar paper 'The Organisation of Medical Practice in Malpighi's Italy', kindly sent to me. Benadusi 1996, ch. 5 on Poppi and Tuscany more broadly.
23 Lane 1987, 180; D'Amico 1994, 89–93; Grubb 1996, 123–9; Partner 1990, esp. 6, 22, 60; Nussdorfer 1992, esp. 67–71, 89, 189; 1994.
24 Marshall 1999, xv, 8–9, 72, 102–3, 116.
25 Tuscany: Angiolini 1992; Benadusi 1996; Brown 1982; Fasano Guarini 1973; Litchfield 1986.
26 Zannini 1992 and 1993; AA.VV. 1992–7, IV, Zannini, 'L'impiego pubblico', 415–63, esp. 423–6 for two individuals cited.
27 Chambers and Dean 1997.
28 Gigli 1994 is a good modern annotated edition; Nussdorfer 1994, 109–14 on his life, *passim* for much use of Gigli's diary for 1608–70.
29 Angiolini 1992.
30 Romano 1996, 101–3; Lotto 1969.
31 M. Barbagli 1988, esp. Tables IV – 5, 6, 29–31 for figures here and most to follow.
32 Romano 1996, 109, Table 3.3.
33 Klapisch-Zuber 1986; Gross 1990, esp. Table 18; Arru 1990.
34 Gavitt 1990; Black 1989, 200–6; Klapisch-Zuber 1985, esp.132–64.
35 Cohn 1996b, esp. 14, 159–60.
36 Walker 1998a, ch. 6, 1998b; Garzoni 1996, 1263–8, esp. 1267.
37 Walker 1998b, 87.
38 Rapp 1976, 24–7. See also: D'Amico 1994, Goldthwaite 1980; Lee 1982; Pullan 1968; Scavizzi 1968.
39 Gross 1990, 99.
40 Garzoni 1996, 1459–64; Hughes 1988, 100, quoting Rainaldo.
41 Chambers and Dean 1997.
42 Hughes 1988; Wright 1980; Zorzi 1994.
43 Pullan 1978, 1026.
44 Calvi 1989, 147–54.
45 Brackett 1992, esp. ch. 3 on Florence; Zorzi 1994, esp. 48–51; Chambers and Dean 1997 *passim* on those serving magistrates sent out from Ferrara and Mantua. On Venice and Veneto, Povolo 1980 and other articles in Cozzi 1980–5; Nussdorfer 1992, 224–5; Mackenney 1987.
46 Brackett 1993; Davidson 1994; Trexler 1981; Delumeau 1957–9, I, 416–29; Menetto and Zennaro 1987.
47 AS Perugia Editti e Bandi, vol. 2 fols. 27v–8r, 35v, 56r–v, and Riformanze 1492 fol.109v.
48 D'Amico 1994, 140–3.
49 ASB, Ufficio delle Bullette, 1598: Campsonus Meretricum volume.
50 Masson 1975; Rosenthal 1992.
51 Santore 1988.
52 Martin 1989, 130.

53 Ruggiero 1993, 31.
54 Cohen and Cohen 1993, esp. 189–99 quote from 195.
55 Black 1989, 181.
56 Pullan 1994, no. IV, untranslated 'Poveri, mendicanti e vagabondi, ' reprinted from AA.VV. *Storia d'Italia* Einaudi *Annali* 1 1978; Woolf 1986; Zardin 1995, esp. D'Amico 273–90; Black 1989, esp. ch. 8. See also Cowan 1998, esp. ch.7, for European context, by a Venetian specialist.
57 Pullan 1978, 994–5.
58 Cipolla 1981, 16.
59 Black 1989, 158 quotes and precis two stanzas. For a modern edition of his poetry, Rouch 1982.

7 THE FAMILY AND HOUSEHOLD

1 M. Barbagli 1988, 1991; Hajnal 1965, 1983; Herlihy and Klapisch-Zuber 1985; Kertzer and Brettell 1987; Laslett 1983; Tamassia 1910/1971.
2 Cited Gottlieb 1993, 252, 244.
3 Romano 1996, Part III, esp.209.
4 Notably undermined by Herlihy and Klapisch-Zuber 1985, using the 1427 Tuscan *catasto* records, and by Barbagli's work on the eighteenth and nineteenth centuries, Barbagli 1988, 1991.
5 Barbagli 1991, 255.
6 Herlihy and Klapisch-Zuber 1985. See especially Table 10.1 for types of household.
7 Herlihy and Klapisch-Zuber 1985, esp. 282–6.
8 Douglass 1991, esp. 290, Table 15.2 for details.
9 Douglass 1991; cf. Douglass 1980; Delille 1985, esp. 188–97, with Tables 34–8.
10 Chojnacki 1974, esp. 179 n. 10.
11 Pilliod 1992.
12 Delille 1985, 30–1.
13 Klapisch-Zuber 1985, ch. 10, at 214. See generally Hughes 1985.
14 Molho 1994.
15 Kuehn 1991, 212–37.
16 Klapisch-Zuber 1985, ch. 9, esp. 192–3.
17 Kuehn 1991, 200; see Alberti 1969, 114–16.
18 Astarita 1992, esp. ch. 5; Delille 1983 and 1985, esp. Part III; Visceglia 1983; Merzario 1981; Kertzer and Brettell 1987, 90–1, 104.
19 Garrard 1989 has a translation of the surviving trial record in an Appendix; Cavazzini 1997; Bissell 1999, ch. 1 and Appendices.
20 E. S. Cohen 1991.
21 Ariès 1962; Stone, 1977; See also Gottlieb 1993; Chojnacki 1992 on adolescence; Ross 1974, Haas 1998 on Italian childhood; Heers 1977. On Florence particularly: Brucker 1986; Goldthwaite 1968; Kent 1977; Phillips 1987. AA.VV. 1966; Tamassia 1910/1971; Novi Chavarria 1988 on preaching about the family.
22 Giovanni Maria Cecchi, *The Horned Owl* 1981; Girolamo Bargagli, *The Female Pilgrim* 1988. Both plays have interesting and varied sets of characters, and are valuable for reflecting diverse attitudes and prejudices.
23 Especially De Maio 1987. In English: Constance 1990 has some valuable studies of Italian writings; Brown and Davis 1998.
24 Pitkin, 1984, esp. 25, 109–10, 120–1, using her translations, and ch. 6 'Fortune'. For the connection between Machiavelli's sexual attitudes and sexual politics see Freccero 1993, esp. 163.
25 See Moss 1993, 137–53, esp.142; I have used *Il Novellino* 1975 reprint edn, S. S. Nigro, of 1940 Bari edn, A. Mauro, citing phrases from 180, 201, and quote from 10.

26 Kuehn 1991, 1998.
27 Jordan 1990, 167–71.
28 Francesco Barbaro 'De re uxoria liber', cited by Herlihy 1985, 117. Part of this treatise is translated as 'On Wifely Duties' in Kohl and Witt 1978, 189–228.
29 W. Thomas 1963, 16, 82–3, 108.
30 See esp. Cantarella, 1991, 229–44. The Latin versions of the unusual names have not been translated here; Moss 1993, 140–41.
31 See the letters of Alessandra Macinghi Strozzi, Gregory 1997; discussed by e.g. Phillips 1989, ch. 3 and *passim*; Molho 1994, 222–32; Goldthwaite 1968, chs. 2 and 3. [The roles of the Baglioni women are suggested by various letters in ASP, Carteggio Alfani, and Archivio Comunale, Todi, Lettere Diverse vol. 3 (3); Archivio Segreto Vaticano, Lettere di Principi, vol. 7 fol. 138, Monaldesca Baglioni to Pope Clement VII 3 July 1532.]
32 Astarita 1992, ch. 5.
33 Chojnacki 1974, 1985, 1991, 1992.
34 Chojnacki 1974, 198 n. 73, 1991, 149; Cohn 1998.
35 Davidson 1994, esp. 77–8, 87; Heers 1977, 61. Cf. McLaren, 1990 esp. ch. 5 ; Bell 1999; Haas 1998; Cohn 1996b, esp. ch. 6, 'Sex and violence on the periphery'.
36 Black 1989, 200–205; Trexler 1973; Gavitt 1990; Kertzer 1992, 1993; Cohn 1996b.
37 Cowan 1991, 136–7, and 1999.
38 Zanetti 1972, 1977; Johansson 1987, 361.
39 Haas 1998.
40 Trexler 1991, esp. 159–86, with extensive quotations from Morelli's *Ricordi*; Ross 1974.
41 King 1994, quoting from 16–17 and 32; the codex of consoling writings is in the Hunter Collection in Glasgow University Library.
42 Davidson 1994; R. C. Davis 1994; Heywood 1904. On youth confraternities Black 1989, 47–9; Weissman 1982, esp. 116, 189–90, 213–14, 230; Trexler 1991, 367–99; Grendi 1992; Eisenbichler 1998.
43 *Ragionamento del Sig. Annibal Guasco ad Lavinia sua figliuola della maniera del governarsi elle in corte; andando per Donna* (Turin, 1586), unpaginated. Dedicated to the Infanta Caterina, Duchess of Savoy. Cf. Bell 1999, 192.
44 Ago 1990, 62.
45 Calvi 1994; 1999.
46 Calvi 1992 and 1994, 37–64; Ago, 1992; Klapisch-Zuber 1985, ch. 6.
47 Brucker 1967. Generally see Goody 1972; Heers 1977; Laslett 1983; Wall and others 1983. Specific studies: Clarke 1991, ch. 5; Delille 1985, part 3; Grendi 1987, ch. II; F. W. Kent 1977.
48 Cited by F. W. Kent 1977, 154. Perosa 1960.
49 Kent 1977, quotes from 14, 96.
50 Black 1970 esp; and see Banker 1997; Black 1967a, 1981; Blanshei 1979. Burckhardt 1955, 16–21 omitted the heart-eating episode recorded by the chronicler Francesco Matarazzo 1905, 116.
51 Scalvanti 1903, 306–7. The word *zeie* is printed and, unless a misreading, would suggest aunts not uncles.
52 Black 1970, 263–4; Luchs 1983.

8 THE SOCIAL ELITES

1 Scott 1995, I Introduction by Scott and Storrs, ch. 7 by Donati; Astarita 1992, 1999; Bush 1983, 1988; Davis 1962; Stumpo 1984; Tagliaferri 1984; Visceglia 1983, 1988a, 1988b; Visceglia 1992.
2 For a critical and balanced discussion of interpreting mentalities or, better, the French *mentalités*, Vovelle 1990.
3 Scott 1995, I, esp. ch. 7; Donati 1988; Berengo 1965, 254–63; Walker 1998a.

4 Donati, 1995, 239.
5 Cowan 1986, 51–2, n. 181.
6 Zanetti 1972, 21.
7 Donati 1988, 126–8, 147. Cf. Grubb 1988, esp. 86–93 on 'patriciate into nobility' in Vicenza.
8 Muto 1984, 287–303, esp. 295. Tutini 1644, *Dell'origine e fundation de seggi di Napoli*, Naples.
9 Cited by Borelli 1984, 13.
10 Politi, *Aristocrazione e potere politico nella Cremona di Filippo II* Milan, 1976, cited by Vigo 1984, 248. The comments on Perugia are derived from impressions gained years ago when reading the council records, the *Riformanze* in the ASP from the mid fifteenth to mid sixteenth centuries, and a few later volumes; the ten *Priori* are listed at the start of each session (of two or three months). The stress on status and title becomes notable by the 1530s.
11 Vigo 1984, 248; Berner, 1972, 9–10.
12 Borelli 1984, 17–18; Vigo 1984, 218; Zanoli 1973, esp. 293–4.
13 Borelli 1984, 16–17 lists some of the major works on agriculture.
14 Burke 1995; Black 1993; Donati 1988; Elias 1983, esp. ch. IV.
15 Hanlon 1998.
16 Hanlon 1998, 342–3; Walker 1998a.
17 Astarita 1992, 221.
18 Astarita 1992, 17, 220, Table 6.1; Donati 1995; Muto 1989.
19 Stumpo 1984, 163–4, 168.
20 Cowan 1986.
21 Stumpo 1984, 154.
22 Bush 1983; Grubb 1988; Astarita 1992, 1999.
23 Stumpo 1984.
24 Litchfield 1986, 33.
25 Zenobi 1992 provides a useful analysis of elites in the different parts of the Papal State; see also Black 1967a, 1970, 1981, 1984; Blanshei 1979; Chiacchella 1974; Polverini Fosi 1985, 1992.
26 Ago 1990; Hortubise 1985; Reinhard 1991. Wider context: Caravale and Carraciolo 1978; Gross 1990; Nussdorfer 1992.
27 Litchfield 1986, 37, n. 38 (quote, my translation).
28 Burke 1994, ch. 4.
29 Berner 1972; Litchfield 1986.
30 Diaz 1983; Cochrane 1973.
31 Hortubise 1985; Berengo 1965.
32 Donati 1995; Zanetti 1972.
33 Zanetti 1972.
34 Borelli 1974 for the 29 families; Berengo 1975, has some criticisms of the selection and adds other families to the elite.
35 Cowan 1986, 1999, and cf. Burke 1994; Pullan 1999c. Generally: Lane 1987; AA.VV. 1992–7, VI, Part II/I 'La società veneziana'.
36 Cozzi, Knapton, and Scarabello 1992, 169.
37 Finlay 1980; Queller 1986.
38 Bellavitis 1995; Cowan 1986; Chambers and Pullan 1992, Part VI.4; Zannini 1992, 1993; Pullan 1999c.
39 Zannini 1992.
40 Lewis 1981, 362 and Pl. 14.6; Allerston 1998; Chambers and Pullan 1992, 263–6 for documents.
41 Grubb 1988.
42 Colapietra 1961, reviewed by E. Gencarelli, *ASI* 120 1962, 238–42.
43 Visceglia 1992, her Introduction and contributions esp. by A. Spagnoletti on Bari and A. Musi on Salerno.
44 Berner 1972.

9 SOCIAL GROUPINGS AND LOYALTIES

1 Key conceptual works, backed largely by research on Florence include: Trexler 1991, with a stress on the importance of ritual, drawn from e.g. Geertz 1973/1993; Kent and Kent 1982; Eckstein 1995; Weissman 1982, 1985, 1987.
2 F. W. Kent 1987, 80. Thomas 1995 now provides a major study of Neri di Bicci's workshops based on his *Ricordanze*.
3 Black 1967a, 1970, 1981; Heywood 1904, 1910.
4 Falassi 1975; Hook 1979; Silverman 1984.
5 Quotes from Kent and Kent 1982, 14 and 15, with my modification of the last one; Landucci 1969, 87, cf. 61, 64, 73.
6 Notably Kent and Kent 1982 and Eckstein 1995; see also Cohn 1980a, Trexler 1991.
7 Polizzotto 1994.
8 Zago 1982.
9 Gianighian and Pavanini 1984, 166 no. 32 for the Fondamenta Tron housing; cf. Maretto 1992, 416–17.
10 R. C. Davis 1993, 1994, 1997.
11 R. C. Davis 1994, 1999.
12 Ferraro 1993; Burke 1997, ch. 7.
13 A. Dunning's work for his Courtauld Institute thesis, including the 1644 celebrations, generates these comments.
14 Allerston 1996; Brandes 1996; Calabi and Lanaro 1998, essays by Calabi and S. Zaggia; Calimani 1987; Concina and others 1991; Goy 1997, 231–34; Cozzi 1987; Pullan 1971 Part III, 1977, 1983, 1988b; Ravid 1999; Toaff 1996. AA.VV. 1972–; *Annali* 11: *Gli Ebrei in Italia*, Vivanti 2 vols., 1996–7, esp. R.Segre on 'La Controriforma' 709–78, and 'La formazione di una communità marrana: I Portoghesi a Ferrara' 779–841, S. Siegmund, 'La vita nei ghetti' 845–92, Molho, 'Ebrei a marrani fra Italia e Levante ottomano' 1011–43, J-P. Filippini, 'La nazione ebrea di Livorno' 1046–66.
15 Ioly Zorattini 1987.
16 Hsia 1992.
17 Pullan 1977; Black 1989, 268–9, and 1999b; Molho (cited above, note 14).
18 ASVen SU Busta 59; Martin 1989, 168; Ruggiero 1993, 118–19, 249; Pullan 1983, 161.
19 Black 1989, esp. 38–41 on guild/confraternity inter-connections, and 2000; Fanfani 1959; Grimagna and others 1981; Guenzi and others 1998; Mackenney 1987, 1997, 1998; Manno 1997; Rosser 1997 for European-wide background; Spicciani 1984.
20 Black 1967a, 1970, 1981 and sources.
21 Mackenney 1998.
22 ASR Camerale II. Arti e Mestieri, Busta 19, folder dated 1786.
23 Black 1989 and 1992 for major overview, 1996 for quick guide, while 1999b surveys the literature over the last 30 years. Terpstra 1999b, and Donnelly and Maher 1999, are the latest contributions with varied approaches. See also: Eisenbichler 1997, 1998; Henderson 1994; Mackenney 1994, 1997, 1998; Pullan 1994, esp. nos IX and XII updating his views from his pioneering 1972 study of the Venetian Scuole Grandi; Paglia 1990; Terpstra 1995.
24 Chambers and Pullan 1992, 287–8.
25 Arrizabalaga and others 1997.
26 Mackenney 1998; Olson 1998 supplementing Black 1989.
27 Châtellier 1989; O'Malley 1993, 1994.
28 Fanucci 1601.
29 Black 1989, ch. 2; Gentilcore 1992; Paglia 1990, esp. 96 for Benevento; Bertoldi Lenoci 1988–90.
30 Black 1989, 34.
31 Black 1999b; Casagrande 1999; King 1998, 202–6.
32 Biblioteca Comunale, Bologna [L'Archiginnasio], Fondo Ospedale, vol. 14. On inner and outer groups: Black 1999b; Terpstra 1995.

33 Weissman 1982, 98, 102.
34 Black 1989, ch. 5; Wisch 1990, 1992.
35 ASP Sodalizio di San Martino, vol 1.
36 Black 2000 updates my 1989 discussion; Dandelet 1997; Seidel 1994; Calabi and Lanaro 1998, with broader discussions of foreigners settling in cities.
37 ArchVicR: S.Cecilia in Trastevere I – Matrimoni 1 1572–1610; S.Ivo dei Bretani I – Matrimoni 1 1566–1602; S.Lorenzo in Lucina, Matrimoni I 1564–80; S.Maria in Aquiro I – Battesimi 1 1562–9 (but also including marriages 1563–93).

10 PAROCHIAL SOCIETY

1 Hay 1977b, for fifteenth century church, with ch. 2 on parochial situation. Black 1999a deals with evolution of the parochial system, with bibliography. Counter-Reformation and the Council of Trent: Jedin and Dolan 1980; Bossy 1970, 1985; Cochrane 1988a, 1988b. Davidson 1987; Delumeau 1977; Jedin, 1964; Wright 1975a, 1975b, 1982; Hsia 1998 and Mullett 1999 latest on European-wide scene. In Italian: Allegra 1981 is a wide-ranging study of the parish priest; De Rosa and Gregory 1994.
2 Cohn 1999b.
3 Gentilcore 1992, esp. 37–8; Gentilcore 1994a esp. 282–3; Carroll 1992, 96–104; see also Salimbeni 1977; Lopez, 1983, esp. 234–5.
4 *Canons and Decrees of the Council of Trent* 1951, 200–02; G.Alberigo 1973, 767–8. Black 1984 for problems of implementation of Trent, with case study of Perugia.
5 Sbrana and others 1977; Ebner 1973, 1974; Jedin 1943, 323–36; Volpe 1973.
6 I looked for example at: (a) ArchVicR., vols. concerning S.Cecilia in Trastevere; S.Giovanni dei Fiorentini; S.Ivo dei Bretani; S.Lorenzo in Lucina; S.Maria in Aquiro; (b) ASR: Stato Civile – Appendice: Libri Parrocchiale, Reg. III: no. 1 S.Sebastiano; no. 2 S.Vicolo di Funari; no. 3 S.Maria in Aquiro; no. 5 S.Susanna; no. 6. S.Susanna e S.Sebastiano a Termini; no.8 S.Maria in Aquiro.
7 McArdle 1978, 182–8.
8 Alberigo 1973, 753–9 (decrees). On marriage and Trent: *New Catholic Encyclopedia* IX, 'Marriage', XIII: 'Tametsi', New York and London; Brundage 1987, 1995; Brandileone 1896; Jedin 1964; Jemolo 1948; von Pastor 1898–1953, XV, 355–6, 376; Tamassia 1971.
9 Nubola 1993, esp. chs 5–7; Preto 1970; Rosa 1976, 167–8, 178–9; Prodi 1960, 353 on Cardinal Paleotti's worries.
10 Davidson 1984; Chambers and Pullan 1992, 183–8, 193–5; Muir 1989. On Pisa: Greco 1984, esp. 25–37, 43–4, 58–61, 64–5.
11 Rosa 1976, 167–8; Donvito and Pellegrino 1973, 8, 11.
12 Toscani 1986, quoting 586.
13 Mezzadri 1969, 39; Cohn 1988, 219–22.
14 Alberigo 1958, 251; Monticone 1953, 237–8; Davidson 1984, 25; Wright 1975b, 454; Greco 1984, 70; Lopez 1965, 34–5; Preto 1970, 800–01; Scarano 1958, esp. 290.
15 Black 1984, 441–2, with refs; Deutscher 1981, 1989; Guasco 1986; Pelliccia 1946. Borromeo provided model legislation in his *Constitutiones et Decreta Condita in Provinciale Synodo Mediolanensi* (Brescia, 1567), 47–50 'De Seminario Clericorum'; on his seminaries, Rimoldi 1965; Nubola 1993.
16 Burke 1978, 271; Alberigo 1958, 288; Rimoldi 1965, 452.
17 Masi 1957, 93 quote. Papers and supporting documents from several conferences published in *Ravennatensia* (see Bibliography) are of considerable value on legislation, and the evidence of investigations, Visitations, etc.
18 Pelliccia 1946; Deutscher 1984 on Novara. On the *concorso*: Masetti Zannini 1976; Greco 1984, esp. 42–3.
19 Black 1984.
20 Fanti 1979–80, 1981.

21 ASB Tribunale del Torrone vol. 5743 1628–30, ff. 126r–204v, *passim*; Niccoli 1995.
22 ASB Arcivescovile Liber Criminalium 1624, fols. 49v–51r.
23 APVen Curia Patriarcale - Archivio 'Segreto': Criminalia S.Inquisitionis 1586–99, fols. 85–102.
24 Di Simplicio 1994a.
25 Davidson 1984.
26 Ciammitti 1990, 151 (quote).
27 Franchi 1980, esp. 16–23, 56–7, cc. 64r, 70r–v, 78r.
28 Bossy 1970, 1985, esp. ch. 4; N. Z. Davis 1974. Corrain and Zampini 1970, 1971, survey, rather uncritically, much episcopal legislation, and relate condemned popular practices with later ethnographic studies of the nineteenth and twentieth centuries.
29 Bossy 1998.
30 Bossy 1984, 1985; Carroll 1992, 107–11, 114; Klapisch-Zuber 1985, 89–93, 287; Trexler 1971, 66–7; Ebner 1973, 1974; Volpe 1977, esp. 234–47.
31 Scalvanti 1903, 272–3.
32 Brucker 1967, 114, 123, 134. Klapisch-Zuber 1985, esp. chs 9 and 11 focusing on Altieri's dialogue. Brucker 1998, 29–37; Brucker 1986, esp. 82–4; F. W. Kent 1977, 91–4, 134, 218, 242–3; Molho 1994, esp. 182–92; Trexler 1971, 124–6, includes quote from 1517 synod; Vaussard 1962, ch. ix; Tamassia 1971, esp. 181–95; Herlihy 1995, ch. 5, 96–109 for prohibited degrees of consanguinity and affinity.
33 Stevenson, 1983, for world-wide comparisons and 91–3, 169–73 for Italy and Trent; Dean and Lowe 1998; Rasi, 1941, I, 235–81, esp. for Veneto area.
34 Gabriele Paleotti, *Del Sacramento del matrimonio. Avvertimenti alli reverendi curati* Bologna, 1577; rev. edn Venice, 1607 used; cf. Prodi 1959–67, II, 126–8. Cf. Carlo Borromeo, *Le piu belle pagine delle omelie*, Gorla, Milan, 1926, 119–20.
35 Brandileone 1896; Manzoni 1959, ch. 8, 95–6 and 1960, 128–9.
36 Bossy, 1975, 21–38; Hay 1977a, 79–80; Black 1989, esp. 14, 95–7 for Cacciaguerra; Trexler 1971, 62–5, 70, 205–7, 286–7, on confession as the pre-eminent activity of a priest; Fumo, *Summa* 1554, Venice edn, 95v–103r 'Confessio Sacramentalis', 'Confessor'; J. Martin 1993, 185–7, indicating the pressure of confessors on Venetians to confess possible heresies. On confessionals: Headley and Tomaro 1988, 179, 202–3.
37 E.g. on trying to ensure Mass was better said, and worshippers behaved better: *Statuti et Constitutiones Synodi* Perugia, 1564, 'De Honestate' Const.I; Samaritani 1971; Lopez 1965, 14–15; Corrain and Zampini 1970; Scaduto 1960, 380–1; Nubola 1993, 139–40, 381–3.
38 Bossy 1983; Black 1989, esp. 29–30, 45, 89–100, 272; Black 1998b; Weissman 1982, 229–34, quoting an account of a *Quarantore* celebration; Voelker 1988 on altars and equipment.
39 Bossy 1985, 42–5 on Carnival; Burke 1987, ch. 13; Black 1989, ch. 5; Andrieux 1968, 124–32; Gentilcore 1992, 57–9; Trexler 1991, esp. 191–2, 215–78, 399–418, 414–18 (fifteenth-century changes in Carnival); Vaussard 1962, 133–151; Wisch 1990, 1992; Reato 1988, with illustrations of Venetian Carnival activity.
40 Burke 1978, 340; Gentilcore 1992, 59–61; Corrain and Zampini 1970; Lanternari 1955.
41 Bossy 1970, 61; Imberciadori 1959, esp. 437–41; Prodi 1959–67, II, 385; Olivieri 1972, esp. 635–8.
42 Ariès 1981; Bossy 1985, 26–34; N. Z. Davis 1974, 335 and 1977, 92–6; Black 1989; Strocchia 1992; Cohn 1988, esp. 179–84, 217–19, 225–30, and 1992 for earlier period; Vaussard 1962, ch. ix on eighteenth century.
43 Grendler 1989, esp. chs 12 and 13; Black 1989, 1992, ch. 10.3.
44 Mullett 1987, esp. ch. 4; Delumeau 1990, esp. 357–72 on 'Sermons and Hymns'; Camporesi 1990; O'Malley 1993, esp. ch. 3; Ridolfi 1959, pays much attention to Savonarola's sermons; Weinstein 1970; Meneghin 1974; Novi Chavarria 1982, 159–85; Imberciadori 1959, 446.
45 Alberigo 1973, 667–70; Carlo Borromeo, *Instructiones praedicationes Verbi Dei* (Milan, 1581, and later edns); Wright 1975a, 454; Altieri 1969; Sposato 1965, 25. There is an interesting

diary of a Milanese layman who became an enthusiast for Christian Doctrine teaching: Marcora 1965, part translated in Cochrane and Kirshner 1986, 409–26.

46 ArchVicR Arciconfraternita della Dottrina Cristiana, palchetto 168, vol. 417 Congregationi 1599–1608; Black 1989, 223–8, 1992, 287–93, 430–1; Franza 1958, esp. 25–58, 95–6, 219–32; Pelliccia 1980.

47 Grendler 1989, esp. ch. 2.

48 Lopez 1965, 101–4; Del Re 1968, 143.

49 Bossy 1975; Burke 1978, 223–34, esp. 224–5; Stone 1977, 139–42; Wright 1975b; Fragnito 1997.

50 Black 1999a.

11 SOCIAL TENSIONS, CONTROL AND AMELIORATION

1 Cellini 1995; Dean and Lowe 1994; Muir and Ruggiero 1994; Martines 1972; Muir 1993; Villari 1993.

2 von Greyerz 1984; N. Z. Davis 1974; Black 1989, esp. 8, 133–7, 150, 275–7.

3 Muir 1993; Bossy 1998.

4 Larner 1972 usefully exemplifies these interlocking factors.

5 See the works of E. Cohen and T. Cohen in the Bibliography; Rossi 1994; Burke 1987; Burke's starting quotation, the vulgar sexual libel against Ferdinando Fredini and his wife, posted on their door in 1620, is translated by P. Cohen 1991–2, 874 n. 30.

6 ASR, Tribunale del Governatore, Processi, Busta 298.

7 P. Laven 1994; Brackett 1993, esp. ch. 4 for Tuscany; Villari 1993, esp. 33–55 for Kingdom of Naples. Ortalli 1986, with papers in English by N. S. Davidson, E. J. Hobsbawm, J. S. Grubb; Polverini Fosi 1985, 1993 on Papal State; Caravale and Caracciolo 1978, 343–6; Villari 1983, ch. 4 on Naples; Povolo 1980; Delumeau 1957–9, II, 541–66, bandits in the Papal State.

8 Villari 1993, 49–50; Polverini Fosi 1985; Hobsbawm 1971, esp. 13–28.

9 Davidson 1986, 421.

10 Raggio 1986.

11 Starn 1982, 148–54 on the turning-point of Montalcino.

12 Pastore and Sorcinelli 1990, 51–75.

13 Galasso 1982, II, 278–80.

14 Cohn 1999a.

15 Muir 1993, 1998; Bianco 1994.

16 Coniglio 1978, 149; Larner 1972, 59; Pullan 1964.

17 Coniglio 1978, esp. ch. 4.

18 Burke, 1987, ch. 14; R.Villari 1993, 'Afterword One'; Merriman, 1938, 17–27, 127–35, provided the old narrative account; Elliott 1970, context for the Naples and Palermo revolts. Fiorentino 1984, II, 43–9 highlights the visual impact of Masaniello and his myth.

19 Galasso 1967, 403–4, 1977, 188–93, and 1982, esp. I, 254–62. Cf. on Francesco d'Andrea; Comparato 1974, 49, 92, 124–30, 417.

20 Calisse 1969, esp. 165–80; Stern 1994; Brackett 1992; Cozzi, 1973; Ruggiero 1980 Part One; Cozzi 1980–85; Cohen and Cohen 1993 have translated transcripts from the Roman Governor's court; Nussdorfer 1992, ch. 4; Gross 1990 ch. 9; Fornili 1991.

21 Rossi, 1969; Mallett and Hale 1984, 218–20, 328–9.

22 A. di S. Bologna, Torrone vols. 5742 1630, 5743 1628–30; Arcivescovile 1624: Liber Criminalium 1624 [formerly Torrone, 5360/2]; cf. Niccoli 1995; Pastore 1991; Crouzet-Pavan 1997.

23 A di S. Bologna, Assunteria del Governo, Lettere di Varie Comunità vol. 7 Bolognese 1644–76, esp. letters of 17 Jan., 2 July 1662, 9 May 1663, 26 April 1665, 15 July 1668, 3 Sept. 1670, 16 Nov. 1672.

24 Brackett 1992, with Figures 2 and 3; Franzoi 1997, with illustrations.
25 Davidson 1994; Burke 1987, ch. 8.
26 E. Cohen 1991a; see above Chapter 7.
27 Rocke 1996; Pavan 1980; Labalme 1984; Ruggiero 1985; Saslow 1986; Scarabello 1980.
28 Mirollo, 1963, 12; Cellini, 1995; Martini 1988, esp. 104–11, and n. 73.
29 T. Cohen 1992; T. Cohen and E. Cohen 1993.
30 Grendler 1977 esp. ch. 2; Martin 1989; Pullan 1983; Tedeschi 1991; Di Simplicio 1994b; Del Col 1996, 1998; Prosperi 1996. Archival research in Venice, Florence and Bologna on Inquisitions and ecclesiastical courts (see Bibliography), for my forthcoming book on the Counter-Reformation in Italy.
31 ASVen SU Busta 33; APVen. 'Criminalia S.Inquisitionis 1586–99', fols 12–17.
32 See cases of Anzola Civrana, June 1646, and Giulia *meretrice*, December 1652: ASVen SU Buste 103 and 106.
33 ASVen SU Busta 103, Contra Iom. Paulum Sorratinun 10 April 1646; accused of swearing by the puttana [whore] di Dio, puttana di Signore, Sangue [blood] di Dio, potta [cunt] di Dio. Busta 106, 'Contra Franciscum Matthei [2 Dec. 1653].
34 AAF S.Uffizio Filze 2–3, fols 55–7; ASVen Busta 103, 'Joannis Jons. Q. Jois. De Sazonia, 24 March 1639', 'Fugarola Lodovico' 10 July 1646. Cf. Monter and Tedeschi 1986, 141.
35 Ginzburg 1983; Harner, 1973; Riddle 1994.
36 Hoak, 1985, 499.
37 Black 1989, esp. 137–50; subsequently useful works in English have appeared: Geremek 1994; Jütte 1994; Grell, Cunningham, Arrizabalaga 1999.
38 Black 1989, 159 quotes Cardinal Odoardo Farnese's reactions.
39 Black 1989, esp. 214–16, and sources; Cavallo 1991, 1995; Terpstra 1995.
40 Black 1989, 1992, chs. 6–9, 1998a; Albini 1993; Cavallo 1995; Fanti 1997; Henderson 1994, Mackenney 1994, Pullan 1971, 1988, 1994; Ricci 1996; Terpstra 1994, 1995, 1999a, Zardin 1995. While revising this section I received, thanks to Alessandra Bonzi, copies of the provisional papers prepared for discussion at the Bologna conference *Forme di povertà e innovazioni istituzionali in Italia dal Medioevo ad oggi*, May 1999. Ahead of official publication of revised versions, I would note that contributions by G. Albini, S. Cavallo, M. Fanti, J. Henderson, B. S. Pullan, G. Ricci and N. Terpstra have influenced this section. Grell, Cunningham, Arrizabalaga 1999, with key articles by B. C. Pullan (general), J. Henderson (Tuscany), R. Palmer (Veneto), S. De Renzi (Rome) and D. Gentilcore (Naples).
41 San Bernardino da Siena 1950–65, III, 64.
42 Alessandro Sperelli, *Della pretiosita della limosina* (Venice, 1666), 239, 243; de Angelis, *Della limosina overo opere che si assicurano nel giorno del final giuditio* (Rome, 1615 edn), 59; cf. Black 1989, 17, 138, 145–6.
43 San Bernardino da Siena 1950–65, VIII, 86–8; see Black 1989, 139; Spicciani 1982, 829.
44 Black 1998a.
45 Gazzini 1997.
46 Pullan 1999a.
47 ASVen Scuole Piccole e Suffragi, SS.Trinita, scuola vicino alla Salute. Busta 706, Libro 3 'Notariato della Scola della S.ma Trinita', 1649–1710; Black 1989, 186–7; Pullan 1994, no. X.
48 R. Mackenney's translation of parts of Caravia's *Il Sogno di Caravia* 1541 in Chambers and Pullan 1992, 213–16. Full Italian text reproduced in *Venezia Cinquecento. Studi di storia dell'arte e della cultura* 1/1, 1991.

12 EPILOGUE

1 Venturi 1969–90, V, part 2, ch. 2 deals with the famine years; quotes from 245, 265.
2 Venturi 1969–90, I, II and V, parts 1 and 2, and essays in English, 1972; cf. for recent assessment and context, Robertson 1992, 1997; Verga 1998. Carpanetto and Ricuperato 1987; Chorley 1965; Woolf 1979.

3 Venturi 1972, 52–62; Bellamy 1995, best annotated translation of Beccaria's short book, 7 (quote).
4 Eisenbichler 1998, 297.
5 Venturi 1969–90, II; Chadwick 1981, esp. ch. 5.
6 Bettinelli 1786 edn, xli–ii; Venturi 1969–90, V/1, 622–9.
7 Chittolini 1995.
8 Chard 1999, 92.

BIBLIOGRAPHY

Archival sources

This listing of Archives and series is confined to material used specifically for this book; more material from these archives can be identified via my previous publications.

Bologna:

Archivio di Stato (ASB)

Tribunale del Torrone, vols 5742, 5743, 5758 (1628–32); Tribunale della Plebe: Querele, Mazzo (1573–88), Visite al Contado, Mazzo I (1579–1692). Assunteria del Governo, Lettere di Varie Comunità, vol. 7. Arcivescovile Liber Criminalium 1624. Ufficio delle Bullette, 1598.

Florence:

Archivio Arcivescovile (AAF)

S.Uffizio, Filze 2–3.

Perugia:

Archivio di Stato (ASP)

Iura Diversa vol. 190, (1535–70); Giudiziari, vol. for 1522; Riformanze volumes; Sodalizio di San Martino, vol. 1; Fondo Notarile, vols 676, 825; Monti di Pietà, Debitori e Creditori, vol. 1. Carteggio Alfani.

Archivio di S.Pietro

Mazzo xxxvi; Diverse 38.

Rome:

Archivio di Stato (ASR)

Tribunale del Governatore, Processi, Busta 298 (1595–6). Camerale II. Arti e Mestieri, Buste 6, 19, 25, 33. Stato Civile – Appendice: Libri Parrocchiali: 1 S.Sebastiano, inhabitants in 1580, deaths and burials 1578–81, baptisms 1565–81, deaths 1566–70; no. 2 S.Vicolo di Funari, two books with entries on deaths 1568–1622; no. 3 S.Maria in Aquiro Libro dei Morti 1597–1644; no. 8 S.Maria in Aquiro. Liber Status Animarum 1601–34; no. 5 S.Susanna, list of families 1593–1609; no. 6. S.Susanna e S.Sebastiano a Termini, record of totals from no. 5.

Archivio del Vicariato (ArchVicR)

Libri Parocchiali: S.Cecilia in Trastevere I – Matrimoni 1 (1572–1610), confirmations 1577–92, deaths 1575–1610, and Stati d'anime 1602–17; S.Giovanni dei Fiorentini, 2 Battesimi, 1571–90); S.Ivo dei Bretani I – Matrimoni 1 (1566–1602); S.Lorenzo in Lucina, Matrimoni I (1564–80); S.Maria in Aquiro I – Battesimi 1 (1562–69), but also including marriages 1563–93, deaths 1568–85, lists of communicants 1564–94.

Venice:

Archivio di Stato (ASVen)

Scuole Piccole e Suffragi, Busta 706 (SS.Trinita alla Salute). Sant'Uffizio [SU], Buste 33, 59, 103, 106.

Archivio Patriarchale (APVen)

Curia Patriarcale - Sezione Antica, Atti patriarcale riguardanti le monache, vols for 1591–9 and 1620–30. Archivio 'Segreto': Criminalia S.Inquisitionis 1586–.

Secondary works

[AA.VV. = Autori Varii; collected studies with no clear identification of editor(s); here arranged chronologically.

ASI = *Archivio Storico Italiano*

EHR = *English Historical Review*

JMH = *Journal of Modern History*

MEFRM = *Mélanges de l'école française de Rome*

RSI = *Rivista Storica Italiana*

SCJ = *Sixteenth Century Journal*]

AA.VV., 1966, *Vita privata a Firenze nei secoli xiv e xv* (Florence).

—— 1972– , *Storia d'Italia* (Einaudi). Initially 5 vols (Turin, 1972–8), co-ordinated by R. Romano and C. Vivanti; supplementary vols, series of *Annali* or *Documenti*, have appeared since under various editors.

—— 1979, *Contadini e proprietari nella Toscana moderna. Atti del Convegno di studi in onore di Giorgio Giorgetti*, I *Dal Medioevo all'età moderna* (Florence).

—— 1980, *Tiziano e venezia. Convegno Internazionale di Studi, Venezia, 1976* (Vicenza).

—— 1980, *Venezia a la peste 1348/1797* (Venice, 2nd edn).

—— 1983, *Firenze e la Toscana dei Medici nell'Europa del '500* (2 vols, Florence).

—— 1984, *Artigiani e salariati. Il Mondo del Lavoro nell'Italia dei secoli xii–xv. Decimo Convegno Internazionale, Pistoia, 1981* (Pistoia).

—— 1992–97, *Storia di Venezia. Dalle Origine alla Caduta della Repubblica* (Rome, Istituto della Enciclopedia Italiana), General Editor, G. Benzoni. III, 1997: *La formazione dello Stato Patrizio*, eds G. Rinaldi, G. Cracco and A. Tenenti; IV, 1996: *Il Rinascimento. Politica e Cultura*, eds A. Tenenti and U. Tucci; V, 1996: *Il Rinascimento. Società e Economica*, eds A. Tenenti and U. Tucci; VI, 1994: *Dal Rinascimento al Barocco*, eds G. Cozzi and P. Prodi.

Abbondanza, R. (ed.), 1973, *Il Notariato a Perugia. Mostra documentaria e iconografica per il xvi congresso nazionale del notariato* (Perugia) Rome.

Abel, W., 1980, *Agricultural Fluctuations in Europe: From the Thirteenth to Twentieth Centuries*, London.

Abelove, H. and others (eds), 1983, *Visions of History*, Manchester.

Abulafia, D. (ed.), 1995, *The French Descent into Renaissance Italy 1494–5*, Aldershot and Brookfield, Vermont.

Adams, N. and Nussdorfer, L., 1994, 'The Italian City, 1400–1600', in H. A. Millon and V. Magnago Lampugnani (eds), 205–30.

Accati, L., 1987, 'The larceny of desire: The Madonna in seventeenth-century Catholic Europe', *Disciplines of Faith. Studies in Religion, Politics and Patriarchy*, (eds) J. Obelkevich, L. Roper and R. Samuel, London and N.Y.

Ackerman, J. S. and Rosenfeld, M. N., 1989, 'Social Stratification in Renaissance Urban Planning', in S. Zimmerman and R. F. E. Weissman (eds), 21–49.

Ago, R., 1980, 'Inserimento dei forestieri nella communità: il caso di Anguillara', in *La popolazione Italiana del Settecento*, Bologna, 529–36.

—— 1990, *Carriere e clientele nella Roma barocca*, Rome and Bari.

—— 1992, 'Giochi di Squadra: uomini e donne nelle famiglie nobili del xvii secolo', in M. A. Visceglia (ed.), 256–64.

Alberigo, G., 1958, 'Studi e problemi relativi all'applicazione del Concilio di Trento in Italia, (1945–58)', *RSI*, 70, 239–98.

—— (ed.), 1973, *Conciliorum Oecumenicorum Decreta*, 3rd edn, Bologna.

Alberti, Leon Battista, 1969, *The Family in Renaissance Florence*. A translation by Renée Neu Watkins of *I Libri della Famiglia*, Columbia, South Carolina.

Albini, G., 1993, *Città e ospedali nella Lombardia medievale*, Bologna.

Allegra, L., 1981, 'Il parroco: un mediatore fra alta e bassa cultura', in AA.VV. *Storia d'Italia*, 1972– , *Annali*, 4, 895–947.

Allerston, P., 1996, 'The Market in Second-hand Clothes and Furnishings in Venice, *c.* 1500 – *c.* 1650', Doctoral Dissertation, European University Institute, Florence.

—— 1998, 'Wedding Finery in Sixteenth-century Venice', in Dean and Lowe (eds), 25–40.

—— 1999, 'Reconstructing the Second-hand Clothes Trade in Sixteenth- and Seventeenth-century Venice', *Costume. The Journal of the Costume Society*, 13, 46–56.

Altieri, P., 1969, 'Attività sinodale della Chiesa Cesenate,' *Ravennatensia*, 1, 143–53.

Andrieux, M., 1968, *Daily Life in Papal Rome in the Eighteenth Century*, London.

Angiolini, F., 1992, 'Dai segretari alle 'Segreterie': uomini ed apparati di Governo nella Toscana Medicea (metà xvi secolo – metà xvii secolo', *Società e Storia*, 58, 701–20.

—— 1996, 'La Società', in Greco and Rosa (eds), Rome and Bari, 297–331.

Argan, G. C., 1969, *The Renaissance City*, London.

Ariès, P., 1962, *Centuries of Childhood: a social history of family life*, New York.

—— 1981, *The Hour of Our Death*, London.

Arrizabalaga, Jon, Henderson, John and French, Roger, 1997, *The Great Pox. The French Disease in Renaissance Europe*, New Haven and London.

Arru, A., 1990, 'The Distinguishing Features of Domestic Service in Italy', *J. Family Hist.*, 15, 547–66.

Astarita, T., 1992, *The Continuity of Feudal Power. The Caracciolo di Brienza in Spanish Naples*, Cambridge.

—— 1999, *Village Justice. Community, Family, and Popular Culture in Early Modern Italy*, Baltimore and London.

Balestracci, D., 1999, *The Renaissance in the Fields. Family Memoirs of a Fifteenth-Century Tuscan Peasant*, trans. P. Squatriti and B. Meredith, 'Introd.' by E. Muir, University Park, PA.

Banker, J., 1997, 'The Social History of Perugia in the Time of Perugino', in J. A. Becherer (ed.), *Pietro Perugino. Master of the Italian Renaissance*, Grand Rapids, MI, 37–51.

Barbagli, M., 1988, *Sotto lo stesso tetto. Mutamenti della Famiglia in Italia dal xv al xx secolo*, 2nd edn, Bologna.

—— 1991, 'Three Household Formation Systems in Eighteenth- and Nineteenth-century Italy', in Kertzer and Saller (eds), 250–70.

Bargagli, Girolamo, 1988, *The Female Pilgrim (La Pellegrina)*. Translated with Introduction and Notes by Bruno Ferraro, Dovehouse Editions, Canada.

Basini, G. L., 1970, *L'uomo e il pane. Resorse, consumi a carenze alimentari della popolazione modenese nel cinque a seicento*, Milan.

Battara, P., 1937, 'Botteghe e pigione nella Firenze del '500', *ASI*, 95, 3–28.

Belfanti, C. M., 1988, 'Della città alla campagna: industrie tessili a Mantua tra carestie ed epidemie (1550–1630)', *Critica Storica*, 25, 438–53.

—— 1993, 'Rural Manufactures and Rural Proto-industries in the "Italy of the Cities" from the Sixteenth through the Eighteenth Century', *Continuity and Change*, 8, 253–80.

—— 1998, 'A Chain of Skills: the production cycle of firearms manufacture in the Brescia area from the sixteenth to the eighteenth centuries', in A. Guenzi and others (eds), 266–83.

Bell, R. M., 1999, *How to Do It. Guides to Good Living for Renaissance Italians*, Chicago and London.

Bellamy, R. (ed.), 1995, *Beccaria. On Crimes and Punishments and Other Writings*, Cambridge.

Bellavitis, A., 1995, '"Per Cittadini Metterete ...". La stratificazione della società veneziana cinquecentesca tra norma giuridica e riconoscimento sociale', *Quaderni Storici*, 30, 359–83.

Bellavitis, G. and Romanelli, G., 1989, *Venezia* (Le città nella storia d'Italia), 2nd edn, Rome and Bari.

Bellettini, A. 1978, 'Ricerche sulle crisi demografiche del seicento', *Società e Storia*, I.i, 35–64.

Belli, C., 1983, 'Famiglia, proprietà e classi sociali a Montefusco nella prima metà del xvii secolo', *MEFRM*, 95, 339–92.

Beloch, G., 1959, [Giulio = Karl as next] 'La popolazione d'Italia nei secoli sedecesimo, diciasettesimo e diciottesimo', in Cipolla (ed.), 450–500.

Beloch, K. J., 1937, 1939, 1961, *Bevölkerungsgeschichte Italiens*, 3 vols, Berlin.

Beltrami, D., 1955, *Saggio di storia dell'agricoltura nella repubblica di Venezia durante l'età moderna*, Venice and Rome.

—— 1959, 'Lineamenti di storia della popolazione di Venezia dal Cinquecento al Settecento', in Cipolla (ed.), 501–31.

—— 1962, *La penetrazione economica dei Veneziani in terraferma; forze di lavoro e proprietari fondaria nelle campagne venete dei secoli xvii e xviii*, Venice.

Benadusi, G., 1995, 'Rethinking the state: family strategies in early modern Tuscany,' *Social History*, 20,157–78.

—— 1996, *A Provincial Elite in the Creation of the State*, Baltimore and London.

Berengo, M., 1965, *Nobili e mercanti nella Lucca del Cinquecento*, Turin.

—— 1975, 'Patriziato e Nobiltà: il caso veronese', *RSI*, 493–517.

Berner S., 1972, 'The Florentine Patriciate in the Transition from Republic to Principato, 1530–1609', *Studies in Medieval and Renaissance History*, 9, 2–15.

Bertoldi Lenoci, L., 1988–90, *Le Confraternite Pugliesi in Età Moderna*, 2 vols, Fasano Br.

Bettinelli, S., 1786, *Risorgimento d'Italia Negli Studj, nelle Arti, e ne' Costumi dopo il Mille*, Venice.

Bianco, F., 1994, 'Mihi Vindictam: aristocratic clans and rural communities in a feud in Friuli in the late fifteenth and sixteenth centuries', in Dean and Lowe (eds), 249–73.

Bissell, R. Ward, 1999, *Artemisia Gentileschi and the Authority of Art*, University Park, PA.

Black, C. F., 1967a, 'Commune and the Papacy in the government of Perugia, 1488–1540', *Annali della Fondazione per la storia amministrativa*, 4, 163–91.

—— 1967b, 'Politics and Society in Perugia, 1488–1540', B.Litt. Thesis, Oxford.

—— 1970, 'The Baglioni as Tyrants of Perugia, 1488–1540', *EHR*, 85, 245–81.

—— 1981, 'Perugia and Papal Absolutism in the Sixteenth Century', *EHR*, 96, 509–39.

—— 1984, 'Perugia and Post-tridentine Church Reform', *J. Eccl. Hist.*, 35, 429–51.

—— 1989, *Italian Confraternities in the Sixteenth Century*, Cambridge.

—— 1992, *Le Confraternite Italiane del Cinquecento* (rev. and trans. of above), Milan.

—— 1993, 'The High Renaissance,' in Black and others, 76–103.

—— 1996, 'Confraternities', in H. Hillerbrand (ed.), *The Oxford Encyclopedia of the Reformation*, 4 vols, IV, 406–8, New York and Oxford.

—— 1998a, 'Early Modern Venice – An Ideal Welfare State?,' in C. A. Maltezou (ed.), *Ricchi e Poveri nella società dell'oriente grecolatino. Simposio Internazinale*, 145–58, Venice.

—— 1998b, '"Exceeding every expression of words"; Bernini's Rome and the Religious Background', in A. Weston-Lewis (ed.), *Effigies and Ecstasies. Roman Baroque Sculpture and Design in the Age of Bernini*, National Gallery of Scotland exhibition catalogue, 11–21, Edinburgh.

—— 1999a, 'Confraternities and the Parish in the Context of Italian Catholic Reform', in Donnelly and Maher (eds), 1–26.

—— 1999b, 'The Development of Confraternity Studies over the last Thirty Years', in Terpstra (ed.), 9–29.

—— 2000, 'Early Modern Italian Confraternities: Inclusion and Exclusion,' forthcoming in *Historein* (Athens), vol. 2.

—— and others, 1993, *Atlas of the Renaissance*, London. [American edn titled: *Cultural Atlas of the Renaissance*.]

Blanshei, S., 1979, 'Population, Wealth and Patronage in Medieval and Renaissance Perugia', *J. Interdisciplinary Hist.*, 9, 597–619.

Bonelli Conenna, L., 1980, 'Cenni sulle comunità del contado senese dopo la conquista medicea', in L. Rombai (ed.), *I Medici e lo Stato Senese 1555–1609 Storia e Territorio*, 225–37, Rome.

Borelli, G., 1974, *Un Patriziato della Terraferma Veneta tra xvii e xviii secolo (Ricerche sulla nobiltà veronese)*, Milan.

—— 1984, 'I ceti dirigenti italiani tra realtà e utopia', in Tagliaferri (ed.), 9–19.

Bossy, J., 1970, 'The Counter Reformation and the People of Catholic Europe', *Past and Present*, 47 (May), 51–70.

—— 1975, 'The Social History of Confession in the Age of the Reformation', *Trans.Roy. Hist.Soc.*, 25, 21–38.

—— 1983, 'The Mass as a Social Institution 1200–1700', *Past and Present*, 100 (August), 29–61.

—— 1984, 'Godparenthood: the Fortunes of a Social Institution in Early Modern Christianity', in von Greyerz (ed.), 194–201.

—— 1985, *Christianity and the West 1400–1700*, Oxford.

—— 1998, *Peace in the Post-Reformation*, Cambridge.

Brackett, J. K., 1992, *Criminal Justice and Crime in Late Renaissance Florence 1537–1609*, Cambridge.

—— 1993, 'The Florentine *Onestà* and the Control of Prostitution, 1403–1680', *SCJ*, 24, 273–300.

Brandes, F., 1996, *Veneto Jewish Intineraries. Places, History and Art*, Venice.

Brandileone, F., 1896, *La celebrazione del Matrimonio in Roma nel secolo xv e il Concilio di Trento*, Rome.

Braudel, F., 1972, *The Mediterranean and the Mediterranean World in the Age of Philip II*, 2 vols, (trans.), London. There is a one volume edn. abridged by R. Ollard, same title with no notes, but more lavishly illustrated, 1992, London and New York.

—— 1984, *Civilization and Capitalism 15th-18th Century*, I: *The Structures of Everyday Life*; II: *The Wheels of Commerce*; III: *The Perspective of the World*, trans. S. Reynolds, London.

—— 1991, *Out of Italy*, trans S. Reynolds (Paris, 1991) from French edn. 1989, with lavish illustrations. (First published as chapters in Italian in AA.VV (1971) *Storia d'Italia*, (Einaudi, Turin)).

Braunfels, W., 1990, *Urban Design in Western Europe. Regime and Architecture 900–1900*, Chicago.

Briganti, A., 1910, *Le Corporazioni delle Arti nel Comune di Perugia*, Perugia.

Brown, J. C., 1982, *In the Shadow of Florence. Provincial Society in Renaissance Pescia*, Oxford.

—— 1986a, 'A Woman's Place was in the Home: Women's Work in Renaissance Tuscany', in M. W. Ferguson, M. Quilligan, and N. J. Vickers (eds), *Rewriting the Renaissance: the Discourses of Sexual Difference in Early Modern Europe*, 206–24, Chicago.

—— and Davis, R. C. (eds), 1998, *Gender and Society in Reniassance Italy*, London and New York.

—— and Goodman, J., 1980, 'Women and Industry in Florence' *J. Econ. Hist.* 40, 73–80.

Brucker, G., 1986, *Giovanni and Lusanna. Love and Marriage in Renaissance Florence*, London.

—— (ed.), 1967, *Two Memoirs of Renaissance Florence. The Diaries of Buonaccorso Pitti and Gregorio Dati*, trans. J. Martines, New York and London.

—— (ed.), 1998, *The Society of Renaissance Florence. A Documentary Study*, Toronto and London.

Brundage, J. A., 1987, *Law, Sex, and Christian Society in Medieval Europe*, Chicago.

—— 1995, *Medieval Canon Law*, London and New York.

Burckhardt, J., 1955, *The Civilization of the Renaissance in Italy. An Essay* [1860 original], Phaidon 5th edn used, trans. S. G. C. Middlemore, London.

Burke, P., 1978, *Popular Culture in Early Modern Europe*, London.

—— 1987, *The historical Anthropology of Early Modern Italy. Essays on Perception and Communication*, Cambridge.

—— 1994, *Venice and Amsterdam. A Study of Seventeenth-century Elites*, 2nd edn, Cambridge and Cambridge, MA.

—— 1995, *The Fortunes of the Courtier. The European Reception of Castiglione's Cortegiano*, Cambridge.

—— 1997, *Varieties of Cultural History*, Cambridge.

Burroughs, C., 1990, *From Signs to Design. Environmental Process and Reform in Early Modern Rome*, Cambridge, MA and London.

Bush, M., 1983, *Noble Privilege*, Manchester.

—— 1988, *Rich Noble, Poor Noble*, Manchester.

Cairns, C., 1985, *Pietro Aretino and the Republic of Venice*, Florence.

Calabi, D., 1993, *Il Mercato e la città. Piazze, Strade, architetture d'Europa in età moderna*, Venice.

—— and Lanaro, P. (eds), 1998, *La Città Italiana e I Luoghi Degli Stranieri XIV–XVIII secolo*, Rome and Bari.

—— and Morachiello, P., 1987, *Rialto. Le Fabbriche e il Ponte*, Turin.

Calimani, R., 1987, *The Ghetto of Venice*, trans. K. S. Wolfthal, New York.

Calisse, C., 1969, *A History of Italian Law*, South Hackensack.

Calvi, G., 1989, *Histories of a Plague Year. The Social and the Imaginary in Baroque Florence*, Berkerley, Los Angeles and Oxford.

—— 1992, 'Maddalena Nerli and Cosimo Tornabuoni: A couple's narrative of family history in early modern Florence', *Renaissance Quarterly*, 45, 312–39.

—— 1994, *Il contratto morale. Madri e figli nella Toscana moderna*, Rome and Bari.

—— 1999, 'Widows, the State and Guardianship of Children in Early Modern Tuscany', in S. Cavallo and L. Warren (eds), *Widowhood in Medieval and Early Modern Europe*, 209–19, London.

Camporesi, P., 1980, *Bread of Dreams. Food and Fantasy in Early Modern Europe (Il pane selvaggio)*, trans. D. Gentilcore, Oxford.

—— 1990, *The Fear of Hell. Images of Fear and Salvation in Early Modern Europe*, Cambridge.

—— 1992, *Le belle contrade. Nascita del paesaggio italiano*, Milan.

—— 1993, *The Magic Harvest. Food, Folklore and Society*, trans. J. K. Hall, Cambridge.

Canons and Decrees of the Council of Trent, trans. T. A. Buckley, 1951, London.

Cantarella, E., 1991, 'Homicides of Honor: the development of Italian adultery law over two millenia', in Kertzer and Saller (eds), 229–44, New Haven and London.

Caravale, M. and Caracciolo, A., 1978, *Lo Stato pontificio da Martino V a Pio X*, Turin.

Carmichael, A. G., 1991, 'Contagion Theory and Contagian Practice in Fifteenth-century Milan', *Renaissance Quarterly*, 44, 213–56.

Carpanetto, D. and Ricuperati, G., 1987, *Italy in the Age of Reason 1685–1789*, trans. C. Higgitt, London.

Carroll, M. P., 1992, *Madonnas that Maim. Popular Catholicism in Italy since the Fifteenth Century*, Baltimore and London.

Casagrande, G., 1999, 'Confraternities and Lay Female Religiosity', Terpstra (ed.), 48–66.

Cattola, F., 1988, 'Il "ritorno alla terra"', in Cherubini (ed.), 103–68.

Cavaciocchi, S. (ed.), 1990, *La Donna nell'economia secc. xiii–xviii*, Florence.

Cavallo, S., 1991, 'Conceptions of Poverty and Poor-relief in Turin in the Second Half of the Eighteenth Century', in Woolf (ed.), 148–99.

—— 1995, *Charity and Power in Early Modern Italy. Benefactors and their Motives in Turin, 1541–1789*, Cambridge.

Cavazzini, P., 1997, 'Agostino Tassi and the Organization of his Workshop: Filippo Franchini, Angelo Caroselli, Claude Lorrain and the others', *Storia dell'Arte*, 91, 401– 31.

Cecchi, Giovanni Maria, 1981, *The Horned Owl.* Translated with an Introduction and Notes by K. Eisenbichler (Carleton Renaissance Plays in Translation), Wilfred Laurier U.P., Waterloo, ON.

Cellini, B., 1956, *The Autobiography of Benevenuto Cellini*, trans. G. Bull, London.

—— 1995, *The Life of Benvenuto Cellini*, trans. J. A. Symonds, edited by J. Pope-Hennessy, London.

Cerutti, S., 1991, 'Group Strategies and Trade Strategies: the Turin tailors' guild in the late seventeenth and early eighteenth centuries', in Woolf (ed.), 102–47.

Chadwick, O., 1981, *The Popes and European Revolution*, Oxford.

Chambers, D. S. and Dean, T., 1997, *Clean Hands and Rough Justice. An Investigating Magistrate in Renaissance Italy*, Ann Arbor.

—— and Pullan, B. S., with J. Fletcher (eds), 1992, *Venice. A Documentary History, 1450–1630*, Oxford and Cambridge, MA.

Chard, C., 1999, *Pleasure and Guilt on the Grand Tour. Travel Writing and Imaginative Literature 1600–1830*, Manchester and New York.

Chastel, A., 1983, *The Sack of Rome, 1527*, Princeton, NJ.

Châtellier, L., 1989, *The Europe of the Devout. The Catholic Reformation and the Formation of a New Society*, trans. Jean Birrell, Cambridge and New York.

Cherubini, G. (ed.), 1988, 1989, *Storia della Società Italiana*, X: *Il Tramonto del Rinascimento*, 1988; XI: *La Controriforma e il Seicento*, 1989, Milan.

Chiacchella, R., 1974, *Economia e Amministrazione a Perugia nel Seicento*, Reggio Calabria.

Chittolini, G., 1989, 'Cities, "City-states", and Regional States in North-central Italy', *Theory and Society*, 18, 689–706.

—— 1995, 'The "Private", the "Public", the "State"', *JMH.*, 67, [Supplement], S34–S61.

Chojnacki, S., 1974, 'Patrician Women in Early Renaissance Venice', *Studies in the Renaissance*, 21, 176–202.

—— 1985, 'Kinship ties and Young Patricians in Fifteenth-century Venice', *Renaissance Quarterly*, 38, 240–70.

Chojnacki, S., 1991, '"The Most Serious Duty": motherhood, gender, and patrician culture in Renaissance Venice', in Migiel and Schiesari (eds), 133–54.

—— 1992, 'Measuring Adulthood: Adolescence and Gender in Renaisance Venice', *J. Family Hist.*, 17, 371–95.

—— 1998, 'Daughters and Oligarchs: gender and the early renaissance state', in Brown and Davis (eds), 63–86.

Chorley, P., 1965, *Oil, Silk and Enlightenment. Economic Problems in Eighteenth Century Naples*, Naples.

Chubb, T. C. (ed.), 1967, *The Letters of Pietro Aretino*, Hamdon, CT.

Ciammitti, L., 1990, 'One Saint Less: The story of Angela Mellini, a Bolognese seamstress, 1667–17[?]', in Muir and Ruggiero (eds), 141–76.

Cipolla, C. M., 1965, 'Four Centuries of Italian Demographic Development', in Glass and Eversley (eds), 570–87.

—— 1968, 'The Economic Decline of Italy', in Pullan (ed.), 127–45.

—— 1973, *Cristofano and the Plague. A Study in the History of Public Health in the Age of Galileo*, London.

—— 1976, *Public Health and the Medical Profession in the Renaissance*, Cambridge.

—— 1977, *Faith, Reason and the Plague. A Tuscan Story of the Seventeenth Century*, Brighton.

—— 1979, *I pidocchi e il granduca: crisi economica e problemi sanitari nella Firenze del 1600*, Bologna.

—— 1981, *Fighting the Plague in Seventeenth-century Italy*, Madison.

—— 1992a, *Miasmas and Disease. Public Health and the Environment in the Pre-industrial Age*, New Haven and London.

—— 1992b, *Il burocrate e il marinaio. La 'Sanità' toscana e le tribolazioni degli inglesi a Livorno nel xvii secolo*, Bologna.

—— 1993, *Before the Industrial Revolution. European Society and Economy, 1000–1700*, 3rd edn rev., London.

—— (ed.) 1959, *Storia dell'economia italiana. Saggi di storia economica*, I, Turin.

Ciriacono, S., 1988, 'Mass Consumption Goods and Luxury Goods: the de-industrialization of the Republic of Venice from the sixteenth to the eighteenth century', in van der Wee (ed.), 41–61.

Clark, P. (ed.), 1985, *The European Crisis of the 1590s*, London.

Clarke, P. C., 1991, *The Soderini and the Medici. Power and Patronage in Fifteenth-century Florence*, Oxford.

Cochrane, E., 1973, *Florence in the Forgotten Centuries 1527–1800*, Chicago and London.

—— 1988a, 'Counter Reformation or Tridentine Reformation? Italy in the Age of Carlo Borromeo', in Headley and Tomaro (eds), 31–46.

—— 1988b, *Italy 1530–1630*, edited by J. Kirshner, London.

—— and Kirshner, L. (eds), 1986, *Readings in Western Civilisation, V: The Renaissance*, Chicago and London.

Coffin, D. R., 1988, *The Villa in the Life of Renaissance Rome*, Princeton.

Cognasso, F., 1965, *L'Italia del Rinascimento*, 2 vols, Turin.

Cohen, E. S., 1991a, 'No Longer Virgins: Self-representation by young women in late Renaissance Rome', in Migiel and Schiesari (eds), 169–91.

—— 1991b, '"Courtesans" and "Whores": Words and behavior in Roman streets', *Women's Studies*, 19, 201–8.

—— 1992, 'Honor and Gender in the Streets of Early Modern Rome', *J. Interdisciplinary Hist.*, 22 (Spring 1992), 597–625.

—— 1994, 'Between Oral and Written Culture: The social meaning of an illustrated love letter', in B. B. Diefendorf and C. Hesse (eds), 181–201.

Cohen, T. V., 1991, 'A Long Day in Monte Rotondo: the politics of jeopardy in a village uprising, (1558)', *Comparative Studies in Society and History*, 33, 639–68.

—— 1991–2, 'The Lay Liturgy of Affront in Sixteenth-century Italy', *J. Social Hist.*, 25, 857–77.

—— and Cohen E. S., 1993, *Words and Deeds in Renaissance Rome. Trials before the Papal Magistrates*, Toronto, Buffalo and London.

Cohn, S. K., 1980a, *The Laboring Classes in Renaissance Florence*, New York.

—— 1980b, 'Criminality and the State in Renaissance Florence, 1344–1466', *J. Social Hist.*, 13, 211–33.

—— 1988, *Death and Property in Siena, 1205–1800. Strategies for the Afterlife*, Baltimore and London.

—— 1992, *The Cult of Remembrance and the Black Death. Six Renaissance Cities in Central Italy*, Baltimore and London.

—— 1996a, 'Inventing Braudel's Mountains: The Florentine Alps after the Black Death', in Cohn and Epstein (eds), 383–416.

—— 1996b, *Women in the Streets. Essays on Sex and Power in Renaissance Italy*, Baltimore and London.

—— 1998, 'Women and Work in Renaissance Italy', in Brown and Davis (eds), 107–26.

—— 1999a, *Creating the Florentine State. Peasants and Rebellion, 1348–1434*, Cambridge.

—— 1999b, 'Piety and Religious Practice in the Rural Dependencies of Renaissance Florence', *EHR*, 114, 1121–42.

—— and S. A. Epstein (eds), 1996, *Portraits of Medieval and Renaissance Living. Essays in Honor of David Herlihy*, Ann Arbor.

Colapietra, R., 1961, *Vita pubblica e classi politiche nel viceregno napoletano, 1656–1734*, Rome.

Comparato, V. I., 1974, *Uffici e Società a Napoli (1600–1647). Aspetti dell'ideologia del Magistrato nell'età moderna*, Florence.

Concina, E., 1988, *L'Arsenale della Repubblica di Venezia. Tecniche e istituzioni dal medioevo al'età moderna*, 2nd edn, Milan.

—— 1994, *Venezia nell'età moderna. Strutture e funzioni*, 2nd edn, Venice.

—— 1998, *A History of Venetian Architecture*, trans. J. Landry, Cambridge and New York.

—— Camerino, U. and Calabi, D., 1991, *La Città degli Ebrei. Il Ghetto di Venezia. Architettura e Urbanistica*, Venice.

Coniglio, G., 1978, *Aspetti della società nel secolo xvi*, Naples.

Constance, J, 1990, *Renaissance Feminism. Literary Texts and Political Models*, Ithaca and London.

Conti, E., 1965, *La formazione della struttura agraria moderna nel contado fiorentino*, I: *Le campagne nell'età precommunale*; III, part 2, *Monografie e Tavole Statistiche*, Rome.

Corradi, A., 1973, *Annali delle epidemie occorse in Italia dalle prime memorie fino al 1850*, 5 vols, Bologna.

Corrain, C. and Zampini, P., 1970, *Documenti etnografici nei sinodi diocesani italiani*, Bologna; reprinting articles from *Palestra del Clero*, 1964–9, Rovigo.

—— —— 1971, 'Costumanze superstiziose bolognesi rilevate nel diritto ecclesiastico locale', *Ravennatensia*, 2, 57–69.

Cosgrove, D., 1993, *The Palladian Landscape. Geographical Change and its Cultural Representations in Sixteenth-century Italy*, Leicester and London.

Cowan, A. F., 1986, *The Urban Patriciate. Lübeck and Venice 1580–1700*, Cologne and Vienna.

—— 1991, 'Urban Elites in Early Modern Europe: an endangered species?', *Historical Research*, 64, 121–37.

—— 1998, *Urban Europe 1500–1700*, London and New York.

—— 1999, 'Patricians and Partners in Early Modern Venice', in Kittell and Madden (eds), 276–93.

Cozzi, G., 1973, 'Authority and the Law in Renaissance Venice', in Hale (ed.), 293–345.

—— (ed.), 1980–85, *Stato Società e Giustizia nella Repubblica Veneta (sec. xv-xviii)*, 2 vols, Rome.

—— (ed.), 1987, *Gli Ebrei e Venezia. Secoli xiv-xviii*, Milan.

—— Knapton, M., and Scarabello, G., 1992, *La Repubblica di Venezia nell'età moderna. Dal 1517 alla fine della Repubblica* (*Storia d'Italia*, (ed.) G. Galasso, vol. XII/2, UTET), Turin.

Crispolti, C., 1648, *Perugia Augusta*, Perugia (also Bologna 1974 photo reprint).

Croce, B., 1970, *History of the Kingdom of Naples*, edited by H. S. Hughes, Chicago and London.

Crouzet-Pavan, E., 1992, *'Sopra Le Acque Salse'. Espaces, Pouvoir et Société à Venise à la fin du Moyen Âge*, 2 vols, Rome.

D'Ambrosio, A. and Spedicato, M., 1998, *Cibo e Clausura. Regimi alimentari e patrimoni monastici nel mezzogiorno moderno (sec. xvii–xix)*, Bari.

D'Amico, S., 1994, *Le Contrade e la Città. Sistema produttivo e spazio urbano a Milano fra Cinque e Sericento*, Milan.

—— 1995, 'Poveri e gruppi marginali nella società milanese Cinque-Seicento', in Zardin (ed.), 273–90.

—— 2000, 'Crisis and Transformation: Economic organization and social structures in Milan, 1570–1610', *Social Hist.*, 25, 1–21.

Dandelet, T., 1997, 'Spanish Conquest and Colonization at the Center of the Old World: The Spanish nation in Rome, 1559–1625', *JMH*, 60, 479–511.

Davanzo Poli, D. (Curator), 1997, *I Mestieri Della Moda a Venezia. The Arts and Crafts of Fashion in Venice, from the 13th to the 18th Century*, [European Academy and Accademia Italiana exhibition catalogue; revised edition from versions of the exhibition in different locations since 1988], London.

Davidson, N. S., 1984, 'The Clergy of Venice in the Sixteenth Century', *Bull. Soc. Renaissance Studies*, 2 (Oct), 19–31.

—— 1986, 'An Armed Band and the Local Community on the Venetian Terraferma in the Sixteenth Century', in G. Ortalli (ed.), 401–22.

—— 1987, *The Counter-Reformation*, Historical Association Studies, Oxford.

—— 1994, 'Theology, Nature and the Law: Sexual sin and sexual crime in Italy from the fourteenth to the seventeenth century' in Dean and Lowe (eds), 74–98.

Davis. J. C., 1962, *The Decline of the Venetian Nobility as a Ruling Class*, Baltimore.

Davis, N. Z., 1974, 'Some Tasks and Themes in the Study of Popular Religion', in Trinkaus and Oberman (eds), 307–36.

—— 1975, *Society and Culture in Early Modern France*, London.

—— 1977, 'Ghosts, Kin and Progeny; Some features of family life in early modern France', *Daedalus*, 106, 87–114.

—— 1981, 'The Sacred and the Body Social in Sixteenth-century Lyon,' *Past and Present*, 90 (Feb), 40–70.

—— and Farge, A. (eds), 1993, *A History of Women in the West. III: Renaissance and Enlightenment Paradoxes*, Cambridge, MA and London.

Davis, R. C., 1991, *Shipbuilders of the Venetian Arsenal. Workers and Workplace in the Preindustrial City*, Baltimore and London.

—— 1993, 'Arsenal and *Arsenalotti*: Workplace and community in seventeenth-century Venice', in T. M. Safley and L. N. Rosenband (eds), *The Workplace before the Factory. Artisans and Proletarians 1500–1800*, 180–203, Ithaca and London.

—— 1994, *The War of the Fists. Popular Culture and Public Violence in Late Renaissance Venice*, Oxford.

—— 1997, 'Venetian Shipbuilders and the Fountain of Wine', *Past and Present*, 156 (May), 55–86.

—— 1999, 'The Spectacle almost fit for a King: Venice's *Guerra de'canne* of 26 July 1574', in Kittell and Madden (eds), 181–212.

Dean T. and Lowe K. J. P. (eds), 1994, *Crime, Society and the Law in Renaissance Italy*, Cambridge.

—— —— (eds), 1998, *Marriage in Italy 1300–1650*, Cambridge.

—— and Wickham, C. (eds), 1990, *City and Countryside in Late Medieval and Renaissance Italy. Essays presented to Philip Jones*, London and Ranceverte.

Del Col, A., 1996, *Domenico Scandella Known as Menocchio. His Trials Before the Inquisition, 1583–1599*, trans. J. and A. C. Tedeschi, Binghampton, NY.

—— 1998, *L'Inquisizione nel Patriarcato e Diocesi di Aquileia 1557–1559*, Trieste.

Delille, G., 1983, 'Dots des filles et circulation des biens dans les Pouilles aux xvie–xviie siècles', *MEFRM*, 95, 195–224.

—— 1985, *Famille et Propriété dans le Royaume de Naples (XVe – XIXe siècle)*, Rome.

—— 1990, 'Agricultural systems and demographic structures in the Kingdom of Naples', in A. Calabria and J. A. Marino (eds), *Good Government in Spanish Naples*, 79–126, New York, Bern, Frankfurt am Main, and Paris.

Della Casa, G., 1994, *Galateo. A Renaissance Treatise on Manners*, translated and edited by K. Eisenbichler and K. R. Bartlett, Toronto.

Delumeau, J., 1957–9, *Vie économique et sociale de Rome dans la seconde moitié du xvie siècle*, 2 vols, Rome.

—— 1974, *L'Italie de Botticelli à Bonaparte*, Paris.

—— 1977, *Catholicism between Luther and Voltaire. A New View of the Counter-Reformation*, with an Introduction by J. Bossy, London and Philadelphia.

—— 1990, *Sin and Fear. The Emergence of the Western Guilt Culture 13th–18th Centuries*, New York.

Del Panta, L., 1996, 'I processi demografici', in Greco and Rosa (eds), 215–47.

Del Re, N., (ed.), 1968, *Roma Centro Mondiale di Vita Religiosa e Missionaria*, Bologna.

De Maddalena, A., 1964, 'Il mondo rurale italiano nel Cinque a nel Seicento', *RSI.*, 76, 349–426.

De Maio, R., 1987, *Donna e Rinascimento*, Milan.

De Renzi, S., 1999, '"A Fountain for the Thirsty" and a Bank for the Pope: Charity, conflicts and medical careers at the Hospital of Santo Spirito in seventeenth-century Rome', in O. P. Grell, A. Cunningham and J. Arrizabalaga (eds), 102–31.

De Roover, F. E., 1966, 'Andrea Banchi, Florentine Silk Manufacturer and Merchant in the Fifteenth Century', *Studies in Medieval and Renaissance History*, 3, 223–85.

De Rosa, G. and Gregory, T. (eds), 1994, *Storia dell'Italia Religiosa, II: L'Età Moderna*, Rome and Bari.

De Seta, C., 1994, 'The Urban Structure of Naples: Utopia and Reality', in Millon and Magnago Lampugnani (eds), 349–70.

Deutscher, T., 1981, 'Seminaries and the Education of Novarese Parish Priests, 1593–1627', *J. Eccl. Hist.*, 32, 303–19.

—— 1989, 'The Growth of the Secular Clergy and the Development of Educational Institutions in the Diocese of Novara I (1563–1772)', *J. Eccl. Hist.*, 40, 381–97.

De Vries, J., 1976, *Economy of Europe in an Age of Crisis 1600–1750*, Cambridge, 1976.

Diaz, F., 1983, 'L'idea in una nuova élite sociale negli storici e trattatisti del Principato', in AA.VV., 1983, *Firenze e la Toscana*, II, 665–81.

Diefendorf, B. B. and Hesse, C. (eds), 1994, *Culture and Identity in Early Modern Europe, 1500–1800. Essays in Honor of Natalie Zemon Davies*, Ann Arbor.

Di Simplicio, O., 1994a, 'Perpetuas: the women who kept priests, Siena 1600–1800,' in Muir and Ruggiero (eds), 32–64.

—— 1994b, *Peccato Penitenza Perdono Siena 1575–1800. La formazione della coscienza nell'Italia moderna*, Milan.

Donati, C., 1988, *L'Idea di Nobiltà in Italia Secoli xiv–xviii*, Rome and Bari.

—— 1995, 'The Italian Nobilities in the Seventeenth and Eighteenth Centuries', in Scott (ed.) I: *Western Europe*, 237–68, 280–82, London and New York.

Donnelly, J. P. and Maher, M. W. (eds), 1999, *Confraternities and Catholic Reform in Italy, France and Spain*, Sixteenth Century Essays and Studies, vol. 44, Kirksville, MO.

Donvito, L. and Pellegrino, B., 1973, *L'Organizzazione Ecclesiastica degli Abruzzi e Molise e della Basilicata nell'età postridentina, 1585–1630*, Florence.

Dooley, B., 1989, 'Social Control and the Italian Universities: from Renaissance to Illuminism', *JMH*, 61, 205–39.

Dorigato, A., 1986, *Murano Glass Museum*, trans. M. Langley, Milan.

Douglass. W. A., 1980, 'The South Italian Family: A critique', *J. Family Hist.*, 5, 338–59.

—— 1991, 'The Joint-Family Household in Eighteenth-century Southern Italian Society', in Kertzer and Saller (eds), 286–303.

Dué, A. (ed.), 1994, *Atlante Storcio della Toscana*, Florence.

Ebner, P., 1973, 'I libri parrocchiali di Vallo della Lucania dal xvi al xix secolo', *Ricerche di Storia Sociale e Religiosa*, II/3, 109–57.

—— 1974, 'I libri parrocchiali di Novi Velia dal xvi al xix secolo', *Ricerche di Storia Sociale e Religiosa*, III/5–6, 65–140.

Eckstein, N. A., 1995, *The District of the Green Dragon. Neighbourhood Life and Social Change in Renaissance Florence*, Florence.

Eisenbichler, K., 1997, 'Italian Scholarship on Pre-modern Confraternities in Italy', *Renaissance Quarterly*, 50, 567–80.

—— 1998, *The Boys of the Archangel Raphael. A Youth Confraternity in Florence, 1411–1785*, Toronto.

Elias, N., 1983, *The Court Society*, trans. E. Jephcott, Oxford.

Elliott, J. H., 1970, 'Revolts in the Spanish Monarchy', in R. Forster and J. P. Greene (eds), *Preconditions of Revolution in Early Modern Europe*, 109–30, Baltimore and London.

Epstein, S. R., 1993, 'Town and Country: Economy and institutions in late medieval Italy', *Economic Hist. Rev.*, 46, 453–77.

—— 1994, 'Regional Fairs, Institutional Innovation, and Economic Growth in Late Medieval Europe', *Economic Hist. Rev.*, 47, 459–82.

Fabretti, A., 1885, *La prostituzione in Perugia nei secoli xiv e xv*, Turin.

Faccini, L., 1988, *La Lombardia fra '600 e '700*, Milan.

Fairchilds, C., 1993, 'Consumption in Early Modern Europe. A Review Article,' *Comparative Studies of Society and History*, 35, 850–8.

Falassi, A., 1975, *La Terra in Piazza. An Interpretation of the Palio in Siena*, Berkeley.

Fanfani, A., 1959, *Storia del Lavoro In Italia. III: Dalla fine del secolo xv agli inizi del xviii*, Milan.

Fanfani, T., 1998, 'The Guilds in Italian Economic Development in the Early Modern Era: Guilty or innocent?', in A. Guenzi, P. Massa and F. Piola Caselli (eds), 409–22.

Fanti, M., 1979–80, 'Il fondo delle 'Visite pastorali' nell' Archivio Generale Arcivescovile di Bologna', *Archiva Ecclesiae*, 22/23, 151– 67.

—— 1981, *Una Pieve, un Popolo Le visite pastorali nel territorio di Lizzano in Belvedere dal 1425 al 1912*, Lizzano del Belvedere.

—— 1997, 'Carità e Assistenza: istituzioni e iniziative ecclesiastiche e laicali nel medioevo e nell'età moderna,' extract from P. Prodi and L. Paolini, II, 141–201.

Fanucci, C., 1601, *Trattato di tutte le opere pie dell'alma citta di Roma*, Rome.

Farr, J. R., 1997, 'On the Shop Floor: Guilds, artisans, and the European market economy, 1350–1750', *J. Early Mod. Hist.*, 1, 24–53.

Fasano Guarini, E., 1973, *Lo Stato Mediceo di Cosimo I*, Florence.

—— (ed.), 1978, *Potere e società negli stati regionali italiani fra '500 e '600*, Bologna.

—— (ed.), 1986, *Prato storia di una città, II: Un microcosmo in movimento, 1494–1815*, Prato and Florence.

Fei, S., Gobbi Sica, G. and Sica, P., 1995, *Firenze Profilo di Storia Urbana/Florence An Outline of Urban History*, Florence.

Ferraro, J. M., 1993, *Family and Public Life in Brescia, 1580–1650*, Cambridge.

Filippini, N. M., 1993, 'The Church, the State and Childbirth: The midwife in Italy during the eighteenth century', in H. Marland (ed.), *The Art of Midwifery. Early Modern Midwives in Europe*, 152–75, London and New York.

Fiorentino, K., 1984, 'La rivolta di Masaniello del 1647', in *Civiltà del Seicento a Napoli*, (Exhibition catalogue), 2 vols, II, 43–9, Naples.

Finlay R., 1980, *Politics in Renaissance Venice*, London.

Finzi, R., 1979, *Monsignore al Suo Fattore. la 'Istruzione di agricoltura' di Innocenzo Malvasia, 1609*, Bologna.

Fontaine, L., 1991, 'Family Cycles, Peddling and Society in Upper Alpine Valleys in the Eighteenth Century', in Woolf (ed.), 43–68.

—— 1996, *History of Pedlars in Europe*, trans. V. Whittaker, Cambridge and Oxford.

Fornili, C. C., 1991, *Delinquenti e Carcerati a Roma alla metà del '600. Opera dei Papi nella riforma carceria*, Rome.

Fragnito, G., 1997, *La Bibbia al rogo. La censura ecclesiastica e I volgarizzamenti della Scrittura, 1471–1605*, Bologna.

Franchi, Giorgio da Berceto, 1980, *Nove. Diario di un paese dell'Appennino (1544–1557)*, ed. G. Petrolini (La Pilotta, n.p., n.d., *c.* 1980).

Franza, C., 1958, *Il Catechismo a Roma dal Concilio di Trento a Pio VI*, Rome.

Franzoi, U., 1997, *The Prisons of the Doge's Palace in Venice* (Electa Art Guide), Milan.

Freccero, J., 1993, 'Medusa and the Madonna of Forlì: Political sexuality in Machiavelli', in A. R. Ascoli and V. Kahn (eds), *Machiavelli and the Discourse of Literature*, 161–78, Ithaca and London.

Galasso, G., 1967, *Economia e società nella Calabria del Cinquecento*, Naples.

—— 1977, *Il Mezzogiorno nella Storia d'Italia*, Florence.

—— 1982, *Napoli Spagnola dopo Masaniello. Politica, cultura, società*, 2 vols, Florence.

—— and Russo, C. (eds), 1982, *Per la Storia Sociale e Religiosa nel Mezzogiorno d'Italia*, II, Naples.

Gambi, L., 1964, 'Per una storia della abitazione rurale in Italia', *RSI.*, 76, 427–54.

Garrard, M. D., 1989, *Artemisia Gentileschi. The Image of the Female Hero in Italian Baroque Art*, Princeton.

Garzoni, T., 1595, *La Piazza Universale di Tutte le Professioni del Mondo*, Venice (Vincenzo Somasco).

—— 1617, *Opere di Tomaso Garzoni Da Bagnacavallo, Cioè La Piazza Universale di tutte le Professioni del Mondo. La Sinagoga de gli Ignoranti. L'Hospitale de' Pazzi Incurabili. and Il Theatro de' varij and diversi Cervelli Mondani*, Venice (Giorgio Valentini and Antonio Giuliani).

—— 1996, *La Piazza Universale di Tutte le Professioni del Mondo*, edited by P. Cherchi and B. Collina, 2 vols, Turin.

Gavitt, P., 1990, *Charity and Children in Renaissance Florence. The Ospedale degli Innocenti, 1410–1536*, Ann Arbor.

Gazzini, M., 1997, *"Dare et habere". Il mondo di un mercante milanese del Cinquecento (con l'edizione del libro di conti di Donato Ferrario da Pantigliate)*, Milan.

Geertz, C., 1993, *The Interpretation of Cultures. Selected Essays*, New York.

Gentilcore, D., 1992, *From Bishop to Witch. The system of the sacred in early modern Terra d'Otranto*, Manchester and New York.

—— 1994a, '"Adapt Yourselves to the People's Capabilities": Missionary strategies and impact in the Kingdom of Naples, 1600–1800', *J. Eccl. Hist.*, 45, 269–96.

—— 1994b, '"All that pertains to medicine": *Protomedici* and *Protomedicati* in early modern Italy', *Medical Hist.*, 38, 121–42.

—— 1995a, '"Charlatans, Mountebanks and other Similar People": the regulation and role of itinerant practitioners in early modern Italy', *Social Hist.*, 20, 297–314.

—— 1995b, 'Contesting Illness in Early Modern Naples: Miracolati, physicians and the Congregation of Rites', *Past and Present*, 148 (Aug), 117–48.

—— 1997, 'The Fear of Disease and the Disease of Fear', in W. C. Naphy and P. Roberts (eds), *Fear in Early Modern Society*, 184–208, Manchester and New York.

—— 1998, *Healers and Healing in Early Modern Italy*, Manchester and New York.

—— 1999, '"Cradle of saints and useful institutions": Health care and poor relief in the Kingdom of Naples,' in Grell, Cunningham and Arrizabalaga (eds), 132–150.

Geremek, B., 1994, *Poverty. A History*, trans. A. Kolakowska, Oxford and Cambridge, MA.

Ghisalberti, C., 1985, '"Flos Caeli". Un trattatello inedito dal codice 494 della Biblioteca Casanatense', in Troncarelli (ed.), 175–184.

Gianighian, G. and Pavanini, P. (eds), 1984, *Dietro I Palazzi. Tre secoli di Architettura Minore a Venezia 1492–1803*, Venice.

Gigli, G., 1994, *Diario di Roma*, edited by M. Barberito, 2 vols, Rome.

Ginori, L., 1977, 'Old Properties of a Florentine Family', *Apollo*, 105 (Jan), 34–9.

Ginzburg, C., 1980, *The Cheese and the Worms. The Cosmos of a Sixteenth-century Miller*, trans. J. and A. Tedeschi, London.

—— 1983, *The Night Battles. Witchcraft and Agrarian Cults in the Sixteenth and Seventeenth Centuries*, trans. J. and A. Tedeschi, London.

Giorgetti, G., 1973, 'Contratti agrari a rapporti sociali nelle campagne', in AA.VV. *Storia d'Italia* (Einaudi), V, 701–58.

Giusberti, F., 1986, 'Le botteghe di una città pre-industriale, un paessaggio regolato', in *Mercati e Consumi: organizzazione e qualificazione del commercio in Italia dal xii al xx secolo, 1o Convegno Nazionale di Storia del Commercio in Italia, Reggio Emilia/Modena, 1984*, 671–90, Bologna.

Glass, D. V. and Eversley, D. E. C. (eds), 1965, *Population and History*, London.

Gnavi, A., 1990, 'Valori urbani e attività marginali nella Piazza Univerale di Tomasso Garzoni', *Ricerche Storiche*, 20, 47–71.

Goldthwaite, R. A., 1968, *Private Wealth in Renaissance Florence: A study of four families*, Princeton.

—— 1980, *The Building of Renaissance Florence. An Economic and Social History*, Baltimore and London.

—— 1993, *Wealth and the Demand for Art in Italy 1300–1600*, Baltimore and London.

Goody, J., 1972, 'The Evolution of the Family', in P. Laslett and R. Wall (eds), *Household and Family in Past Time*, 103–24, Cambridge.

Gottlieb, B., 1993, *The Family in the Western World, from the Black Death to the Industrial Age*, New York and Oxford.

Goy, R. J., 1989, *Venetian Vernacular Architecture. Traditional Housing in the Venetian Lagoon*, Cambridge.

—— 1997, *Venice. The City and its Architecture*, London.

Greco, G., 1984, *La parrocchia a Pisa nell'età moderna (secoli xvii–xviii)*, Pisa.

—— and Rosa, M. (eds), 1996, *Storia degli antichi stati italiana*, Rome and Bari.

Gregory, H., 1997, *Selected Letters of Alessandra Strozzi. Bilingual Edition*, trans. with an Introduction by H. Gregory, Berkeley, Los Angeles and London.

Grell, O. P., Cunningham, A. with Arrizabalaga, J. (eds), 1999, *Health Care and Poor Relief in Counter-Reformation Europe*, London and New York.

Grendi, E., 1987, *La Repubblica Aristocratica dei Genovesi*, Bologna.

—— 1992, 'Le Società dei Giovani a Genova fra il 1460 e la reforma del 1528', *Quaderni Storici*, 80, 509–29.

Grendler, P. F., 1977, *The Roman Inquisition and the Venetian Press 1540–1605*, Princeton.

—— 1989, *Schooling in Renaissance Italy. Literacy and Learning, 1300–1600*, Baltimore and London.

Greyerz, K. von, (ed.), 1984, *Religion and Society in Early Modern Europe 1500–1800*, London.

Grimagna, S., Perissa, A. and Scarabello, G., 1981, *Scuole di Arti Mestieri e Devozione a Venezia*, Venice.

Grohmann, A., 1981, *Città e territorio tra medioevo ed età moderna, (Perugia, secc. xiii–xvi)*, 2 vols, Perugia.

Gross, H., 1990, *Rome in the Age of Enlightenment*, Cambridge.

Grubb, J. S., 1988, *Firstborn of Venice. Vicenza in the Early Renaissance State*, Baltimore and London.

—— 1996, *Provincial Families of the Renaissance. Public and Private Life in the Veneto*, Baltimore and London.

Guasco, M., 1986, 'La formazione del clero: i seminari', in AA.VV. *Storia d'Italia*, (1972–), *Annali* 9, 631–715.

Guenzi, A., Massa, P. and Caselli, F. P., (eds), 1998, *Guilds, Markets and Work Regulations in Italy, 16th–19th Centuries*, Aldershot, Brookfield USA.

Guerrieri, G., 1967, 'L'Abbazia di S. Pietro nell'economia e nella tecnica agraria in Umbria', *Bollettino della Storia Patria dell'Umbria*, 64, 300–34.

Guiton, S., 1977, *A World by Itself. Tradition and change in the Venetian Lagoon*, London.

Haas, L., 1998, *The Renaissance Man and His Children. Childbirth and early childhood in Florence, 1300–1600*, London.

Hajnal, J., 1965, 'European Marriage Patterns in Perspective', in Glass and Eversley, (eds), 101–43.

—— 1983, 'Two Kinds of Pre-industrial Household Formation Systems', in Wall, Robin and Laslett (eds), 65–104.

Hale, J. R., (ed.), 1973, *Renaissance Venice*, London.

Hanlon, G., 1998, *The Twilight of a Military Tradition. Italian Aristocrats and European Conflicts, 1560–1800*, London.

Hannawalt, B. A., (ed.), 1986, *Women and Work in Renaissance Europe*, Bloomington, Indiana.

Harner, M. J., 1973, 'The Role of Hallucinogenic Plants in European Witchcraft', in Harner, M. J. (ed.), *Hallucinogens and Shamanism*, 125–50, New York.

Hay, D., 1977a, *The Italian Renaissance in its Historical Background* (rev. edn), Cambridge.

—— 1977b, *The Church in Italy in the Fifteenth Century*, Cambridge.

—— and Law, J., 1989, *Italy in the Age of the Renaissance 1380–1530*, London and New York.

Headley, J. M. and Tomaro, J. B., (eds), 1988, *San Carlo Borromeo. Catholic Reform and Ecclesiastical Politics in the Second Half of the Sixteenth Century*, Washington, London and Toronto.

Heers, J., 1977, *Family Clans in the Middle Ages. A Study of Political and Social Structures in Urban Areas*, Amsterdam, New York and London.

Henderson, J., 1994, *Piety and Charity in Late Medieval Florence*, Oxford.

—— 1998, '"Mal Francese" in Sixteenth-century Rome: the Ospedale di San Giacomo in Augusta and the "Incurabili"', extract from *Popolazione e società a Roma dal medioevo all'età contemporanea*, ed. E. Sonnino, 483–523, Rome.

—— 1999, 'Charity and Welfare in Early Modern Tuscany,' in Grell, Cunningham with Arrizabalaga (eds), 56–86.

Herlihy, D., 1985, *Medieval Households*, Cambridge, MA and London.

—— 1990, *Opera Muliebria. Women and work in Medieval Europe*, New York.

—— 1995, *Women, Family and Society in Medieval Europe. Historical Essays, 1978–1991*, Providence, RI and Oxford.

—— and Klapisch-Zuber, C., 1985, *Tuscans and Their Families*, New Haven and London.

Hersey, G., 1969, *Alfonso II and the Artistic Renewal of Naples 1485–95*, New Haven.

Heywood, W., 1904, *Palio and Ponte; an account of the sports of central Italy from the age of Dante to the XXth century*, London.

—— 1910, *A History of Perugia*, London.

Hibbert, C., 1975, *The House of the Medici. Its Rise and Fall*, New York.

Hoak, D., 1985, 'Art, Culture and Mentality in Renaissance Society: the meaning of Hans Baldung Grien's Bewitched Groom (1544)', *Renaissance Quarterly*, 38, 488–510.

Hobsbawm, E. J., 1971, *Primitive Rebels. Studies in the Archaic Forms of Social Movement in the 19th and 20th Centuries*, 3rd edn, Manchester.

Hook, J., 1979/1988, *Siena. A City and its History*, London. Italian translation, *Siena. Una città e la sua storia* (Siena, 1988), has better illustrations, and a valuable appreciation of the author's work by R. Barzanti.

Hortubise, P., 1985, *Une Famille-Témoin. Les Salviati*, Vatican City.

Howard, D., 1990, *Jacopo Sansovino. Architecture and Patronage in Renaissance Venice*, New Haven and London.

—— 1980, *The Architectural History of Venice*, London.

Hsia, R. Po-Chia, 1992, *Trent 1475. Stories of a Ritual Murder Trial*, New Haven.

—— 1998, *The World of Catholic Renewal*, Cambridge.

Hughes, D., 1975, 'Domestic Ideals and Social Behaviour: Evidence from Medieval Genoa', in C. E. Rosenberg, ed., *The Family in History*, 115–43, Philadelphia.

Hughes, D. O., 1985, 'From Brideprice to Dowry in Mediterranean Europe', in Kaplan, (ed.), 13–58.

Hughes, S., 1988, 'Fear and Loathing in Bologna and Rome. The Papal Police in Perspective', *J. Social Hist.*, 21, 97–116.

Huse, N. and Wolters, W., 1990, *The Art of Renaissance Venice. Architecture, Sculpture, and Painting, 1460–1590*, Chicago and London.

Imberciadori, I., 1959, 'Spedale, scuola, e chiesa in popolazioni rurali dei secoli xvi–xvii', *Economia e Storia*, 6, 423–49.

Ioly Zorattini, P. C., 1987, 'Gli insediamento ebraici nel Friuli', in Cozzi (ed.), 261–80.

Jedin, H., 1943, 'Le origini dei registri parrocchiali e il Concilio di Trento', in *Il Concilio di Trento. Rivista commemorativa del IV Centinario*, 2 no. 4 (Oct), 323–36.

—— 1964, *Crisis and Closure of the Council of Trent*, London.

—— and Dolan J. (eds), 1980, *History of the Church. V: Reformation and Counter-Reformation*, London.

Jemolo, A. C., 1948, 'Riforma Tridentina nell'ambito matrimoniale', in L. Russo (ed.), *Contributi alla Storia del Concilio di Trento e della Controriforma*, 1948, 45–51, Florence.

Johannsson, S. R., 1987, 'Centuries of Childhood/Centuries of Parenting: Philippe Ariès and the modernization of privileged infancy', *J. Family Hist.*, 12, 343–65.

Jones, P. J., 1964, 'Per la storia agraria italiana nel medio evo: lineamenti e problemi', *RSI.*, 76, 287–348.

—— 1966, 'Medieval Agrarian Society in its Prime. 2: Italy', in *The Cambridge Economic History of Europe*, I, 2nd edn, 340–431, Cambridge.

—— 1968, 'From Manor to Mezzadria: A Tuscan case-study in the medieval origins of modern agrarian society,' in N. Rubinstein (ed.), *Florentine Studies*, 193–241, London.

Jordan, C., 1990, *Renaissance Feminism. Literary Texts and Political Models*, Ithaca and London.

Jütte, R., 1994, *Poverty and Deviance in Early Modern Europe*, Cambridge.

Kaplan, M. A., (ed.), 1985, *The Marriage Bargain: Women and dowries in European history*, New York, Binghampton.

Kennet, W. and Young, E., 1990, *Northern Lazio. An Unknown Italy*, London.

Kent, D. V. and Kent, F. W., 1982, *Neighbours and Neighbourhood in Renaissance Florence: The District of the Red Lion in the fifteenth century*, Locust Valley, NY.

Kent, F. W., 1977, *Household and Lineage in Renaissance Florence. The Family Life of the Capponi, Ginori, and Rucellai*, Princeton.

—— 1987, 'Ties of Neighbourhood and Patronage in Quattrocento Florence', in Kent and Simons (eds), *Patronage, Art and Society in Renaissance Italy*, 79–98, Canberra and Oxford.

—— and Simons, P. (eds), 1987, *Patronage, Art and Society in Renaissance Italy*, Canberra and Oxford.

Kertzer, D. I., 1992, 'Child Abandonment in European History', *J. Family Hist.*, 17, 13–19.

—— 1993, *Sacrificed for Honor. Italian infant abandonment and the politics of reproductive control*, Boston.

—— and Brettell, C., 1987, 'Advances in Italian and Iberian Family History', *J. Family Hist.*, 12, 87–120.

—— and Saller, R. P. (eds), 1991, *The Family in Italy from Antiquity to the Present*, New Haven and London.

King, C., 1998, *Renaissance Women Patrons*, Manchester.

King, M. L., 1991, *Women of the Renaissance*, Chicago and London.

—— 1994, *The Death of the Child Valerio Marcello*, Chicago and London.

King, R., 1985, *The Industrial Geography of Italy*, London and Sydney.

Kittell, E. E. and Madden, T. E. (eds), 1999, *Medieval and Renaissance Venice*, Urbana and Chicago.

Klapisch-Zuber, C., 1985, *Women, Family and Ritual in Renaissance Italy*, Collected essays, Chicago and London.

—— 1986, 'Women Servants in Florence During the Fourteenth and Fifteenth Centuries', in Hannawalt (ed.), 56–82.

Koenigsberger, H. G., 1960, 'Decadence or Shift? Change in the Civilisation of Italy and Europe in the 16th and 17th centuries', *Trans. Roy. Hist. Soc.*, 10, 1–18.

Kohl, B. C. and Witt, R. G. (eds), 1978, *The Earthly Republic. Italian Humansists on Government and Society*, Manchester.

Krautheimer, R., 1985, *The Rome of Alexander VII, 1655–1667*, Princeton.

Kuehn, T., 1991, *Law, Family and Women. Toward a legal anthropology of Renaissance Italy*, Chicago.

—— 1998, 'Person and Gender in the Laws', in Brown and Davis (eds), 87–106.

Labalme, P. H., 1982, 'Personality and Politics in Venice: Pietro Aretino', in D. Rosand, ed., *Titian. His World and his Legacy*, 119–32, New York.

—— 1984, 'Sodomy and Venetian Justice in the Renaissance', *Legal Hist. Rev.*, 52, 217–54.

Lanaro, P., 1999, *I mercati nella Repubblica Veneta. Economie cittadine e stato territoriale, secoli xv–xviii*, Venice.

Landucci, L., 1969, *A Florentine Diary from 1450 to 1516 by Luca Landucci continued by an anonyomous writer till 1542*, trans. Alice de Rosen Jervis, New York.

Lane, F. C., 1987, *Venice. A Maritime Republic*, Baltimore and London.

—— 1992, *Venetian Ships and Shipbuilders of the Renaissance*, Baltimore and London.

Lanternari, V., 1955, 'La politica culturale della Chiesa nelle Campagne: le Feste di S. Giovanni', *Società*, 11, 64–95.

Larner, J., 1972, 'Order and Disorder in Romagna, 1450–1500', in Martines (ed.), 38–71.

—— 1980, *Italy in the Age of Dante and Petrarch 1216–1380*, London.

—— 1990, 'Crossing the Romagnol Appennines in the Renaissance', in Dean and Wickham (eds), 147–70.

La Roncière, C-M. de, 1983, 'L'approvisionnement des villes italiennes au moyen âge (xive–xve siècle), Extract from *L'Approvisonnement des Villes* (reprinted from *Flaran*, 5, 1983), 33–51.

Laslett, P., 1983, 'Family and Household as Work Group and Kin Group: areas of traditional Europe compared', in Wall, Robin and Laslett (eds), 513–87.

Laven, D., 1995, 'Machiavelli, *italianità* and the French invasion of 1494', in Abulafia (ed.), 355–69.

Laven, P., 1994, 'Banditry and Lawlessness on the Venetian *Terraferma* in the late *Cinquecento*' in Dean and Lowe (eds), 221–48.

Lee, E., 1982, 'Women and Work in Quattrocento Rome', in P. A. Ramsay (ed.), *Rome in the Renaissance. The City and the Myth*, 141–52, Binghampton, N.Y.

Lewis, D., 1981, 'Patterns of Preference: Patronage of sixteenth-century architects by the Venetian Patriciate', in G. F. Lytle and S. Orgel (eds), *Patronage in the Renaissance*, 354–82, Princeton, NJ.

Litchfield, R. B., 1986, *Emergence of a Bureaucracy. The Florentine Patricians 1530–1790*, Princeton, NJ.

Livi Bacci, M., 1976, *La Société Italienne devant les crises de mortalité*, Florence.

—— 1990, *Nutrition and Population. An essay on European Demographic History*, Cambridge.

Logan, O., 1972, *Culture and Society in Venice 1470–1790*, London.

Lopez, P., 1965, *Riforma Cattolica e vita religiosa e culturale a Napoli. Dalla fine del Cinquecento ai primi anni del Settecento*, Naples and Rome, n. d. [*c.* 1965].

—— 1983, 'Sulla diffusione dell'eterodossia nella Napoli del Cinquecento', in *L'Uomo e la Storia. Studi in onore di Massimo Petrocchi*, 229–66, Rome.

Lotto, L., 1969, *Il 'Libro di spese diverse' con aggiunta di lettere e d'altri documenti*, edited by P. Zampetti, Venice and Rome.

Lowry, M., 1979, *The World of Aldus Manutius: business and scholarship in Renaissance Venice*, Oxford.

Luchs, A., 1983, 'A Note on Raphael's Perugian Patrons', *The Burlington Magazine*, 125, 29–31.

Luise, F., 1983, 'Solofra tra il 1640 e il 1676 nei capitoli matrimoniali e nei testamenti', *MEFRM*, 95, 299–338.

Mack, C. R., 1987, *Pienza. The Creation of a Renaissance City*, Ithaca and London.

Mackenney, R., 1987, *Tradesmen and Traders. The World of the Guilds in Venice and Europe,* c. *1250–*c. *1650*, London and Sydney.

—— 1994, 'Continuity and Change in the scuole piccole of Venice, c. 1260–c. 1600', *Renaissance Studies*, 8, 388–403.

—— 1997, 'The Guilds of Venice: State and Society in the *Longue Duree*', *Studi Veneziani*, 34, 15–43.

—— 1998, 'Public and Private in Renaissance Venice', *Renaissance Studies*, 12, 109–30.

Maczak, A., 1995, *Travel in Early Modern Europe*, trans. U. Phillips, Cambridge, Oxford and Cambridge MA.

Maiden, M., 1995, *A Linguistic History of Italian*, London and New York.

—— and Parry, M., (eds), 1997, *The Dialects of Italy*, New York and London.

Majarelli, S. and Nicolini, U., 1962, *Il Monte dei Poveri di Perugia*, Perugia.

Malanima, P., 1977, *I Riccardi di Firenze. Una famiglia e un patrimonio nella Toscana dei Medici*, Florence.

—— 1979, 'La proprietà fiorentina e la diffusione della mezzadria nel contado pisano nei secoli xv e xvi', in AA.VV. (1979), *Contadini e Proprietari*, 345–75.

—— 1990, *Il lusso dei Contadini. Consumi e industrie nelle campagne toscane del Sei e Settecento*, Bologna.

Labalme, P. H., 1996, 'L'economia', in Greco and Rosa (eds), 249–95.

Mallett, M. E. and Hale, J. R., 1984, *The Military Organization of a Renaissance State. Venice* c. *1400 to 1617*, Cambridge.

Manno, A., 1997, *I Mestieri di Venezia. Storia, arte e devozione delle corporazioni dal XII al XVIII secolo*, 2nd edn, Cittadella [Padua].

Manzoni, A., 1959, *The Betrothed*, trans. A. Colquhoun, London.

—— 1960, *I Promessi Sposi*, edited by A. Asor Rosa, Milan.

Marangoni, G., 1974, *Associazioni di Mestiere nella Repubblica Veneta, (vittuaria – farmacia – medicina)*, Venice.

Marcora, C., (ed.), 1965, 'Il Diario di Giambattista Casale (1554–1598), *Memorie Storiche della Diocesi di Milano*, 3, 209–437.

Maretto, P., 1992, *La casa veneziana nella storia della città dalle origini all'Ottocento*, 4th edn, Venice.

Marino, J. A., 1988, *Pastoral Economics in the Kingdom of Naples*, Baltimore and London.

Marshall, R. K., 1999, *The Local Merchants of Prato. Small Entrepreneurs in the Late Medieval Economy*, Baltimore and London.

Martin, A. L., 1996, *Plague? Jesuit Accounts of Epidemic Diseases in the 16th Century*, Sixteenth Century Studies, xxviii, Kirksville.

Martin, J., 1993, *Venice's Hidden Enemies. Italian Heretics in a Renaissance City*, Berkeley, Los Angeles and London.

—— 1996a, 'The Imaginary Piazza: Tomasso Garzoni and the Late Italian Renaissance', in Cohn and Epstein (eds), 439–54.

—— 1996b, 'Spiritual Journeys and the Fashioning of Religious Identity in Renaissance Venice', *Renaissance Studies*, 10, 358–70.

Martin, R., 1989, *Witchcraft and the Inquisition in Venice 1550–1650*, Oxford.

Martines, L., (ed.), 1972, *Violence and Civil Disorder in Italian Cities, 1200–1500*, Berkeley, Los Angeles and London.

Martini, G., 1988, *Il 'Vitio Nefando' nella Venezia del Seicento. Aspetti sociali e repression di giustizia*, Rome.

Masella, J., 1979, 'Economia e società nel periodo spagnola', in G. Musca, (ed.), *Storia della Puglia*, 2 vols, 27–44, Bari.

Masetti Zannini, G. L., 1976, 'Ricerche sulla cultura del clero Piceno. I', *Studia Picena*, 43, 60–89.

—— 1980, *Stampatori e librai a Roma nella seconda metà del Cinquecento*, Rome.

Masi, G., 1957, *Organizzazione ecclesiastica e ceti rurali in Puglia nella seconda metà del Cinquecento*, Bari.

Masson,, G., 1975, *Courtesans of the Renaissance*, London.

Matarazzo, F., 1905, *Chronicles of the City of Perugia 1492–1503 written by Francesco Matarazzo*, trans. E. S. Morgan, London.

Mazzei, R., 1977, *La Società Lucchese del Seicento*, Lucca.

—— 1979, 'The Decline of the City Economies of Central and Northern Italy in the Seventeenth Century', *J. Italian Hist.*, 2, 197–208.

McArdle, F., 1978, *Altopascio. A Study in Tuscan Rural Society, 1587–1784*, Cambridge.

McCray, W. P., 1999, *Glassmaking in Renaissance Venice. The Fragile Craft*, Aldershot and Brookfield, USA.

McLaren, A., 1990, *A History of Contraception*, Oxford and Cambridge.

Meneghin, V., 1974, *Bernardino da Feltre e I Monti di Pietà*, Vicenza.

Menetto, L. and Zennaro. G., 1987, *Storia del Malcostume a Venezia nei secoli xvi e xvii*, Abano Terme, Padua.

Merriman, R. B., 1938, *Six Contemporaneous Revolutions*, Oxford.

Merzario, R., 1981, *Il Paese Stretto: strategie Matrimoniali nella Diocesi di Como. Secoli xvi-xviii*, Turin.

Metzger Habel, D., 1990, 'Alexander VII and Private Builders: two case studies in the development of Via Del Corso', *J. Soc. Architectural Historians*, 49, 293–309.

Mezzadri, L., 1969, 'Il Seminario nell'epoca dell'assolutismo e dell'Illuminismo', in F. Molinari, (ed.), *Il Seminario di Piacenza e il suo fondatore*, Piacenza.

Migiel, M. and Schiesari, J., 1991, *Refiguring Woman: Perspectives on gender in the Italian Renaissance*, Ithaca and London.

Miller, N., 1989, *Renaissance Bologna. A Study in Architectural Form and Content*, New York and Bern.

Millon, H. A. and Magnago Lampugnani, V. (eds), 1994, *The Renaissance from Brunelleschi to Michelangelo. The representation of Architecture* [Catalogue of Exhibition in Venice], Milan.

Mirollo, J. V., 1963, *The Poet of the Marvelous. Giambattista Marino*, New York and London.

Moioli, A., 1998, 'The Changing Role of the Guilds in the Reorganisation of the Milanese Economy Throughout the Sixteenth and the Eighteenth Centuries', in Guenzi, Massa and Caselli (eds), 32–55.

Molho, A., 1994, *Marriage Alliance in Late Medieval Florence*, Cambridge, MA and London.

Montaigne, M. de, 1955, *Journal de Voyage en Italie en 1580 et 1581*, edited by M. Rat, Paris.

—— 1983, *Travel Journal*, trans. and edited by D. M. Frame, San Francisco.

Montanari, M., 1966, *Mille Anni della Chiesa di S. Pietro in Perugia e del suo patrimonio*, Foligno.

—— 1994, *The Culture of Food*, trans. C. Ipsen, Oxford and Cambridge, MA.

Monter, E. W. and Tedeschi, J., 1986, 'Toward a Statistical Profile of the Italian Inquisitions, Sixteenth to Eighteenth Centuries', in G. Henningsen and J. Tedeschi (eds), *The Inquisition in Early Modern Europe*, 130–57; reprinted in Tedeschi, 1991, 89–126.

Monticone, A., 1953, 'L'applicazione a Roma del Concilio di Trento. Le Visite del 1564–1566', *Rivista della Storia della Chiesa in Italia*, 7, 225–50.

Morton, H. V., 1966, *The Waters of Rome*, London.

Moss, H., 1993, 'Anti-feminism in the Renaissance Short Story: the case of Masuccio Salernitano', in C. E. J. Griffiths and R. Hastings (eds), *The Cultural Heritage of the Italian Renaissance. Essays in honour of T. G. Griffith*, 137–53, Lewiston, Queenston and Lampeter.

Muir, E., 1989, 'The Virgin on the Street Corner. The place of the Sacred in Italian Cities', in S. Ozment (ed.), *Religion and Culture in the Renaissance and Reformation*, 25–40, Kirksville, MO.

—— 1993, *Mad Blood Stirring. Vendetta and Factions in Friuli during the Renaissance*, Baltimore and London.

—— 1998, *Mad Blood Stirring. Vendetta in Renaissance Italy. Reader's Edition*, Baltimore and London.

—— and Ruggiero, G., (eds), 1990, *Sex and Gender in Historical Perspectives. Selections from Quaderni Storici*, Baltimore and London.

—— —— (eds), 1994, *History from Crime. Selections from Quaderni Storici*, Baltimore and London.

Mullett, M., 1987, *Popular Culture and Popular Protest in Late Medieval and Early Modern Europe*, London, New York and Sydney.

Mullett, M. A., 1999, *The Catholic Reformation*, London and New York.

Muraro, M. and Marton, P., 1986, *Venetian Villas*, Cologne.

Musgrave, P., 1992), *Land Economy in Baroque Italy. Valpolicella, 1630–1797*, Leicester and London.

Muto, G., 1984, 'Gestione del potere e classi sociali nel Mezzogiorno spagnolo', in Tagliaferri (ed.), 287–303.

—— 1989, 'Il regno di Napoli sotto la dominazione spagnola', in Cherubini (ed.), XI, 225–36.

Niccoli, O., 1990, *Prophecy and People in Renaissance Italy*, trans. L. G. Cochrane, Princeton.

—— 1995, *Il seme della violenza. Putti, fanciulli e mammoli nell'Italia tra Cinque e Seicento*, Rome and Bari.

—— (ed.), 1991, *Rinascimento al femminile*, Rome and Bari.

Nicolini, F., 1934, *Aspetti della vita italo-spagnola nel Cinque e Seicento*, Naples.

Novi Chavarria, E., 1982, 'L'attività missionaria dei Gesuiti', in Galasso and Russo (eds), 159–85.

—— 1988, 'Ideologia e comportamenti familiari nei predicatori italiani tra cinque e settecento. Tematiche e modelli', *RSI.*, 678–723.

Nubola, C., 1993, *Conoscere per governare. La diocesi di Trento nella visita pastorale di Ludovico Madruzzo, 1579–1581*, Bologna.

Nussdorfer, L., 1992, *Civic Politics in the Rome of Urban VIII*, Princeton.

—— 1994, 'Writing and the Power of Speech: Notaries and artisans in Baroque Rome', in Diefendorf and Hesse (eds), 103–18.

Olivieri, A., 1972, 'Sensibilità religiosa urbana e sensibilità religiosa contadina nel Cinquecento veneto', *Critica Storica*, 9, 631–50.

Olson, R. J. M., 1998, 'The Rosary and its Iconography', *Arte Cristiana*, 787, 263–76; 788, 334–42.

O'Malley, J., 1993, *The First Jesuits*, Cambridge, MA and London.

—— 1994, 'The Society of Jesus', in R. L. De Molen, ed., *Religious Orders of the Catholic Reformation*, 139–63, New York.

Ortalli, G., (ed.), 1986, *Bande armate, Banditi, Banditismo e repressione di giustizia negli stati europei di antico regime*, Rome.

Pagano de Divitiis, G., 1997, *English Merchants in Seventeeth-century Italy*, Cambridge.

Paglia, V. (ed.), 1990, *Confraternite e Meridione nell'età moderna Rome; Ricerche di Storia Sociale e Religiosa*, vols 37–38.

Palmer, R., 1982, 'The Church, Leprosy and Plague in Medieval and Early Modern Europe', in W. J. Sheils, ed., *The Church and Healing*, Studies in Church History, XIX, 79–99.

—— 1993, 'Physicians and the Inquisition in Sixteenth-century Venice', in O. P. Grell and A. Cunningham (eds), *Medicine and the Reformation*, 118–33, New York and London.

—— 1999, '"Ad una sancta perfettione": Health care and poor relief in the Republic of Venice in the era of the Counter-Reformation', in Grell, Cunningham and Arrizabalaga (eds), 87–101.

Palumbo-Fossati, I., 1984, 'L'interno della casa dell'artigianato e dell'artista nella Venezia del Cinquecento', *Studi Veneziani*, 8, 109–53.

Park, K., 1985, *Doctors and Medicine in Early Renaissance Florence*, Princeton, NJ.

Parker, D., 1996, 'Women in the Book Trade in Italy, 1475–1620', *Renaissance Quarterly*, 49, 509–41.

Partner, P., 1976, *Renaissance Rome 1500–1559. A Portrait of a Society*, Berkeley, Los Angeles and London.

—— 1990, *The Pope's Men. The Papal Civil Service in the Renaissance*, Oxford.

Pastor, L. von, 1898–1953, *History of the Popes*, 40 vols, London.

Pastore, A., 1991, *Crimine e giustizia di peste nell'Europa moderna*, Rome and Bari.

—— and Sorcinelli, P. (eds), 1990, *Emarginazione, Criminalità e Deviazione in Italia tra '600 e '900*, Milan.

Pavan, E., 1980, 'Police des moeurs, société et politique à Venise à la fin du Moyen Age', *Revue Historique*, 264, 241–88.

Pavanini, P., 1981, 'Abitazioni popolari e borghesi nella Venezia cinquecentesca', *Studi Veneziani*, 5, 63–126.

Pazzi, P., (ed.), 1996a, *L'Oro di Venezia. Oreficiere, Argentieri e Gioielli di Venezia e delle Città Veneta (da collezioni private)* (Exhibition catalogue, Biblioteca Marciana), Venice.

—— (ed.), 1996b, *Contributi per la Storia dell'Oreficeria, Argenteria e Gioielleria*, Venice.

Pelliccia, G., 1946, *La Preparazione ed ammissione dei chierici ai santi ordini nella Roma del secolo xvi*, Rome.

—— 1980, 'Scuole di Catechismo e scuole rionali per fanciulle nella Roma del Seicento', *Ricerche per la Storia Religiosa di Roma*, 4, 237–68.

Pepe, G., 1952, *Il Mezzogiorno d'Italia sotto gli Spagnoli*, Florence.

Perosa, A. (ed.), 1960, *Giovanni Rucellai ed il suo Zibaldone, 1: 'Il Zibaldone Quaresimale'*, London.

Petrocchi, M., 1972, *Aspirazione dei Contadini nella Perugia dell'ultimo trentennio del Cinquecento, ed altri scritti*, Rome.

Phillips, M., 1989, *The Memoir of Marco Parenti. A Life in Medici Florence*, London.

Pignatti, T., 1969, *Pietro Longhi. Paintings and Drawings. Complete Edition*, London.

Pilliod, E., 1992, 'Bronzino's household', *The Burlington Magazine*, 134, 92–100.

Pitkin, H. F., 1984, *Fortune is a Woman. Gender and Politics in the Thought of Niccolò Machiavelli*, Berkeley and London.

Piva, L., 1991, *Le Pestilenze nel Veneto*, Camposanpiero, Padua.

Polizzotto, L., 1994, *The Elect Nation. The Savonarolan Movement in Florence 1494–1545*, Oxford.

Pollak, M. D., 1991, *Turin 1564–1680. Urban Design. Military Culture and the Creation of the Absolute State*, Chicago and London.

Polverini Fosi, I., 1985, *La società violenta. Il banditismo nello Stato pontificio nell seconda metà del Cinquecento*, Rome.

—— 1992, 'Signori e tribunali. Criminalità nobiliare e giustizia nella Roma del Cinquecento', in Visceglia (ed.), 214–30.

—— 1993, 'Justice and its Image: Political propaganda and judicial reality in the pontificate of Sixtus V', *SCJ*, 26, 73–95.

Pomata, G., 1994, *La Promessa di Guarigione. Malati e Curatori in Antico Regime*, Rome and Bari.

Poni, C., 1989, 'Norms and Disputes: The shoemakers's guild in eighteenth-century Bologna', *Past and Present*, 123 (May), 80–108.

—— 1991, 'Local Market Rules and Practices. Three Guilds in the Same Line of Production in Early Modern Bologna', in Woolf (ed.), 69–101.

Povolo, C., 1980, 'Aspetti e problemi dell'amminstrazione della giustizia penale nella Repubblica di Venezia, secoli xvi–xvii', in Cozzi (ed.), 1980–85, 153–258.

Preto, P., 1970, 'Benefici parrocchiali e altari dotati dopo il Tridentino a Padova', *Quaderni Storici*, 5, 795–813.

—— 1984, *Peste e società a Venezia nel 1576*, 2nd edn., Vicenza.

Primum (-quartum), volumen statutorum Perusie (Perugia, 1523–8).

Prodi, P., 1959–67, *Il Cardinale Gabriele Paleotti, 1522–1597*, 2 vols, Rome.

—— 1960, 'Lineamenti dell'organizzazione diocesana in Bologna durante l'episocopato del card. G. Paleotti (1566–1597)', in *Problemi di Vita Religiosa in Italia. Convegno di Storia della Chiesa in Italia*, 323–94, Padua.

—— and Paolini, L., 1997, *Storia della Chiesa di Bologna*, 2 vols, Bergamo.

Prosperi, A., 1996, *Tribunali della coscienza. Inquisitori, confessori, missionari*, Turin.

Pullan, B. S., 1964, 'The famine in Venice and the new Poor Law 1527–1529', *Bollettino dell'Istituto della Società e dello Stato Veneziano*, 5–6 (1963–4), 141–202.

—— 1968, 'Wage-earners and the Venetian Economy, 1550–1630', in Pullan (ed.), 146–74.

—— 1971, *Rich and Poor in Renaissance Venice: the social institutions of a Catholic State, to 1620*, Oxford.

—— 1977, '"A Ship with Two Rudders": Righetto Marrano and the Inquisition in Venice', *Historical J.*, 20, 25–58.

—— 1978, 'Poveri, mendicanti e vagabondi (secoli xiv–xvii)', in AA.VV. *Storia d'Italia. Annali 1*, 981–1047. [Reprinted, untranslated, in B. S. Pullan, (1994), no. IV].

—— 1983, *The Jews of Europe and the Inquisition of Venice 1550–1670*, Oxford.

—— 1988a, 'Support and Redeem: Charity and poor relief in Italian cities from the fourteenth to the seventeenth century', *Continuity and Change*, 3, 177–208.

—— 1988b, 'The Conversion of the Jews: the style of Italy', *Bull. John Rylands University Library of Manchester*, 70, 53–70. [Reprinted in Pullan, (1994), no. XI].

—— 1994, *Poverty and Charity: Europe, Italy, Venice 1400–1700* [collected essays], Aldershot and Brookfield, VM.

—— 1999a, 'Town Poor, Country Poor: The Province of Bergamo from the sixteenth to the eighteenth century', in Kittell and Madden (eds), 213–36.

—— 1999b, 'The Counter-Reformation, Medical Care and Poor Relief', in Grell, Cunningham and Arrizabalaga (eds), 18–39.

—— 1999c, ' 'Three Orders of Inhabitants': Social hierarchies in the Republic of Venice', in J. Denton, ed., *Orders and Hierarchies in Late Medieval and Renaissance Europe*, 147–66, 190–95, Basingstoke and London.

—— (ed.), 1968, *Crisis and Change in the Venetian Economy in the Sixteenth and Seventeenth Centuries*, London.

Queller, D. E., 1986, *The Venetian Patriciate. Reality versus Myth*, Urbana and Chicago.

Raggio, O., 1986, 'Parentele, fazioni e banditi: la Val Fontanabuona tra Cinque e Seicento', in Ortalli (ed.), 233–75.

Rapp, R., 1976, *Industry and Economic Decline in Seventeenth-century Venice*, Cambridge, MA.

Rasi, P., 1941, 'L'applicazione delle norme del Concilio de Trento in materia matrimoniale', in *Studi di Storia e Diritto in onore di Arrigo Solmi*, I, Milan.

Ravennatensia. Centro Studi e Ricerche sulla Antica Provincia Ecclesiastica Ravennate, Cesena: 1 *Atti dei Convegni di Cesena e Ravenna (1966–7)*, (1969); 2 *Atti del Convegno di Bologna (1968)*, (1971); 3 *Atti dei Convegni di Piacenza e Modena (1969–70)*, (1972); 4 *Atti del Convegno di Ferrara (1971)*, (1974); 6 *Atti dei Convegni di Faenza e Rimini (1974–5)*, 1977.

Ravid, B., 1999, 'Curfew Time in the Ghetto of Venice', in Kittell and Madden (eds), 237–75.

Reato, D., 1988, *Storia del Carnivale di Venezia*, Venice.

Reinhard, W., 1991, 'Papal Power and Family Strategy in the Sixteenth and Seventeenth Centuries', in R. G. Asch and A. M. Birke (eds), *Princes, Patronage and the Nobility. The Court at the Beginning of the Modern Age, c. 1450–1650*, 329–56, Oxford.

Revel, J., 1975, 'Les privilèges d'une capitale: l'approvisionnement de Rome à l'époque moderne', *Annales ESC.*, 30, 563–74.

Ricci, G., 1996, *Povertà, vergogna, superbia. I declassati fra Medioevo e Età moderna*, Bologna.

Riddle, J. M., 1994, *Contraception and Abortion from the Ancient World to the Renaissance*, Cambridge MA and London.

Ridolfi, R., 1959, *The Life of Girolamo Savonarola*, London.

Rimoldi, A., 1965, 'Istituzioni di S. Carlo Borromeo per il clero diocesano Milanese', *La Scuola Cattolica*, 93, 427–58.

Robertson, J., 1992, 'Franco Venturi's Enlightenment', *Past and Present*, 137, 183–206.

—— 1997, 'The Enlightenment above National Context: Political economy in eighteenth-century Scotland and Naples', *Historical J.*, 40, 667–97.

Rocke, M., 1996, *Forbidden Friends. Homosexuality and Male Culture in Renaissance Florence*, New York and Oxford.

Romano, D., 1996, *Household and Statecraft. Domestic Service in Renaissance Venice, 1400–1600*, Baltimore and London.

Romby, G. C. and Tarassi, M., 1992, *Vivere nel contado al tempo di Lorenzo* (Comitato per le celebrazioni del V centenario dela morte di Lorenzo il Magnifico, Exhibition Catalogue), Florence.

Rosa, M., 1976, *Religione e Società nel Mezzogiorno tra Cinque e Seicento*, Bari.

Rosenthal, M. F., 1992, *The Honest Courtesan. Veronica Franco, Citizen and Writer in Sixteenth-century Venice*, Chicago and London.

Ross, J. B., 1974, 'The Middle-class Child in Urban Italy, Fourteenth to Early Sixteenth Century', in L. deMause (ed.), *The History of Childhood*, 183–228, New York.

Rosser, G., 1997, 'Craft Guilds and the Negotiation of Work in the Medieval Town', *Past and Present*, 154 (Feb), 3–31.

Rossi, F., 1969, 'Le armature da munizione e l'organizzazione delle cernide nel bresciano', *Archivio Storico Lombardo*, 8, 169–86, plus Tables.

Rossi, P. L., 1994, 'The Writer and the Man. Real Crimes and Mitigating Circumstances: *Il caso Cellini*', in Dean and Lowe (eds), 157–83.

Rouch, M. (ed.), 1982, *Storie di vita popolare nelle canzoni di piazza di G. C. Croce. Fame fatica e mascherate nel '500*, Bologna.

Ruffo, V., 1916, 'La galleria Ruffo nel secolo xvii a Messina', *Bollettino d'Arte*, 10, 21–64, 95–108, 165–92, 284–320, 369–88.

Ruggiero, G., 1980, *Violence in Early Renaissance Venice*, New Brunswick.

—— 1985, *The Boundaries of Eros. Sex Crime and Sexuality in Renaissance Venice*, New York and Oxford.

—— 1993, *Binding Passions. Tales of Magic, Marriage and Power at the End of the Renaissance*, Oxford.

Sakellariou, E., 1995, 'Institutional and Social Continuities in the Kingdom of Naples between 1443 and 1528', in Abulafia (ed.), 327–53.

Salimbeni, F., 1977, 'La parrocchia nel Mezzogiorno nell'età moderna e contemporanea', *Ricerche di Storia Sociale e Religiosa*, 12, 239–66.

Samaritani, A., 1971, 'Fonti inedite sulla riforma cattolico-tridentina in diocesi di Comacchio nel sec. xvi', *Ravennatensia*, 2, 467–550.

San Bernardino da Siena, 1950–65, *Omnia Opera*, Florence.

Santore, C., 1988, 'Julia Lombardo, "Somtuosa meretrize": A Portrait by Property', *Renaissance Quarterly*, 41, 44–83.

Saslow, J. M., 1986, *Ganymede in the Renaissance. Homosexuality in Art and Society*, New Haven and London.

Sbrana, C. and others, 1977, *Gli 'Stati delle Anime' a Roma dalle origini al secolo XVII. Fonti per lo studio della popolazione di Roma*, Rome.

Scaduto, M., 1960, 'Le "Visite" di Antonio Possevino nei domini dei Gonzaga', *Arch. St. Lombardo*, 10, 336–410.

Scalvanti, O. (ed.), 1903, 'Cronaca di Pietro Angelo di Giovanni', *Bollettino della [Regia] Deputazione di Storia Patria per l'Umbria*, 9, 33–380.

Scarabello, G., 1980, 'Devianza sessuale ed interventi di giustizia a Venezia nella prima metà del xvi secolo', in AA.VV. (1980), *Tiziano e Venezia*, 75–94.

Scarano, P., 1958, 'Una Visita Pastorale personale nella diocesi di Mottola nel 1631', *Rivista di Storia della Chiesa in Italia*, 12, 281–90.

Scavizzi, P., 1968, 'Considerazioni sull'attività edilizia a Roma nella prima metà del Seicento', *Studi Storici*, 9, 171–92.

Scott, H. M. (ed.), 1995, *The European Nobilities in the Seventeenth and Eighteenth Centuries*, I: *Western Europe*, London and New York.

Seidel, M., 1994, 'The Social Status of Patronage and its Impact on Pictorial Language in Fifteenth-century Siena', in E. Borsook and F. Superbi Giofreddi (eds), *Italian Altarpieces 1250–1550. Function and Design*, 119–39, Oxford.

Sella, D., 1979, *Crisis and Continuity. The Economy of Spanish Lombardy in the Seventeenth Century*, Cambridge, MA and London.

—— 1997, *Italy in the Seventeenth Century*, London and New York.

Sereni, E., 1961, *Storia del paesaggio agrario italiano*, Bari.

—— 1997, *History of the Italian Agricultural Landscape*, trans. with Introduction by R. Burr Litchfield, Princeton, NJ.

Sestan, E., 1950, 'Per la storia di un idea storiografia: l'idea di una unità della storia italiana', *RSI*, 62, 180–98.

Silverman, S., 1989, 'The Palio of Siena: Game, Ritual or Politics?', in S. Zimmerman and R. F. E. Weissman (eds), 224–39.

Slicher van Bath, B. H., 1963, *The Agrarian History of Western Europe 500–1850*, London.

Smith, A. A., 1998, 'Gender, Ownership and Domestic Space: Inventories and family archives in Renaissance Verona', *Renaissance Studies*, 12/3, 375–91.

Spicciani, A., 1982, 'La povertà involuntaria', in D. Maffei and P. Nardi (eds), *Atti del simposio internazionale Cateriniano-Bernardiniano . . . 1980*, Siena.

—— 1984, 'Solidarietà, previdenza e assistenza per gli artigiani nell'Italia medioevale (secoli xii–xv)', in AA.VV. (1984), *Artigiani e Salariati*, 293–343.

Sposato, P., 1965, *Aspetti e figure della Riforma Cattolico-Tridentino in Calabria*, Naples, (n.d. [*c.* 1965]).

Starn, R., 1982, *Contrary Commonwealth. The Theme of Exile in Medieval and Renaissance Italy*, Berkeley, Los Angeles and London.

Stearns, P. N., 1997, 'Stages of Consumerism: Recent work on the issues of periodization', *JMH.*, 69, 102–17.

Stern, L. I., 1994, *The Criminal Law System of Medieval and Renaissance Florence*, Baltimore and London.

Stevenson, K., 1983, *Nuptial Blessing. A Study of Christian Marriage Rites*, New York.

Stone, L., 1977, *Love, Sex and Marriage in England 1500–1800*, London.

Stortoni, L. A. (ed.), 1997, *Women Poets of the Italian Renaissance. Courtly Ladies and Courtesans*, New York.

Strocchia, S. T., 1992, *Death and Ritual in Renaissance Florence*, Baltimore and London.

Stumpo, E., 1984, 'I ceti dirigenti in Italia nell' età moderna. Due modelli diversi: nobiltà piemontee e patriziato toscano', in Tagliaferri (ed.), 151–97.

Tagliaferri, A. (ed.), 1984, *I Ceti Dirigenti in Italia in età moderna e contemporanea. Atti del Convegno Cividale del Friuli . . . 1983*, Udine.

Tamassia, G., 1910/1971, *La famiglia italiana nei secoli decimoquinto e decimosesto*, Milan, 1910; Rome, 1971 reprint.

Tarabotti, Arcangela, 1994, *Che le Donne siano della spezie degli uomini. Women are no Less Rational than Men*, edited with an introductory essay by Letizia Panizza, Institute of Romance Studies, University of London.

Tedeschi, J., 1991, *The Prosecution of Heresy. Collected Studies on the Inquisition in Early Modern Italy*, Binghampton, NY.

Terpstra, N., 1994, 'Apprenticeship in Social Welfare: From confraternal charity to municipal poor relief in early modern Italy', *SCJ.*, 25, 101–20.

—— 1995, *Lay Confraternities and Civic Religion in Renaissance Bologna*, Cambridge and New York.

—— 1999a, 'Confraternities and Public Charity: Modes of civic welfare in early modern Italy', in Donnelly and Maher (eds), 97–121.

—— (ed.), 1999b, *The Politics of Kinship. Confraternities and Social Order in Early Modern Italy*, Cambridge.

Thomas, A., 1995, *The Painter's Practice in Renaissance Tuscany*, Cambridge.

Thomas, W., 1963, *The History of Italy, 1549, by William Thomas*, edited by George B. Parks, Ithaca, NY.

Thornton, D., 1997, *The Scholar in His Study. Ownership and Experience in Renaissance Italy*, New Haven and London.

Thornton, P., 1991, *The Italian Renaissance Interior 1400–1600*, London.

Toaff, A., 1996, *Love, Work, and Death. Jewish Life in Medieval Umbria*, trans. J. Landry, London and Portland, OR.

Toscani, X., 1986, 'Il reclutamento del clero (secoli xvi–xix)', in AA.VV. *Storia d'Italia* (Einaudi), *Annali*, IX, 573–628.

Travaglini, C. M., 1998, 'The Roman Guilds System in the Early Eighteenth Century', in Guenzi and others (eds), 150–70.

Trexler, R. C., 1971, *Synodal Law in Florence and Fiesole 1306–1518*, Vatican City.

—— 1973, 'The foundlings of Florence, 1395–1455', *History of Childhood Quarterly*, 1/2, 259–84.

—— 1981, 'La prostitution florentine au xve siècle: patronages et clientèles', *Annales E.S.C.*, 36, 983–1015.

—— 1991, *Public Life in Renaissance Florence*, Ithaca and London.

Trincanato, E., 1995, *A Guide to Venetian Domestic Architecture, 'Venezia Minore'*, edited by R. Salvadori, Venice.

Trinkhaus, C. and Oberman, H. O. (eds), 1974, *The Pursuit of Holiness in late Medieval and Renaissance Religion*, Leiden.

Troncarelli, F. (ed.), 1985, *La Città dei Segreti. Magia, Astrologia e Cultura Esoterica a Roma*, (xv–xviii), Milan.

Tucci, U., 1980, 'Venezia Industriale e 'L'Arsenale', in AA.VV. (1980), *Tiziano e Venezia*, 15–19.

Ulvioni, P., 1989, *Il Gran Castigo di Dio. Carestia ed epidemie a Venezia e nella Terraferma 1628–1632*, Milan.

Van Der Wee, H. (ed.), 1988, *The Rise and Decline of Urban Industries in Italy and the Low Countries*, Leuven.

Vanzan Marchini, N-E., 1995a, *I Mali e I Rimedi della Serenissima*, Venice.

—— (ed.), 1995b, *Le Leggi di Sanità della Repubblica di Venezia*, I, Venice.

Vaussard, M., 1962, *Daily Life in Eighteenth Century Italy*, London.

Ventura, A., 1964, *Nobiltà e popolo nella società veneta del '400 e '500*, Bari.

Venturi, F., 1969–90, *Settecento Riformatore*, Turin; esp. I: *Da Muratori a Beccaria 1730–1764*, (1969); II: *La chiesa e la repubblica dentro I loro limiti 1758–1774*; V 1 (1987) and 2 (1990): *L'Italia dei lumi, 1764–1790.*

—— 1972, *Italy and the Enlightenment. Studies in a Cosmopolitan Century*, edited by S. Woolf, London.

Verga, M., 1998, 'Le XVIIIe siècle en Italie: Le "Settecento" réformateur', *Revue d'histoire moderne et contemporaine*, 45, 89–116.

Vertova, L., 1995, 'A Late Renaissance View of Rome', *The Burlington Magazine*, 137 (July), 445–51.

Vianello, A., 1993, *L'Arte dei Calegheri e Zavateri di Venezia tra xvii e xviii secolo*, Venice.

Viazzo, P. P., 1989, *Upland Communities. Environment, Population and Social Structure in the Alps since the Sixteenth Century*, Cambridge and New York.

Vigo, G., 1984, 'Solidarità e conflitti sociali nella Lombardia Spagnola', in Tagliaferri (ed.), 247–58.

Villari, R., 1967, *La rivolta antispagnola a Napoli: Le origini*, Bari.

—— 1983, *Ribelli e riformatori dal xvi al xviii secolo*, 2nd edn, Rome.

—— 1993, *The Revolt of Naples*, Cambridge. [Translation of Villari (1967) from its 5th edn (1987), with additional Afterwords translated from his *Elogio della dissimulazione*, Bari.]

Villone, A., 1983, 'Contratti matrimoniali e testamenti in una zona di latifondo: Eboli a metà '600 ', *MERFM*, 95, 225–98.

Visceglia, M. A., 1983, 'Linee per uno studio unitario dei testamenti dei contratti matrimoniali dell'aristocrazia feudale napoletana tra fine Quattrocento e Settecento', *MEFRM*, 95, 393–470.

—— 1988a, *Il bisogno di eternità; comportamenti aristocratici a Napoli in età moderna*, Naples.

—— 1988b, *Territorio, feudo et potere locale: Terra d'Otranto tra Medioevo ed età moderna*, Naples.

—— (ed.), 1992, *Signori, Patrizi, Cavalieri nell'età moderna*, Rome and Bari.

Voelker, E. C., 1988, 'Borromeo's influence on Sacred Art and Architecture' in Headley and Tomaro (eds), 172–87.

Volpe, F., 1973, 'Il libri parrocchiali come strumento di indagine dalla popolazione meridionale', in *La società religiosa nell'età moderna*, 1063–81, Naples.

—— 1977, 'Il libri parrocchiali del Cilento', *Ricerche di Storia Sociale e Religiosa*, 2, 229–97.

Vovelle, M., 1990, *Ideologies and Mentalities*, trans. E. O'Flaherty, Cambridge and Oxford.

Waddy, P., 1990, *Seventeenth Century Palaces in Rome. The Art of the Plan*, New York, Cambridge, MA and London.

Walker, D. S., 1967, *A Geography of Italy*, 2nd edn, London.

Walker, J., 1998a, 'Honour and the Culture of Male Venetian Nobles, *c.* 1500–1650', Ph.D. Thesis, Cambridge.

—— 1998b, '*Bravi* and the Venetian Nobles, *c.* 1550–1650', *Studi Veneziani*, 36, 85–114.

—— 1999a, 'Gambling and Venetian Noblemen *c.* 1500–1700', *Past and Present*, 162 (Feb), 28–69.

Wall, R., Robin, J. and Laslett, P. (eds), 1983, *Family Forms in Historic Europe*, Cambridge.

Wallerstein, I., 1974, 1980, *The Modern World System.* I: *Capitalist Agriculture and the Origins of the European World-Economy in the Sixteenth-century*; II: *Mercantilism and the Consolidation of the European World-Economy*, New York and London.

Weinstein, D., 1970, *Savonarola and Florence: Prophecy and patriotism in the Renaissance*, Princeton.

Weissman, R. F. E., 1982, *Ritual Brotherhood in Renaissance Florence*, New York and London.

—— 1985, 'Reconstructing Renaissance Sociology: The "Chicago School" and the study of Renaissance society', in R. Trexler (ed.), *Persons in Groups*, 39–46, Binghampton, NY.

—— 1987, 'Taking Patronage Seriously: Mediterranean values and Renaissance society', in Kent and Simons (eds), 25–45.

—— 1989, 'The Importance of Being Ambiguous: Social relations, individualism and identity in Renaissance Florence', in Zimmerman and Weissman (eds), 269–80.

Wiesner, M. E., 1987, 'Spinning out Capital: Women's work in the early modern economy', in R. Bridenthal, C. Koonz and S. M. Stuard (eds), *Becoming Visible. Women in European History*, 2nd edn, 221–49, Boston and Dallas.

—— 1993, *Women and Gender in Early Modern Europe*, Cambridge.

Wills, C., 1997, *Plagues. Their Origin, History and Future*, London.

Wilton, A. and Bignamini, I. (eds), 1996, *Grand Tour. The Lure of Italy in the Eighteenth Century* (exhibition catalogue, Tate Gallery), London.

Wisch, B., 1990, 'The Roman Church Triumphant: Pilgrimage, Penance and Processions Celebrating Holy Year of 1575', in *Triumphal Celebrations and the Rituals of Statecraft. Papers in Art History from the Pennsylvania State University*, VII, 83–117.

—— 1992, 'The Colosseum as a Site for Sacred Theatre: A Pre-history of Carlo Fontana's Project', in *An Architectural Progress in the Renaissance and Baroque. Sojourns in and out of Italy, Papers in Art History from the Pennsylvania State University*, VIII, 92–111.

Woolf, S. J., 1979, *A History of Italy 1700–1860*, London.

—— 1986, *The Poor in Western Europe in the Eighteenth and Nineteenth Centuries*, London and New York.

—— (ed.), 1991, *Domestic Strategies: Work and family in France and Italy 1600–1800*, Cambridge.

Wright, A. D., 1975a, 'The Significance of the Council of Trent', *J. Eccl. Hist.*, 26, 353–62.

—— 1975b, 'The People of Catholic Europe and the People of Anglican England', *Historical J.*, 18, 451–66.

—— 1980, 'Venetian Law and Order: a Myth?', *Bull. Inst. Historical Research*, 53, 192–202.

—— 1982, *The Counter Reformation. Catholic Europe and the non-Christian World*, London.

Zago, R., 1982, *I Nicolotti*, Padua.

Zanetti, D., 1972, *La demografia del Patriziato Milanese nei secoli xvii, xviii, xix*, Pavia.

—— 1977, 'The Patriziato of Milan from the Domination of Spain to the Unification of Italy: An outline of the social and demographic history', *Social Hist.*, 6, 745–60.

Zannini, A., 1992, 'Un ceto di funzionari amministrativi; i cittadini originari veneziani 1569–1730', *Studi Veneziani*, xxiii, 131–45.

—— 1993, *Burocrazia e burocratici a Venezia in età moderna: i cittadini originari, sec. xvi–xviii*, Venice.

Zanoli, P., 1973, 'Il patrimonio della famiglia Litta sino alla fine del Settecento', *Arch. St. Lombardo*, 10, 284–346.

Zardin, D. (ed.), 1995, *La Città e I Poveri. Milano e le terra lombarde dal Rinascimento all'età spagnola*, Milan.

Zenobi, B. G., 1992, 'Feudalità e patriziati cittadini nel governo della "periferia" pontificia del cinque-seicento', in Visceglia (ed.), 94–107.

Zimmerman, S. and Weissman, R. F. E. (eds), 1989, *Urban Life in the Renaissance*, Cranbury NJ and London.

Zompini, G., 1980, *Le Arti che vanno per via nella Città di Venezia*, preface by G. Parise, Milan.

Zorzi, A., 1994, 'The Judicial System in Florence in the Fourteenth and Fifteenth Centuries', in Dean and Lowe (eds), 40–58.

Zucconi, G., 1995, *Venice an architectural guide, with an essay by Donatella Calabi*, 2nd edn, Venice.

INDEX

[Includes modern authors whose work is highlighted in the main text. Some names of minor places and persons mentioned only once in the text have been omitted to avoid an excessive index. Indications are given on which map(s) places may be located.]